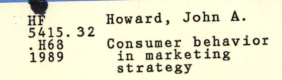

HF
5415.32
.H68
1989

Howard, John A.
Consumer behavior
in marketing
strategy

$28.50

DATE		

© THE BAKER & TAYLOR CO.

CONSUMER BEHAVIOR
IN
MARKETING STRATEGY

CONSUMER BEHAVIOR
IN
MARKETING STRATEGY

JOHN A. HOWARD

Graduate School of Business
Columbia University

PRENTICE HALL, Englewood Cliffs, NJ 07632

LIBRARY OF CONGRESS
Library of Congress Cataloging-in-Publication Data

Howard, John A.
    Consumer behavior in marketing strategy / John A. Howard.
        p.   cm.
    Includes bibliographies and indexes.
    ISBN 0-13-169666-1 :
    1. Consumer behavior.   2. Marketing--Management.   I. Title.
HF5415.32.H68 1989
    658.8'342--dc19   88-15542
                                                          CIP

Editorial/production supervision and
    interior design: Maureen Wilson
Cover design: Edsal Enterprises
Manufacturing buyer: Margaret Rizzi

Printed in the United States of America

10 9 8 7 6 5 4 3 2 1

ISBN 0-13-169666-1

Prentice-Hall International (UK) Limited, *London*
Prentice-Hall of Australia Pty. Limited, *Sydney*
Prentice-Hall Canada Inc., *Toronto*
Prentice-Hall Hispanoamericana, S.A., *Mexico*
Prentice-Hall of India Private Limited, *New Delhi*
Prentice-Hall of Japan, Inc., *Toyko*
Prentice-Hall of Southeast Asia Pte. Ltd., *Singapore*
Editora Prentice-Hall do Brasil, Ltda. *Rio de Janeiro*

Contents

PART III   APPLICATION

CHAPTER 8

Strategy for Extensive Problem Solving   122

CHAPTER 9

Strategy for Limited Problem Solving   148

CHAPTER 10

Strategy for Routine Problem Solving   175

CHAPTER 11

Strategy for Organizational Buying   197

PART IV   SOCIOCULTURAL ENVIRONMENT

CHAPTER 12

Culture and Subcultures   224

CHAPTER 13

Social Class and Reference Groups   237

Preface

The object of this book is to provide conceptual and technical tools that will enable the reader to apply them to marketing practice, both profit and nonprofit, in a way that has not been previously possible. This is accomplished, first, by systematically integrating two independent streams of basic consumer research: the well-established concept formation approach and the newer information-processing approach. Second, it brings together systematically the consumer and the competitor as the two key elements the manager faces. Third, these two fundamental integrations are done in the context of a systematic way of designing marketing strategy and plans, including the personal computer and mathematical modeling for simulating a market.

Simultaneously with the emphasis upon a managerial orientation, the book has an equally strong orientation toward basic research on the consumer. For example, the integration of the role of memory into the study of the consumer has just begun and holds enormous promise. Although consumer behavior is an important issue in itself, the research on memory obviously extends far beyond mere buying behavior. There is concern among those psychologists doing research on memory generally that laboratory research will produce misleading results. Thus, consumer behavior researchers with their skills for the naturalistic setting of the market may be able to make a major contribution to our understanding of human thinking generally. After all, Herbert A. Simon, trained in political science and economics, received the Nobel laureate for his work in psychology.

This book on consumer behavior grew out of earlier efforts by the author to formulate a systematic understanding of the consumer. These efforts were

initiated by the Ford Foundation's request for him to do a study of the state of marketing knowledge as taught and researched in American business schools. Later, General Foods cooperated by collecting a splendid body of data from its instant breakfast test market in terms of the emerging theory. John U. Farley saw the power of these data and the theory and modeled these consumers of instant breakfast. This led to two parallel paths of development over the past 15 years. The author, often with the support of John Farley and Don Lehmann, proceeded to apply the theory to a variety of company situations and products such as General Motors, General Foods, IBM, Pfizer, and General Electric. In a parallel fashion, John Farley and Don Lehmann, aided by others, undertook many analyses of groups of studies of consumer modeling efforts in developing their concept of the meta-analysis of marketing. The results of these two parallel paths supported each other.

Procter & Gamble Company early provided ideas as seen in the book and has continued to provide essential financial support throughout the development of the book. The author is extremely grateful for this support.

MORE ABOUT THIS BOOK

Consumer behavior is a field of knowledge that explains and predicts how consumers buy. It has arisen largely in response to the needs of managers of profit and nonprofit organizations and of public policymakers.

To facilitate our understanding of this field, this text has been segmented into five parts, as follows: Part I, Introduction; Part II, Psychological Foundations of the Consumer Decision Model; Part III, Application; Part IV, Sociocultural Environment; and Part V, Extensions of the Consumer Decision Model.

The Introduction is comprised of three chapters. Chapter 1 discusses the uses that consumer behavior as a body of theory serves and how it has arisen. Its usefulness has been greatly enhanced first because of the acceptance of marketing strategy as a centerpiece for managing any organization that serves consumers. Second, the computer is playing an essential role in the development of theory and in applying that consumer theory to marketing practice.

Chapter 2 illustratively introduces and explains three basic concepts upon which the field rests. The first is the concept of a *product category*, which explains much about how consumers buy. Second, the concept of the *product life cycle* enables us to classify consumers into three very meaningful patterns of buying behavior. Third, the concept of a *market* made up of consumers and competitors is basic to all consumer behavior because it represents the environment in which the consumer buys.

Chapter 3 introduces a simple six-variable model—the Consumer Decision Model (CDM)—which is the vehicle that enables us to understand quickly how consumers behave. The model immeasurably clarifies the field by integrating it and serving as the engine of application.

Part II, which includes Chapters 4 through 7, is concerned with how

consumers adapt over the product life cycle. In Part I, we learned the three types of consumer behavior depending upon where the product category is on the product life cycle: extensive problem solving (situation 1), limited problem solving (situation 2), and routine problem solving (situation 3). These will be distinguished throughout the book.

The major purpose here in Part II is to describe a logic for the behavior in each situation. This logic gives far more detailed understanding than that found in Chapter 3 of how the CDM operates in explaining and predicting the way consumers buy.

With this foundation of understanding, the reader might now like to know of some other consumer models with which to compare the CDM. To meet this need, Chapter 7 compares the CDM with two well-known models: the Engel, Kollat, and Blackwell (EKB) model and the Bettman model. These two are quite different, the first being originally designed for teaching and the second for basic research. Each serves a vital role.

With Part II providing a logic for understanding each type of consumer according to the stage of the product life cycle, we are now ready in Part III to apply that logic to practice in building marketing strategy. The problems are quite different for each of the three, and so a separate chapter is devoted to each (Chapters 8, 9, and 10). In addition, formal organizations, be they profit or nonprofit, sometimes buy quite differently from individual consumers because they often have "buying centers" that do the buying. Consequently, a fourth chapter (Chapter 11) is included to provide a logic for organizational buying that is very commonly encountered in marketing to health organizations that have received a great amount of attention in recent years.

Repeatedly in Part III we needed to know if differences existed among the consumers making up a market to decide whether we should consider segmenting it, and if so what those segment differences were. More specifically, those customer differences were an essential part of core strategy, the foundation of marketing strategy. The profit potential of identifying a market niche becomes greater as the product category reaches the higher levels of the product life cycle and begins to level off. Competition becomes sharper.

The simple CDM avoided this profit potential to simplify. Also, it is easy to exaggerate how often these market niches occur. Because people are different doesn't necessarily mean they buy differently. Further to utilize those differences to get a competitive advantage can be very complex, and so we delayed it until we could examine the problem systematically in Chapters 12 through 14.

These differences occur for a number of reasons. Cultural differences are among the most common. European advertising is quite different from American advertising. European ads are less direct and more nostalgic, they employ humor far more extensively, and "emotion is not worn on the sleeve to the same extent as it is in America."[1] Social classes also often buy some

---

[1] W. Slootweg, "What American Advertisers Can Learn from Europe," *Viewpoint* (September/October 1986), 27.

products differently. Finally, even within the members of a single family, needs and tastes can differ. Consequently, we examine each of these three groups in Chapters 12, 13, and 14, respectively. Later, in Part V (Chapter 15), we attempt to find a common denominator of them so that we can better understand them.

One area of consumer differences that is often discussed is "situational differences."[2] These arise because of the purpose for which the product is purchased. If you are having the boss in for dinner, you may buy a higher quality of steak than for a regular family dinner. These situational differences are difficult to deal with, and some evidence indicates that they are not as frequent as we thought.[3]

Other extensions of the CDM to incorporate individual differences among consumers follow in Part V.

Because of its simplicity the six-variable CDM has powerful advantages, as described in Chapter 7. However, this simplicity comes at the price of missing conditions that in some uses can be limiting. Consequently, in Part V we extend the CDM in five directions to incorporate these missing conditions. The first extension is to include explicitly the fact that within each of the three types of consumers, there are individual differences. This fact is, of course, a central part of core strategy, namely, market segmentation, which is Chapter 15 and grows out of Part IV, Sociocultural Environment.

The second extension is to recognize that in applying the CDM there are feedbacks operating in the consumer's thinking. If he buys a brand and likes it, he will more probably buy it next time. The third extension is to catch nonlinear and interactive relations among the CDM variables. When they do exist, much better explanation and prediction is possible if these are incorporated.

Finally, we have been assuming up to this point that the purpose of consumer behavior research is to serve the profit or nonprofit organization. This avoids the important question of the consumer's interest, however. Does the consumer need protection such as from untruthful advertising? This last extension will explore how the CDM can be useful in issues involving the protection of the consumer, which has come to be called "consumerism." The federal government has long been concerned with protecting the consumer. Because that policy is now undergoing major change and also because it is important to an organization's consumers, a substantial review is made of the history of that policy to guide future thinking about it. Finally, this need for consumer protection sometimes raises doubts about the social desirability of marketing activity. Also, marketing is a relatively new function of an organization, and its practitioners have lacked a logic to guide them and to help them articulate and justify their proposed strategies. Consequently, the social acceptability of

---

[2] R. W. Belk, "Situational Variables and Consumer Behavior," *Journal of Consumer Reaearch*, 2, no. 3 (December 1975), 162.

[3] J. U. Farley, D. R. Lehmann, and M. J. Ryan, "Patterns in Parameters of Buyer Behavior Models: Generalizing from Sparse Replication," *Marketing Science*, 1, no. 2 (Spring 1982), 181–204.

marketing and probable future developments in our knowledge of consumer behavior will be examined.

ACKNOWLEDGMENTS

As the foregoing indicates, this effort involved the participation of many other people, especially faculty, MBAs, and doctoral students. John Farley and Don Lehmann, each as advisor, critic, and friend, has played an enormous role in the development of the material. Harold Kassarjian did an imaginative, thorough, and remarkably honest review of an early draft of the manuscript. It provided important encouragement as well as a realistic appraisal of the work yet to be done. To receive this kind of criticism is one of the greatest rewards of academia. Morris Holbrook has been a constructive critic and with his remarkable creativity has contributed many new ideas. Don Morrison has often been a splendid critic. Rajeev Batra read the entire current manuscript and provided new sources and many helpful comments. Michel Laroche, as a doctoral student, developed a new way of doing nonlinear analysis, and the reader will encounter numerous important contributions that characterize him as a major innovator. Ann L. Beattie provided much help with information processing theory. Victor Micati, a former student and now a senior executive at Pfizer, Inc., was of immense help educating the author into the practical problems of marketing, especially in a large international corporation. Kapil Jain, as a research assistant, was highly creative in reviewing criticism and discussing the manuscript. Debra Stephens carefully read a portion of one draft of the manuscript. Harrison W. Wood was one of the earliest contributors. He quickly saw the merit of the general approach and helped immensely in converting the case material to teachable form. In that early stage he had an enormous impact. Finally, I am especially grateful to Pat Murphy of Notre Dame and Manoj Hastak of the University of Illinois who evaluated three successive drafts of the manuscript. They were of inestimable help in pointing out flaws in content and presentation and suggesting additional sources. They went far beyond the usual role of a reviewer. Dave Stewart of Vanderbilt did a helpful review of one of the early manuscripts.

The Graduate School of Business of Columbia University has for many years provided me with support and a stimulating intellectual environment. I am especially grateful to Maxine Braiterman, supervisor of the Word Processing Center, and her crew. She was most creative and helpful in seeing this project through, and she was always in the forefront of the technology.

In preparing a manuscript today, the author is faced with the difficult issue of how to deal with sexism in this modern age. The procedure used here has been to alternate, first dealing in terms of one sex and later shifting to the other sex as examples.

CONSUMER BEHAVIOR
IN
MARKETING STRATEGY

CHAPTER 1

Study of Consumer Behavior

1. INTRODUCTION

In 1973 Miller Brewing introduced its low-calorie Lite beer to the American public.[1] At the time, competitors ridiculed the idea that a market existed for such a product. They felt that to drink a low-calorie beer would be "sissy," that "macho men" drank beer, and that these "he-men" wanted real beer. Today Lite beer represents a category making up 20% of total American beer sales, and competitors have hastened to get on the bandwagon but probably will never catch up.[2]

This new product grew out of new consumer tastes and new technology. The changing consumer tastes arose from an enhanced desire for better health, which would be aided by eating less sugar. The technology involved a new enzyme that could remove the residue of sugar from beer. This pattern of development—new tastes and new technology leading to a new product category—is today being repeated in industry after industry. To help management understand consumers' needs so as to be able to recognize the potential for this pattern of development of change in consumer tastes and new technology and be able to articulate the new thing in terms of the consumers' needs so that it will be accepted in the market is what this book is all about.

[1] *The Wall Street Journal* (New York edition), May 16, 1986, p. 27.
[2] Monci Jo Williams, "Betting on a Beer Without a Buzz," *Fortune*, 109, no. 16 (June 25, 1984), 76.

Consumer behavior is the study of how and why consumers buy and consume. This textbook describes and explains the process, assuming that the reader has no prior knowledge of consumer behavior. We will explore how consumers think and act in buying and consuming products and services from both profit and nonprofit organizations. In some situations, such as buying a can of soup, behavior can be a very simple process. But, in other situations, such as buying a first home computer, the process is very complex. In either case, however, it is now possible to articulate an understanding of that behavior, which can provide assistance to all managers involved in marketing a good or service.

To explain why differences exist in buying is one of the several roles of consumer behavior theory. This theory, combined with the tools such as the consumer survey to put it to work, makes up the field of "consumer behavior."

2. PURPOSE OF TEXT

A marketing manager will want to know how consumer behavior will help him to design better marketing plans and to get those plans accepted within the company, a problem Miller faced in 1973 with Lite beer. It will guide him in collecting the most useful information, in analyzing that information, and in interpreting it in terms of marketing plans for his product.

In a nonprofit service organization such as a hospital, an individual in the marketing department will want to know the patients' needs and how best to serve those needs. The words will be different, but the problems will be similar to those a brand manager at Procter & Gamble encounters. Further, health care, which has been traditionally nonprofit, has now in many cases become for-profit; for example, Hospital Corp. of America is now borrowing $1.25 billion in its business as an operator of hospital and health care facilities.[3] Thirty percent of all general hospital beds are now for-profit.[4]

A recent report on the New York City government in the *Public Administration Review* also suggests the need for consumer behavior applications.

> Part of the explanation for the imperfect link between spending and services in New York City involves changes in consumer behavior. Examples include the declining number of false alarms and the drop in the amount of refuse to be collected. Because consumer behavior is an important determinant of service levels, public policy should be concerned with modifying this behavior. In fact, the significance of the consumers' role has received growing recognition among municipal officials in recent years. They now engage in explicit programs to alter citizen demand for services through a combination of educational efforts (that are called marketing in the private sector), regulation, and pricing.[5]

[3] *The Wall Street Journal* (New York edition), February 25, 1986, Sec. 2, p. 36.

[4] *The Wall Street Journal* (New York edition), March 18, 1986, Sec. 2, p. 31.

[5] C. Brecher and R. D. Horton, "Retrenchment and Recovery: American Cities and the New York Experience," *Public Administration and Review*, 45, no. 2 (March/April 1985), 273.

Moreover, colleges and universities now recognize that they need to know about consumer behavior to aid in recruiting students. "Marketing admissions" has become an accepted term to mean marketing to potential students. An example of such a college is Blackburn College, a four-year liberal arts school in Carlinville, Illinois, with one of the finest records in preparing students for graduate work in the health sciences. Yet like most liberal arts schools, it is facing enrollment problems with the decline of that age group as a segment in the national population. Blackburn's president, Bill Denman, is sensitive to the need for systematic student recruiting. In April 1984 he commissioned the Admissions Marketing Group, a private consulting group in Chicago, to do a study and come up with a strategy. Since then, one member of his staff has the major full-time responsibility to do consumer behavior analyses and make strategy recommendations. In light of these recommendations, changes are being made in its recruiting practices.

3. CONSUMER BEHAVIOR THEORY

An understanding of how the theory of consumer behavior and its application tools evolved will enable you to appreciate the validity of the theory and will give you guidance in its practical application. Let us discuss the reasons for consumer behavior theory's importance, its sources, and why it is easy to use.

Consumer behavior theory like all theory is a simplified, abstract representation of reality. Consumer behavior, like all human behavior, is complex, and the more simplified picture of consumers provided by theory helps us enormously in understanding consumers. It not only helps us think about consumers but also provides us with a language to talk about them. Having this language is very useful because to be effective in an organization—company or nonprofit organization—you have to persuade others to accept your ideas. In fact, lacking this language has been one of the greatest weaknesses of modern marketers. Finance has to accept your plans or you will lack financing. Manufacturing must accept them or else your product may not come out of the factory the way you want it—and when you want it. Research and development must see your logic to go along with your proposed product improvement.

More specifically, to do this persuading, it is helpful to have some information, facts, data. Theory guides you in deciding what data on consumers to collect. It helps you in analyzing that data. And, above all, it helps you in interpreting the results of the analysis in terms of designing marketing strategy and setting plans.

3.1   Source of Consumer Behavior Theory

Market research has been developing especially since "marketing," which brings together all customer elements, grew out of "sales" in the early 1950s. Insofar as there was much consumer behavior theory guiding the market research, that theory drew heavily upon the psychologist, Freud. It emphasized the nonutilitarian or emotional reasons for buying.

The field of consumer behavior really began to develop in the early 1960s when the Ford Foundation commissioned a two-year study of the state of knowledge of marketing in American business schools,[6] as a part of its $35 million effort over a decade to raise the level of teaching and research in American business schools. In that study it became apparent that consumer behavior was at that time the only really researchable area in marketing and that there was a substantial foundation in the social sciences upon which to build. Professors and doctoral students began systematic research on how and why consumers buy. Today that research output has become a flood of knowledge in learned journal articles. For example, taking only the two leading basic journals, the *Journal of Consumer Research* and the *Journal of Marketing Research*, they appear four times each year and each averages about 10 articles. These 80 articles have been appearing for more than a decade. These approximately 800 articles each reporting new research on some aspect of consumer behavior give you some idea of the magnitude of the flow.

This same effort has simultaneously led to the development of market research. While creating these pieces of knowledge about the consumer, researchers were also creating marketing research techniques for collecting information about consumers. This information is badly needed for making marketing decisions that pay off. Market research has become a multimillion-dollar business as companies have come to recognize the necessity to know their customers better. Market research companies such as A. C. Nielsen and other large firms that are now merging have recognized the profit opportunity in providing this information. *Science 86*, in its regular review of American science, includes an article entitled "The Supermarket Snoop." Marketing scientists are using the Universal Product Code to look over your shoulder and into your grocery bag."[7] It is a fascinating article on the nature and use of supermarket scanning data in providing market research information. A major conclusion from all this new technology and merging of corporate entities, however, is the greater need for consumer behavior theory to guide the marketing manager in what data to collect and how to interpret this mass of data. Rather than describe marketing research in general terms here, market research techniques will be discussed in connection with specific problems in later chapters.

Second, in consumer theory as in all fields of science, knowledge first evolves in small pieces. When viewed individually, these small pieces of knowledge are not very useful in meeting the manager's needs. Practical problems are too complex. In the next stage, however, these pieces are assembled, integrated, and synthesized into a body of theory so that the manager can apply it to his needs. The theory portrays the hidden order in this very complex activity we

---

[6] For the report of the Ford Foundation study, see J. A. Howard, *Executive and Buyer Behavior* (New York: Columbia University Press, 1963).

[7] Laura B. Ackerman, "The Supermarket Snoop," *Science 86* (April 1986), 24–25.

call consumer behavior. On the surface the exceedingly complex and highly varied behavior displayed by consumers seems essentially unknowable. Then, wonderfully, through the development of a theory, the hidden pattern emerges describing the order we suddenly see and explaining why that pattern of behavior happens to take place.

What is this magic stuff called consumer behavior theory that does these wonderful things? As stated earlier, a theory is a simplified, abstract representation of reality. But it is much more than this. It is something that helps us to make better marketing decisions for profit and nonprofit enterprises. But this is the end result; it amounts to putting the cart before the horse. Let us first examine the characteristics of theory that enables it to do this for us.

Zaltman and Wallendorf have thought carefully and at length about what constitutes a theory and have come up with 10 essential characteristics of a good theory.[8]

1. A theory both *explains* how consumers buy and *predicts* what consumers will buy.
2. It *unifies* previously unrelated areas of knowledge; for example, it relates information that consumres get from advertising to what brands they buy.
3. The theory is *simple*. If not, it can be so complex that we can't understand it well enough to apply it to our problems.
4. It is *testable* so that we can verify whether the theory is valid and therefore dependable.
5. Implied in the previous characteristic, it is *supported by the facts*. What we mean by testing is to lay the theory up against data describing how consumers buy in the market and thereby determine if the facts confirm the theory. If they don't, you should either modify the theory until the facts do verify it or junk the theory.
6. The theory is *general* by being applicable to a wide range of products and services. If a theory isn't general, it cannot be very useful.
7. It has *heuristic value* by which is meant that it poses new questions for us that had not been previously asked. In attempting to answer these questions, new knowledge is created that then becomes a part of the theory.
8. It is *internally consistent*. If it is not internally consistent and contains some logical incongruities, we have reason to doubt any predictions made from it. Lacking this quality, a theory can obviously be a dangerous tool.
9. It is *original*. Unless it is original, it adds little to existing knowlege.
10. It is *plausible*. Unless the theory is seen by others as making sense, they will not likely accept it and so it will not be useful.

These 10 benefits lead to an eleventh:

11. It can be applied to *designing marketing strategy* and plans.

[8] G. Zaltman and M. Wallendorf, *Consumer Behavior: Basic Findings and Management Implications* (New York: John Wiley & Sons, 1983), pp. 622–24; for another list, see J. A. Howard and J. N. Sheth, *The Theory of Buyer Behavior* (New York: John Wiley & Sons, 1969), Chapter 1.

This is where we started out discussing what a theory is. If the characteristics hold, the theory helps us make better marketing decisions, and in Chapter 7, we will verify how well they do apply to the theory here.

3.2   Consumer Behavior and Marketing Strategy

Theory has also become more easily used. Fortunately, parallel with the emerging consumer theory, the concept of marketing strategy has evolved as the implementing mechanism for divisional strategies in a company that guides the development of annual marketing plans. Once the marketing manager acquires the understanding of the consumer provided by the theory, to use it he has to relate that understanding to his company needs. The vehicle to accomplish this is the marketing strategy. In the past decade this role of marketing strategy in a company has been a major development in management practice. Marketing strategy is the thinking and organizing framework through which the annual marketing plans for a brand are created. The marketing manager's task is the complex one of designing this strategy for a brand.

The strategy links the division's objectives to the annual plan in such a way that the annual plan, when properly implemented, will serve those objectives. The strategy is a timeless "superplan" and is changed only when major changes occur in the company's environment. This is illustrated by IBM in introducing its first Personal Computer. The Customer Decision Model (CDM) presented in Chapter 3 was used in the important task of selecting retail stores, setting policy for retail stores, and guiding retail stores in managing the sales of the Personal Computer.

Just how the knowledge of the consumer is linked to the other inputs of the strategy, such as to estimates of competitive behavior, is an important issue. This linkage procedure is through the idea of a core strategy, which is discussed at length in Chapter 8. Merrill Lynch's core strategy for its Cash Management Account in 1986 might be stated as follows: "To have a competitive advantage over Shearson and Dean Witter, we will emphasize the client benefits of personal service, rate of return, and comprehensiveness of transaction statement to middle-income investors." Implicit in this core strategy is the things that Merrill Lynch believes its investors want and that market research guided by theory can discover.

The Personal Computer has also made theory easier to use. The Personal Computer has affected our lives in many ways, especially in marketing. New products are possible. The managed cash account just mentioned and discussed in Chapter 2, for example, has had a profound effect on Wall Street, and it was possible only because of the computer. Also, computer-aided design (CAD) brings a more general tool to the factory that ensures much closer coordination between the research and development people and marketing personnel in meeting the customers' needs. Linking marketing and technology is a story in itself, but this can be delayed until Chapter 8, where we are concerned with marketing strategy for product innovations.

Equally important, the personal computer permits the middle-level marketing manager, if he is guided by good theory, to sit at his desk and analyze consumer behavior in a way undreamed of a few years ago. Because of his position as marketing manager, his knowledge of the market is typically superior to others in the company for judging the potential of new directions. By using his theory and computer, he can explore the new brand franchise represented in each of these directions and thus answer tomorrow's questions. But people like Kent Mitchell, former senior vice president at General Foods, point out that business school education and company experience have weakened the capacity of brand managers to develop new brand franchises because of the greater emphasis upon short-term financial criteria. Less emphasis is being placed on understanding the consumer. They maintain that this is being relegated to the market research department.

However, both domestic and international events such as technology and invasion of our markets by foreigners have enormous effect. Our automobile industry was almost bankrupted by the Japanese in the 1970s. Events have awakened many higher-level managers to the need to understand better their customers as industry after industry has encountered these serious marketing difficulties and setbacks. Nonprofit organizations are becoming aware that they too need to understand their customers, as we have already noted.

The new technology—the computer and the theory—will enable brand managers to model consumers and so learn a new way of developing brand franchises so essential in a fast-moving world.

4. SUMMARY OF BOOK CONTENTS

This book is an outgrowth of the foregoing developments. Chapter 2 presents a framework, particularly the product life cycle (PLC), for the application of theory to facilitate applying it to practical problems of the manager. Chapter 3 presents a simple but exceedingly general Consumer Decision Model that serves to summarize and integrate pieces of knowledge about the consumer that enables the manager to understand much better the consumer and so apply that knowledge. Chapters 4 through 6 spell out the supporting information processing and other foundations of that model. These foundations make the theory readily usable in interpreting the model's output into recommendations for management actions. Chapters 8 through 11 focus the model and supporting theory in terms of the product life cycle so as to facilitate application in creating marketing strategy and plans.

Finally, the model of Chapter 3 that simplifies, integrates, and unifies much of consumer theory comes at a price: in this simplifying process some conditions are temporarily assumed away. Once you have become familiar with using the simplified Consumer Decision Model, however, these more complex conditions can be incorporated into the CDM as Chapters 15 through 18 explain.

Included in these extensions are issues of consumerism and marketing's acceptance by management.

This book is organized differently from most consumer behavior texts. It is organized in the way we have just indicated—product life cycle, Customer Decision Model, information-processing underpinnings, and further extensions—so as to present an integrated, synthesized whole. In this form, it facilitates learning and understanding of the nature and roles of consumer behavior knowledge. Because of this integrated and synthesized structure, it covers essentially the same ground, however, as do the more encyclopedic texts.

5. USE OF THE TEXT

The content of this book as just summarized is designed to meet the needs of a wide range of students interested in marketing careers and careers related to marketing of profit and nonprofit products and services.

By providing an integrated review of the available knowledge in the field, this book fulfills the role of a comprehensive textbook on consumer behavior, often referred to as a "principles" approach. It describes the great amount of basic research done on why and how consumers buy and consume. It explains how to apply this knowledge to many and varied marketing situations as has been emphasized. Questions at the end of each chapter will emphasize the principles of consumer behavior instead of their application.

The text can also be used by those who are interested in applying it to conventional cases that deal with consumers in an actual buying situation but in a qualitative, nonquantitative way. This is the conventional case analysis such as the Harvard-type case. Also, the cases on a computer disk described shortly can be used in this conventional qualitative way.

Finally, the text can be used by students who prefer a more theory-based, systematic, and quantitative approach, with emphasis upon application to practice. In the quantitative approach, an extensive set of data collected systematically for each brand in terms of the simple model in Chapter 3 is available on a computer disk for each of four cases. Each case is from consulting experience and regards a different product and different set of marketing conditions.

In using this quantitative approach, the first case (set of data) is about RCA's introduction of the videodisk player. About 80 consumers report their answers about their knowledge, understanding, liking, sources of information, and so on of the RCA videodisk. These data are available for you to readily access by your personal computer, and no prior computer knowledge is assumed. To facilitate accessing the data with your personal computer, a very simple, "hands-on" set of instructions called "Quick'n Easy I" for using the PC developed with great effort is made available to you.

To take advantage of the PC in analyzing these consumer data, you will use the theory of the text to apply the simple six-equation model (CDM) described in Chapter 3. The material assumes that you have had no prior exposure to statistics. This statistical review material appears in *Computer Applications*, which accompanies this text.

The end result of the quantitative approach is a mathematical model of the RCA data. With that model you can make predictions about the effects of various changes in marketing expenditures, which is the most vital information that managers need. Modeling consumer behavior, then, is the third way this text may be used. However, no prior modeling experience is assumed. From your model you can derive recommendations for fundamental improvements in the company's offering and its marketing.

Finally, the output of that simple model can also be used as input to the Financial Model. The Financial Model quickly tells you what the optimum price and advertising budget are for your product, which could have been useful to Miller introducing Lite Beer more than a decade ago. The Financial Model was constructed as part of $3.5 million grant from IBM to Columbia University to develop computer management aids. It not only tells you the optimum price and advertising but dramatically portrays the role of each level of management in carrying out this complex process of bringing new consumer tastes and new technology together to build a new product category as Miller Lite did in 1973.

Recently, the assertion was made that "some influential B-school professors argue that business schools are too quantitative and theoretical, that they produce narrow-minded technicians who lack interpersonal and communications skills."[9] This statement can be seriously misleading. The marketing manager armed with the theory in this book and the Personal Computer can bring that splendid experience he has acquired in his market and merge the artistic and scientific in a way not previously possible. Because of his unique knowledge of his market, he can do this far more effectively than anyone else in the company. Furthermore, it will greatly improve his communication skills for explaining to others why his strategy makes sense and should be followed. Traditionally, marketers have been seriously handicapped by their inability to communicate this. This theory provides a vocabulary that was previously lacking. John Peterson, senior vice president of Combustion Engineering, Inc., has written and spoken at length on the marketer's inability to interact effectively with others in the company because of this lack of an appropriate marketing vocabulary.[10]

In summary, the adaptability of the book to such a variety of students' needs—comprehensive principles textbook, conventional case analysis, and computer modeling—is one of its major strengths. Another strength is the simple six-variable CDM, which is used throughout the text and ties it all together as described earlier. Finally, still another strength is its sharp focus upon practical applications to management problems, both profit and nonprofit.

---

[9] John A. Byrne, "20 Leading Business Schools—By the Numbers," *Fortune* (March 24, 1986), p. 67.

[10] J. R. Peterson, "Preparing for the Next Marketing War," presentation to the Conference Board (New York, 1984), p. 7.

Questions

1. What is meant by new consumer tastes and new technology as the basis for new products?
2. Define consumer behavior.
3. What are the characteristics of a good theory of consumer behavior?
4. Define a marketing strategy.
5. Describe the three different ways that this text may be used.

.

CHAPTER 2

Foundations of Consumer Behavior

1. CONSUMER BEHAVIOR: AN EXAMPLE

When Merrill Lynch launched its major advertising campaign in 1971, its ad agency, Ogilvy and Mather introduced the "Bullish on America" theme. A commercial showed a bull joining up with a herd that was charging across the prairie. While the ad seemed to strike a responsive note among some investors, Merrill Lynch wasn't totally satisfied with the results. So it dropped Ogilvy and Mather as its ad agency and asked Young & Rubicam to redesign its campaign.

Young and Rubicam, upon reading Stanford Research Institute's VALS (values and lifestyle typology) for classifying customers, concluded from the VALS analysis that the Merrill herd was appealing to the wrong instincts in potential consumers. It was felt that the ad conjured up an image of gun-shy investors who want to feel secure, to run with the crowd—and, by extension, who didn't mind getting only average results. On the other hand, the truly bullish investors that Y & R believed Merrill Lynch wished to attract were "achievers," those who want to stand out from the pack and to be identified as unique individuals. Instead of seeking safety in numbers, they think of themselves as bold risk-takers who beat the odds and reap higher than average returns. So Y & R came out with a commercial in which a lone bull glides smoothly through a china shop—without breaking a single vase. The new slogan "A Breed Apart" and the bull's successful maneuverings were thought to suggest innovativeness, resourcefulness, and an appealing combination of brute strength and finesse.

This saga of advertising in an investment house probably sounds like a lot of bull to the average consumer. After all, who *really* cares whether five animals storm around a field or one of the same species steps sedately around a china shop? A lot of marketing managers, that's who. This is what consumer behavior is all about.

In 1977, this same bull with its "Breed apart" slogan became the centerpiece of a massive advertising campaign when Merrill Lynch introduced its Cash Management Account. The Cash Management Account offered the individual consumer a mass of financial services in one bundle. It is generally thought to be the most important innovation ever to hit Wall Street.

The standard features of all such accounts have become a brokerage account, a checking account or a cash deposit or money market mutual fund, a debit or credit card, and a single monthly statement that outlines the transactions that have occurred during the monthly billing period. In addition, the service provides periodic "cash sweeps" of any idle cash resulting from deposits, sale of stock or bonds, dividends, and interest income into the available money market fund(s). Such funds may be invested in government securities, bank instruments, or tax-exempt instruments as specified by the investor. Checks or debit card withdrawals may be drawn directly on the cash deposit or money market fund, which is the account owned by a bank, if it is a deposit, or "managed" by the brokerage house, if it is a money fund. Additions made to "managed cash accounts" offered by banks are made in person at a branch office, through an automatic teller machine (ATM), or by mail.

This Cash Management Account example happens to illustrate a fundamental element of marketing and consumer behavior, the product life cycle. In 1977 the "bull" as "A breed apart" marked the beginning of the product life cycle for the category of managed cash accounts. Today the managed cash account has reached its growth stage and represents a major financial industry. This chapter describes how the product life cycle acts as a basic influence in shaping the nature of consumer behavior.

One of the complexities of consumer behavior is the immense variety of buying situations. Some of these differences will be incorporated here; others will be introduced in later chapters, especially Chapters 12, 13, 14, and 15. Three concepts are discussed in this chapter—product category, product life cycle (PLC), and market—and they can help in making sense of this variety. They are the foundation to an understanding of consumer behavior for marketing purposes.

2. PRODUCT CATEGORY

Product category is the means by which consumers group similar brands so as to simplify their thinking. The formation of product category is an essential part of consumer behavior. Once a consumer places a new brand in its product category in his mind, he knows a lot about the brand because he assumes it is like other brands in that category. When Shearson in 1982 offered its Financial

Management Account, investors could assume that as a "managed cash account" it would be substantially similar to Merrill Lynch's Cash Management Account.

Obviously, buying a managed cash account is different from buying a can of soup. Let us examine why some of these differences exist. First, the "*product* category," as it is commonly called, is the group of brands that the consumers view as close substitutes for each other. For example, some investors may treat all railroad stocks as being in the same product category, but they break computer stocks into two classes, "the biggies" such as IBM and the "little ones." Economists have found the concept of product category useful in defining a market as indicated by the economist's assumption of "separability" whereby they assume that consumers do group brands in their minds and so "separate" brands in terms of groups of brands.[1] Also, they use the label "industry" for product category, because traditionally they have not been as much concerned about brand comparisons as marketers have. But marketing managers sometimes define an industry incorrectly because they do not carefully examine how consumers actually group brands into product categories. A well-known company thought it was selling a brand of soup, but discovered that consumers were using it as an ingredient in a cocktail spread. Consumers were grouping the brand of soup with the product category of cocktail spreads, not with the category of soups.

These examples all illustrate the basic principle of the product category, which is that the consumer groups or categorizes similar brands into a product category to simplify her buying behavior.

3. PRODUCT LIFE CYCLE

3.1 Introduction

Consumers are always learning about and responding to a product category from the time when the first brand in it is introduced, as the Cash Management Account was in 1977, and throughout its "life cycle." The *product life cycle* is very useful as an organizing device to show the process by which both buyers and sellers change their behavior while interacting in the market. Managers find it especially useful, because not only does marketing vary over the PLC but so do manufacturing, finance, human resources, research and development, and as Abernathy and Utterback well described.[2]

The product life cycle suggests that a different strategy be followed for a brand in a product category at each of the three stages. Richard Foster, a director of McKinsey & Company, the large international consulting company,

---

[1] K. Lancaster, *Variety, Equity and Efficiency* (New York: Columbia University Press, 1979), p. 25.

[2] W. J. Abernathy and J. M. Utterback, "Innovation and the Evolution of Technology in the Firm," unpublished paper, HBS-75-18R (Harvard Business School, Cambridge, Mass., rev. June 1976).

takes the product life cycle as his basic concept in advising companies how to adapt continually in his new book, *Innovation*, and has dramatically articulated its central role in a company's attempt to innovate.[3] Phil Kotler has pointed how these three stages can be used in marketing nonprofit services and for another text systematically using this product life-cycle framework, see R. L. Horton.[4]

3.2   An Example of Product Life Cycle

The product life cycle begins when the first brand in a new *product category* is first introduced, such as Merrill Lynch's Cash Management Account was in 1977. Consumers usually accept an innovation slowly. In Figure 2-1, another innovation that was very important at the time because coffee was such a vital part of peoples' lives was Nescafe, which used the new technology of instant or soluble coffee. It was slow at the starting gate when Nestle Company introduced it in 1937. It is important to see this 31-year sweep of the life cycle of a product category because this pattern of change is one of the most important features of a consumer's life and, therefore, of the marketer's life as well.

Previously, consumers had known only regular ground coffee. The new coffee was brewed at supernormal pressure and temperature and then sprayed into a column of hot air in a drying tower. When it fell to the bottom, it was a fine, soluble powder. As Figure 2-1 shows, Nescafe finally took off in about 1950. As you also see in Figure 2-1, it continued to grow rapidly throughout that decade. By 1962, however, not only did the rate of growth level off once again, but the absolute level of consumption began to decline. This trend in total coffee sales has continued down every year since, including 1982. Coffee sales as a whole have lost out particularly among the younger people since 1962 to soft drinks and beer.[5] In fact, just in the last two years, the number of coffee drinkers has become smaller than the number who consume soft drinks.[6] However, soluble coffee has continued to increase its share of all coffees.

Not all new products conform to this theoretical pattern of the product life cycle, but most do, and in terms of the theory of buyer behavior, it is a highly useful description. Products tend to go through these three stages: introduction, growth, and maturity. Growth is slow at first (Fig. 2-1), then rises rapidly, and levels off. Sometimes it begins to decline.

The inevitability of the decline has come to be questioned, and the evidence to date is mixed. Many criticized the concept of decline because they supposed that managers, if they believed it, would tend to assume a brand

---

[3] Richard Foster, *Innovation* (New York: Summit Books, 1986).

[4] R. L. Horton, *Buyer Behavior: A Decision-Making Approach* (Columbus, Ohio: Charles E. Merrill, 1984); and P. Kotler, *Marketing for Non-Profit Organizations*, 2nd ed. (Englewood Cliffs, N.J.: Prentice Hall, 1982).

[5] *The Wall Street Journal* (New York edition), March 19, 1986, p. 33.

[6] John C. Maxwell, Jr., "Coffee Sales Dip Continues," *Advertising Age*, May 9, 1983, p. 82.

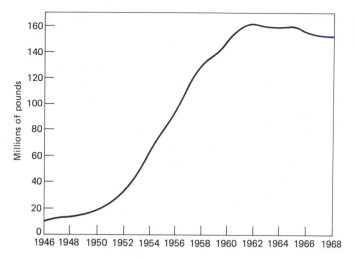

Figure 2-1
Product Life Cycle of Instant Coffee,
1946–1968

should be dropped once its sales have leveled off. Consequently, it was thought that managers would probably be less attentive to new opportunities for the old brand.

Three comments are in order about the use of the product life-cycle concept in this book. First, it is used here as an explanatory concept.[7] Second, we will not be concerned with the decline stage. Indeed, we could just as well use the term "product *growth* curve," except that it is less familiar. Third, the product life cycle is useful only in describing the behavior of a product category, not of an individual brand. This is important because it is sometimes mistakenly applied to brands. Now you can see why the product class concept was introduced first. Brands grow by gaining a greater share of their category.

Nescafe, for example, was the first to introduce the new product class of instant coffee. Other coffee makers rolled out their own version of instant during the decade of the product's rapid growth, such as General Foods with Maxwell House Instant. The individual brand patterns of growth, however, may have been quite different from that of the total product category.

It is this rise of an innovation—the creation of a new product category—that characterizes any postindustrial society. In preindustrial societies, new products are almost nonexistent. In industrial societies, new products exist, but they are likely to fit into established classes. Radically new products are not so frequent.

3.3   Consumers Adapt to Product Life Cycle

3.3.1 Introduction.   In adapting to these three stages of the PLC, consumers acquire a pattern of behavior that is different for each stage.

Consider the individual consumers who were buying instant coffee in the three decades from 1940 to 1970. In 1940, few had ever seen an instant

[7] G. S. Day, "The Product Life Cycle: Analysis and Applications Issues," *Journal of Marketing*, 45 (Fall 1981), 60–67.

coffee, so there was no reason to need the product. Consequently, they had to develop criteria (benefits) by which to judge its relevance. This required obtaining extensive information and processing (thinking about) it. Consumers faced such decisions as: Was it good to want and buy such a convenient food? Or would using instant coffee violate established social values? At that time, the typical consumer was likely to be a female homemaker proud of her ability to brew *regular* coffee. As was shown in a classic study by M.I.T. psychologist Mason Haire, almost half the homemakers surveyed felt that friends would think them lazy and extravagant if they used instant coffee.[8]

This example points to a basic premise of consumer behavior. Consumers are always solving problems when they buy something and especially if it is quite new. Psychologists have found that consumers are actually learning "concepts" or "images," first, of the product category and then of the brands as they go through the product life cycle. This is a part of the patterns of behavior just mentioned. Each of the three stages of the product life cycle reflects a specific pattern of problem solving or decision making on the part of the buyer: initially, *extensive problem solving* (EPS), then *limited problem solving* (LPS), and finally, *routine problem solving* (RPS). This notion of how consumers change their behavior will be developed at length. We emphasize it, not because it is a new idea; for example, it was used as early as 1963.[9] Nor is the notion of dubious validity; for example, it is consistent with some of the latest developments in cognitive science, the study of how people think.[10] But it is so highly useful in designing marketing strategy that the book has been organized in terms of it. Consequently, you do need to be familiar with it.

Each consumer's behavior then can be classified into one of the three stages of the cycle according to two characteristics: amount of information available and speed of decision, as summarized in Table 2-1. For example, in EPS the amount of information needed is great, and the decision is slow. As you will see in the following paragraphs, consumer behavior is highly interdisciplinary. All three social scientists—economists, psychologists, and marketing scientists—recognize the role of the product life cycle in consumer behavior. This interdisciplinary character of marketing you will see throughout the book.

3.3.2 Extensive Problem Solving. Let us continue with the Nescafe example but, if you don't wish to, have a cup, take Coke, which today may be much more to your liking. There were two noticeable characteristics of consumers at the bottom of the product life cycle as in Figure 2-1. First, they needed a great amount of information to decide whether to buy instant coffee and so searched for the information by talking to friends, reading ads, and so on. Second, they

---

[8] M. Haire, "Projective Techniques in Marketing Research," *Journal of Marketing*, XIV, no. 5 (April 1950), 649–56.

[9] J. A. Howard, *Marketing Management* (Homewood, Ill.: Richard D. Irwin, 1963), Chapters 3 and 4.

[10] J. R. Anderson, *The Architecture of Cognition* (Cambridge, Mass.: Harvard University Press, 1983), Chapter 6.

Table 2-1   Characteristics of Stages of Decision

Stage of PLC	Stage of Decision	Amount of Information Used	Speed in Making Decision
Introduction	EPS	Large	Slow
Growth	LPS	Medium	Medium
Maturity	RPS	Small	Fast

pondered the decision and made up their minds slowly. This kind of behavior is called "extensive problem solving" by marketers as in Table 2-1.

It occurs when consumers are confronted with a brand from an unfamiliar product category, a category that they have never encountered. In the extensive problem-solving stage, therefore, a consumer must form a concept of the product category. Psychologists refer to this stage as *concept formation* as in Table 2-2. Before she can buy a brand in an informed way, the consumer must form in her mind a concept of the category. Another word used for this concept is "product category image."

To learn to buy an innovation, which by definition is "new to the world," as instant coffee was in 1940, consumers must learn what the product will do for them—how it will fit into their lives and what criteria they should use to judge it. This is the *grouping and distinguishing* principle. When consumers first encountered instant coffee, they grouped it with something it resembled. Since it was more like regular coffee than anything else, they grouped it with coffee. They then began to distinguish it from regular coffee and so formed an instant coffee product category different from regular coffee. To do this, they used criteria, for example, convenience and taste. (It was more convenient but less tasty than regular coffee, they concluded.)

Table 2-2   Three Views of the Stages of Consumers' Decision Processes

PLC	Stage 1, Introduction	Stage 2, Growth	Stage 3, Maturity
Marketer	Extensive problem solving (EPS)	Limited problem solving (LPS)	Routine problem solving (RPS)
Psychologist	Concept formation	Concept attainment	Concept utilization
Economist	Changing utility function	Constant utility function Changing consumer technology	Constant utility function Constant consumer technology

Criteria that are used to choose a product are usually termed "benefits," which can be either positive or negative. Price is usually negative. In this way, consumers formed a concept of the product category called "instant coffee." This process of concept formation is the psychologists' counterpart of the manager's notion of extensive problem solving. As will be discussed in later chapters, the psychologists' view helps to explain the speed of consumers' decision and the amount and kind of information they need to make their judgments.

Let's look at the economist's version of stage 1 in Table 2-2 and compare it with the marketer's corresponding "extensive problem solving" and the psychologist's "concept formation." The economist, as you may recall from your introductory economics course, refers to this stage of the consumer's thinking as "changing her utility function." He means that to buy an innovation, the consumer must first *change* (or develop anew in her mind) the benefits by which she judges this new thing. In buying regular coffee she may have used "taste," "sharpness," and "price" as the benefits. But this new stuff often was weak on smelling like coffee. Consequently, for instant coffee she learned to use "taste," "smell," and "price." She must learn a new set of benefits for the new product category, as regular coffee drinkers and noncoffee drinkers had to do when instant came along.

According to the economist, the consumer's "utility function" is the thing that allows her to distinguish between the brands in this new product class, and so when she learns new criteria for choosing brands, she is, in the economist's terminology, "changing her utility function" to include new benefits by which she can evaluate brands in this new product category.

Extensive problem solving is an important concept that will be used throughout this text. Chapter 4 will discuss the implications of how this stage relates to the consumer decision model of Chapter 3, and Chapter 8 will deal with its role in marketing strategy.

3.3.3 Limited Problem Solving.

When more brands of instant coffee appeared as competition for Nescafe, in the decade of the 1950s, such as General Foods with its Maxwell House version of instant, the consumers' problem was much simpler. They merely put it in the right grouping (right product category) in their minds and then proceeded to distinguish it from other brands in that category.

They had already determined the benefits, but each brand was a little different in odor, taste, and price. Thus, to choose among brands, consumers had to evaluate the new brand based on each of these benefits. Each consumer judged the new brand on each of the benefits and decided whether it was better than, the same as, or not as good as Nescafe.

The benefits do not have to be learned all over again when she encountered a new brand in this familiar class. Consequently, consumers need less information than in extensive problem solving, and their decision time is faster, as seen in Table 2-1. This kind of behavior, called limited problem solving, occurs when consumers encounter a new brand in a familiar product category.

An example of this today is any new "managed cash account." Psychologists call this process of learning to evaluate a new brand in a familiar category *concept attainment*. A consumer must attain a new concept for the brand, but she already has a concept of the category.

As indicated earlier, economists view EPS as an instance of a "changing utility function" where the consumer must acquire his ability to distinguish a product category. But once having acquired a "utility function" for this product category, he must "change his *consumer technology*" to buy a new brand in that category. He chooses a new means for satisfying his needs. Just as changing production technology for the firm involves changing the combinations of quantities of land, labor, and capital in a factory, buying a new brand that requires him to change his previously established combination of benefit ratings is changing his consumer technology.[11] This is an important idea in the economist's thinking because it shows that consumers do not want products per se, but that they want certain quantities or amounts of the "characteristics" or benefits that a brand offers; for example, in a car, it might be durability, convenience, maintenance cost, and price.

Here we have seen that the economist's theory is in line with that of the marketer and psychologist. However, economists do not deal with the specific psychological *processes* of thinking by which consumers form their judgments in evaluating a brand on characteristics in the LPS stage such as they did with instant coffee. More important, economists do not deal with the still more fundamental issue of the processes by which consumers decide which set of product characteristics to use in judging any brand in a product class as required by stage 1 in Table 2-2.[12] After all, a product has many more characteristics than consumers can actually use in evaluating it. This process of learning his utility function with respect to the product category is the realm of stage 1. The marketer feels that she must understand both processes—both stage 1 and stage 2—because through her marketing, for example, advertising, salesmen, and so on, she provides *information the consumer can use* in forming both types of judgments. These and other issues of LPS will be discussed in more detail in Chapter 5.

3.3.4 Routine Problem Solving. By the late 1950s, consumers had become familiar with most of the brands of instant coffee. They had lost their reservations about convenience foods; in fact, convenience foods had become chic. Purchasing a different brand from the one the consumer happened to be using at the moment was a simple task: by this time he knew much about the brands, and so he merely examined prices and compared quality and availability in the supermarket. Buying had become routine in that he had evolved an *evoked set*.

---

[11] K. Lancaster, "A New Approach to Consumer Theory," *Journal of Political Economy,* LXXIV, no. 2 (April 1966), 132–57; D. S. Ironmonger, *New Commodities and Consumer Behavior* (London: Cambridge University Press, 1972); W. J. Baumol, "Calculation of Optimal Product and Retailer Characteristics: The Abstract Product Approach," *Journal of Political Economy,* 75 (October 1967), 674–85.

[12] G. S. Becker, *The Economic Approach to Human Behavior* (Chicago: University of Chicago Press, 1976), p. 144.

The evoked set is defined as, among the available brands, those brands that he would consider buying. To simplify his buying when faced with many brands as is typical in RPS, he will select a few of the most acceptable brands, and these few constitute his evoked set. All judgments about the quality of each brand had largely been made: consumers had already formed a concept, or image, of each brand. To decide in this situation, consumers merely consider the price and availability of the brand, which they have already learned to evaluate in forming their concept or mental picture of the brand. This situation is thus called *concept utilization* by psychologists and routine problem solving by marketers. For economists this is the only case they thought much about until recently, when they developed the concept of "changing consumer technology" for the LPS case. They refer to the RPS case as "constant consumer technology".

This kind of behavior is characterized by little need for information and by quick decisions as noted in Table 2-1. If prices tend to be stable and suppliers consistently make products readily available in retail stores, routine problem solving says that consumers' behavior becomes habitual and less thoughtful. A consumer may simply buy the same brand as before: he becomes somewhat *brand loyal*. However, as prices and availabilities change, he tends to shop around, which is sometimes called "variety seeking," as discussed in Chapter 6. While RPS seems to be the simplest for the marketer to deal with, Chapter 6 outlines some of the very real problems of trying to meet the needs of consumers in RPS.

These stages can be used by marketing managers in designing advertising, sales presentations, and other promotions to meet the consumer's needs for information about products. To do this, the manager must know how much and what kind of information to provide and how quickly consumers are likely to respond. For example, some consumers have become aware of the ill effects of too much sugar and so are looking for less heavily sweetened food. In response, Duffy-Mott produced an unsweetened applesauce. But talking with consumers reveals that they do not know this. Consequently the product sits on shelves unsold, because the company did not provide the amount of information—through advertising—that the consumer requires.

3.4 Evidence on Consumer Behavior over the PLC

First, a German study of mothers buying baby food for their first child was designed specifically to test how buyers change their behavior over the product life cycle.[13] The product category was well known by mothers of older children, but it was a new product category to these particular mothers. Thus, to a segment of the population, it was a true innovation.

The study confirms that as mothers gain experience buying baby food and move from EPS to LPS and RPS (see Table 2-1), they reduce their information search, use fewer sources of information, and use the sources less frequently.

[13] K. P. Kaas, "Consumer Habit Forming, Information Acquisition and Buyer Behavior," *Journal of Business Research*, 10 (1982), 13–15.

Table 2-3 Amount of Information Acquired Each Week

	Total Number of Bits of Information	Number of Brands Searched	Number of Attributes Accessed
Week 1	17.20	4.89	4.83
Week 2	11.81*	4.33*	3.89†
Week 3	10.18†	3.94‡	3.79
Week 4	7.33*	3.33*	2.99*
Week 5	6.21*	3.07	2.37*
Week 6	4.52*	2.36*	1.81*

* Decrease from previous week is significant at .001 level.

† Decrease from previous week is significant at .01 level.

‡ Decrease from previous week is significant at .05 level.

SOURCE: D. R. Lehmann and W. L. Moore, "Validity of Information Display Boards: An Assessment Using Longitudinal Data," *Journal of Marketing Research*, XVII, no. 4 (November 1980), 453.

In addition, they shift from product category–specific information to brand-specific information. Also, when they are less familiar with a product as in LPS, they assign more importance to digestibility, freshness, and vitamin content. But with more experience, their behavior becomes RPS. Specifically, they emphasize such "situational benefits" as price, availability, and special bargains. Their feeling of confidence increases, and, in turn, they buy larger quantities of the product at each purchase. Further, they intend to change from buying it in specialty shops to discount stores where the prices are lower as they became more familiar.

Second, in an experimental study of bread purchasing by Don Lehmann and Bill Moore, 120 students and staff members of the Columbia Business School were given a choice of a free loaf of bread from among five special types of bread each week for seven weeks.[14] They were also given access to choices of information just prior to when they selected the bread each time. You can see in Table 2-3 how their search behavior declined from week to week in terms of amount of information selected (col. 1), number of brands searched (col. 2), and the number of bread attributes that were searched (col. 3). The conclusion, as you can see, is in agreement with the baby food study in that the amount of information used declined from week to week as they moved from EPS to LPS to RPS as shown by the decrease from week to week. Obviously, EPS would be much simpler with bread than with a personal computer.

Also, there was clear evidence of "the existence of two distinct segments and a growing number of people in the RRB (RPS) segment over time."[15] Further,

[14] W. L. Moore and D. R. Lehmann, "Individual Differences in Search Behavior for a Non-Durable," *Journal of Consumer Research*, 7, no. 3 (December 1980), 296–307.

[15] D. R. Lehmann, W. L. Moore, and T. Elrod, "The Development of Distinct Choice Process Segments over Time: A Stochastic Modeling Approach," *Journal of Marketing*, 46 (Spring 1982), 55.

there was evidence of cyclic behavior, shifting back into LPS from RPS, which will be discussed at length in Chapter 6. Lehmann, Moore, and Elrod's methodology did not fully capture this cyclic shifting. However, they report "a substantial fraction of the population becomes so routinized that they collect no external information prior to purchase."[16] In summary, Lehmann, Moore, and Elrod provide us with more evidence of the validity that consumer behavior of a frequently purchased item represents three stages over the product life cycle—EPS, LPS, and RPS—in the sense that they found that the two upper stages clearly exist.

Third, a study by Jim Bettman and Whan Park throws light on the lower two stages—EPS and LPS—of the PLC and is devoted to microwave ovens.[17] We wouldn't expect purchasers of such a product to attain routine problem-solving status, since the product is both infrequently purchased and expensive. Here the effects of consumer familiarity with the product class were tested. A sample of 99 housewives was divided into three groups: low familiarity (LF), medium familiarity (MF), and high familiarity (HF). The MF group processed more of the available information and depended less on prior knowledge. The authors suggest that the LF group always processes information more extensively because they find it difficult, and the HF group processes less, because they don't need it.

The authors also maintain that consumers with more knowledge are more likely to use *brand* processing, which means that they make their choices by thinking of the brand as a whole instead of examing the individual attributes of the brand. On the other hand, the LF consumers are more inclined to examine the individual attributes of each brand. Finally, earlier in developing their choice process, they use comparison with absolute standards such as the brand is "*very sweet*." Later they shift to trade-offs and compare it with alternative brands; that is, brand A is chosen because it is sweeter than brand B.

Fourth, in another study of the same data on the microwave product, these ideas were further developed.[18] Unfamiliar customers (LF) used a fewer number of values on the attributes or benefits than did either medium familiarity (MF) or high familiarity (HF). Also, the LF were more confident in judging price and brand name than in judging product quality in terms of benefits. Finally, the choice of microwaves tended to be a two-stage choice process: first, reduce the number of brands to be compared and then choose from among this reduced number.

For this decision to reduce the number of brands being considered, LF took the least time, MF the most. But after the reduction process had actually taken place and she was choosing a specific brand, LF took the most time and

---

[16] Ibid., p. 56.

[17] J. R. Bettman and C. W. Park, "Effects of Prior Knowledge and Experience and Phase of the Choice Process on Consumer Decision Processes: A Protocol Analysis," *Journal of Consumer Research*, 7 (December 1980), 234–48.

[18] C. W. Park and V. P. Lessig, "Familiarity and Its Impact on Consumer Decision Biases and Heuristics," *Journal of Consumer Research*, 8 (September 1981), 223–30.

HF the least. Further, the consumer's confidence in her buying increased with familiarity in the reduction stage between LF and HF, although the difference between MF and HF is not significant. Similar results to reducing the brands being considered were found in selecting the specific brand, except that in the latter, the difference between LF and MF was not significant.

A final body of evidence supports the three stages at a still more fundamental level. It deals with how consumers actually "process information" or think. Johnson and Russo did a creative study using automobiles of how consumers with different levels of knowledge think about the product category of cars. They found that people with different levels of knowledge processed information differently.[19] At lower levels of knowledge, consumers tended to organize their information and think about the *attributes* of the brand as individual "chunks" of information in their memory. This we would call a late EPS or LPS case, depending upon the level of knowledge. Consumers with a higher level of knowledge organized their information around the *brand* as a whole, as one big "chunk" in their memory. This we would call moving toward RPS. Thus, we find consistency with the three-stage view and the specific way of structuring these three levels as you will see in each Chapter 4, 5, and 6, respectively.

Further, they point out that with increasing knowledge, consumers limit their search for information. They do this because they develop more efficient decision procedures:

> For example, experienced consumers would ignore the attribute "cruising range" since they realize that it is simply the product of fuel capacity and estimated miles per gallon. This procedural knowledge appears to be a major advantage that experienced consumers bring to the decision task.[20]

In summary, from this more fundamental study—Johnson and Russo—has come still more evidence that the three-stage view is a valid conceptualization of how consumers process information that is the foundation of their buying behavior.

3.5   Clarification of Complications

The joint concept of stages of the PLC and of changing consumer decision has two complications that should be clarified. First, Figure 2-1 pictures the product life cycle of instant coffee as though one person went through each of the stages in the period between 1940 and 1970. Of course, one consumer does not really require 30 years to pass through these stages, but only a few weeks or months, depending on how frequently she buys the product in question, which in turn depends on the amount consumed.

What is accurate, however, is that in the *1940s most consumers* were *becoming*

[19] E. J. Johnson and J. E. Russo, "Product Familiarity and Learning New Information," *Journal of Consumer Research*, 11, no. 1 (June 1984), 542–50.
[20] Ibid., p. 548.

familiar with this new product for the first time, as shown in Figure 2-2. By the 1950s, most consumers knew about instant coffee and were simply discriminating between one brand and another as other new brands came along; see Figure 2-2. By the 1960s, no new brands were appearing; most consumers had become familiar with a number of brands and were simply buying from the brands within their evoked set according to information on price and availability of a particular brand.

Yet, even in the 1940s, there were probably some people who quickly came to like Nescafe, and thereafter for quite sometime—perhaps the rest of their lives—bought only Nescafe, ignoring all new brands. Also, in the 1950s and extending even into the 1960s, there were some people—in the more remote areas of the United States, for instance—who were first learning about this new product. Finally, new households were being set up, and these people, too, were often buying coffee for the first time.

Consequently, by no means had all the consumers reached the same stage of learning at any point in time. Nevertheless for a frequently purchased, low-priced product, there is a tendency for one of the three stages of decision to be typical at any time, and it is this *typical* market that must be the focus of the marketing manager's attention.

Second, consumers of important and infrequently purchased products— "consumer durables" like refrigerators, for instance—do not conform as closely to Figure 2-2. Some of these consumers may forget the relevant benefits in the long period between purchases of refrigerators. More important, technological changes occurring between purchases results in a new product design, which sometimes requires that the consumer learn new criteria for choosing (benefits), which makes it EPS. Finally, consumers' personal values may also change in the interim between purchases, and so they weigh the benefits differently, as

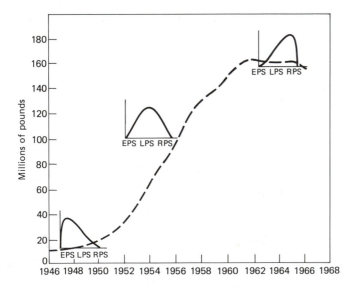

Figure 2-2
Product Life Cycle and Stages of the Decision Process for Instant Coffee, 1946–1968

will be discussed in Chapter 4. All three of these effects tend to cause each purchase to be something of an extensive problem-solving situation requiring substantial information and time. Thus, routine problem-solving behavior seldom exists for most consumers of expensive infrequently purchased items.

3.6 Summary of Product Life Cycle

The product life-cycle concept contributes in a number of very essential ways to designing effective marketing strategy. First, it guides the marketer in deciding the stage of consumer decision. If the consumers do not yet have a product category concept in their minds, it is EPS. If they do but do not yet have a concept of the brand they are considering, it is an LPS. If they have both—a brand concept in a familiar product category—it is RPS.

Second, it guides the marketer in selecting the information that should be disseminated to that market. Third, it guides him in deciding when to disseminate the information; for example, in EPS the customer first needs some vague notion of what that product category is like. Once having acquired this, the consumer can then handle more specific information about the brand's benefits. Fourth, it tells him how much information the customer needs as emphasized in Table 2-1.

Finally, it guides him in how to convey the needed information. He can use advertising, salesmen, direct mail, and so on. If he goes the advertising route, he can use television, newspapers, radio, cable, and so on. For example, advertising has been found more effective for brands early in the product life cycle and word-of-mouth later in the cycle.

4. MARKET

Here we introduce the third concept, the market. The *market* concept is one of the most widely used words in management's vocabulary. For example, a manager would think of an "RPS market." What does he mean by a market? The market is defined as "where" the companies and their consumers "interact" over the product life cycle.

The economist thinks of a *market* as geographically defined, as a *place* where people meet to buy and sell. This is an apt description of a market in a less advanced country, where personal contact is the usual means of trading. It is even an apt view of some markets in advanced countries, including the floor of the New York Stock Exchange or the meat market of 125th Street on Manhattan's West Side, where truck drivers from the Corn Belt unload meat to be resold to distributors in the New York area. However, because of improved technology of communication, such as, telecommunication and television, most markets in advanced countries have become quite impersonal. General Foods, for instance, makes Sanka coffee, stocks it in supermarkets, and advertises it over television, and the typical consumer never sees a representative of General Foods and may not even associate Sanka with General Foods.

To define his specific market is one of the most important tasks of a marketing manager because he usually serves only a part of a market. He obviously must specify the consumers he plans to serve so that he can reach them with his advertising, for example. But equally important, he must specify the competitors against whom he plans to compete. These are the consumer targets and the competitor targets that he must specify to design the core strategy for his product. This core strategy concept, which is discussed in Chapter 8 and used thereafter throughout the book, is the foundation out of which all marketing strategy and planning for his product should flow.

5. CONCLUSIONS

The study of consumer behavior is described by consumer behavior theory that is made up of concepts and relations among these concepts. Three fundamental concepts were presented: product category, product life cycle, and market. All three are a foundation to understanding the consumer, but the product life cycle is the most essential, especially for frequently purchased products.

The three stages of the product life cycle were presented as giving rise to three patterns of behavior: EPS, LPS and RPS. Also, the need for the buyer to have information about a product in order to buy it was emphasized. Thus, consumer information was another concept, and the buyer's information needs were related to the stage of the cycle. This is a relationship that helps us understand the consumer and greatly increase our marketing effectiveness. Finally, the consumer in his concept or image of a product category has benefits by which he evaluates any brand in that category. In this evaluation he builds a brand image in his mind of each brand in his evoked set. This brand image tells him how good this brand is in serving his needs.

These are the concepts and relations among those concepts that make up buyer behavior theory. In Chapter 3, this idea will be described more in detail in the form of a simple model, which in that form applies only to the buyers of a new brand in a familiar product class (LPS). To apply it to EPS and RPS, the model must be slightly modified for each of these two other stages.

Questions

1. What is the significance of the term "product category" in trying to understand how consumers buy?
2. Why is the product life cycle such an important concept for marketing?
3. What evidence do you have for believing that consumers really do change their buyer behavior over the life cycle of a product category?
4. What are the key complications that you should recognize in using the product life-cycle concept?
5. How would you describe a "market" for any product of your own choosing?

CHAPTER 3

A Basic Tool:
The Consumer Decision Model

1. INTRODUCTION TO CONSUMER DECISION MODEL

The purpose of Chapter 3 is to present a simple model of buyer behavior that describes consumer behavior in the growth stage and will be used throughout the rest of the book. Consumers live in a complex environment, and hence, their behavior is complex. A model is defined as a simplified description of that complex behavior. The model is made up of only six components and the relations among these components.

Why do we use a model? With this simplified picture, the marketer can be much more effective in understanding how consumers respond to his marketing effort. Knowing this, he can design still better marketing plans to encourage them to buy his product. For example, in his advertising he can tell them that his product has features they like, if he knows the features they like.

You may ask, "Why use this particular model? Aren't there other models available?" There are others, and two will be discussed in Chapter 7. To our knowledge none has been tested as much in the market as this one. In Table 3-1 are some of the instances where it has been applied. As you can see, a variety of products and conditions were deliberately included. In each of these applications something was learned about how to use the Consumer Decision Model (CDM) more effectively. Also, John Farley, Donald Lehmann, et al. over the past six years have done a series of meta-analyses of a number of these

Table 3-1   Some Applications of Consumer Decision Model

Company	Product	Time	Location
General Foods	Instant breakfast	1966	Domestic
Jabon Federal	Toilet soap	1969	Argentina
General Motors	Subcompact	1970	Domestic
General Foods	Vegetable bacon	1974	Domestic
Bristol Myers	Shampoo	1974	Domestic
Emery Air Freight	Air freight	1974	Domestic
IBM	Videodisk	1978	Domestic
Pfizer, Inc.	Antiarthritic	1980	Domestic
General Electric	Factory automation consulting	1982	Domestic
Ford Foundation	Condoms	1982	Kenya
Merrill Lynch	Managed cash account	1985	Domestic

applications to improve the methodology.[1] These will be discussed at the end of the chapter in terms of extending the CDM.

A model can be applied either qualitatively or quantitatively. It is applied qualitatively when it is used with a typical marketing case that describes some actual marketing situation. There it is used to organize the facts so that they can be better interpreted as the basis of action that should be taken. It is applied quantitatively when the data from one of the actual computer cases discussed in Chapter 1 are used mathematically to describe the relations among those facts. In this way predictions can be made about the payoff of different kinds of marketing actions. The model presented here in Chapter 3 can be used either qualitatively or quantitatively.

A review of the consumer's buying process will help us understand the model of that process. We found in Chapter 2 that buyers learn about a product by categorizing it, by placing it in their minds—memorizing it—in a category of equivalent brands called a "product category," for example, managed cash accounts. The product category has a label that makes it easier for the buyer to discuss equivalent things with acquaintances—both to get their advice and to give them his own advice about the new brand. When someone tells the buyer that new car X is a "compact," since he knows what a compact is, he immediately knows this offering is smaller, cheaper, more maneuverable, and easier on gas than are mid-sized or full-sized cars but it is larger than a subcompact.

Once the buyer groups an unfamiliar brand in a known product category, she learns more about it by distinguishing it from other brands in the class. She compares it on certain attributes, such as size, price, and, in the case of cars, gas consumption. Her judgments of the features of the new brand contribute to her image, which is impressed upon her memory. This grouping and distinguishing to produce a brand image roughly describes buyer behavior as discussed in Chapter 2, but now let us be more precise.

---

[1] See J. U. Farley and D. R. Lehmann, *Meta-Analysis in Marketing: Generalization of Response Models* (Lexington, Mass.: Marketing Science Institute and D. C. Heath, 1986).

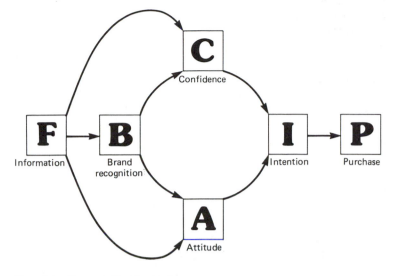

Figure 3-1   Consumer Decision Model

Brand image is defined as the consumer's total understanding of the brand. It is made up of three components. First, it is the physical characteristics by which the customer recognizes the brand. Second, it is the strength of the brand of each of the relevant benefits on a "favorable-unfavorable" scale as judged by the customer. Third, it is the strength of the consumer's feeling about his ability to determine accurately the quality of the brand. In Chapter 4 another component will be added, the consumer's product hierarchy.

This chapter is about the process by which the consumer groups a *new* brand in an *established* product class and then distinguishes it from existing brands in that class. It is important for you to remember that this is a case of "limited problem solving," developed at length in Chapter 2. The process of buying in a limited problem-solving (LPS) situation is explained through the CDM (see Figure 3-1). The CDM can be applied to the other two stages of consumer behavior—extensive problem solving (EPS) and routine problem solving (RPS)—described in Chapter 2, but to do this, it must be slightly modified as you will see in Chapters 4 and 6. Later, in Chapter 3, when you have an overall view of the model, we will introduce more of the detailed psychological processes that operate in the CDM and discuss them at length in later chapters.

2. CONSUMER DECISION MODEL

2.1 Introduction

The CDM is defined as a model made up of six interrelated components (variables) that are related to each other as shown in Figure 3-1: information (F), brand recognition (B), attitude (A), confidence (C), intention (I), and purchase (P).

Of these six, the three central components—brand recognition (B), attitude toward the brand (A), and confidence in judging the brand (C)—make up the buyer's brand image and can be thought of as the ABC's of consumer behavior. They are formed in the consumer's mind by the grouping and distinguishing process discussed in Chapter 2.

2.2 Information

Information or "facts" (F) has to be defined with care, as a massive amount of research indicates. First, as a stimulus, it is some physical event that one or more of the buyer's five sense organs—seeing, hearing, smelling, touching, and tasting—are exposed to, either voluntarily or involuntarily. Typically, brochures, newspapers, radio, television, and word-of-mouth are sources of information for the buyer. Sight and hearing are the two major sense organs by which he absorbs the information. But in food, taste, and smell are generally important. Touch is highly significant for blind people, but we believe that marketers have yet to use that sense fully among normal people.

Second, our concern is much more with the percept than with the stimulus. The percept is defined as that which the buyer perceives from being exposed to the stimulus. Since our interest is in the percept, we define *information* (F) as the percept that is caused by the stimulus.[2] The standard measure of the consumer's percept (F) is recall. But a simple straightforward question about what the consumer recalls is usually not adequate for eliciting the percept in the consumer's mind as you will see in Chapter 5.

Facts of various kinds and from varied sources are often critically important to the consumer when she makes an LPS purchase. As the CDM shows, information (F) causes the buyer to recognize the brand (B), to evaluate it in terms of her needs, which is attitude (A), and to create in her mind a level of confidence (C) or certainty of how well she can judge if the brand will yield satisfactory or unsatisfactory results.

2.3 Brand Recognition

Brand recognition (B) is defined as the extent to which the buyer knows enough about the criteria for categorizing, but not for evaluating and distinguishing it from other brands in its product category. Recognition helps the consumer to build both an attitude (A) toward the brand and confidence (C) in his judgment of it (see arrows in Figure 3-1).

Recognition attributes of a brand tend to be physical: the color, size, shape, and texture of the box. A simple outline of the object with little data is

---

[2] For someone in marketing and so likely to be interested in perception, a splendid relevant review of research in perception can be found in G. A. Miller and P. N. Johnson-Laird, *Language and Perception* (Cambridge, Mass.: Harvard University Press, 1976), Chapters 1 and 2.

adequate. Thus, packaging and product design are extremely important. A new vegetable bacon, Lean Strips, was introduced to the market by General Foods in 1974. In the test market questionnaire, the characteristics used to represent brand recognition (B) included the kind of package, the picture on the package, the size of the package, and manner of storing (frozen or refrigerated) the product.

You can think of brand recognition as referring to the product's *form* in contrast to the consumer's attitude toward the brand, which has to do with its *function,* namely, what the product does to cause the buyer to like or dislike it. This distinction is basic, since form and function can perform markedly different roles in the buyer's thinking. However, a consumer needs information about both form and function to be able to categorize a brand in a product class.[3]

Equally important, these physical attributes are a major reason why marketing a product and marketing a service, such as a health service, pose different problems. Increasingly the physical attributes are being emphasized in practice. They have not been studied in depth, but there has been some attention to trademarks and related ideas.[4] Practitioners are at least intuitively aware of them. That's why service companies sometimes outfit their employees in standard uniforms—a substitute for the physical product. For example, salespersons at Century 21, a national real estate firm that sells residential properties, wear standard uniforms bearing the same insignia that appear on its TV advertising and front-lawn signs. Merrill Lynch, as noted in Chapter 2, uses the figure of a bull in its advertising for the Cash Management Account to project a "bullish" image and a slogan, "More resources, better solutions." They make Merrill Lynch people "a *breed apart*," which associates the bull symbol to the service offered.

In a recent attempt to describe these differences between service and packaged goods advertising, Grey Advertising, Inc., wrote;

> While some of the marketing and advertising strategies that apply to packaged goods industries occasionally work for service industries, the fact is that service companies have unique characteristics that require special insights and special solutions from marketers. The most helpful ingredient in service business advertising is the development of a strong, distinctive enduring Brand Character that can be used effectively and simultaneously in marketing, advertising, promotion, employee motivation, and all other corporate activities.[5]

Financial institutions, in particular, have no physical product to give them identity, an irksome problem now that they seek to expand their consumer services. Merrill Lynch a decade ago recognized this with its trademark of a bull.

Product designer Walter Margulies has said, " 'corporate identity' and

---

[3] Ibid., p. 232.

[4] S. J. Levy and D. W. Rook, "Brands, Trademarks and the Law," in B. M. Enis and K. J. Roering, *Review of Marketing, 1981* (Chicago: American Marketing Association, 1981), pp. 185–94; D. Cohen, "Trademark Strategy," *Journal of Marketing*, 50, no. 1 (January 1986), 61–74.

[5] "Service with a Difference," *Grey Matter*, 51, no. 1 (1980), p. 2.

'corporate image' are not synonymous, but are opposite sides of the same coin."[6] What he means is that the image of a corporation or brand in the buyer's mind can be favorable or unfavorable and so reflect correspondingly upon the identity that he attaches to the corporation or brand.

Brand image as you will recall is the total picture of the brand in the buyer's mind and is made up of all three elements: his brand recognition, his attitude toward the brand, and his confidence in his ability to judge the quality of the brand. These we call the ABCs of marketing. The concept of brand recognition is not widely recognized in practice at present, but it probably will be as its role in consumer thinking is better understood. Recently, however, product designers have been talking about "visual clues" and "product semantics," and advertisers have been using "semiotics," which deals with signs, symbols, and their functions in communicating.[7]

2.4 Attitude

Attitude (A) toward the brand, the second part of brand image, is defined as the extent to which the buyer expects the brand to yield satisfaction of his particular needs. To the extent the buyer does, it spurs her intention to buy the brand.

Attitude is probably the most basic and widely accepted concept throughout the social sciences. To give you some appreciation for it, you can say that attitude is as pervasive to the social sciences as the concept of the atom is to the natural sciences. Great progress has been made in the past two decades in understanding the nature of attitude and its relation to behavior both in marketing and the basic social sciences.[8] This discussion is only an overview, however, to build upon in developing a coherent theory of consumer buying.

Discussing the measurement of it is probably the most useful at this point. Attitude can be measured in at least two ways: unidimensionally and

---

[6] Walter P. Margulies, "How Banks Stress Corporate Image," *Advertising Age*, May 19, 1980, pp. 85–86.

[7] J. C. Houghton, "Semiotics on the Assembly Line," *Advertising Age*, March 16, 1987, p. 18.

[8] For a careful review, see R. Batra, "Affective Advertising: Role, Processes and Measurement," in R. A. Peterson, W. D. Hoyer and W. R. Wilson, eds., *The Role of Affect in Consumer Behavior: Emerging Theories and Applications*, (Lexington, Mass: D. C. Heath, 1986), pp. 53–85.

For a review of research on the general topic of attitude, see R. H. Fazio and M. P. Zanno, "Direct Experience and Attitude Behavior Consistency," in R. Berkowitz, ed., *Advances in Experimental Social Psychology* (New York: Academic Press, 1981), Vol. 14, pp. 161–202. It also shows how attitude is beginning to be viewed as related to confidence (C) and brand identification (B) as done in the CDM. Further, see R. E. Petty, J. T. Cacioppo, and D. Schumann, "Central and Peripheral Routes to Advertising Effectiveness: The Moderating Role of Involvement," *Journal of Consumer Research*, 10 (September 1983), 135–46, for an extensive discussion of how attitudes are formed and especially the role of motivation.

multidimensionally. An example of unidimensional attitude is when the buyer is asked: "Will you please rate brand X on a 1-to-5 scale, where 5 is favorable and 1 unfavorable?" To that question, the buyer has a single—or unidimensional—answer, any one of five numbers.

A multidimensional measurement, often called an "expectancy value" measure, has several stages. First, the marketer asks a pilot group of buyers to tell him the attributes or *benefits* by which they evaluate a brand in this product class. *Benefit* is defined as a characteristic of the product or service that the consumer values either positively or negatively. Then, each buyer in the regular sample is asked to rate the relative *importance* of these benefits. Next, he is asked to rate how well the brand *performs* on each of the more important of these benefits. The benefits can be either negative or positive; for example, price is usually negative.

With this kind of measurement one brand's high rating on a certain benefit offsets or compensates for its low rating on another benefit in the consumer's mind, and so it is called the *linear compensatory* rule. For example, the buyer may like the style of one car but finds the price too high—the positive style compensates for the negative price. The marketer takes each of the buyer's answers and multiplies her ratings on the *importance* of each benefit times her ratings on the *amount* of each benefit she perceives in the brand. These products are then added together to produce the "attitude" variable in the CDM. This is the multidimensional measure of the buyer's attitude toward the brand.

An example of this multidimensional measure is the client's attitude toward Merrill Lynch's Cash Management Account in Table 3-2. As you see, in the first column are the client's benefits: personal service, rate of return on investments, reputation of Merrill Lynch, and convenience of monthly transaction statement. The second column is how important each of these benefits is to the client on a 1-to-7 scale in evaluating any brand of managed cash account. The third column contains a particular client's ratings of the specific brand, Cash Management Account, on these benefits. The two ratings for each benefit are multiplied together and the product inserted in the fourth column. These products are then summed to give a measure of "attitude."

As you can imagine, the multidimensional measure is more useful than is the unidimensional as a guide to allocating advertising, research and develop-

Table 3-2 Multidimensional Measure of Attitude Toward the Cash
Management Account

Benefits	Importance	Performance	
Personal service	6.14	6	36.8
Rate of return	6.10	4	24.4
Reputation of the firm	6.00	4	24.0
Transaction statement	5.98	3	17.9
			Attitude = 103.1

ment dollars, and other uses.[9] Obviously, devoting funds to improving the more important benefits provides a better payoff than does heaping money into the less important benefits. The multidimensional measure is also a guide to designing the promotional message and deciding the amount of promotional expenditures.

2.5   Confidence in Judgment

Confidence is the third element in the buyer's image of a brand. It is defined as the buyer's degree of certainty that his evaluative judgment of a brand is correct. The buyer's confidence in a particular brand is increased when his thinking is clarified by repeated reminders from marketers and from peers, that his peers like it, that it is distinct from other brands, and that the information is consistent with what he already knows about the brand. In turn, confidence causes intention to buy (see Figure 3-1) by removing the hesitancy to act caused by uncertainty.

It might seem strange that increasing the consumer's confidence (C) necessarily increases her intention to buy (I). You might argue that if her attitude (A) toward the brand is low—she doesn't care for it—increasing her confidence (C) would merely be adding to her belief that it is a poor brand. This should *decrease* her intention to buy it, contrary to what the model indicates. The reason that her confidence (C) does affect her intention (I) favorably is because that when her confidence (C) is low she "looks" for information. That she does look for informaton when her attitude is low is supported by studies of car purchasing. There is substantial evidence,[10] much of it unpublished, that a positive relationship holds between confidence (C) and intention (I). Also, attitude affects confidence to some extent, but this relation is complex and is not shown in Figure 3-1. It will be discussed in Chapter 17.

Although shown as three separate elements making up brand image, in fact, brand recognition, attitude toward a brand, and a buyer's confidence in his judgment of the brand are all intimately interrelated. Brand recognition forms a mental foundation, or "chunk," in his memory upon which the other two components of brand image build. Thus, B causes both A and C in Figure 3-1. Technically, B is an eidetic image, which means that it can be seen in the consumer's mind's eye in vivid detail.[11] The sharper it is, the more effective it

[9] In a forthcoming review of attitude research, W. J. McGuire is critical of this general type of attitude measure. His criticism may stimulate a healthy review of the field. See W. J. McGuire, "Attitude Structure," in A. R. Pratkanis, S. J. Breckler, and A. G. Greenwald, eds., *Attitude Structure and Function* (Hillsdale, N.J.: Lawrence Erlbaum Associates, forthcoming).

[10] R. E. Smith and W. R. Swinyard, "Attitude-Behavior Consistency: The Impact of Product Trial vs. Advertising," *Journal of Marketing Research*, XX, no. 3 (August 1983), 257–68. See Fazio and Zanno, "Direct Experience." See, also, P. D. Bennett and G. D. Harrell, "The Role of Confidence in Understanding and Predicting Buyer Attitudes and Purchase Intentions," *Journal of Consumer Research*, 2 (September 1975), 110–17; and M. Laroche and J. A. Howard, "Nonlinear Relations in a Complex Model of Buyer Behavior," *Journal of Consumer Research*, 6 (March 1980), 385.

[11] D. O. Hebb, "Concerning Imagery," *Psychological Review*, 75, no. 6 (1968), 466–77.

will be in affecting attitude and confidence and, therefore, influencing behavior indirectly.

Attitude also helps determine into which product category the buyer will group the brand.[12] For example, if the gas consumption of a car is rated favorably—meaning low gas consumption—the car is more likely to be grouped as a subcompact car. Attitude also aids brand recognition in distinguishing a particular brand from other brands in its category. Likewise, confidence, which is the result of information and built on brand recognition, adds strength to the brand image.[13]

A successful marketer helps the buyer to group a brand into the appropriate category and to distinguish it from other brands in that category. Unless the buyer can put the new brand into a category in his mind, he is less likely to buy it. If the marketer's information isn't clear enough, she could lose a prospective buyer who is too busy to use the time and effort required to learn about the product category.

2.6   Intention

Intention (I) to buy is defined as a mental state that reflects the buyer's *plan* to buy some specified number of units of a particular brand in some specified time period.[14]

It is useful for the marketer to understand buyer intention. If he surveys consumers, he can get a feel for the typical consumer's current intentions. Simultaneously, he can tap other elements of the customer's thinking—F, B, A, and C. Consequently, since he finds out intention to buy at that time, he can measure the effects of B, A, and C on I and thus measure indirectly the effect of B, A, and C on P. This works well for frequently purchased products, but for infrequently purchased items some problems may arise because of the time lag between when intention is measured and when the purchase is executed.

In addition, events in the buyer's life other than information may affect her intention, and these too can be fed into intention if desired. The marketer is often able to identify these events and thus estimate their future effects on intention and indirectly upon purchase. For example, a consumer's expectations about her future income can strongly shape her intention to buy consumer durables.

Again, as seen in Figure 3-1, attitude and confidence affect intention. Intention in turn affects purchase.

---

[12] Miller and Jonson-Laird, *Language and Perception*, p. 232.

[13] G. S. Day, *Buyer Attitudes and Brand Choice Behavior* (New York: The Free Press, 1970), p. 83.

[14] G. A. Miller, E. Galanter, and K. Pribram, *Plans and the Structure of Behavior: Basic Findings and Management Implications* (New York: Holt, Rinehart and Winston, 1960).

2.7 Purchase

To the marketer, *purchase* (P) is obviously the most important variable in the entire system. It represents the payoff—or lack of it—for marketing expenditures.

In the buyer's decision process, purchase is defined as when the buyer has paid for a brand or has made some financial commitment to buy some specified amount during some specified time period. It is caused by intention to buy.

Measurement of purchase (P) is relatively simple: the customer did or did not buy, or make a financial commitment to buy, during a certain time period. Depending upon the frequency of purchase, it is sometimes useful to distinguish between the decision to purchase and the act of purchase such as with a Cash Management Account, where intervening events may interrupt.

3. ILLUSTRATIVE APPLICATION OF CDM

3.1 Introduction

Like all models, the CDM can be used both qualitatively and quantitatively as mentioned at the outset of this chapter. You can use it qualitatively when, for example, you are doing a business case for class, and use it to organize your facts so as to obtain a clearer picture of events happening in the case.

3.2 Explanation of Using It Quantitatively

If a marketer were using the CDM quantitatively to explain how his consumers buy, he would restate the diagram in Figure 3-1 but include estimates of relationships among the variables. Assume that you have surveyed 100 buyers by telephone interview and by a series of carefully stated questions about their purchasing of managed cash accounts obtained data for each of the six variables for Merrill Lynch's brand. These telephone answers are then converted into numbers by *regression analysis*, which is a statistical tool that provides a measure of the relation between each of the variables. Thus, the regression coefficient can be obtained. For instance, the regression coefficient between information (F) and brand recognition (B) is .28 (see Figure 3-2).

As essential background to applying the model to the Cash Management Account let us briefly discuss the raw data from which these numbers are derived. We have been careful to define each of the six variables. These were *conceptual* definitions, however, in which each variable was defined in terms of other concepts. But where we want measurements as we must in consumer behavior as in any other science, we need an *operational* definition of each variable as well. How can we define "attitude (A)" so as to get a measure of it as seen at the bottom of Figure 3-2? As implied earlier we asked the consumer to rate a selected list of benefits in terms of how important each is to him on a 1-to-7 scale, in

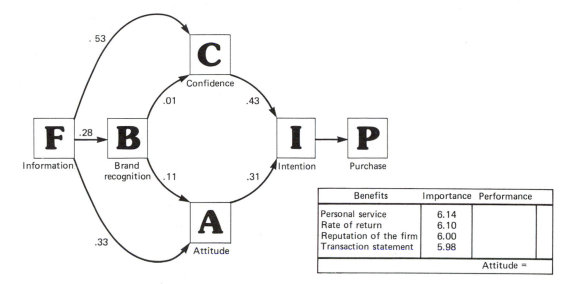

Figure 3-2 Consumer Decision Model of Merrill Lynch's Cash Management Account

Benefits	Importance	Performance
Personal service	6.14	
Rate of return	6.10	
Reputation of the firm	6.00	
Transaction statement	5.98	
		Attitude =

buying this product category. Then, he is asked to rate the brand on each of the four or five most important benefits according to how well the brand *performs* on a corresponding 1-to-7 scale. This is what we mean by an operational definition. Thus, an operational definition is a set of procedures or operations employed in distinguishing the object (brand) referred to from others in the same category. An operational definition is needed for each variable to apply the CDM. Further, each product category requires a different operational definition; for example, with a car the benefits are likely to be things like style and gas consumption while with a food they are things like taste and nutrition. Regression analysis as in the scatter diagram of Figure 3-3 estimates a linear relationship between two variables—an independent or causal variable (F) and a dependent or caused variable (A)—by minimizing the vertical distances from the data points to a line. The slope of that line (.33) is the regression coefficient and the constant (2) is the intercept:

$$A = 2 + .33F$$

What ".33" means is that if F is increased one unit on its scale, A correspondingly increases by .33, or 33% as much on its scale. Translating the regression coefficient into percentage of change helps the marketing manager to understand what his marketing can accomplish and to present his results to others in the company. More generally, you can say that if advertising (F) (the independent or causal result) is increased 10%, attitude (A) (the dependent or caused variable) increases by 3.3%, the proportionate amount that .33 is of 10%. This rule is a very helpful device for understanding the usefulness of the CDM. It will be used repeatedly throughout the rest of the book. If the regression coefficients are standardized to correct for differences in scales units as those in

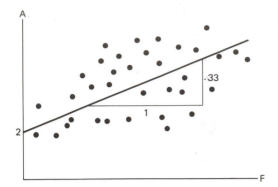

Figure 3-3
Relation Between Information and
Attitude

Figure 3-2 are, then scales of different length can be compared. For example, attitude was measured on a 1-to-7 scale, but confidence was measured on a 1-to-5 scale. Yet the two scores are fully comparable when standardized.

Using standardized coefficients, the marketer can tell which relationship is most powerful. For example, he can compare the $F \rightarrow A$ and $F \rightarrow C$ relations and note that F has less of an effect on A (33%) than upon C (53%). This tells him something about where the greatest payoff is in terms of advertising copy, namely, that maybe it is better to put money into information about the distinctiveness of the brand to affect the buyer's confidence instead of about the benefits of the brand to affect the buyer's attitude.

One final point: although the numbers shown in Figure 3-2 vary from product to product, they do tend to be stable over time for a particular product.

3.3   Prediction

A model can be used to *explain* what is happening in the market as we did in suggesting that advertising copy be changed. It can also be used *predictively*, by simulating the market. For example, one simplified use of the model is to find the total effect that increasing information (F) has upon actual purchase (P). The marketer can simulate the market by simply multiplying the regression coefficients through a chosen critical path in the system represented by Figure 3-2. Using arithmetic, he can determine whether it's wise to spend more or less funds on advertising. Alternatively, the marketer can calculate all the relations and thus incorporate the entire model. Simulation will be described more fully later in the course.

Using the CDM to simulate buyer behavior is very useful for the short-term planning that occupies most of the life of a brand or product manager. By comparing the content of the "attitude" box of his own brand against competing brands, the marketer can formulate strategy. Equally, if not more important, however, is the CDM's role in long-term planning. Over a product life cycle, for instance, these regression coefficients for buyers may change, although these relations are surprisingly stable as will be discussed in Chapter 4. This change probably occurred with instant coffee discussed in Chapter 2. Knowing how they change helps the marketing chief understand the market dynamics and make *long-term* predictions. Victor C. Micati, executive vice president of Pfizer, Inc., Europe (the largest element of Pfizer, International, America's largest international drug company), has described the usefulness of the CDM in strategic planning:

> there is an incredible tendency to interpret the future in terms of the way things exist today, or more generally, the way things existed retrospectively and make judgments from that. I believe that as you begin to force yourself to understand the *mental processes* and *relationships* involved, you can begin to design studies that get at those mental processes for your market, and thus attempt to simulate the future. That's what's so meaningful in planning. And that is the true value of this type of research.
>
> One of the incredible things you find in the young MBA coming into industry is his/her skills and the ability to look at today and define the marketplace and define competition and do it down to a very fine level of detail. But they frequently do not focus enough attention on what the future will hold.
>
> It is more difficult; you can't be precise about the future. You can't predict exactly what is going to happen. You can predict or try to predict from *behavioral trends* what might happen. And that is what the planning game is all about.
>
> When Ford invests in a three-year development program or Pfizer invests in a ten-year development program, they are investing against some *speculation* about what the *future will be like*. The extent to which you are good at projecting the future will determine to what extent you will be successful. *When this form of analysis is carried to the point of forcing the future*, it makes its most magnificent contribution to the planning process.[15]

4. EXTENSIONS OF THE CDM

The CDM provides profound insight into the nature of consumer buying and consuming. Only a model can do this because the human mind cannot grasp the immense complexities of this phenomenon without a model. Imagine yourself as part of a family planning program in Africa, as T. R. L. Black, a doctor, and John Farley, a professor, were, in the middle 1970s trying to learn how a brand of male contaceptives called Kinga (Swahili for "protection") should be marketed.[16] This was a part of the Ford Foundation's program. They faced this very complex problem knowing little more than that the market was comprised of 600,000 low-income people of Kenya. However, the marketing program they developed led 26% of the couples to try the condom, largely because the advertising caused them to lower their perceptions of the price.

To take full advantage of this insight into consumer buying provided by the CDM, however, requires two conditions. First, it must be possible to explain how the model can produce this insight. In Chapter 2, three concepts

---

[15] Personal correspondence.

[16] T. R. L. Black and J. U. Farley, "Responses to Advertising Contraceptives," *Journal of Advertising Research*, 17, no. 5 (October 1977), 49–56.

implied in Figure 3-3 were introduced: product category, product life cycle, and the market. They are really components of the CDM. The CDM is based on a product category and stage of cycle. It also implies including the market in that the CDM is typically applied to key competitors' brands as well. Further, you will recall that although the CDM as described in Chapter 3 applies specifically to only the growth stage of the cycle, which is limited problem solving, it can easily be modified as we will see in Chapters 4 and 6 to fit EPS and RPS as well. These three concepts of product life cycle, product category, and market are treated as supporting components of the CDM. Another component is the explanation of consumer information processing—how he is able to take in information and make sense of it—which will be covered in Chapters 4 through 6. This fuller explanation gives much additional leverage to the simple model as you will see there. Other supporting components will be added as we go along.

Second, it must be possible to explain why the simple CDM doesn't always apply. Under some conditions that we will now specify, the CDM's simplicity comes at a price. You need to be able to predict when this is likely to happen so that you can decide whether the additional power gained by extending the CDM is worth the time and effort required to make the change or whether its simple answers will suffice. These conditions will now be specified so that you can be aware of them.

First, and as implied in Figure 3-1, the CDM is homogeneous, recursive, and linear. The *homogeneous* aspect implies that all consumers are alike, that your market is not segmentable, and therefore that you have defined your market as all customers buying the product category and hence that you are competing with all supplying companies in the industry. The model can easily be made *heterogeneous*, however, simply by inserting segmenting characteristics such as age, sex, income, and sociocultural variables discussed in Part IV. These variables have usually been found to impinge upon intention to buy, so that their respective boxes in Figure 3-1 would have arrows leading to "Intention." The variables are inserted into the regression equation to determine intention. Segmentation is discussed at length in Chapters 12, 13, 14, and 15 because it is basically a complex but very important topic, as you probably know, and you need more concepts to understand it well.

The recursive model assumes that causation goes only one way, from information forward, but it can be made *nonrecursive* by adding feedbacks. Buyer feedback—her reaction to using a brand that she has just purchased—also influences her next purchase just as well and usually more than does current information, so that a nonrecursive (feedback) model is more realistic than is a recursive (nonfeedback) model. In this way some of the actual consumption process can be incorporated into the model. If the buyer likes the product when she buys it, she will obviously be more likely to buy it next time. The CDM can take this feedback into account with a box called "Satisfaction" when it is connected to "Purchase" with an arrow. There are also two dotted arrows running back from "Satisfaction," one arrow to "Confidence" and one to "Attitude." Thus, if buyer satisfaction is high, confidence and attitude will be higher still on the next purchase. (This feedback is described in detail in Chapter 16.)

Linear relations can limit the CDM. The arrow from F to A in Figure 3-1 is represented by a straight line in Figure 3-3, the scatter diagram. While the straight line simplifies the marketer's analysis of the data, some of the relationships are really *nonlinear*. To treat them as linear can make a marketer's predictions less precise, and sometimes, seriously wrong. Also by doing nonlinear analyses, she can determine whether some of the independent variables are *interactive*. For example, if a buyer's attitude is high, her confidence will have a stronger effect upon intention than when her attitude is low. In this case, confidence is interacting with attitude in causing intention. (Both nonlinear and interactive relations are explained in detail in Chapter 17).

Going beyond homogeneity, recursiveness, and linearity, situational differences such as buying for different needs—buying steak for the family dinner versus buying steak when having the boss for dinner—are not included in the CDM as described here. Situational differences are often referred to and cited in the textbooks. However, Farley, Lehmann, and Ryan find situational differences not to be nearly as important as we thought.[17]

In addition, the CDM uses utilitarian motives. It may well be that for some products such as buying artwork, attending concerts, buying lingerie (bras and panties), and so on, a more emotional analysis should be incorporated. The emotional aspects will be added in Chapter 10.

Also, the CDM assumes that all the marketing variables take effect in about the same length of time. Research has shown, however, that there are substantially greater lags, or "carryover" effects, in advertising than with price.[18] You can expect consumers to respond to a price change much more quickly than to a change in advertising.

Finally, all the discussion here is about using the CDM to make better profit and nonprofit management decisions but omitting the important issue of consumerism. Doesn't the consumer have problems he needs help on? For example, should he believe the advertising? Chapter 18 deals with how to use the CDM to help the consumer by guiding the development of appropriate consumer protection laws.

5. CONCLUSIONS

This chapter has presented a model composed of cetain components of human behavior. It has attempted to capture the core of consumer behavior from among the myriad influences that actually operate in the typical buying situation.

[17] J. U. Farley, D. R. Lehmann, and M. J. Ryan, "Patterns in Parameters of Buyer Behavior Models: Generalizing from Sparse Replication," *Marketing Science*, I, no. 2 (Spring 1982), 181–204.

[18] G. Assmus, J. U. Farley and D. R. Lehmann, "How Advertising Affects Sales: Meta-analysis of Econometric Results," *Journal of Marketing Research*, XXI (February 1984), 65–74.

By little more than a mechanical application, a brand manager can use the model for short-term market planning, since it provides estimates of marketing effects. With a little more imagination, the model can be a useful strategy tool for the divisional marketing vice president, who needs to position products against both customers and competitors. And, with substantial creativity, the model can be used to design the marketing element of corporate strategy—for example, to guide R & D spending toward technologies that will provide the products of tomorrow. But to design strategy, the marketer also needs to know the basic theory contained in Chapters 4 to 6. Basic theory is essential in defining the variables used in a case study. But for other reasons, too, the marketer cannot use the CDM effectively without applying this more advanced theory— a point that is crucially important and requires more explanation.

The theory supplies the basis for drawing the arrows in Figure 3-1. It substitutes for the reams of data that would be needed to check out all possible relations between the variables and to find the right variables for each particular situation if no theory is available. For a model of only three variables, there are 12 possible ways that the arrows can be arranged.[19] Hence, it would be terribly laborious to check out even a three-variable model. How about checking out this six-variable model?

A quantitative model can be built without theory, but it is much more limited in what it can contribute to explaining and predicting consumer behavior. For example, Pfizer, Inc., can develop a useful model for each of its domestic products, telling the marketing manager how much promotion expenditures for drugs influence the doctor's prescription level. But to use it, the company must have had three years of experience with the particular drug. This requirement renders the model much less useful because the most crucial period in a product's marketing life is the first three years. With the CDM, it is necessary to have data at only one point in time to get the same information. Thus, the model with a theoretical foundation—a structural model—is far more powerful and economical and easier to use than is an estimation model like the promotion model. Without the theory, the marketer is a mechanic instead of an engineer.

Questions

1. What are the ABCs of consumer behavior? Define them.
2. What is a brand image?
3. Describe how a multidimensional measure of the attitude variable can be carried out.
4. Explain the difference between explanation and prediction in using a consumer behavior model.
5. Describe at least five possible extensions of the Consumer Decision Model.

---

[19] F. N. Kerlinger and E. J. Pedhazur, *Multiple Regression in Behavioral Research* (New York: Holt, Rinehart and Winston, 1973), p. 321.

CHAPTER 4

Theory Underlying Extensive Problem Solving

1. INTRODUCTION

This chapter will describe the consumer's behavior when he is confronted with an innovation—a new brand or service in a new product category. Examples are IBM's introduction of the Personal Computer and Sony's marketing of the first VCR (video cassette recorder), the Betamax. Specifically, the chapter deals with one of the most difficult but most important problems that especially advanced nations face: how to put their advanced technology to work on developing new categories of products and services. It also shows why and how the CDM must be modified to explain this type of buying behavior.

An innovation requires the consumer to engage in extensive problem solving (EPS) to form a new product category concept. Typically it is the first stage of the product life cycle as described in Chapter 2. In Chapter 3 we discussed how the buyer assimilates a new brand within an existing product category. This has required him to use only limited problem solving (LPS). Typically, EPS involves two levels of choice, choice among categories and then a choice of whether this brand is satisfactory. From a marketing standpoint, it requires a much longer planning horizon.

In the first stage of development of a product category, the consumer must call upon mental processes above and beyond those he uses in LPS or routine problem solving (RPS). He is not simply adding another brand to the lowest level of his product hierarchy; he is creating a new category at the next highest level: the product or category level. It is described by a slightly modified CDM as shown in Figure 4-1.

To make a well-informed buying decision in the circumstances of EPS, the consumer needs a great amount of information. This is especially true in the case of such a high-priced unfamiliar product as the Personal Computer. This is represented in Figure 4-1, which is a modified version of the CDM. In Figure 4-1 you notice that the "importance" column of benefits making up attitude (A) is empty. This empty column is an indicator that the consumers are in EPS. They have not even yet learned what the appropriate benefits are. Much less are they able meaningfully to attach importance weights to those benefits to the extent the weights will contribute to predicting their behavior represented by the second column in the box.

However, in the case of a very-low-priced item that offers no social or health cost, for example, the consumer may simply try it and learn by trying it. For these customers there is a direct relation, a bypass of the thinking process, as discussed later in Chapter 6 and shown by the direct F to I arrow in Figure 4-1. This was found to exist, for example, with some people buying a vegetable bacon called Lean Strips.

We will examine the four subprocesses of supporting theory—attention, search, memory, and choice—but also emphasize motivation because benefits that are related to motives as you saw in Chapter 3 must be formed in extensive problem solving. We must first, however, examine the notion of the product hierarchy, which can clarify complex situations.

Figure 4-1 CDM Modified for EPS

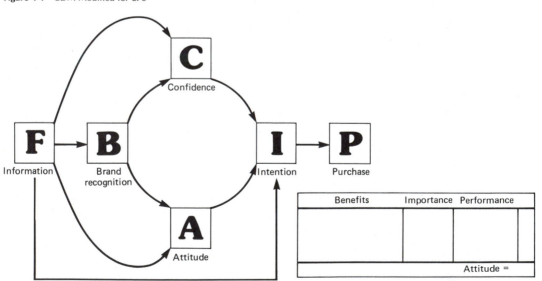

2. PRODUCT HIERARCHY

2.1   Introduction

Many of us are inclined to underrate the capacity of the consumer. That this should happen is not surprising. For example, most of us instinctively think of someone walking into a supermarket as confronting mental chaos. How can he conceivably make sense of those literally thousands of brands that he faces and so make rational purchases?

The answer is that our view of him is quite wrong. He usually makes remarkably rational decisions. The reason he does is because this experienced consumer has for each of most products a product hierarchy in his mind that serves as a framework and guides him. The car product hierarchy in Figure 4-2 is a good example because a car is something with which we are all familiar. It is a *thing* that *transports* a *few* people contrasted with a bus that transports many people and a truck that transports freight. Consequently, we have little trouble making good sense out of even such a complex thing as a four-wheeled piece of transportation driven by a complicated internal combustion engine and a complex series of gears called a "car." From our culture and experience, each of us has built in our minds a "buy map" of cars something like that in Figure 4-2. It completes the concept of the consumer's brand image.

The concept of product hierarchy is a convergence of five different parallel strands of scientific development. First, marketers developed it to identify

Figure 4-2   Product Hierarchy for Automobiles

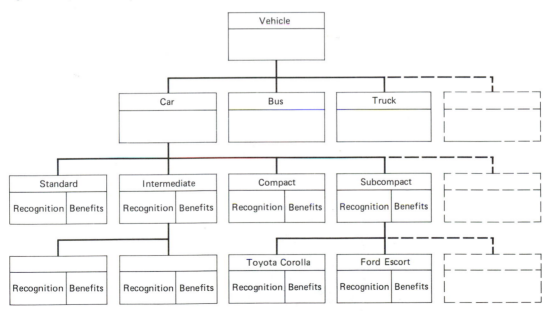

and describe competition as they pursued their practical problem of marketing a product or service.[1] Companies selling in the same category are in direct competition. A company selling into another category is in indirect and usually less demanding competition. Second, the psychologist was interested in how people categorize natural objects.[2] The product hierarchy is the means that a consumer uses to recognize and understand a new brand by "categorizing" it in its category in his mind. Third, psycholinguists were concerned with how people were able to perceive information and convert it into words to form sentences and paragraphs and so communicate effectively about the brand.[3] When the consumer places a new brand in a category, it is thereby labeled in her mind as a "subcompact," and associated with that particular noun is a set of adjectives (brand recognition: B) by which she recognizes that brand and another set of adjectives by which she evaluates that brand (attitude: A). This noun and associated adjectives are her means of thinking and communicating about the brand. Fourth, the influence of product hierarchy upon human memory—how people remember information about brands—such as about cars, has been a major area of research, as you will see in Chapter 5. Finally, psychometricians have been concerned with designing scaling procedures that will enable them to measure similarities among objects in the consumer's mind.[4] This last step of measurement of the hierarchy is obviously essential if the product hierarchy concept is to be useful to marketers. The product hierarchy, like the atom in the natural sciences and the attitude concept in the behavioral sciences, is one of those seminal concepts that brings together many hitherto seemingly unrelated areas of human thought and action.

There are two dimensions of this hierarchy in Figure 4-2, vertical and

---

[1] H. W. Boyd, Jr., and J. Larreche, "The Foundations of Marketing Strategy," in G. Zaltman and T. V. Bonomo, eds., *Review of Marketing 1978* (Chicago: American Marketing Association, 1978), pp. 41–72.

[2] E. Rosch, "Principles of Categorization," in E. Rosch and B. B. Lloyd, eds., *Cognition and Categorization* (Hinsdale, N.J.: Lawrence Erlbaum Associates, 1978), pp. 27–48.

[3] G. A. Miller and P. N. Johnson-Laird, *Language and Perception* (Cambridge, Mass.: Harvard University Press, 1976).

[4] A. Tversky and S. Sattath, "Preference Trees," *Psychological Review,* 86, no. 6 (November 1979), 542–73. The measurement of the concept of product hierarchy under field conditions as required for application is now being developed. As is typical in science, the basic research measures used were slow and expensive. E. Hirschman and S. P. Douglas in "Hierarchical Cognitive Content: Towards a Measurement Methodology," in K. B. Monroe, ed., *Advances in Consumer Research* (Ann Arbor, Mich.: Association for Consumer Research, October 1980), Vol. VIII, pp. 100–5, made one of the earliest attempts to devise a field measure. More recently the work of Tversky has stimulated new effort. He reconceptualized the problem of measuring similarity in A. Tversky and I. Gati, "Studies of Similarity," in E. Rosch and B. Lloyd, eds., *Cognition and Categorization* (Hinsdale, N.J.: Lawrence Erlbaum Associates, 1978), pp. 79–98. For some very promising recent work that draws upon Tversky, see D. R. Lehmann and W. L. Moore, "Two Approaches to Estimating Hierarchical Models of Choice," unpublished working paper (School of Business, Columbia University, New York, August 1985). This particular piece is in terms of preference for objects that can be just as well applied to similarity of objects. Also, for a stochastic model, see R. Grover and W. R. Dillon, "A Probabilistic Model for Testing Hypothesized Hierarchical Market Structures," *Marketing Science,* 4, no. 4 (Fall 1985), 312–35.

horizontal. The vertical dimension is made up of each of the various levels. Research has shown us that the "car" level of Figure 4-1 is the most important and is called the *basic level*. For example, if you meet a friend at a trade show in Atlantic City, he may ask, "How did you come down?" You would most likely reply "by car," not by vehicle: superordinate, subcompact (subordinate), or Escort (sub-subordinate). However, if you were considering the purchase of a car, you would think and talk at the brand level. Marketers need to be aware of these differences in levels of thinking and vocabulary to communicate properly.

The horizontal dimension of the product hierarchy is also important because consumers make comparisons across a given level of the hierarchy in buying products and services. Specifically, for each category at each level, there is in the consumer's mind a middlemost or "prototypical" position on the identifying and evaluative dimensions discussed in Chapter 3. For example, assume that you know what a subcompact car is. Ford introduces the Escort, and so you compare the Escort with the prototype of the subcompact category to decide whether the Escort is a subcompact.

The prototype is the middlemost position of the representation that the customer has in his mind of brands that belong in that category. To be concrete, the representation will be referred to as a "scale." That scale is made up of those dimensions of the brand that consumers use to recognize and those used to evaluate brands in that category. This middlemost position is well recognized by consumers and agreed on. Hence, it is a dependable position. On the other hand, the boundaries of that representation or "scale" are not well defined and hence are not always agreed on. It is essential to recognize these characteristics of the protoype in understanding how the consumer uses information in making buying decisions.

The prototype allows the buyer to compare an innovation to existing products—or existing brands to one another—by merely comparing them with the prototype. He does not have to rehearse all their individual characteristics and dimensions mentally. This capacity adds immensely to the consumer's efficiency in processing information. The prototype, in other words, is the *standard* she automatically uses to gauge everything else that falls in the same category. It is her standard of comparison.

The role of the prototype is indicated by the finding that a longer time is required to evaluate what he considers nonprototypical brands in a category. This has been found in quite diverse types of research, which gives us confidence that it is true! The more nonprototypical an innovation is, the longer it takes a consumer to absorb new information on that innovation. Fortunately, consumers are able to articulate what this prototypical position is and so marketers are able to learn about consumers' conceptions of typical and atypical brands. Psychologists have shown this to be true.[5] A marketer can use the knowledge

---

[5] C.B. Mervis and E. Rosch, "Categorization of Natural Objects," *Annual Review of Psychology*, 32 (1981), 89–115. Also that the scale in which the prototype is located is made up of both the identifying and evaluative dimensions of a product may come as a surprise. For this, see Rosch and Lloyd, eds., *Cognition and Categorization*, pp. 214–15, 309–11.

to learn what the new item will be compared with and infer how easily information about it will be processed, and how long a time it will take him to do it. EPS takes the most time, LPS less time, and RPS the least.

We have been using the familiar car to illustrate the concept of a product hierarchy, but this misses some of the possible complexities. Assume that you are faced with considering a personal computer. Although we are long used to a mainframe, most of us in buying our personal computer have no idea what that superordinate category is, much less what the vital basic level is. We are literally facing mental chaos when we think about buying it. Worse still, we are lost in making comparisons with the jumble of "prototypes" at the subordinate level. Further, even the much better informed computer buyer doesn't know whether there should be only three levels or four levels in his computer product hierarchy. A still more difficult problem for the consumer was probably Merrill Lynch's Cash Management Account in 1977. This was horrendously complex, and, worse yet, it was a service instead of a physical product. What did they compare it with, a bank account? You will recall from Chapter 2 that the Cash Management Account is far more than an ordinary bank account. The purpose of this contrast between cars, computers, and managed cash accounts is to show how different and more difficult EPS can be as compared with LPS and RPS cases described in Chapters 5 and 6, respectively.

Not only does the consumer need a lot of information to decide whether to buy it, but he has very limited capacity to process it. He has little information already in his memory to help him make sense of what he is seeing. Consequently, the nature of the information available can make a lot of difference in how easily he can process the information and understand the innovation. The consumer in EPS needs at least two general kinds of information: "practical knowledge" and "lexical or word knowledge," as George Miller has called them.[6] Let us treat these separately. It is essential that the two be carefully distinguished in your thinking.

2.2 Practical Knowledge

At the time when a customer is trying to build a level in a product hierarchy such as the product category level in Figure 4-1, he needs a description of how the product will be used. For example, if it is a vegetable bacon, will he use it only for breakfast, at lunch or dinner on a salad, or as a snack to feed hungry kids when they come home from school of an afternoon? It is this general kind of functional information or "practical knowledge" that gives the busy consumer some hint as to whether the product holds any interest for

---

[6] G. A. Miller, "Practical and Lexical Knowledge," in Rosch and Lloyd, eds., *Cognition and Categorization*, pp. 305–19. Miller and Johnson-Laird, *Language and Perception*, pp. 290–91, postulate that a product hierarchy is divided into two parts, a conceptual core and lexical concepts. "Practical knowledge" is the conceptual core, which is their way of incorporating EPS. The lexical concepts are represented by adjectives that label the identifying and evaluative dimensions of the brand-level items.

him and will justify him taking his valuable time in thinking further about it. In this way *practical knowledge* is defined as information that sets the *framework*—typically the product category concept—within which the lexical knowledge operates for the buyer to identify and evaluate a particular brand. In contrast to practical knowledge, lexical or word knowledge is specific information about the content of the recognition criteria (B) and evaluative criteria (A) or benefits, shown on the bottom row of Figure 4-2. These are the two key variables in the CDM.

Conveying practical knowledge can be a very difficult communication task, which probably explains why so many innovations fail in the market. In building this level of the product hierarchy in the consumer's mind, as many small computer manufacturers are now unconsciously trying to do, figures of speech—analogies, similes, and metaphors—can play an effective role in communicating this new thing. These bypass logic and appeal to the imagination. As George Miller has put it, "the human mind is constantly on the alert for analogies that will relate new experience to something already known and familiar."[7]

In an analogy, we reason that if two things agree in one or more respects, they probably agree in yet other respects: "Vegetable bacon resembles regular bacon in taste and appearance." Also similes can be useful: "The computer *is like* a pocket calculator." A more common example of a simile perhaps was when the author's wife was adding a small front porch to the house. The architect suggested a prehung metal door to replace the fitted wooden door. The wife was fearful metal door might look cheap and not keep out the New England winds as well. The carpenter said, "The metal door fits *like* a refrigerator door." This simile was far more persuasive than endless sentences of ordinary prose could have been. Finally, metaphors can be especially helpful, for example, "The computer *is* a thinking machine." Or as a news reporter who was describing "windowing" in the small computer said, "The underlying concept . . . of Lisa [the first to use the windowing idea] is an electronic desk with a built-in filing cabinet and trash can."[8] Such a metaphoric way of communicating is the most useful way of making our abstractions concrete, but it can be very ambiguous to an audience lacking the essential cultural background to grasp its meaning readily.

2.3 Lexical or Word Knowledge

Considerable attention is devoted to language here because it is not only important for EPS consumers but LPS and RPS as well, as will be used throughout the book. To a large extent, marketing is communicating to consumers.

"Lexical" as described earlier refers to the words of a language as opposed to the grammar and construction of that language. Specifically, it is the adjectives that consumers use to recognize a brand when they see it, which is the brand

---

[7] G. A. Miller, *Language and Speech* (San Francisco, Calif.: W. H. Freeman, 1981), p. 141.

[8] *Christian Science Monitor* (Boston edition), December 12, 1983, p. 30.

recognition (B) that you first encountered in Chapter 3 as one of the variables in the CDM. For General Foods' vegetable bacon Lean Strips, these adjectives dealt with size and shape of the package.

Second, the consumer in building his lexical background develops a set of adjectives for evaluating a brand. These are the benefits that make up the customer attitude (A) in the CDM as described in Chapter 3. Again, in the case of Lean Strips, they were taste, cost, and nutritiousness.

This second type of information is much more precise than practical knowledge. Also, it applies as well to LPS and RPS, where the customer has the recognizing and evaluating adjectives already formed in his mind.

There are three media by which this lexical information is communicated. The first is language. And, of course, the words of the language are supplemented by both pictures and music as the other two communication media. Here we will focus on the language medium. "Personal computer" is a noun, and the words by which he recognizes and evaluates the IBM PC in that class are adjectives. In EPS a major task of the customer is to learn the correct adjectives to describe the product for his purposes. A set of adjectives is needed for recognizing the brand (B), for example, the Escort, and another set for evaluating it (A). When the customer is in LPS, you will recall that he already knows what the adjectives are, which is what we mean when we say he already has a product category image formed in his mind. All he needs then to deal with a new brand in that category is to position that brand on his available adjectival benefits and recognition dimensions.

One of the much discussed questions in information processing has been whether the customer uses both recognizing and evaluative adjectives to place a brand in a product category. Earlier it had been assumed by psychologists that she used only recognition adjectives and by marketers that she used only evaluative adjectives, but more recently research has shown that she uses both, and to communicate with her we must do likewise.[9] This makes EPS more complicated. To form a concept in her product hierarchy, she must learn both. In identifying the IBM PC, in relation to other personal computers, the buyer selects an adverb to modify each relevant adjective. If she considers personal computers "small," she might use the adverb "very" to define the IBM as "*very* small." She does the same with the evaluative attributes. If one of the evaluative adjectives is "inexpensive," the adverb could be "*somewhat* inexpensive." Thus adjectives and adverbs together communicate both recognition (B) and evaluation (A).

Further, a particular kind of adjective called a polar adjective is most likely to be used to recognize and evaluate a brand because it makes her judgments about brands more precise. It is an adjective that has a polar opposite, that is, hard-soft, high-low, large-small, new-old. There are 39 polar adjectives shown in Table 4-1 that do most of our work for us in communicating.[10] These 39

---

[9] Miller and Johnson-Laird, *Language and Perception.*

[10] J. Deese, *The Structure of Associations in Language and Thought* (Baltimore, Md.: Johns Hopkins University Press, 1965), pp. 121–24.

Table 4-1   Polar Adjectives

Words		Response Frequencies		Words		Response Frequencies	
Alone	Together	10	6	Hard	Soft	28	15
Active	Passive	17	21	Heavy	Light	18	5
Alive	Dead	44	22	High	Low	17	31
Back	Front	22	25	Inside	Outside	40	40
Bad	Good	43	29	Large	Small	23	13
Big	Little	14	15	Left	Right	51	19
Black	White	39	23	Long	Short	21	11
Bottom	Top	25	28	Married	Single	21	20
Clean	Dirty	15	21	Narrow	Wide	15	12
Cold	Hot	20	41	New	Old	13	20
Dark	Light	16	16	Old	Young	7	25
Deep	Shallow	10	19	Poor	Rich	19	26
Dry	Wet	19	25	Pretty	Ugly	13	18
Easy	Hard	17	5	Right	Wrong	39	41
Empty	Full	17	23	Rough	Smooth	10	16
Far	Near	17	35	Short	Tall	14	15
Fast	Slow	19	27	Sour	Sweet	18	12
Few	Many	41	21	Strong	Weak	13	26
First	Last	28	21	Thick	Thin	21	13
Happy	Sad	16	19				

Source: J. Deese, *The Structure of Associations in Language and Thought* (Baltimore: Johns Hopkins University Press, 1965), Table 24, p. 123.

adjectives were derived systematically. Response frequencies refer to the person's tendency to cite one adjective when another is mentioned. For example, in Table 4-1, when subjects were asked "What word comes to mind when you think of 'Alone'?" "Together" was cited six times as you see at the top left portion of the table. If you read through the list, you will probably agree that these are widely used in normal speech and writing. First, from the Thorndyke-Lorge word count of thousands of words, 278 "common adjectives" were selected. These were adjectives that occurred in the Thorndyke-Lorge list with a frequency of 50 instances or more per million words. Second, from the 278 common adjectives, 39 pairs were found to be associated in the subject's mind as polar opposites. These were concentrated in the most widely used words of the original Thorndyke-Lorge list, which adds validity to the role of polar adjective. Thus, these are the most commonly used adjectives from a list of very commonly used adjectives.

Their relevance can be seen in preparing a questionnaire for market research. A market researcher can present the following scale to a buyer:

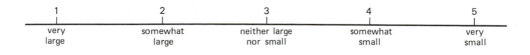

and ask him to rate, for example, the IBM PC on that scale. Contrast this scale with an alternative scale, "large"—"not large." You will agree that "not large" is more ambiguous than is "small." Polar adjectives can be treated as equal interval instead of ordinal scale; that is, the psychological distance from "very large" to "somewhat large" is the same as that from "somewhat small" to "very small." This is very important because the researcher can then apply powerful statistical techniques such as regression referred to in Chapter 3 for analyzing the data.

The consumer combines nouns, adjectives, and adverbs with verbs[11] to form sentences, such as "The IBM is somewhat expensive." This is called a kernel sentence. This type of sentence is particularly useful in marketing because it is the form in which the buyer stores information about a product in his memory. If it is not in this form when he receives the information, then he must convert it to this form in order to store it. Storage takes more time and he will store less of the ad in his memory. This form is defined as a simple, declarative, active, and affirmative sentence, for example, "The IBM processes very rapidly." the opposite is a complex, negative, passive, and interrogative sentence. In the latter form, to communicate the same meaning the kernel sentence content becomes, "Is it that the computer that does not process slowly is an IBM?" Such a sentence would obviously win no advertising copywriter's prize for clarity and ease of understanding by the consumer.

The second medium of communication used is pictures. Typically, these are pictures of the size, shape, and/or color of the brand. These characteristics are especially important because they communicate the recognition of the brand (B). The buyer can easily discriminate by mere outline of an object. Thus, a simple picture of a brand will suffice. Recognition plays an especially powerful role in understanding why the consumer buys as you will see later in the chapter. Pictures can also draw attention, add detail, and eliminate ambiguity. For example, the sentence—"I saw the man on the hill with a telescope"—is ambiguous.[12] It isn't clear whether the man who is the speaker has the telescope, the man on the hill has it, or the telescope is just lying on the hill beside the man. The picture in Figure 4-3 quickly clarifies this ambiguity: the speaker has the telescope.

The third medium of communication is music. Unfortunately, our understanding of it is almost entirely intuitive. Everyone would agree it can draw attention and aid memory, but not much evidence is yet available.[13] Recent research has shown that background music on television advertising facilitated the consumer to form an attitude toward the brand if the consumer were not

---

[11] Verbs are substantially more complex to deal with than are nouns, adjectives, and adverbs. We will say no more about their nature. The interested reader can consult Miller and Johnson-Laird, *Language and Perception,* Chapter 7.

[12] H. A. Simon, *The Sciences of the Artificial* (Cambridge, Mass.: M.I.T. Press, 1969), pp. 49–50.

[13] G. J. Gorn, "The Effects of Music in Advertising on Choice Behavior: A Classical Conditioning Approach," *Journal of Marketing,* 46, no. 1 (Winter 1982), 94–101; R. E. Milliman, "Using Background Music to Affect the Behavior of Supermarket Shoppers," *Journal of Marketing,* 46, no. 3 (Summer 1982), 86–91.

Figure 4-3
An Ambiguous Sentence Clarified
by a Picture

SOURCE: H. A. Simon, *The Sciences of the Artificial* (Cambridge, Mass.: M.I.T. Press, 1969), p. 51.

highly involved. If the consumer were highly involved, this background music interfered and decreased the tendency for the consumer to form an attitude.[14]

2.4   Additional Complications

Another complicating factor in communicating with EPS customers is that brands obviously vary in how much they are like the prototype or middlemost brand in the buyer's product category, as discussed earlier in the chapter. "Good" brands are at one end of the evaluative (A) scale, and "bad" brands are on the other end. Some are very similar to and therefore close to the prototype, the middlemost, while others may be close to the boundary of a category prototype.

Moreover, the boundaries of a category, especially of a category that is new to them, are themselves somewhat vague and movable in the consumer's mind. The boundaries are not well identified, and as new brands similar to the new product category appear to compete with the innovation, the consumer may force them into the category by creating information that really is not there. Both conditions mean that the learning problem that EPS customers face is greater than would otherwise be true.[15]

Finally the learning process for EPS is extensive and also quite different between learning to recognize a brand (B) and learning to evaluate a brand (A). The effects of this difference in learning difficulty show up even in tasks that are much simpler than buying.[16] For example, from a sentence verification

[14] C. W. Park and S. Young, "Consumer Response to Television Commercials: The Impact of Involvement and Background Music on Brand Attitude Formation," *Journal of Marketing Research*, XXIII (February 1986), 11–24.

[15] Mervis and Rosch, "Categorization of Natural Objects," 101–3.

[16] E. Hunt, "On the Nature of Intelligence," *Science*, 219 (January 1983), 144–45.

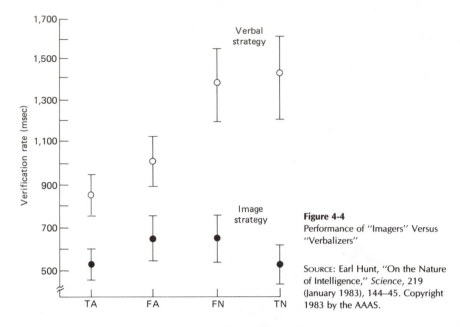

Figure 4-4
Performance of "Imagers" Versus "Verbalizers"

SOURCE: Earl Hunt, "On the Nature of Intelligence," *Science*, 219 (January 1983), 144–45. Copyright 1983 by the AAAS.

experiment, we know that if you show someone the phrase "plus above star" until they indicate they understand it, then show them "+" you can get one of the four results shown in Figure 4-4. In col. 1 (TA) they "imaged," which is the process involved in *recognition*—that is, read the sentence, generated an image of the expected picture, and then compared the image to the percept— and verified the phrase as true. They did this in a little more than half the time (lower portion of col. 1) required when they "verbalized" it (upper portion of col. 1), which is the process involved in *evaluating* a brand. The verbalizers memorized the phrase, described the picture to themselves, and then compared the description to the memorized phrase. As you can see, when they imaged it they required 550 milliseconds, when they verbalized it they required 850 milliseconds.

When the phrase was false, the difference between imaging and verbalizing was still greater as you see in col. 2 (FA). Finally, when a negative was inserted—"plus not above star"—and the two steps repeated, you see even still greater differences in cols. 3 (FN) and 4 (TN) of Figure 4-4.

Now you can understand why it takes so much longer to make a decision in EPS. You will find in Chapter 5 that it requires 5 to 10 seconds to memorize— to fix a chunk of information in long-term memory—if recall is required. However, if only recognition—of a picture—is all that is necessary, only 2 to 5 seconds are required. Also, this study gives further support to the notion that brand recognition content and attitude content are processed differently.

2.5   Summary

We can summarize the additional information content required in EPS discussed up to this point as the following:

Practical knowledge
Lexical knowledge
Adjectives for identifying the brand
Adjectives for evaluating the brand
Appropriate adverbs to give distance or numerosity to the adjectives

Also, the form of the information needs to be different as we have seen: for example, pictures are often better than words, providing they are properly "framed"; polar adjectives are better than nonpolar adjectives; kernel sentences are better than more complex sentences; and so on.

However, we have omitted one key point, and that is how the consumer learns to weight the importance of the evaluative adjectives, the benefits of the CDM. This is a matter of motivation, which we discuss next.

3. MOTIVATION

3.1 Introduction

How the *recognition* dimensions are learned as the customer develops his product hierarchy is not difficult to understand. About any physical attribute that the buyer can use to discriminate among products at each of the levels—product classes and superclasses—will suffice for recognition purposes. However, for him to select the appropriate *evaluative* dimensions is much more complicated, since the boundary lines of a category can be both vague and movable. For a dimension to serve the evaluative role requires that it be connected in some way to the *consumer's* objectives. These personal objectives are called his motives.

A key manifestation of motives is the importance weights that the consumer attaches to the evaluative attributes of the CDM. The consumer's values are a key source of the importance weights in forming a product hierarchy or some portion of it. The values will be referred to as long-term motives as distinguished from the more physiological motives such as hunger and sex—often called "drives"—that can be referred to as short-term motives.

3.2 Long-Term Motives

A consumer in EPS is by definition making at least a *two-level choice*: which product category to buy and which brand within the category. To amplify this view, Figure 4-5 is an elaboration of the CDM, although brand identification (B), confidence (C), and intention (I) are left implicit to simplify. Also, the "not buy" option is excluded to simplify. It shows how the CDM can be applied to quantify choice at different levels in the product hierarchy, but first let us discuss the values that underlie choice. Important for the purpose here is that it explains the role of customer values when a customer is developing a product hierarchy.

First, in box 1 "terminal values" are the more general personal values

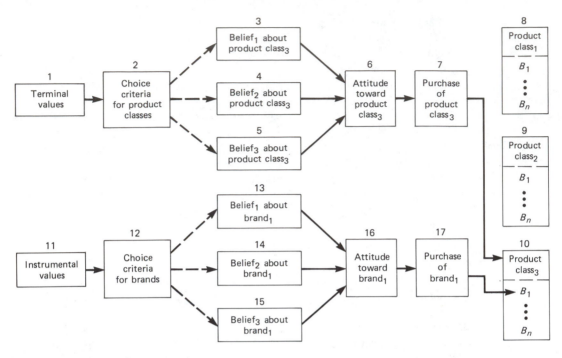

Figure 4-5   Specification of Structure of EPS

referring to end-states of existence, for example, a comfortable life, an exciting life. Broken lines connect box 2 with boxes 3, 4, and 5 because there is no causal relation implied. Further, in box 2 "choice criteria" refer to benefits, and "belief" in boxes 3, 4, and 5 refers to where the consumer "believes" a brand is located on those respective benefits. These lead to attitude (box 6), which leads to the purchase of a particular product class (box 7) and of a particular brand in that class (box 10), indicating that she has now formed product class 3. The lower-level system shows the process by which brand choice is made once the new thing—the innovation—is categorized by the higher (product category) system. Box 12 is the weighting of the benefits required for choice among the brands because the weightings grow out of box 11, instrumental values that are the less general, more specific personal values referring to modes of behavior such as ambitious, loving, and so on.

To derive this system Al Boote used *models* of home appliances for his product categories.[17] For instance, he divided up washing machines by whether they were full-size automatics with one or two cycles, full-size automatics with three or more cycles, miniautomatics, or compacts. The choice criteria or benefits for the product category were found to be reputation for dependability, good

[17] A. S. Boote, "An Explanatory Investigation of the Roles of Needs and Personal Values in the Theory of Buyer Behavior" unpublished Ph.D dissertation (Columbia University, New York, 1975).

style and appearance, and good value for the money. At the level of brand choice, Boote found it necessary to add a fourth criterion: reputation for modern, up-to-date features.

The sample used in the study was relatively homogeneous in terms of age, income brackets, and ethnic backgrounds. And the results were based on each subject's (or her spouse's) intention to purchase, within three months, one or more of a list of household appliances. After considering the benefits, the buyers in Figure 4-5 formed attitudes, and their attitudes led to decisions of whether or not to purchase a particular product category and brand. In this case, most buyers concluded, based on information available to them, that they wanted to purchase brand 1 within product class 3.

An illustration could be Mrs. Smith who has decided she needs a new washing machine. Her old one, which she bought 15 years ago, is worn out. Since that time she hasn't bothered to think about a washing machine and so has forgotten all about the different kinds (categories). Further, there has been a great amount of technological change bringing many improvements. Finally, prices have changed. Consequently, she has to go through a whole new learning process.

Mrs. Smith enjoys working in the garden and has two sons, ages 4 and 6, respectively, who delight in playing in the mud. Consequently, she will have a preference for a full-size automatic washer with three or more cycles. However, it will be substantially more expensive and take up more room in the house than would a miniautomatic. She could get by with a full-size automatic with one or two cycles. A compact is much too small for her purposes.

Her terminal values, box 1, cause her to begin to think in terms of more specific criteria (box 2). They are

> Reputation for dependability (box 3)
> Good style and appearance (box 4)
> Good value for the money (box 5)

Out of this process comes her choice of box 6 and decision to buy (box 7) a full-size automatic with three or more cycles (box 10).

Now the question is, Which brand of this category of full-size automatic with three or more cycles will she buy? For this decision, from her instrumental values (box 11) she adds a fourth benefit (box 12):

> Reputation for modern up-to-date features (which is not shown)

In forming her attitude toward the available brands, she would use her importance weights. Specifically, you will recall from Chapter 3 where in the CDM each benefit or criterion is multiplied by its importance weight, and then she adds these products to obtain an attitude. However, Chapter 3 deals with LPS, not EPS. This raises an important question. Is Mrs. Smith in EPS or LPS?

Probably she is moving rapidly into LPS out of EPS. Although she had not thought about buying a washing machine until quite recently, she uses a washing machine regularly. So she learns quickly about the modern machine she is now confronted with. Therefore, her attitudes (box 16) probably do contain importance weights.

A key conclusion implied here is that to fit the CDM to EPS consumers the importance weights are omitted. Put another way, including the weights will not improve the fit of the model. For LPS consumers, including the weights will substantially improve the fit of the model. Now proceeding with Mrs. Smith, she has formed her attitude and proceeds to purchase (box 17) brand B_1 in box 10.

Something to keep in mind is that the two-level choice structure that the buyers faced in Figure 4-5 isn't confined to brand and product class levels; it can, indeed, be applied at the higher levels of the hierarchy.

In this total causal system of Figure 4-5, the role of values is not only to motivate search and attention but to endow the benefits with importance weights and so give direction as to which brand. It is this role of providing benefit weights that we want to emphasize here because in EPS a major task of the buyer is to form these weights. As you noticed in box 11, instrumental values are the source of weights for brand choice. Thus, you would conclude from Figure 4-5 that terminal values determine choice at the product class level but instrumental values at the brand choice level.

Boote's data supported this conclusion that terminal values operate at the higher level and instrumental at the lower level. However, a later study using cars and personal deodorants did not support it.[18] But in the later study the key issue that values do determine attribute weights was supported as it has been in other studies. In summary, you have seen an example of two-level choice that makes explicit the motivational detail of this two-level process in the consumer's mind. Also, it describes how the consumer forms the weighting that he attaches to each of the benefits.

The major reason for this two-level choice diagram for the purposes here is that consumers are making choices across categories of products. Holbrook asserts, "too little consumer research involves macro-level analysis across products . . . across-products perspective appears more central to questions about how people organize the activities that shape their lives."[19] This cross-product analysis presented here and using the CDM is the way we get to understand those fundamental consumer changes that open up opportunities for product innovations that are so crucial to marketing success in industrially advanced countries.

But let us now return to the motivational features of that two-level

---

[18] R. E. Pitts and A. G. Woodside, "Personal Values and Market Segmentation: Applying the Value Construct," in R. E. Pitts and A. G. Woodside, eds., *Personal Values and Consumer Psychology* (Lexington, Mass.: Lexington Books, 1984), pp. 55–67.

[19] M. B. Holbrook, "O, Consumer How You've Changed: Some Radical Reflections on the Roots of Consumption," unpublished mimeo (Columbia University, New York, November 1985), pp. 8–9.

choice to get a fuller understanding of the information processing that a consumer makes use of in EPS.

3.3 Short-Term Motives

Short-term motives that also influence search, attention, memory, and choice appear under various headings: arousal, emotion, feelings, affect, and so on. Recent research has been able to sweep up much of these under the title of *affect*,[20] which is defined as feeling, emotion, mood, and temperament. Also, this research has shown some of the relation between affect and how consumers process information, in receiving advertising, for example. In reviewing the research evidence on how affect may influence the consumer's response to advertising, Ray and Batra conclude that it may have four effects.[21] It can cause greater attention, encourage more processing, yield more positive judgments of the message, and cause ads to be better remembered. It can also operate through liking for the ad, but this is greater in low-involvement situations, which are less likely to occur in EPS.

Thus, both long-term motives, via benefit importance ratings, and short-term motives, via affect, influence consumer information processing, which we turn to next. However, short-term motives play a more important role in EPS since the customer, being unfamiliar with the situation, has few expectations to guide him, and so the motives must help the customer adapt his information processing to a wider range of conditions than in LPS.

4. SEARCH

The consumer's product hierarchy guides the buyer's search, attention, memory, and choice in EPS just as it does in LPS and RPS. However, of course, the control in EPS is weaker than in LPS and RPS, because his product hierarchy is less fully developed in EPS.

Consequently, short-term motives will play a greater role. The buyer's search for information will have to be substantially greater in EPS than in RPS or LPS. He will need (1) *more information* on the innovation than he would if it were an existing product category,[22] for example, he will need practical knowledge in addition to the lexical knowledge needed in LPS. And attention will

---

[20] R. B. Zajonc, "Feeling and Thinking," *American Psychologist*, 35, no. 2 (February 1980), 151–75.

[21] M. L. Ray and R. Batra, "Emotion and Persuasion in Advertising: What We Do and Don't Know About Affect," in A. Tybout and R. Bagozzi, eds., *Advances in Consumer Research* (Ann Arbor, Mich.: Association for Consumer Research, 1983), Vol. X, 543–48.

[22] G. N. Punj and R. Staelin, "A Model of Consumer Information Search Behavior for New Automobiles," *Journal of Consumer Research*, 9, no. 4 (March 1983), 379, based upon car data that may not be appropriate because cars in the American market do not typically involve an innovation. On the other hand, they find that the most important determinant of search is the lack of relevant knowledge.

be (2) *less automatic* because (a) more of the information will be new to him and (b) his *expectations will be less well formed*. So he must decide whether the innovative product is important enough to justify his making a greater effort to search for information to understand it.

That decision is based on whether he perceives that the innovation fits into his values and his life-style. If it is an important, low-priced item, instead of going through extensive prepurchase search, the buyer may find it more economical simply to buy the innovation and learn about it by using it.[23] Buying first can be more economical than spending a lot of time and effort searching, focusing attention, and, in general, processing the information before purchase. However, it is surprising to most of us how much information processing is shown by the buyer of such an ordinary product as the vegetable bacon, Lean Strips, was.

As you have probably observed we are using a "linear view" in this chapter, which asserts that the buyer first searches, then pays attention, remembers, and finally chooses. It is helpful in describing the consumer's thinking process, but it would be misleading to infer that the buyer's actual learning process is really so direct. In fact, the buyer's mind jumps back and forth. He senses this innovation is probably a new product category, and that makes him aware that he should be on the lookout for more information on the subject. Also, there may be conflict between benefits—perhaps a car offers him comfort but not economy—then he must go back and conduct a more careful search of the product's benefits and identifying criteria. These feedbacks that we are ignoring here by using the linear view do operate, and they will be discussed at length in Chapter 16. However, their omission here is not too limiting, and the simplification of a linear view is helpful to grasping the complex process of buying.

The *type* of information the customer needs obviously influences this search process. At the earliest stage of searching, he needs "practical" information to begin to position properly that new thing in his product hierarchy. It tells him what this thing will do for him in a broad brush sense and helps him begin to form the criteria (B) for recognizing it. He needs the recognition criteria (B) and where the product is located on these criteria. Second, he needs the evaluation criteria of benefits (A) and where it stands on these, both in locating the brand in the product hierarchy and in deciding how good it is for him. The sooner he can begin to weight these benefits, the better will be his choice. Finally, he needs information to build his confidence (C). For this, he needs to know how his peers judge the brand, how different it is from anything like it, and how consistent these messages are with each other in terms of input for him. Inconsistent messages will raise doubts in his mind and depress his confidence.

Another element that directs the buyer's search—besides the *type* of

---

[23] This has been recently confirmed among new car buyers by Punj and Staeling, ibid., 378.

information—is the *source* of information. Evidence suggests that innovative buyers use both personal and impersonal sources. It also suggests that they use mass media (impersonal) early and word-of-mouth (personal) sources late in the choice process.[24] Therefore, we could hypothesize that buyers are initially looking more for "practical" information than "lexical" information, specifically, recognition (B) information. Later, they are seeking evaluative information (A), and here credibility of the source such as one's friends is relevant, as you will see in reading about social diffusion of innovation in Chapter 13.

Because of its importance, let us elaborate a little upon source credibility. It has a number of dimensions:

> *Expertise*—the extent to which a source is perceived as being capable of providing correct information
>
> *Trustworthiness*—the degree to which a source is perceived as providing information that reflects actual feelings or opinions
>
> *Attraction*—the extent to which a source elicits positive feelings from audience members, such as a desire to emulate the source in some way
>
> *Referent other*—the degree to which a source is similar to the target audience members, or is depicted as having similar problems or other characteristics relating to use of a particular product or brand[25]

Also, in EPS, the buyer must process *more* information that in LPS, since she is tying a lot of loose, unknown ends together. This means it is harder for her to absorb the information. And, if she is retrieving the information from memory, it will be from several different locations in her memory. All these factors will lengthen the processing task. However, the greater the time pressure the buyer is under, the less searching she will do, and the more quickly she will decide whether to purchase.

In summary, we have dealt with the amount of information searched for, the type of information, the source of that information, and other aspects.

5. ATTENTION

The consumer's search focuses his attention upon some and not other information. The buyer in EPS lacks the conceptual machinery of a well-developed product hierarchy. Therefore, he has fewer expectations of the nature of the information he will encounter. Thus, his attention is less guided, and, consequently, he has less information-processing capacity. Let us distinguish between his involuntary and voluntary attention.

The buyer's involuntary attention is different in EPS than in LPS. He is less apt to be involuntarily interrupted by information about a new product

---

[24] E. M. Rogers, *Diffusion of Innovations*, 3rd ed. (New York: The Free Press, 1983).

[25] T. S. Robertson, J. Zielinski, and S. Ward, *Consumer Behavior* (Glenview, Ill.: Scott, Foresman, 1984), p. 228.

in EPS, since lacking any prior knowledge, he will be less likely to *notice* it. In other words, it won't stand out as distinct from his expectations, since he has no expectations. Still, the sheer novelty of the new brand sometimes jolts him and focuses his attention on the product.

In EPS, the *voluntary attention* process is also different from LPS. In the first stage, "feature analysis," in which the consumer looks at each specific feature of a brand, she probably relies more heavily upon brand recognition (B) in EPS than she does in LPS, and brand recognition is more concrete and easily understood than are the product's benefits. Without a product category image, the EPS buyer who is voluntarily paying attention, just as with involuntary attention, has less previous knowledge to guide her in making a choice between products.

It is believed that the brand name can serve as a "chunk" in his memory upon which the buyer can begin building a brand image.[26] The buyer adds the typical characteristics of the product to the brand name in his mind to give a fuller picture. He first labels the product by its brand name and physical characteristics, rather than as a set of benefits, which are more abstract. For example, he would label the Lean Strips vegetable bacon according to its physical attributes—its shape and color—or its brand name and not on such evaluative features as taste and economy.

Knowing that attributes are chunks in memory and that short-term memory can hold no more than five chunks, it is not surprising that the buyer typically uses no more than three or four attributes to evaluate a brand. After all, if he requires two attributes to recognize the brand and three to evaluate it, he has no more thinking capacity (his short-term memory is full). This comparison is an oversimplification, but it conveys the point.

Once he has the physical features of the innovation in his mind, the buyer moves to the second step—"active synthesis." Here, he combines the key physical characteristics and the benefits. Just as in the first step, he has no previous product class image, and therefore he has fewer expectations of the innovation. Imagine how much harder it is to decide whether to choose an IBM PC if you have never heard of a personal computer. When there is a conflict between these expectations and the actual product characteristics, he must go back and look for more information. These expectations make for efficiency, because he doesn't waste time looking for irrelevant information.

6. MEMORY

The consumer's product hierarchy in EPS dominates his memory just as in LPS, but not so strongly because the product hierarchy is less fully formed: the product category is missing.

---

[26] J. R. Bettman, *An Information Processing Theory of Consumer Choice* (Reading, Mass.: Addison-Wesley, 1979), p. 62.

The greater need for thinking places heavier demands upon short-term memory. Many more formerly unrelated ideas have to be brought together, especially with a complex innovation such as a home computer. The capacity of short-term memory—five chunks—would seem to be a major barrier to handling the great amount of information required. In addition, fewer chunks will be available to call upon. Using analogies, similes, and metaphors as discussed earlier in the chapter would seem to be especially helpful in lessening the burden. Also, polar adjectives would help. Further, using the kernel sentence in all copy would appear desirable since it does not have to be retranslated to be stored in long-term memory. In addition, long-term memory will have to be searched substantially more.

Finally, the use of pictures, such as of the brand (B), can play even a greater role in EPS than in LPS. Recognition of the picture requires only about one-half as long to transfer information to long-term memory as does recall, which necessitates reconstructing the original stimulus.

In summary, the current principles of memory give you guidance in making predictions about the EPS process. If you wish to see the effects of the structure of memory upon buying behavior in LPS, refer to Chapter 5. However, you will need to make the connections to the EPS situation.

7. CHOICE

7.1   Introduction

Through processing information, our innovating customer has built his "practical" understanding of what the new product does in a general sense. Also, he has formed his recognition criteria labeled by adjectives and where the brand is located on these adjectives in terms of adverbs (B). Also, he has selected his evaluative criteria or benefits and correspondingly estimated how good the brand is on each one using adverbs to modify the adjectives (A). Finally, these activities have caused his confidence (C) to begin to build. Now, the only question is "How does he put all this together to make a choice of whether he should buy this new thing?" Put another way, "What is his decision rule?"

7.2   How Buyers Combine Information

It will be recalled from Chapter 3 that in the CDM when buyers in LPS combine information, they use a weighted-attitude response. In EPS, however, the brand benefits tend not to be well enough understood to be differentially weighted. By trying both and testing them in the CDM to discover which fits the best, it can be determined whether the new product is truly an innovation. If so, the unweighted version should fit better.

Also, EPS is a two-level choice, and the product category level concept is the first level of that choice. Having fixed the product category in mind, the buyer then moves to the second level of choice by adding an attribute or two to the list. But does a buyer make an overall evaluation or consider a brand on one benefit at a time? The first is called the decision rule of *choice by processing brands* (CPB). Here he does not distinguish among the benefits. The second decision rule is called *choice by processing attributes* (CPA), where he does distinguish among the benefits. Some pioneering research indicates that the higher in the hierarchy the choice is being made (the more incomparable the alternatives), the more he uses CPB.[27] However, he still uses some CPA, some "within attribute choice." This dual approach seems sensible. CPB is easier, but he will need CPA to complete his brand image as he moves down the hierarchy in his choice process.

Another type of decision rule is whether, in CPA, he uses a stored-rule method or a constructive method. In the former, the buyer simply relies upon a rule, such as weighted-attribute response (CDM), that is already in his memory. In the latter, he constructs a rule at the time he makes the choice, by using elements of rules stored in memory. There is evidence that an EPS buyer probably uses CPA and a constructive method.[28]

Usually, an EPS buyer is confronted only with the one new brand; there is only one, the innovation. But it is conceivable that he faces several new brands, as when a consumer moves into a new environment—perhaps he is a foreigner coming to the United States or a potential college student facing high school graduation and the choice of a college.[29] If so, another question the marketer must ask is whether the buyer applies a rule consistently to all brands or instead simplifies by following a *phased strategy*. For example, in the first phase, the buyer may eliminate some of the alternative brands by CPB to form an evoked set, and then, in a second phase, use CPA on the remaining brands. Also, the marketer could question whether the degree of experience, or prior knowledge, the buyer has had makes a difference as to which rule the buyer uses to choose a brand. The buyer with limited experience, such as an EPS buyer, will probably find it easier to use CPA.

8. CONCLUSIONS

Looking at EPS from both the language and information-processing viewpoints and as a two-level choice process gives a substantially more complex picture of buyer behavior than exists in LPS. The burden of communicating both practical knowledge (information on what kind of general thing this innovation is) and lexical knowledge (information on identifying and evaluating characteristics of the innovation) is much greater in EPS than in LPS, depending in part upon

---

[27] M. D. Johnson, "Consumer Choice Strategies for Comparing Noncomparable Alternatives," *Journal of Consumer Research*, 11, no. 3 (December 1984), 751.

[28] Bettman, "An Information Processing Theory," pp. 201–22.

[29] M. Laroche, J. Rosenblatt and I. Sinclair, "Brand Categorization Strategies in an Extensive Problem Solving Situation: A Study of University Choice," in T. C. Kinnear, ed., *Advances in Consumer Research* (Provo, Utah: Association for Consumer Research, 1984), Vol. XI, 175–79.

the number of levels of the product hierarchy the consumer has to construct. Although language is more critical in EPS than in LPS, much of what was said here has relevance for LPS and RPS as well.

An EPS buyer has less structure in his mind to manage his searching for information, to control his attention, to support his memory, and to guide his choice. This structure would help to exploit fully the capacity of his perceptual processes to serve his thinking. A number of characteristics of advertising, however, can facilitate acceptance. Information should be fed to him in smaller quantities, in simpler form, and at a slower pace than in LPS. Yet he needs far more information. The consequence, of course, is that diffusion of an innovation simply takes a lot more time than does LPS.

If the nature of the product lends itself to being dramatized, a promotional program that achieves wide public attention and gets the product talked about can probably speed up the acceptance process, for example, Apple's ad campaign, which emphasized trying out a personal computer just as you test drive a car. Such a metaphor will attract the buyer's attention and a culturally accepted vocabulary can be developed more quickly than if the innovation does not get wide public attention. There should be a heavy emphasis on "framed" pictures (B), that is, where the picture is clearly related to the purpose of the ad.

By identifying the appropriate category in the buyer's product hierarchy, marketers can correctly position the innovation to customers and against potential competitors. This positioning will also tell the marketer how many customers there are—that crucial bit of information on market size needed for the "go–no go" marketing decision. The need for this understanding has been sharply enhanced by the increased attention to corporate strategy, which uses a longer-term planning horizon than traditional marketing strategy.

Another feature of EPS is that marketers need a criterion for determining whether a group of customers are in EPS. After all, serious marketing mistakes will be made if management is unaware of it. One criterion is the magnitude of confidence expressed in the product. Consumers in EPS would be expected to have less confidence. Another criterion is whether the buyers merely add the relevant benefit values in making a choice or whether they weight each benefit value by multiplying its importance weight times the performance rating on each benefit. Buyers in EPS are not expected to use this multiplicative approach because they are not familiar enough with the appropriate benefits. The CDM provides this test.

Finally, knowing the cyclic pattern of buying behavior in RPS as discussed in Chapter 6 is also important in providing clues as to how consumers can be shifted from RPS to an innovation (EPS).

Questions

1. Describe how the consumer's product hierarchy guides his buying as fully as you can.
2. Contrast "practical" and "lexical" knowledge.

3. Why is motivation so important to understanding EPS behavior?

4. How can the understanding of a consumer's search behavior be used to guide you in selecting advertising copy and media in marketing to those consumers?

5. The idea of a consumer using a decision rule may seem like an abstract and not very useful notion. How can knowing the decisions rules that consumers use be helpful to you in marketing to them?

CHAPTER 5

Theory Underlying Limited Problem Solving

1. INTRODUCTION

The focus of this chapter is upon the case of limited problem solving (LPS). The theory applies when the customer is confronted by an unfamiliar brand in a familiar product class. For the well-informed car buyer, the Yugo car is an illustration of limited problem solving. It is the smallest of the subcompacts, as you know. Its minimum price is $3,990. Even a new sporty version with manual transmission or optimal automatic will cost only $4,990. But the well-informed car customer probably has a set of brand recognition dimensions and a set of benefits already developed in her mind. Forming the ABCs of marketing as a concept of this remarkable Yugoslav car is far easier than when confronting a subcompact for the first time. Although it may seem small to be classified as a subcompact, the insurance companies do classify it as such. The theory here explains the relationships among variables in the CDM, shown earlier in Figure 3-1 by connecting arrows for this LPS case.

Let us examine the information variable (F) and explore how F influences the other five variables of the CDM. There are five aspects of this complex process by which consumers think: the media by which they receive information, the customer's search for information, whether he pays attention, his memory for storing information and retrieving it, and the actual choice. The latter four are *sub*processes of the consumer's total information processing. The speed with which a customer passes through them varies greatly. For most of us, the Yugo constitutes a major information-processing problem. With some frequently purchased products, a small proportion of customers may almost completely avoid these subprocesses by first buying to try out the brand. However, substantial experience with the CDM suggests that these customers are typically very much in the minority. Hence, it is crucial to know how consumers process information if we are to understand buying.

2. NATURE OF INFORMATION PROCESSING

2.1 Introduction

You recall from Chapter 3 that the content of the information box (F) in the CDM has an effect on brand recognition (B), attitude (A), and confidence (C). "Information processing" has become the accepted term for describing the buyer's thinking processes as he takes in this information and tries to make sense of it by generating brand recognition (B), attitude (A), and confidence (C), which are the basis of his purchasing decision. The process by which he absorbs that information and makes sense of it is complex.

How consumers "process," take in information, and make sense of it in forming their image toward a brand is called "cognitive response."[1] After having been exposed to an ad about a brand, consumers are asked what *thoughts* came to mind when they saw the ad. Their thoughts tend to be of two kinds. The first, counterarguments, are thoughts that argue against a favorable attitude toward the brand. The second, support arguments, are those that argue for a favorable attitude. More recent research has confirmed these conclusions.[2] (The way the consumer chooses from the mass of information available will be discussed here, and the practical implications will be developed at greater length in Chapters 8, 9, 10, and 11.)

The interrelationships among the product hierarchy and the four subprocesses have been explained as "the ability of the (customer's) conceptual machinery to control attention and to exploit perceptual processes in the service of thought."[3] Taking the first part of this sentence, the "conceptual machinery" of the consumer's world refers to her relevant product hierarchy as shown in Figure 5-1. Her product hierarchy "controls" the buyer in the sense that it causes her to search for, pay attention to, memorize relevant information about the new brand, and choose a brand. Search, attention, and memory, in turn, control the information that the buyer processes as she takes it in. Thus, her

---

[1] P. Wright, "Message-Evoked Thoughts: Persuasion Research Using Thought Verbalizations," *Journal of Consumer Research*, 7, no. 2 (September 1980), 151–75.

[2] D. R. Toy, "Monitoring Communication Effects: A Cognitive Structure/Cognitive Response Approach," *Journal of Consumer Research*, 9, no. 1 (June 1982), 66–76.

[3] George A. Miller and P. N. Johnson-Laird, *Language and Perception* (Cambridge, Mass.: Harvard University Press, 1976), pp. 131–32; though not nearly as explicit, J. R. Bettman, *An Information Processing Theory of Consumer Choice* (Reading, Mass.: Addison-Wesley, 1979), p. 156, implies much the same thing.

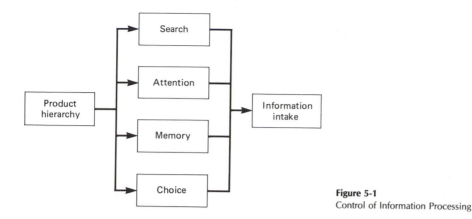

Figure 5-1
Control of Information Processing

product hierarchy plays a very important role. After doing a major pioneering research project on the concept of the product hierarchy as defined here, Mita Sujan concludes, "The categorization approach . . . suggests that consumers have well defined product categories in memory, and that expectations about these categories guide evaluation and decision processes."[4]

More specifically, Sujan found that consumers who are well informed about cameras ("experts"), and when the new brand fits the category in her mind, process information in a particular way. They "rapidly reach final impressions and evaluations (of the brand) and generate more thoughts related to the product category and fewer thoughts related to the product's attributes."[5] This can be called *category processing*.

When the new brand does *not* fit the category, they engage in more analytical processing—more examination of the *individual benefits*—and take longer to form an impression. Also, their final judgment is based on a more constructive piecemeal review of the benefits. Finally, they will try to "subtype" it, to classify it at a more specific level such as by the model of the product.

The less well-informed customer ("novice") but one who also has a product category in her mind, uses category-based processing even more than experts, both when the brand fits the category and when it does not. The novices, however, are less inclined to use information about the benefits than are experts. Put another way, they rely more heavily on their category concept than do the experts.

Before examining each of the four subprocesses of information processing, let us summarize how the product hierarchy controls each of them. As the Sujan research suggests, it is the product hierarchy that gives continuity and order to the total process. Knowing this continuity will contribute immeasurably to your understanding of each of the four subprocesses and, in turn, to your understanding of consumer behavior.

---

[4] M. Sujan, "Consumer Knowledge: Effects in Evaluation Strategies Mediating Consumer Judgments," *Journal of Consumer Research*, 12, no. 1 (June 1985), 31–46.
[5] Ibid., p. 43.

Figure 5-2 Consumer Decision Model, Product Hierarchy, and Information Processing

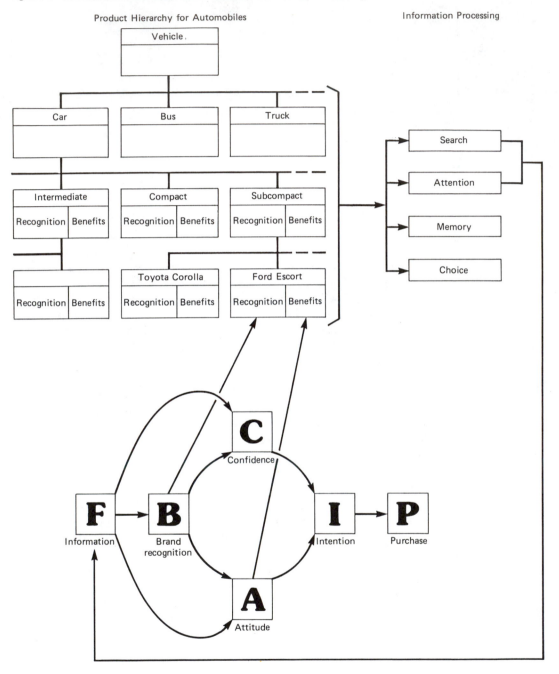

The product hierarchy controls the consumer's *search* by providing tests that the consumer can use in determining the category in which the new product belongs. These tests are of two kinds: those that identify (B) the brand and those that evaluate (A) the brand. The hierarchy controls his *attention* by focusing search, not just upon any of the attributes of the new product but upon those most likely to answer information requirements. These are the recognition attributes and the more important evaluative attributes of those brands in the class that he already knows about. Also, these attributes must facilitate the consumer's discrimination among categories. The hierarchy, by enabling him to choose the correct class or category, permits him to search his *memory* and so to determine how well the new brand performs on each of the relevant evaluative attributes.

Finally, the hierarchy controls *choice* in that, to choose, a customer must bring together the individual brand evaluations and so compare the new brand with existing brands in the appropriate category of the hierarchy and thus form an attitude toward, an intention to buy that brand, and a degree of confidence in his judgment.

But how does all this relate to the CDM? Figure 5-2 answers this question. The product hierarchy relates to the CDM because, if the customer has a category and a brand, for example, Ford Escort, formed in his mind, the physical identification of the Escort is the brand recognition (B) and the quality of the Escort (the benefits he uses to evaluate it) is the attitude (A) in the CDM. The two arrows from the CDM to the product hierarchy represent these two relations.

The product hierarchy, in turn, relates to the subprocesses of the consumer's information processing as shown in Figure 5-1. This is shown in the upper right of Figure 5-2. Finally, two of the four subprocesses feed directly back into the CDM as shown by the arrow, but the nature of feedback processes generally will not be developed in detail until Chapter 16. Search and attention directly shape the information that is fed into information (F) of the CDM. Memory and choice, however, do not directly feed into information (F) but are a part of the information processing that is implicitly going on within the CDM. For example, information (received via (F)) is stored in memory and is later called up from memory to help make sense of and utilize later incoming information. Similarly, information from (F) and memory supports the actual process of evaluating the brand and so leads to the actual choice of whether to buy or not buy an Escort. Consequently, those two connections shown in Figure 5-1 are omitted in Figure 5-2.

We will now examine each of the subprocesses in detail to understand better their roles in the consumer's overall buying process.

2.2 Search

2.2.1 Introduction. *Search* is defined as when the consumer is motivated to expose one or more of her sense organs to information about the new product. When Shearson entered the "managed cash account" market with its Financial

Management Account in 1982, potential buyers looked at ads in magazines or read public relations articles in the daily newspapers.

To be able to think about a new brand, the consumer first must place the brand in a category of equivalent brands; for example, Shearson's Financial Management Account was a brand in the category of managed cash accounts. This entails a *search* of her memory for the potential categories and testing for equivalence between the Financial Management Account and the brands that she already knows in the category. The product hierarchy provides these tests in the form of identifying and evaluating attributes associated with the different product categories, and the new brand will be placed in that category with which its attributes match "best."

A search may also be undertaken if there is need for additional information. If so, this search may be internal or external. In internal search, she searches her memory; for example, her memory could contain information from ads about the Financial Management Account that she has already seen. The customer's product hierarchy will guide her to facts in her memory about the category in which the new brand has been placed.

For external search, her search will be guided by the product hierarchy toward sources such as *The Wall Street Journal* where information for that category is usually available. The directional, or guiding, force for search is the buyer's product hierarchy because it provides the criteria by which she recognizes the product. However, motivation provides both a driving force for her to search and a direction for her to search.

2.2.2. Motivation. Motivation was discussed at length in Chapter 4 because the motivational burden on the consumer is especially heavy in EPS. Therefore, motivation played a major role. The motivational process presented there was "values-norms-brand-benefit importances." These Chapter 4 concepts are pulled together systematically here to form the consumer's *goal hierarchy* and serve as its foundation in LPS and RPS buying situations. The goal hierarchy specified to each product category *focuses motivation* on *brand choice*. It gives both *intensity* and *direction* to buying behavior.

In Chapter 4 a study of buying washing machines and other large home appliances was used to illustrate how EPS consumers are motivated. Buying washing machines will now be used to illustrate how Mr. Baker, an LPS consumer, uses a goal hierarchy to motivate and to guide him during the process of choosing a brand of washing machine. He, however, is in an LPS situation and so is able to use his existing goal hierarchy, learned from a previous experience.

As you see in Figure 5-3 Mr. Baker has a sequence of three broad goals at the top:

1. Determine which *attributes are important*.
2. Evaluate alternatives on these *attributes*.
3. Obtain the *best* alternative.

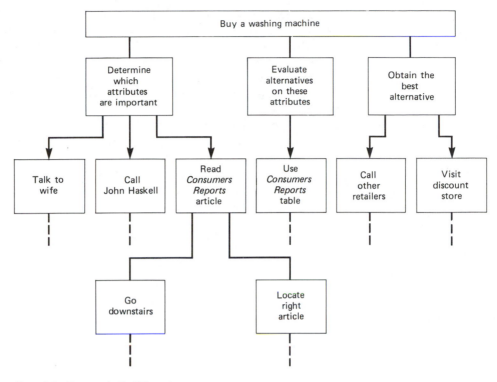

Figure 5-3   Consumer's Goal Hierarchy

SOURCE: J. R. Bettman, *Information Processing Theory of Consumer Choice* © 1979, Addison-Wesley Publishing Co., Inc., Reading, MA, p. 21. Reprinted with permission.

The solid lines in Figure 5-3 represent actual portions of his goal hierarchy. The dashed lines represent portions of the hierarchy that, to simplify, are not detailed in the example. The three goals just mentioned are subgoals of the more general goal "Buy a washing machine."

Being in LPS he knows the relevant attributes, but he reviews the importance of them as the left branch of Figure 5-3 indicates, because it is an important purchase and he hasn't bought one for several years. To answer this question about the importance of the benefits he could, as you see, (1) talk to his wife, (2) call a trusted neighbor, Mr. Haskell, or (3) read *Consumer Reports*. He chooses the last and proceeds to go downstairs and locate the article containing the information.

Having verified the relative importance of each of his relevant benefits from reading *Consumer Reports*, he proceeds next to evaluate the brands against each benefit. Here *Consumer Reports* is especially useful.

Finally, armed with his well-specified beliefs, he proceeds to buy the best washing machine by visiting various retailers, including discount stores. These goal hierarchy elements are the source of high and constant activation of the consumer in LPS and RPS situations.[6] These do not turn off. They cease to be a source only by being changed. They represent expectations of what will happen as he proceeds to search and buy. They are hierarchical, just like the product hierarchy discussed at length in Chapter 4, and for the same reason, this hierarchical structure simplifies the consumer's thinking processes. In this way they provide subgoals that specify the goal more to a particular set of circumstances. These lower levels in the goal hierarchy can be modified to meet the changing conditions that consumers often face as, for example, they move to another community where different shopping facilities exist.

Figure 5-3 is something of an idealized picture, however. Actually, in the process of meeting those goals, the consumer can be distracted. He is continually looking for reasons that might indicate he should be distracted.[7] This is called a *scanner mechanism*. He also has an *interrupt mechanism* that distracts him from following the goals rigidly should his scanner mechanism reveal reasons for interrupting the buying procedure. For example, his scanner mechanism may reveal such as from a newspaper ad that within a couple of weeks there are to be *major sales of washing machines* with large markdowns. He thinks he would be well advised to delay further consideration until then. Another reason is he may find himself in conflict, the two best brands are identically good and for the same price.

A major conclusion about the goal hierarchy is that it gives both intensity and direction to search and attention.

2.2.3 Internal Versus External Search.

Internal search involves retrieving information from memory, whereas external search occurs when the buyer looks for information in the environment around her.[8] For instance, a buyer may search her memory to get sources of information. She recalls that advertising media are likely to carry that information and then she conducts external search by consulting these particular sources.

In internal search she searches her memory for information about a new brand. She evaluates this brand on the basis of the total available information that she has in relation to her images of each of the rest of the brands in that class. From this existing knowledge of the current brands in her product hierarchy she can draw analogies by comparing them with the new brand and thereby conclude how good the new brand is. She looks at the new brand in terms of her brand recognition, her attitude, and her confidence, and as a result of doing this, a budding brand image of the new brand is added to her product hierarchy.

At least four factors influence how much the buyer searches internally— from her memory—instead of externally: the *amount* of information stored in

---

[6] J. R. Anderson, *The Architecture of Cognition* (Cambridge, Mass.: Harvard University Press, 1983), p. 156.

[7] Bettman, *An Information Processing Theory.*

[8] For a discussion of search, see J. W. Newman and D. B. Lockman, "Measuring Prepurchase Information Seeking," *Journal of Consumer Research*, 2, no. 3 (December 1975), 216–22.

memory, the *suitability* of that information for choosing the new brand, the degree of *conflict*, as discussed earlier[9], and the *importance* of the product to the buyer.[10] For example, if (1) she already knows quite a bit, (2) the information is suitable, (3) there is little conflict, and (4) the product is not very important, she may make up her mind about how good the brand is by merely drawing upon her memory. However, in buying an investment, this is most unlikely because being expensive it is typically an important product and also complex.

A number of factors influence the amount or degree to which the buyer searches externally.[11] Very broadly, one factor is cost and the other is benefit. The buyer, in short, tends to take the least costly and most beneficial information. Substantial research supports this generalization; for example, the farther people have to go to shop, the less shopping they will do.

More specifically, the fertility of his environment in terms of the information it offers also makes a difference in how hard the buyer searches. This is manifested in at least three ways. First, he is more likely to search where information is readily available. This is probably why specialty magazines (for example, *Motor Trend*, *Yachting*) have tended to drive out such old standbys as the *American*, *Saturday Evening Post*, and *Life*. The last two have returned but not to their former eminent position by any means. Second, there is some evidence that he will search more when the information-processing load is lighter[12]; for example, if the information is easily processible, such as when kernel sentences are used in the advertising, he will search more. Third, time pressure—an element of the customer's environment—makes a difference. The buyer searches less when he has to make a decision quickly. He may even look longer for Reebok running shoes than for a new refrigerator such as when the old refrigerator breaks down and he must replace it immediately before the food stored in it deteriorates.

Another factor influencing external search is the individual differences among buyers. For example, some buyers have more prior knowledge of a product than others and so use store displays less. Some buyers have more ability to understand—or more interest in—the *best* alternative instead of merely choosing a satisfactory alternative.

A final factor again is conflict. A substantial volume of research has been done here. The researchers using uncertainty, the inverse of confidence (C) in the CDM as an operational measurement of conflict, have generally found a positive relationship between uncertainty and search. Therefore we would

---

[9] Bettman, *Information Processing Theory*, pp. 116–19.

[10] J. Jacoby, R. W. Chestnut, and W. A. Fisher, "A Behavioral Process Approach to Information Acquisition in Nondurable Purchasing," *Journal of Marketing Research*, XV (November 1978), 532.

[11] Bettman, *An Information Processing Theory*, pp. 123–31.

[12] C. Wickens and others, "Performance of Concurrent Tasks: A Psychophysiological Analysis of the Reciprocity of Information Processing Resources," *Science*, 221 (September 9, 1983), 1080–82.

expect a negative relationship between a buyer's confidence and his search. This will be discussed further as a type of feedback in Chapter 16.

A different set of conditions determines *where* the buyer searches—that is, the *direction* instead of the *amount* of external search.[13] There are two sets of forces operating on the direction of search. First, direction is determined by the type of information the buyer seeks. He will search where the information he needs is available, which, in turn, is influenced by five factors. The first factor is the degree of *knowledge* already held; for example, a buyer in limited problem solving already knows from his category concept the benefits for judging a brand but needs to know where the brand is located on these benefits.

A second factor is the relative *availability* of different kinds of information. A customer will read *Consumer Reports* because they give him specific brand ratings. A third factor is the type of conflict; for example, does he have to choose between two desirable benefits or two undesirable (negative) benefits such as prices? A fourth factor is the *purpose* for which the information is to be used; for example, it can be used either for the buyer's own buying problems or for him to inform others such as his friends about what to buy. The fifth is the nature of the *events* that interrupt the buyer's decision process; this interruption directs the buyer's attention away from the information he had been focusing on. For instance if the customer is reading a Procter & Gamble ad for Tide in a newspaper, he may see an ad for a competing brand and focus on it instead as relevant information.

A second set of operating conditions emerges when customers vary their mix of sources of information such as ads, in-store shopping for several brands, multiple store shopping for one brand, and so on. There are two major factors governing this mix: individual differences and stage of choice process. In a study of shopping, great differences among people were found. For appliances, some shopped across stores for a brand, but others compared brands within a given store. In the early stages of the choice process, Rogers found that *mass media* sources such as advertising often enabled one to become aware of the innovation.[14] *Word-of-mouth*, then, tended to be used in the later stages when the choice was being made.

What is the relevance for designing marketing strategy of all these factors influencing how much the buyer searches and where he searches? If he is searching a great amount, an ad can be placed in any one of a variety of media and still reach him. For example, in its introduction of the ill-fated Vega car, General Motors used more than 20 magazines, several television shows, and a great amount of public relations. If the customer is searching but little, the media must be chosen far more carefully to reach him. If the customer is searching in a particular direction, this tells the advertiser the range of media he has from which to choose. Amount of search and direction of search also influences the type of store through which the product should be distributed.

---

[13] Bettman, *An Information Processing Theory*, pp. 119–23.

[14] E. Rogers, *Diffusion of Innovations,* 3rd ed. (New York: The Free Press, 1983).

2.3   Attention

2.3.1 Introduction.   The attention subprocess is one of the most essential elements in human thinking. *Attention* is defined as the allocation of information-processing capacity to a particular stimulus.[15] Unless the buyer is paying attention to information, he is not very likely to process it. Think about the time you have tried unsuccessfully to study without concentrating (without paying attention).

As mentioned earlier, the customer has limited information-processing capacity. The product hierarchy operating within the goal hierarchy plays the crucial role of directing the allocation of the consumer's attention to only those aspects or attributes of the new brand that are relevant for the purpose at hand.[16] Hence, in trying to identify the new brand, attention may be directed to those attributes that best *distinguish* it from other brands or products. On the other hand, while in trying to choose the new brand, attention may be directed at those attributes that are most *important* or heavily weighted in the choice process.[17] The attributes to be focused on are identified by the product hierarchy. The more important an attribute, the more attention she devotes to it. For example, if style in a car is more important to her than is gas consumption, she is more likely to pay attention to information about a car's style.

2.3.2 Voluntary Attention.   As mentioned, increased motivation leads to increased attention. This is called *voluntary attention*.[18] Increased voluntary attention means that the buyer has placed more information-processing capacity at her command. Given this, how does a buyer proceed to process—to make sense of, to interpret—information about a product from an ad, sales representative, friend? She proceeds in two stages.[19]

In the first stage, *feature analysis*, she separates out the key features of the message on which to focus her attention. When the message is a salesperson's verbal statement about the product, this step might not seem very relevant. But if the salesperson also shows the buyer the physical brand, the features in the message can form brand recognition in the CDM. This can make a lot of difference. The buyer processes information by building upon a "chunk" in her memory to form larger collections of information. H. A. Simon says that "a chunk . . . of material . . . is a particular amount that has specific psychological significance."[20] (It can grow as information is integrated into it.) It is essential

---

[15] Bettman, *An Information Processing Theory*, p. 77.

[16] Miller and Johnson-Laird, *Language and Perception*.

[17] M. B. Holbrook, D. A. Velez, and D. G. Tabouret, "Attitude Structure and Search: An Integrative Model of Importance-Directed Information Processing," in K. B. Monroe, ed., *Advances in Consumer Research* (Ann Arbor, Mich.: Association for Consumer Research, 1980), Vol. VIII, pp. 35–41.

[18] Bettman, *An Information Processing Theory*, pp. 78–79.

[19] Ibid., pp. 79–80.

[20] H. A. Simon, "How Big Is a Chunk?" *Science*, 183 (February 8, 1974), 482.

to note that features of brand recognition (B) can serve as that chunk, that is, as the building block upon which the buyer then forms attitude (A), which is the more motivational interpretation and also forms confidence (C). The recognition elements are easier to form because of their concrete nature.

In the second step, the *active synthesis* stage, the buyer interprets the meaning of the message, which helps her to form a brand image. "Meaning," as used here, is an important term, because things have meaning only as they relate to other things. The message, in other words, tells her how one particular brand relates to others in her product hierarchy—both in terms of how she recognizes it (brand recognition) and how she evaluates it (attitude).

Based on her experience, the buyer has *expectations* about what the information will tell her.[21] These expectations are contained in her product category image within that hierarchy. The buyer's expectations make information processing much more efficient, since she needs only limited processing if the information she encounters agrees with her expectations. She must process information in more depth only to the extent that the two do not agree. Thus, both actual characteristics of the product and the buyer's expectations of what the message will tell her about these characteristics shape her interpretation of the message.

Finally, strongly guiding the customer's attention is the relative importance of the benefits she uses in evaluating the brand. She is more likely to notice (pay attention to) information that relates to her more important benefits, as indicated already.

2.3.3 Involuntary Attention.

2.3.3 Involuntary Attention. Involuntary attention, on the other hand, occurs when something interrupts the buyer's train of thought and causes him to notice and learn about something different. He is reading a newspaper public relations story about the Ford Escort, let's say, and an ad in an adjoining column attracts his attention, interrupting his reading. By being interrupted, the buyer involuntarily learns about a brand, even if it is information about a brand that he is not thinking of buying at the moment. He may store the information in his memory and call upon it later if he ever considers buying the brand.

Involuntary attention can also lead to incidental or *latent learning*, when the buyer is not consciously absorbing the information but will use the information later when he needs to buy. This happens when his motivation is low and thus it is related to low-involvement learning. In watching television for entertainment, for example, the buyer probably picks up a lot of information from brand ads and may store it in his memory—without ever being aware that at that moment he is learning about the product. And in storing it, he must seek the relevant product hierarchy with the help of recognition and evaluative attributes.

Latent learning is also important because of the fear often expressed that subliminal advertising has a major detrimental effect upon consumers who are unaware of having experienced it. Several years ago, the dangers of subliminal

---

[21] Bettman, *An Information Processing Theory*, p. 80.

advertising received a lot of attention. Currently, the evidence does not support advertising as having this powerful, hidden effect.[22]

If the marketer knows to which information his customers are voluntarily paying attention, he will be in a much better position to select media and to design copy to insert in those media.

2.4   Memory

2.4.1 Introduction.   Memory is the third subprocess of thinking. The product hierarchy is a part of it, that part that pertains to related categories and brands. The buyer searches his memory, including his product hierarchy and goal hierarchy, for relevant information that he stored earlier. *Memory* is defined as multiple storage places for information; these "places" can be classified as sensory memory, short-term memory, and long-term memory.[23] Sensory memory will not be discussed because information in sensory memory is extremely short-lived—a few milliseconds—unless it is transferred to short-term memory.

The product hierarchy, a part of long-term memory, dominates the memory process for buying. All new information received about the new brand may need to be stored in memory for later use. The product hierarchy helps the consumer to determine what information should be stored (transferred to long-term memory) and how it will be stored. Does one need to remember that the "Escort has wheels" or is it sufficient to remember that the "Escort is a car"? In the same vein, does one need to remember that the "Escort is a small car"? The product hierarchy helps answer these questions, by specifying what the characteristics are that a product must have to fit into that category.

2.4.2 Short-Term Memory.   *Short-term memory* (STM) plays a crucial role in the buyer's thinking. It is defined as the place where his externally obtained information combines with information retrieved from his long-term memory, at which point he is truly "thinking." Information that is not transferred to long-term memory or rehearsed in short-term memory is lost from short-term memory in about 30 seconds or less. You have often rehearsed a telephone number as you dialed someone you never expected to call again. You abruptly forgot it as soon as someone answered.

We deal here with two major aspects of short-term memory: its capacity and the time needed to transfer information from it to long-term memory. The absolute capacity of short-term memory is quite limited, so only a small portion of total memory capacity can be activated at one time. It has a five- to seven-chunk upper limit.[24] A single letter can be a chunk, such as Q, R, or S,

---

[22] T. E. Moore, "Subliminal Advertising: What You See Is What You Get," *Journal of Marketing*, 46, no. 2 (Spring 1982), 27–47.

[23] Recently, there has been some tendency to conceptualize memory as different levels of information processing, instead of as storage places. J. R. Bettman, "Memory Factors in Consumer Choice: A Review," *Journal of Marketing*, 43, no. 2 (Spring 1979), 38.

[24] Simon, "How Big Is a Chunk?" p. 487.

or several words grouped in a meaningful pattern can be a chunk. A phrase is a chunk, just as is an image of a physical object. It is this chunking of information, as mentioned earlier, that makes the buyer's task relatively easy. Also, the five-chunk upper limit can be reduced further to only two or three if the buyer conducts other activities—such as search or counting—at the same time. Thus, short-term memory imposes real limits on a buyer's thinking capacity.

The time it takes for information to be transferred to the long-term memory storage indicates how long the memory processes may take. The viewer requires 5 to 10 seconds to fix a chunk of information from short-term memory in long-term memory, so that he can recall it later. This transfer time is obviously an important part of total information-processing time. The marketer wants to learn the amount of time the buyer requires so he can design, for example, television commercials of the appropriate length.

2.4.3 Long-Term Memory. As illustrated by the product hierarchy, much of the information a customer uses when thinking about whether to buy a new brand comes from her *long-term memory* (LTM). The LTM is defined as an unlimited permanent store. The speed with which she can retrieve that stored information greatly influences her buying behavior. But, first, what content is held in long-term memory?

A buyer usually stores (remembers) *semantic* concepts, or ideas described by words, and the associations among them. Words alone transmit little meaning. For example, the comment "Crispy Strips is a vegetable bacon" is not meaningful unless the buyer already has stored in his long-term memory the meaning of "vegetable bacon." That meaning is how it is related to other products. For example, he probably does not know anything about "vegetable bacon," but he does know about "bacon," which is at the next higher level in his product hierarchy. Consequently, with a limited amount of information, he can associate vegetable bacon with ordinary bacon and vegetable bacon will thus have meaning for him. The marketer needs to transmit that meaning in a sentence.

What is the organization of long-term memory? Whether memory is useful to a customer in buying depends upon the kinds of information he stores in his memory (encoding—words changed into neural events), how fast he can get it into storage (decoding—neural events transformed into meanings), and how fast he can get it out of storage into short-term memory (retrieval). The first two have been discussed. The third, speed of retrieval, is determined by how his memory, (e.g., his product hierarchies) is *organized*.

The organization of memory content is described by the structure of long-term memory as Meyer and Schvaneveldt state.[25] It is very useful in showing how the product hierarchy operates. It is the heart of the consumer purchasing process.

This structure is a network of nodes and links. The nodes are the concepts,

---

[25] D. E. Meyer and R. W. Schvaneveldt, "Meaning, Memory Structure and Mental Processes," *Science*, 192 (April 2, 1976), 27–32.

for example, an Escort, and the links are the relationships among those concepts. Figure 5-4 is a view of these meaning or semantic relationships, as they are stored in memory. As the product hierarchy indicates and this diagram illustrates, the buyer structures the categories of objects from the general to the specific. This memory hierarchy exhibits four kinds of relationships: subsets, supersets, overlaps, and disjoints.

In the experiment from which Figure 5-4 was drawn, subjects were given sentences like "Some birds are animals." In this sentence, the subject (birds) is a *subset* of a higher category (animals) just as an Escort is a subcompact. If the sentence were, "Some animals are birds," then the category, animals, would be a *superset* of the second, "birds" (e.g., "Some subcompacts are Escorts."). If the sentence were "Some birds are female," the relation between the first category, "animals," and the second, "birds," would be an *overlap*, because both, animals and birds, can be female (e.g., "Escorts consume little gasoline."). Finally, if the sentence were "Some birds are tools," the relation would be *disjoint*, because one category (birds) bears no relation to the other (tools) (e.g., "Some Escorts are trains.").

In the experiment, the subjects when presented with each of the sentences were asked to respond "true" or "false." By recording their response times, the experimenter obtained estimates of retrieval time. The conclusion was that the nearer categories are in meaning, for example, subcompact and Escort are closer in meaning than are "subcompacts" and "cars," the shorter are their *response times*. Specifically, subset relationships were closest in meaning, and response time was shortest for these. The consumer uses *subset relations* from his product hierarchies and so remembers easily.

Superset relationships were second closest. Telling a consumer that "Some subcompacts are Escorts" might be useful but typically not nearly as much as telling her specifically that "An Escort is a subcompact." *Overlap relations* were third closest; for example, "some subcompacts are slow." This is still less specific and typically less useful. The fourth case, *disjoint relationships*, is least useful because it is typically *not relevant* information. In summary, response times ranked inversely with closeness of the relationship. We can infer that consumers respond more quickly to closer, and therefore typically more relevant, information. The

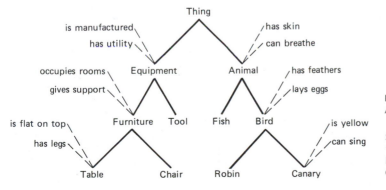

Figure 5-4
A Picture of Long-Term Memory

Source: D. E. Meyer and R. S. Schvaneveldt, "Meaning, Memory Structure and Mental Processes," *Science*, 192 (April 2, 1976), 29. Copyright 1976 by the AAAS.

relevance of this for practice is clear: expect your marketing effort to be slower-acting when the topic is less closely related to what the consumers already know.

What product and product-related concepts the customer has in mind can strongly influence the inferences she makes about your brand. "For example, if a ballpoint pen has an ultra-fine point, and a consumer links the ultra-fine point with greater writing effort, that consumer may infer that the pen requires greater writing effort and not purchase it, even if in fact greater effort is not required."[26] Incidentally, you can also see in Figure 5-4 what it is that the product hierarchy omits; for example, it omits associations that may have little or nothing to do with recognizing and evaluating the brand and also omits a great variety of episodic events.

2.4.4 Buyer Memory Tasks.   To make the foregoing discussion more realistic, let us examine the consumer in terms of her different memory tasks typical of the LPS product situation, namely, both outside the retail store and inside the retail store.

When she is *outside* the retail store, she must receive and store information about the elements of brand image, in order to decide how to evaluate the brand and actually to make her choice. For instance, she learns about the Corolla's attributes primarily from advertising and friends. Whether she stores that information depends upon her *interest* and how *easy* it is to process, such as whether it was given to her in easily processible form. It could be that her short-term memory capacity was overloaded.

Her actual choice of a new brand can also be made outside the store. If, however, that is the case, then the buyer must recall information from her

---

[26] Bettman, "Memory Factors in Consumer Choice," p. 42; for the interested reader, the analysis of Figure 5-4 can be carried much further. When universal affirmative sentences—such as "All birds are animals"—were used, instead of existential affirmative sentences—"Some birds are animals"—the results were somewhat different. The evidence is too elaborate to explain here, but the conclusion was that universal affirmative sentences require extra mental processing. One reason is that, in addition to initially identifying category names, for the buyer to decide whether it is true or false, he must subsequently check for links that connect the location of each category to a collection of basic defining attributes, shown as dashed lines in Figure 5-4.

From Chapter 3, we are already familiar with the notion of the defining attributes of a brand concept that can be identifying (B) or evaluative (A) or both. In the case of universal affirmative sentences, these defining attributes are probably necessary to help verify that the first category mentioned is a subset of the second category. In Figure 3-2, for example, canaries are yellow and can sing, while birds have feathers and lay eggs. It appears that a close relationship between categories—"canaries" and "birds" instead of "canaries" and "animals"—actually slows down the process of retrieval. The similarity of categories requires the buyer to know the defining attributes so as to determine whether the first category mentioned in a universal affirmative is a subset of the second category. "All birds are canaries" would elicit the response "false." Presumably this requires finding a defining attribute of the first category that is generally not an attribute of the second category—having many colors, for instance. Birds are of many colors, but canaries exhibit only one color, yellow. This suggests that a marketer may sometimes want to say in advertising copy what his brand is not, as well as the usual content of what it is; for example, "All subcompacts are small, but VW gives especially good gas mileage and is not heavy."

long-term memory to compare the new brand's characteristics with her knowledge of existing brands.

An important issue because it explains the brand recognition (B) variable in the CDM is whether the buyer takes in information by recognizing it or by having to recall it from long-term memory.[27] If recognition alone is required, not recall, only 2 to 5 seconds are necessary to transfer information from short-term memory. This distinction between *recognition* and *recall* is essential, because it shows how brand recognition (B) facilitates information processing. For recognition, the buyer need only discriminate between the new brand and other brands. But in recall, he has to *reconstruct the stimulus* from his *long-term memory*, since the original stimulus is no longer available in his short-term memory. Five to 10 seconds are required, which is twice as long. Research comparing how consumers process pictures with how they process word messages supports the idea that the buyer processes brand identification by recognition and attitude information by recall.[28] This fact is not yet widely recognized among consumer researchers, however. Most customer research has been done on the verbal memory system instead of the imagery memory system.[29]

Now back to our customer outside the store, if our advertising has provided him with a good brand recognition (B), he will have a stronger favorable attitude toward our brand and probably be able to make his decision to buy it while still outside the store. Then, when he goes into the store to get it, he will be less attracted by competing brands. This holds, providing that in our advertising we have properly "framed" the picture of the brand by explicitly relating the picture to the brand and so made a true brand recognition (B).[30]

Inside the retail store, if he has not already made up his mind, his two major tasks are to decide how to compare the benefits and so be able actually to choose a product. To compare benefits, he can simply compare each brand on the benefits, which reinforces the information he learned before entering the store. If he's in the limited problem-solving stage, as we have been assuming throughout this chapter, the buyer will need to remember information, since explanations on the package will seldom be complete. Also, if his brand recognition is already formed, he can retrieve and process that information much faster. If earlier advertising has pushed up his confidence (C), his chances of forming that intention (I) are better, especially for an important product. Further, the context of the information will make a difference. That is, if the package says something quite different from what he saw in an ad, he will process the informa-

---

[27] Bettman, *An Information Processing Theory of Consumer Choice*, pp. 157–60; also see R. P. Bagozzi and A. J. Silk, "Recall, Recognition, and the Measurement of Memory for Print Advertisements," *Marketing Science*, 2, no. 2 (Spring 1983), 95–134.

[28] J. A. Edel and R. Staelin, "The Information Processing of Pictures," *Journal of Consumer Research*, 10, no. 1 (June 1983), 45–61.

[29] Bettman, "Memory Factors," *Journal of Marketing*, p. 48; R. J. Lutz, "Imagery Eliciting Strategies: Review and Implications of Research," in H. K. Hunt, ed., *Advances in Consumer Research*, (Ann Arbor, Mich.: Association for Consumer Research, 1978), Vol. VI, pp. 611–20.

[30] Edel and Staelin, "The Information Processing of Pictures."

tion—and choose brands—more slowly because his expectations are being contradicted. Moreover, this contradiction will affect his confidence (C) adversely.

2.5 Choice

2.5.1 Introduction.
Choice, too, is significantly controlled by the product hierarchy. The competing brands in the product hierarchy probably become even more important at the choice stage. The buyer compares the new brand with those competing brands in her evoked set more carefully than before.

Choice is made up of two parts, intention (I) and purchase (P). We define intention as a *plan* to purchase as the economists and some psychologists do.[31] Purchase is the execution of that plan, including the financial commitment implied.

2.5.2 Intention to Buy.
The formation of intention—the plan to buy—involves bringing together the weighted benefits making up attitude (A) and developing enough confidence (C) that will permit the customer to act. Research showing that attitude (A) affects intention (I) is well accepted. This was indicated in a recent rare study of car purchasing in which 15,000 people who had bought a car within the last three months were asked whether they bought the car they really wanted.[32] Forty-one percent preferred another car. They mainly wanted a Mercedes-Benz or Chevrolet Corvette. Further, those who preferred another car gave significantly higher ratings to economic-related purchases, such as the importance of gas mileage and fuel economy, interest rate, and costs of maintenance. In other words, their intentions overrode their actual preference, primarily because of major economic reasons.

A number of factors can influence the dependability of the attitude-intention relation.[33] For example, the extent to which the consumer has a strong habit of buying her current brand, *whether* she has had actual experience with the proposed brand, and when the degree of involvement is high, the more likely the relation is to hold.

The effect of confidence (C) on intention (I) is not so well known, but there is substantial evidence for it.[34] Also there is evidence that the effect is greater when attitude (A) is high. But the effects of confidence (C) appear to be stronger for consumer durables than for low-priced frequently purchased items. For example, in a study of subcompact cars, the confidence (C) and intention (I) relationship was twice as strong as the attitude (A) and intention

---

[31] For an extensive discussion of plans, see G. A. Miller, E. Galanter, and K. Pribram, *Plans and the Structure of Behavior* (New York: Holt, Rinehart and Winston, 1960).

[32] J. Stone and J. Schwartz, "What Customers Prefer to Buy May Not Be What They Purchase," *Marketing News*, September 12, 1986, p. 55.

[33] For a fuller discussion, see T. S. Robertson, J. Zielinski, and S. Ward, *Consumer Behavior* (Glenview, Ill.: Scott, Foresman, 1984), pp. 259–62.

[34] For a review of some evidence, see J. A. Howard, *Consumer Behavior* (New York: McGraw-Hill, 1977), p. 56.

(I) linkage. With frequently purchased items, however, the confidence-intention relation is much weaker. K. Moller found the same difference in the relationships when he compared television and toothpaste.[35]

The way data are combined to make a decision is called a *decision rule* or *decision heuristic*, as discussed in Chapter 4. There exists a great variety of logically possible decision rules that a customer might use to combine information to make a choice in LPS. You will recall that the CDM assumes, however, that he uses a linear compensatory rule, in which his attribute performance ratings are weighted by his attribute importance ratings and added together to yield an attitude. In subcompact cars, for example, resale value was the most important benefit, but on performance on this benefit, the VW rated much higher than did GM's new Vega.

How accurate are these importance weightings? There is some evidence that in organizational buying, the lesser important ratings are substantially overstated and that derived weightings from regression analysis are much more accurate. However, the customer's most important stated weightings tended to be accurate.[36]

Which decision rules are actually used under what circumstances is not well understood.[37] Currently, available evidence suggests that a weighted linear compensatory process, exemplified in the CDM, appropriately describes a buyer in limited problem solving confronting a single new product. However, a noncompensatory rule is often used for screening a number of brands. The conditions of limited problem solving obviously omit a number of situations that may exist such as those found in extensive problem solving and discussed in Chapter 4. Also, the CDM assumes that brands in a product category always compete with each other. This may not be so, such as in the case of a product that serves multipurposes such as steak for a family dinner or for guests. A modification of the model can deal with this case, however.[38]

Intention to buy is not only useful for predicting purchase. Data can be collected on it at the same time that data on other variables in the model—information (F), brand recognition (B), attitude (A), and confidence (C)—are being collected. This allows the marketer to analyze all but purchase (P) data without the complications of a time lag. Purchase (P) data can be collected only when the customer obliges by purchasing. A common problem, especially in infrequently purchased durables such as cars, is where the time lag between a stated intention to buy and a later purchase is substantial. Error in the relationship becomes larger.

[35] K. Moller, *Perceived Uncertainty and Consumer Characteristics in Brand Choice* (Helsinki: Helsinki School of Economics, 1979), pp. 198–99.

[36] J. E. Scott and P. Wright, "Modeling an Organizational Buyer's Product Evaluation Strategy," *Journal of Marketing Research*, XIII (August 1976), 211–24.

[37] For an extended discussion of decision rules or heuristics, see Bettman, *Information Processing*, pp. 176–90.

[38] L. McAlister, "Choosing Multiple Items from a Product Class," *Journal of Consumer Research*, 6, no. 3 (December 1979), 213–24.

2.5.3 *Purchase Behavior.*
It is obviously very important to know whether the actual purchase results from the output of information processing—which is, intention.[39] If we regard buying as the execution of a plan, we can still allow for the many events that occur between the time a buyer states her intention to buy and actually makes the purchase. These events can either increase or decrease the firmness of her plans and the probability of that purchase. The earliest evidence of whether intention really causes purchase was generated by economists in their study of product categories in consumer durables. It was an important area of research, because purchases of durables influence the level of economic activity. However, they were concerned with choice of product class, not brand choice.[40]

But M. U. Kalwani and A. J. Silk carefully examined the $I \rightarrow P$ relationship for durable and packaged goods brands both substantively and methodologically. Their conclusion after careful review of a wide range of studies and methods is encouraging:

> For users of intention data, this paper offers welcome evidence that, across a broad range of conditions, such measures do possess a statistically significant degree of predictive validity.[41]

Also, for predicting actual choice, a number of formal choice models have been developed out of economics and psychology.[42] One of these, the hierarchical model, was referred to at the outset of the chapter for measuring the product hierarchy, where we are concerned with measuring similarity of brands instead of preferences for brands. However, there is a great need to incorporate behavioral theory as in the CDM into these choice models that remains yet to be done.

2.6   Implications for Practice

The emphasis in this chapter has been upon information processing—and the effect of this processing upon the relationships between information (F) and recognition (B), attitude (A), and confidence (C). In the end, the customer decides whether to buy and which brand to choose (P). Her attitude, in other words, is reflected in her intention to act (I). Likewise, her intention to buy (I) will likely result in a purchase. Consequently, you can rely upon intention (I) as a good predictor of purchase (P) in the future in most situations. Obviously, the

---

[39] For a discussion of this relation and a model of it, see D. G. Morrison, "Intentions and Purchase Behavior," *Journal of Marketing*, 43, no. 2 (Spring 1979), 65–74.

[40] E. T. Juster, *Anticipations and Purchases: An Analysis of Consumer Behavior* (Princeton, N.J.: Princeton University Press, 1964), p. 211.

[41] M. U. Kalwani and A. J. Silk, "On the Reliability and Predictive Validity of Purchase Intention Measures," *Marketing Science*, 1 (Summer 1982), 243–86.

[42] For an extensive review of such models, see M. L. Sorstjens and D. A. Gautschi, "Formal Choice Models in Marketing," *Marketing Science*, 2, no. 1 (Winter 1983), 19–56.

greater the time lag between the intention (I) and the act of purchase (P), the more the probability that her purchase (P) will deviate from her intention (I) as events she did not anticipate crop up and change her earlier intentions.

As for her confidence (C) and its relation to intention to buy (I), it's clear that low confidence (C) inhibits action. That relationship, however, appears to apply more to consumer durables, perhaps because their price and importance to the buyer are greater than are the price and importance of packaged goods. Also, the effect of confidence (C) upon intention (I) is complex, and it varies directly with the level of attitude (A).

Finally, nothing has been said so far about the stability of these relations among the variables. Specifically, do the coefficients connecting the variables in the CDM remain stable over time, or do they change frequently? Obviously, this is a crucial issue. For example, if the relations are subject to rapid change, the usefulness of the CDM in guiding the manager in deciding what to do in the future is reduced. However, recent basic studies have shown that these relations are remarkably stable.[43] This finding greatly enhances the usefulness of the CDM. Further, from this kind of analysis that revealed the stability of the system, laws of consumer behavior of various product categories and market conditions will ultimately emerge like those we have in the natural sciences such as physics and chemistry.[44]

3. CONCLUSIONS

Marketing is largely (1) communicating with the customer to discover his preferences and then (2) designing the advertising, sales, and so on, to communicate to the consumer the way in which the brand meets those preferences. The primary emphasis here is upon the latter.

The buyer's CDM is linked to his product hierarchy via his brand recognition (B) and attitude (A). His product hierarchy and goal hierarchy guide the process by which information is acquired and used by the customer as shown by the research on category-based choice versus piecemeal choice. The elements of the process are search, attention, elements of memory other than product hierarchy, and choice. Search and action feed directly back into the CDM, and in this way he builds his brand recognition (B), attitude (A), confidence (C), intention (I), and purchase (P), as specified by the CDM. How to quantify these feedbacks as pictured in Figure 5-2 will be further discussed in Chapter 16. The effects of memory and choice are indirect.

[43] J. U. Farley, D. R. Lehmann, R. S. Winer, and J. P. Katz, "Parameter Stability and Carry-over Effects in a Consumer Decision Process Model," *Journal of Consumer Research*, 8, no. 4 (March 1982), 465–70.
[44] J. U. Farley, D. R. Lehmann, and M. J. Ryan, "Patterns in Parameters of Buyer Behavior Models: Generalizing from Sparse Replication," *Marketing Science*, 1, no. 2 (Spring 1982), 181–204.

The buyer's search processes largely control the information to which he is exposed. They also guide how he uses his attention. Motivation—the consumer's goal hierarchy—plays a central role in both of these.

Attention plays a major role in shaping how the customer makes use of information. This is consistent with the marketer's emphasis upon the buyer's attention. In the attention process, the customer first focuses upon the key features of the message. She then puts these key features together with what she already knows to develop a synthesis, which is the meaning to her of the new brand element in her product hierarchy. This synthesis creates an expectation in her mind of what additional information she is likely to encounter. This expectation facilitates her future acquisition of information about the brand by providing a test of consistency. Finally, she can acquire some information involuntarily and without effort.

Memory, the third piece in this complex process, is perhaps the most important of all. The overall guiding role of product hierarchy on memory is supplemented by other elements retained in memory. In this multiple-storage view, the limited capacity (five chunks) and transfer times of short-term memory are serious considerations for marketers. For long-term memory, its organization and differences in process between recognition and recall offer equally serious considerations.

Fourth, the actual choice of brand that emerges from the earlier steps in the complex process is the most central issue for the manager. It is represented by the plan to buy (I) and the execution of that plan (P).

Finally, this complex information-processing accounts well for the relations specified by the CDM, and these relations have been found to be characterized by high stability.

Questions

1. Describe the consumer's goal hierarchy and its purpose.
2. Briefly describe the LPS consumer's search process when buying.
3. What is the role of the consumer's short-term memory in his buying and how is it relevant to you as a marketer?
4. The consumer's long-term memory plays a major role in his buying. Give five examples of how this might happen.
5. Having read the complete chapter, describe how Figure 5-2 ties all the material in Chapter 5 together.

Theory Underlying Routine Problem Solving

1. INTRODUCTION

Chapter 6 deals with the very important buying behavior of the large number of brands that is typically found at the mature stage of the product life cycle. It involves a number of complex issues that we must clarify to make sense of this behavior.

It can be heavily routine or habitual behavior. Here the consumer does not devote much attention to his purchasing task as we learned in Chapter 2. In fact, because of this limited attention, buying here is often referred to as "low-involvement behavior," which Krugman pioneered 20 years ago.[1] Substantial research is now being done comparing "low-involvement" and "high-involvement" behaviors especially in terms of the kinds of advertising that is appropriate for each.[2] Later in the chapter this research will come in handy.

[1] H. E. Krugman, "Impact of Television Advertising: Learning Without Involvement," *Public Opinion Quarterly*, XXIX, no. 3 (Fall 1965), 349–56.

[2] However, see R. Batra and M. L. Ray, "How Advertising Works at Contact," unpublished Research Paper, No. 710 (Graduate School of Business, Stanford University, Palo Alto, Calif., September 1982); R. Batra, "Message Response Involvement: The Construct, It's Involvement, Antecedents and Consequence," unpublished paper (Graduate School of Business, Columbia University, New York, Spring 1984); R. E. Petty, J. T. Cacciopo, and D. Schuman, "Central and Peripheral Routes to Advertising Effectiveness: The Moderating Role of Involvement," *Journal of Consumer Research*, 10, no. 1 (September 1983), 135–46; J. E. Brisoux and M. Laroche, "Evoked Set Formation and Composition: An Empirical Investigation Under a Routinized Response Behavior Situation," in K. B. Monroe, ed., *Advances in Consumer Research* (Ann Arbor, Mich.: Association for Consumer Research, 1981), Vol. VIII, 357–61.

"Repeat purchase" is the marketer's description of the buyer being in a state of routine problem solving (RPS), where he is confronted by familiar brands in a familiar product category. The buyer has already formed an evoked set of the familiar brands. This evoked set is defined as those brands that he considers when he goes to buy. Careful research has shown that he forms this set by establishing a minimum acceptable level for each benefit. If a brand falls below that level on any benefit, the brand is dropped from further consideration.[3] This is called a *conjunctive decision* rule. He will shift among them according to changes in their price and availability. The brands tend to be more standardized than in limited problem solving (LPS), and so brand preferences are not as strong.

As consumers of frequently purchased, low-priced products move up the product life cycle from LPS to RPS, three major changes occur. First, their environment no longer includes much product change. Second, a direct effect from information (F) to intention (I) begins to occur through bypassing the thinking process implied in attitude (A). Third, most consumers begin to develop a cyclic pattern of behavior. Each of these changes will be examined with the degree of brand loyalty as a central idea.

2. BRAND LOYALTY

Brand loyalty is a term widely used in practice to describe how much consumers shift among brands, and it is, of course, particularly appropriate for RPS. It is defined as the inverse of the amount of shifting: the less a consumer shifts among brands, the more brand loyal she is. What is the nature of this brand loyalty?

A sample of 2,500 men and women over age 18 were asked for each of the 21 different categories of products (shown in Table 6-1) their brand preference in the category.[4] Also, they were asked whether they would shift to another brand in that category if there was a price differential between their preferred brand and a generic brand. Finally, they were asked if they would likely be satisfied if they shifted in response to that price differential.

The conclusions were clear. There were enormous differences across categories. For example, in cigarettes, 49% would not shift even with a 50% price differential, and, if they did, 70% said they would not be satisfied. Contrast this with a category at the other extreme, aluminum foil, where only 15% said they would not shift in response to a 50% price differential, and only 36% felt they would not be satisfied if they did shift.

Another conclusion from the study had to do with why this loyalty or

---

[3] N. J. Church, M. Laroche, and J. A. Rosenblatt, "Consumer Brand Categorization for Durables with Limited Problem Solving: An Empirical Test and Proposed Extension of the Brisoux-Laroche Model," *Journal of Economic Psychology*, 6 (1985), 231–53.

[4] D. Johnston, "A Re-examination of the Process of Branding," unpublished paper (Harvard Business School, Cambridge, Mass., January 25, 1979).

Table 6-1   Brand Loyalty

PRODUCT CATEGORY	SHARE LEADER'S LOYALTY RATE	BRAND LOYALTY LEADER
Highest Loyalty Rates		
Cigarettes	Marlboro (42)	Tareyton (74)
Laxatives	Ex-Lax (33)	Metamucil (54)
Cold remedies	Contac (38)	Bayer DCT (50)
Tuna	Chicken of the Sea (42)	Starkist (43)
Vitamins	Miles One-a-Day (38)	Stresstabs (52)
Antacid	Rolaids (37)	Maalox (43)
Coffee	Maxwell House (36)	Hills Brothers (52)
Headache remedies	Bayer (33)	Tylenol (45)
Medium Loyalty Rates		
Toothpaste	Crest (38)	Ultrabrite (39)
Deodorants	Right Guard (33)	Mitchum (56)
Mouthwash	Listerine (34)	Cepacol (47)
Cooking oil	Crisco (36)	Mazola (39)
Shampoo	Head & Shoulders (37)	Selsun Blue (38)
Cola soft drink	Coca Cola (29)	Tab (43)
Margarine	Blue Bonnet (29)	Fleischmann and Imperial (38)
Detergents	Tide (28)	Dash (48)
Rice	Minute (27)	Uncle Ben (32)
		All others (42)
Lowest Loyalty Rates		
Scouring powder	Comet (22)	Bon Ami (22)
Facial tissues	Kleenex (18)	Puffs (28)
Paper towels	Bounty (17)	Brawny (22)
Aluminum	Reynolds (17)	No-name (17)

SOURCE: Don Johnston "A Re-examination of the Process of Branding," unpublished paper (Harvard Business School, Cambridge, Mass., January 25, 1979), pp. 16–17.

lack of it exists. For the category with the highest loyalty, cigarettes (42%), users felt they would most likely not be satisfied if they shifted (70%). This last figure indicates a feeling of risk if they shifted. Thus, the conclusion was that risk is the reason for not shifting.

Finally, and perhaps more relevant for general marketing practice, is comparing the share leader's loyalty rate with the brand leader's loyalty rate. As you see in Table 6-1, for each category, the share leader's loyalty rate is compared with that of the brand with the highest loyalty rate. In every case, as you can see in Table 6-1, the degree of loyalty of the most loyal brand was greater than the loyalty of the market share leader's loyalty.

An implication of this fact is that the largest share brand is practicing "mainstream marketing," that is, selling to everybody in the category. On the other hand, the most loyal brand is practicing "segmented marketing." These are obviously two radically different ways of marketing, and the manager must be aware as to which one he is practicing in order to practice it consistently and effectively.

Table 6-2   Average Number of Category Brands Purchased Six Months in 20 Selected Categories

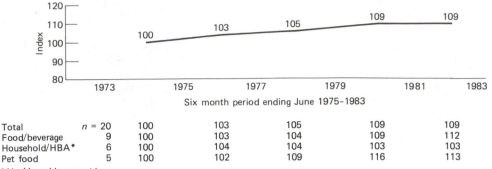

		1975	1977	1979	1981	1983
Total	n = 20	100	103	105	109	109
Food/beverage	9	100	103	104	109	112
Household/HBA*	6	100	104	104	103	103
Pet food	5	100	102	109	116	113

* Health and beauty aids.

SOURCE: Tod Johnson, "The Myth of Declining Brand Loyalty," *Journal of Advertising Research*, 24, no. 1 (February/March 1984), 14. Reprinted from *Journal of Advertising Research*. © Copyright 1984, by the Advertising Research Foundation, Inc.

In conclusion, this analysis of the phenomenon of brand loyalty is very revealing. The variation across product categories tells us that to know brand loyalty is to know a lot about the product. That it is related to the risk of being disappointed suggests sensible behavior. Finally, that it reveals two fundamentally different ways of marketing suggests a logic that we would otherwise miss.

Another important aspect of brand loyalty is whether it is changing. There is a deeply held belief usually expressed with much concern by most marketers, that historically brand loyalty has been severely declining. If true, consumer companies would be seriously damaged, and the value of the enormous investments that companies have made to build brand names would be very seriously threatened.

Because of this widely held concern, Tod Johnson recently subjected 20 categories of products containing 50 leading brands for which his firm had purchase panel data to a very thorough and creative analysis.[5] You see some of the results in Table 6-2. It shows the average number of category brands purchased per buyer per six months in the 20 selected categories. The year 1975 is set at 100. As you can see there, overall the brand loyalty for these products instead of decreasing actually increased between 1975 and 1983, but not by much. Also, as you see, in the lower part of Table 6-2, the increase varied much among the categories. Further, the greatest percentage of increase was with dry cat food, spaghetti sauce, and diet carbonated soft drinks. It happened that these three had the greatest growth. Thus, this growth in brand loyalty was probably because the categories were growing the most.

Johnson concludes that brand loyalty is not declining, but that "marketers' awareness of what brand-loyalty levels really are may be coming closer to *the*

---

[5] T. Johnson, "The Myth of Declining Brand Loyalty," *Journal of Advertising Research*, 24, no. 1 (February/March 1984), 9–17.

truth of where these levels have always been."[6] This evidence should relieve the concern of those who are concerned that it is decreasing.

High brand loyalty, but with great variation among product categories as indicated, is typical behavior for RPS, which characterizes a mature industry where growth has leveled off and product change is small. However, the buyers of all products do not go through the RPS stage. Contrast the foregoing conditions with those of a large consumer durable, such as a television set. Here we would expect only limited problem-solving behavior, since the buyer is probably learning anew about the brand each time he buys. Although some brand loyalty probably still exists, in the four- or five-year interim or longer between purchases, he forgets a lot and learns a lot, too. Also, technological change over those years between purchases may even require him to evaluate the new model with a different set of expected benefits. So he has to form a new product class image, which involves extensive problem solving (EPS). Even his personal values may change in that interval, causing him to look for totally new benefits in the product. This behavior does not fit the RPS pattern.

Probably at the extreme of the non-RPS pattern are refrigerators, ranges, and washing machines, where the service life averages more than 10 years, and these products are even more extreme than automobiles.[7] A large proportion of these buyers, perhaps a majority, engage in considerable search and consult a variety of services, especially salesclerks. But this search occurs near the time of purchase. Because of the infrequency of purchase, however, it may occur long after any earlier attitude measure used as a predictor is likely to have been taken. Most of the remaining buyers in this extreme case are responding to an emergency need, for example, a breakdown of a refrigerator. Typically, they visit only one or two stores; moreover these stores carry only a limited number of brands. A key point is that attitude may not be a strong predictor of purchase for these non-RPS products,[8] but confidence probably will predict well.

Having examined brand loyalty as characterizing RPS where product change is limited, let us get a more specific picture in trying to clarify RPS behavior and the use of the CDM to describe that behavior.

3. RELATION TO THE CDM

The buying process of the RPS buyers cannot be fully represented by the CDM, and the CDM must be modified to accommodate such buyers. In what way should it be modified?

Presumably, the RPS buyer's attitude is already formed, as is brand

---

[6] Ibid, p. 16.

[7] G. S. Day and T. Deutscher, "Attitudinal Predictions of Choices of Major Appliance Brands," *Journal of Marketing Research*, Vol. XIX (May 1982), 192–98.

[8] For an excellent analysis, see ibid.

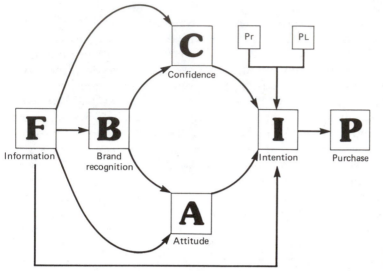

Figure 6-1
RPS Stage of Decision and the CDM

recognition and confidence with respect to the repeat purchase. The market variables, such as price and availability, are subject to change, whereas the product changes much less in RPS. Consequently, price and availability become separated in the consumer's mind from the brand concept. The price (Pr) and availability (place, Pl) are then believed to bear directly upon intention (I) instead of exerting their effects as a part of attitude (A). This direct effect upon I is shown in Figure 6-1. With the changing variables—price and distribution—operating in this way, it would seem that information (F) would affect intention (I) directly and thus bypass the thinking process as shown by the bottom arrow from F to I in Figure 6-1. Mentally some choice tactic could be triggered such as "Buy the cheapest brand in my evoked set"[9] or "Buy brand A." Information (F) would little affect attitude (A), and brand recognition (B) and confidence (C) probably not at all.

However, confidence (C) was shown to be affected by the buyer's state of knowledge of Pr and Pl in a study of toothpaste, where the buyers were highly familiar with most of the brand names.[10] The study concluded that buyers actively acquire amounts of information, particularly about brand names and prices. This contradiction raises doubts about large numbers of consumers bypassing the thinking process in RPS.

We now deal at some length with the issue of whether RPS consumers do bypass their thinking processes. First, it is obviously important for marketing. If it is true, marketing strategy should be different from what it should be if not true. Second, for the CDM to be useful, it must fit the realities of consumer

[9] W. D. Hoyer, "An Examination of Consumer Decision Making for a Common Repeat Purchase Product," *Journal of Consumer Research*, 11, no. 3 (December 1984), 822–29.

[10] J. Jacoby, J. G. Szybillo, and J. Busato-Schach, "Information Acquisition Behavior in Brand Choice Situations," *Journal of Consumer Research*, 3, no. 4 (March 1977), 209–16.

behavior. Third, economists often ascribe irrationality to such consumer behavior as we will see in discussing consumerism in Chapter 18, and whether this is true should be answered.

Pr and Pl can be important variables at the top of the product life cycle when it begins to level off and where most buyers are in RPS, as described in Chapter 2. It is not, however, that the buyer is more responsive to changes per se in Pr and Pl, but that along with some promotion they are the only variables that management can profitably manipulate when buyers are in RPS and the product is fairly stable at the top of the PLC.

4. DIRECT EFFECT OF INFORMATION

Is there other evidence that this bypassing effect may occur in RPS? Following is a review of some of the evidence.

Data on Carnation Instant Breakfast from a study by General Foods of its introduction of Post Instant Breakfast intended to compete with Carnation throws some light on the bypassing issue.[11] The buyers' attitudes toward Carnation were obtained operationally as a unidimensional measure by asking, "How do you rate the brand overall?" Their intention (I) was obtained by the question, "How likely are you to buy the product in the next month?" And their confidence in the product (C) was ascertained by the query, "How confident are you of your ability to judge the product?" Carnation Instant Breakfast had been in the market and heavily advertised for more than two years. Hence, it was familiar to most of the people in the test market area of Portland, Oregon, and was an RPS situation.

With this study we develop evidence for believing that the second major change mentioned at the outset of the chapter—bypassing the thinking process—does occur as the buyer moves up the product life cycle to RPS. First, Figure 6-2 pinpoints some evidence for believing that information can directly affect intention (I). Information (F) often changes the RPS consumer's belief about price (Pr) and availability (Pl), which can create intention since these marketing variables are often changing in RPS. More surprising, however, is that information (F) bypasses the thinking processes required in brand-image formation and goes directly to intention (I) as you will see in Figure 6-2.

"Information sources" (F) was the sum of three items: the consumer's conversations about the product, the direct-mail sample he received, and the number of media messages he recalled having seen and/or heard. Confidence (C), also, was thought to be a factor. Consequently, the 500-plus consumers in the sample were classified into five groups according to the level of their confidence. Then, a separate information source (F) to intention (I) relationship was developed for the confidence level of *each* group as seen in Figure 6-2.

[11] M. Laroche and J. A. Howard, "Nonlinear Relations in a Complex Model of Buyer Behavior," *Journal of Consumer Research*, 6, no. 4 (March 1980), 377–88.

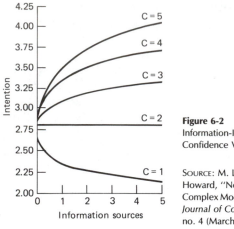

Figure 6-2
Information-Intention Relation,
Confidence Varying

SOURCE: M. Laroche and J. A.
Howard, "Nonlinear Relations in a
Complex Model of Buyer Behavior,"
Journal of Consumer Research, 6,
no. 4 (March 1980), 384.

As you can see in the case of Carnation Instant Breakfast in Figure 6-2, the higher the buyer's confidence (C), the greater the direct effect of information (F) upon intention (I). In fact, at the lowest level of confidence (C = 1) increasing F actually decreases I. Perhaps this occurs because at that point, additional information merely tends to "overload" or confuse the very uncertain consumer rather than inform him. Further and most important, information (F) and confidence (C) interact to cause intention (I), as indicated by the C lines diverging sharply from each other instead of remaining parallel as information (F) increases. Thus, at different levels of C, a change in F has a different amount of effect upon I, or the level of C also influences how much F directly affects I. Put into words, the better informed the consumer, the more likely is the consumer to bypass the thinking process.

One might argue that this effect of information (F) about Carnation on intention (I) to buy it is not as direct as Figure 6-1 shows, but that F is really operating only through A as implied in the CDM in Chapter 3. Actually,

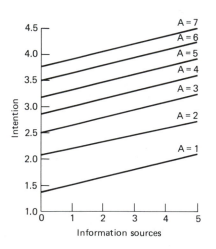

Figure 6-3
Information-Intention Relation,
Attitude Varying

SOURCE: M. Laroche and J. A.
Howard, "Nonlinear Relations in a
Complex Model of Buyer Behavior,"
Journal of Consumer Research, 6,
no. 4 (March 1980), 384.

however, as indicated by the almost perfectly parallel lines in Figure 6-3, information (F) and attitude (A) are not interacting. Information (F) is completely independent of attitude (A). Therefore, information (F) is *not* operating upon intention (I) via attitude (A) as in the simple CDM, but directly on intention (I).
You should remember, however, that this conclusion is based upon a single
study. Nevertheless, no contradictory evidence has been found.

Having concluded that information (F) does have a *direct effect* upon
intention (I) with RPS consumers of Carnation Instant Breakfast, can we say
anything about how strongly this relationship influences purchase behavior,
the *real* payoff variable? This effect of intention (I) upon purchase (P) is shown
in Figure 6-4, where P is defined as the number of units purchased during a
three-week period. The direct effect of information (F) about Carnation on
the purchase (P) of it was particularly powerful when intention (I) was high,
as indicated by the strong nonlinear relation of I to P, seen in Figure 6-4. If in
the sample intention (I) is high, Figure 6-4 shows that a small change in I will
have a very large effect upon purchase (P). However, if intention (I) is low, it
has a very small effect upon purchase (P). It shows how seriously wrong you
could be in making a forecast on the assumption that the intention (I) to purchase
(P) is linear.

In Chapter 5, evidence was cited that for "packaged goods" (frequently
purchased, low-priced products) this relation was nonlinear as shown in Figure
6-4 but linear for consumer durables. The evidence here is consistent with
that because we are dealing with an instant breakfast, a packaged good.

Let us now summarize the evidence. Since we conclude that information
(F) could have a large effect on purchase (P) via the direct effect to I when I is
high as it did with Carnation in Figure 6-4, a key question is whether *I* will be
high when the consumer is in RPS. To answer this important question partially,
we know from Figure 6-2 that intention (I) will be high if confidence (C) is
high, as shown by the top line there. We can assume confidence (C) will be
high in RPS because it increases over the product life cycle. Also, intention (I)
will be high because attitude (A) causes intention (I) and, further, attitude (A)

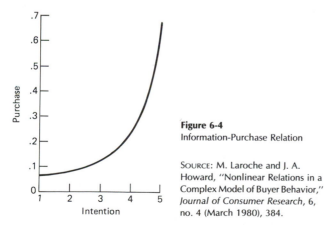

Figure 6-4
Information-Purchase Relation

SOURCE: M. Laroche and J. A.
Howard, "Nonlinear Relations in a
Complex Model of Buyer Behavior,"
Journal of Consumer Research, 6,
no. 4 (March 1980), 384.

has a somewhat larger effect upon intention (I) when confidence (C) is high.[12] So, the *direct effect* of F upon I appears to be occurring in a particular set of circumstances, namely, when the *buyer is in RPS*. This may seem like a roundabout way to come to a conclusion that is intuitively obvious. However, the conclusion is too important to be left to intuition.

Thus, the CDM when applied to RPS consumers should be modified as in Figure 6-1 by incorporating a direct relation between information (F) and intention (I) as we have seen with Carnation Instant Breakfast. With this background we can deal much more effectively with how consumers in RPS process information.

5. INFORMATION PROCESSING

Now let us see what light information processing can throw on our problem of how RPS consumers buy. From Chapter 5 we would expect the RPS buyer to be an efficient information processor. He has both his product category image and brand image well formed, and so he has well-developed expectations. These expectations, along with his previous experience, guide him in paying attention and processing information rapidly. Similarly, they create conflict and sensitize him when the unexpected is encountered. In addition, the kind of information he needs—price and availability—is easily processed. For price, the information is numbers, and in the case of availability, it is a simple yes or no: his retail store either has the brand or doesn't have it. Consequently, he can easily encode this information in his memory.[13]

As for search, internal search in RPS would seem to be quite limited. The demands on the buyer's memory are small in RPS. Mainly, she must merely *recognize* the brand, not recall it. Recognition, you will remember, is substantially easier than is recall.[14] Recognition represents the role of brand recognition (B).

However, it is a low-involving situation that minimizes search and also causes the attractiveness of the ad, for example, to play a greater role. It is low-involvement because the products tend to be frequently purchased and probably low-priced. In addition, the consumer is choosing from an evoked set where all members of that set are acceptable, which greatly reduces the risk of making a bad choice.

---

[12] See R. H. Fazio and M. P. Zanna, "Direct Experience and Attitude-Behavior Consistency," in L. Berkowitz, ed., *Advances in Experimental Social Psychology*, Vol. 14 (San Diego, Calif.: Academic Press, 1981), pp. 179–83. Some unpublished evidence also supports the principle.

[13] E. J. Johnson and J. E. Russo, "Product Familiarity and Learning New Information," *Journal of Consumer Research*, 11, no. 1 (June 1984), 548.

[14] J. R. Bettman, *An Information Processing Theory of Consumer Choice* (Reading, Mass.: Addison-Wesley, 1979), p. 157; R. P. Bagozzi and A. J. Silk, "Recall, Recognition, and the Measurement of Memory for Print Advertisements," *Marketing Science*, 2, no. 2 (Spring 1983), 95–134.

As for the decision rule the consumer uses to combine information and choose a product, we would expect an *established decision rule* instead of a *constructive decision rule* to operate in RPS, where she has had experience with the brand. In the former, the consumer uses a decision rule that she has learned from previous experience. In the latter she uses a rule that is constructed to meet the conditions of this specific decision. Johnson and Russo have shown that the brand itself, being so well defined in RPS, is probably treated as a single attribute or chunk, not a combination of benefits.[15] Thus, we can think of the rule for combining information in RPS as a modified "affect referral." An *affect referral decision rule* has been described this way: "A consumer does not examine attributes or beliefs about alternatives but simply elicits from memory a previously formed over-all evaluation for each alternative."[16] Perhaps a better way to describe the choice is as the application of some simple choice tactic learned over time such as "Buy what you bought last time."[17]

Finally, in RPS, there would seem to be little if any need for advertising. The buyer has all the information she needs, except, of course, about the changing conditions of price and availability. But if we look at actual situations, we often find substantial advertising funds being devoted to brands in a product class that appears to be at the top of the PLC (RPS). Look at the amount of cigarette advertising! Yet, we have been saying that when she is in RPS, she does not need much information. Isn't this a contradiction? It is. Let us explain.

6. DYNAMICS OF RPS

6.1 Introduction

What explains the fairly heavy advertising sometimes found for a product at the top of the PLC? The answer to this question is the third major change as the consumer moves from LPS to RPS. As stated early in the chapter, we can say that most consumers develop a cyclic pattern of behavior, but let us discuss this very important point in explaining what consumers do and why.

Take cigarettes, which were heavily advertised even before tar became an issue. Some of the advertising may be intended to shift buyers across product class boundaries, but probably not much of it is intended for this purpose. Perhaps there is product change. Chairman Harness of Procter & Gamble illustrates: "A significant fact about these five products [Ivory Soap, Crisco, Tide, Crest, and Pampers] is their age. . . . Their combined age is 220 years, and their average age is 44 years. The oldest of these brands is 97 and the youngest

---

[15] Johnson and Russo, "Product Familiarity and Learning New Information," 542–50.

[16] Bettman, *An Information Processing Theory of Consumer Choice*, p. 179.

[17] Hoyer, "An Examination of Consumer Decision Making for a Common Repeat Purchase Product," p. 823.

is 10 years old."[18] His basic message is that products must be continually improved to lead the market year after year as these have. But this is probably somewhat uniquely P&G's strategy. Typically in RPS product change is very limited.

For 15 years there has been a belief that at least most RPS buyers can be surprisingly irregular about the brands they choose, and so they do a lot of shifting among brands. It is called the *ambiguity-arousal hypothesis* meaning that when the consumer encounters an ambiguous, novel situation, his arousal—short-term motivation—increases, causing him to search for information as discussed in Chapter 4.[19] Recent evidence lends strong support. Drawing upon the hypothesis, and using the related empirical evidence, we can verify *why* this shifting in the form of a cyclic pattern of buying behavior occurs.

In Figure 6-5, you note a related view that as buyers progress from EPS to LPS and to RPS, by definition they become increasingly familiar with the product. Consequently their search needs decline. After reaching the RPS stage, however, perhaps they become bored, and their search needs then increase as they seek variety or novelty to offset that boredom in their buying.[20] This is called *boredom problem solving* (BPS). Whether some other motivation than boredom may be the cause of the behavior is an open question.[21]

The consequences of this psychology are that the buyer, instead of repeating a brand purchase, begins to review the existing brands not only in terms of price and availability as we have been saying but also in terms of product benefits. Diagrammatically, in Figure 6-5, he moves via the dashed line from BPS and "cycles" back to LPS, which we can describe as "cyclic behavior." He cycles from LPS to RPS to BPS, then back to LPS, and so on.

This situation would appear to cause the buyer to be confronted with a number of brands from which to choose. Consequently, he would probably use a phased strategy in which he first narrows down the range of alternatives to a manageable number, which we call his evoked set, and which is only those brands he would consider buying.[22] They are brands that (1) he is familiar with and (2) best meet his needs.

It was thought in the original statement of the cycle concept that this cyclic behavior of consumers from RPS to LPS and back again occurred simultaneously among most if not all buyers in the market.[23] If that were the case,

---

[18] E. G. Harness, "Some Basic Beliefs About Marketing," talk, Annual Marketing Meeting of the Conference Board (New York, October 21, 1976).

[19] J. A. Howard and J. N. Sheth, *The Theory of Buyer Behavior* (New York: John Wiley & Sons, 1969), pp. 157–68.

[20] C. W. Park and V. P. Lessig, "Judgmental Rules and Stages of the Familiarity Curve: Promotional Implications," *Journal of Advertising Research*, 6, no. 1 (Winter 1977), 10–16.

[21] P. S. Raju, "Optimal Stimulation Level: Its Relationship to Personality, Demographics, and Exploratory Behavior," *Journal of Consumer Research*, 7, no. 3 (December 1980), 272–82.

[22] J. R. Bettman, *An Information Processing Theory of Consumer Choice*, p. 184; D. A. Lussier and R. W. Olshavsky, "Task Complexity and Contingent Processing in Brand Choice," *Journal of Consumer Research*, 6, no. 2 (September 1979), pp. 154–65.

[23] Howard and Sheth, *The Theory of Buyer Behavior*.

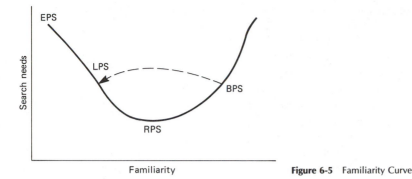

Figure 6-5   Familiarity Curve

the situation would represent a splendid promotional opportunity, but, as will be seen later, this is not so. Buyers, instead, shift brands at different times, and some do not shift at all, as discussed shortly. What the motivation is that triggers this shifting is not well understood.[24] Instead of boredom, it could be called an instinct to avoid missing an opportunity where the opportunity is to buy an improved brand as described earlier by Mr. Harness of P&G.

6.2   Evidence on Cyclic Behavior

Evidence strongly supporting this hypothesis of the cyclical nature of consumer buying was found in a study in Holland, which must be described in some detail to convey its significance.[25] Three low-priced, frequently purchased product categories—beer, margarine, and fopro (a condensed milk used in coffee)—were examined to see if cyclic patterns characterized the behavior of their consumers.

A brief word about the data. At least three of the brands for each category were national brands distributed over Holland as a whole and promoted by newspapers, television, and radio on a national scale. The information was collected from an ongoing 2,000-member commercial purchase panel of families in Holland for a 2-year period.

The "pool-size" concept was used to measure the behavior of the families toward all three products. "*Pool size*" means the number of brands the buyer has bought in his last 10 purchases. Hence, on each purchase of the product,

---

[24] L. McAlister, "A Dynamic Attribute Satiation Model of Variety-Seeking Behavior," *Journal of Consumer Research*, 9, no. 2 (September 1982), 141–50; L. McAlister and E. Pessemier, "Variety Seeking Behavior: An Interdisciplinary Review," *Journal of Consumer Research*, 9, no. 3 (December 1982), 311–22. For a review of measurement problems, see E. Pessemier, "Variety Seeking Behavior: Some Issues Affecting Theoretical and Applied Work," in R. K. Srinivasan and A. D. Shocker, eds., *Analytical Approaches to Product and Market Planning: The Second Conference* (Cambridge, Mass.: Marketing Science Institute, October 1982), pp. 130–34. For a stochastic analysis, see M. Givon, "Variety Seeking Through Brand Switching," *Marketing Science*, 3, no. 1 (Winter 1984), 1–22.

[25] B. Wierenga, *An Investigation of Brand Choice Processes* (Rotterdam, Holland: University of Rotterdam, 1979), Chapter 6.

the buyer's "pool size" either increases by one, or remains the same, or decreases by one. It may help if you recognize that "pool size" is related to the familiar concept of the consumer's evoked set of brands.[26] Specifically, the "pool" is the set of different brands the consumer bought during the last 10 purchases. These brands are acceptable (and therefore in his evoked set) because he has actually chosen them. However, these brands that he purchased in the last 10 purchases probably do not constitute his total evoked set. Consequently, the "pool" is a "truncated evoked set."

In Figure 6-6, pool size (s) is (are) measured on the vertical axis and *purchase occasion* (t) on the horizontal axis for only *1* of the 2,000 families to illustrate the process of buying. You are urged to work through this paragraph and the next very carefully, which will immensely simplify the rest of the chapter. For purchase at time t of fopro, the pool size is 2, as you can see. In other words, during the period of the 10-purchase sequence of $t - 9$, $t - 8$, $t - 7$, $t - 6$, $t - 5$, $t - 4$, $t - 3$, $t - 2$, $t - 1$, t, the family bought two different brands. On its next purchase of fopro ($t + 1$), pool size diminished to 1, which means that during the purchase sequence of $t - 8$ to $t + 1$, the family bought the same brand. This single brand purchasing for fopro continues until $t + 28$, as you can see.

On the $t + 29$ purchase occasion, the family purchases a different brand, and so the pool size increases to 2. The pool size remains 2 for 10 purchases, that is, until $t + 38$. Since the pool size at $t + 38$ is 2, it means that during the 10 purchases $t + 29$ to $t + 38$, the family bought two different brands of fopro. At the next purchase, $t + 39$, the pool size returns to 1, meaning that during the sequence $t + 30$ to $t + 39$, the same brand has been bought and this status is maintained until $t + 62$. The family has, therefore, not switched brands for 33 consecutive purchases, that is, from $t + 30$ till $t + 62$. Then, again an incidental purchase of a different brand occurs at $t + 62$, raising the pool size to 2. The pool size soon reduces to 1 and remains so for a short period till $t + 80$. From $t + 81$, a period of intensive brand switching begins where the pool size increases to as much as 4. Following this turbulent period, the family seems to have made its choice and continues buying the same brand for a long time.

As you see in Figure 6-6, the fopro and beer charts each show one period of extreme search, while margarine exhibits two such periods. Thus "search" is operationally defined by the *number of different brands* bought before settling on a particular brand. It can be contrasted with a straightforward switch from one favorite brand to another favorite brand. Another difference between the products in their switching patterns is that fopro is more subject to single brand periods than is either beer or margarine.

In summary, Figure 6-6 indicates that in a single household there are cycles where, after periods of intensive search, the family may have several long stretches of continuously buying the same brand.

When all 2,000 households are thrown together, a similar picture

---

[26] Ibid., pp. 160–61.

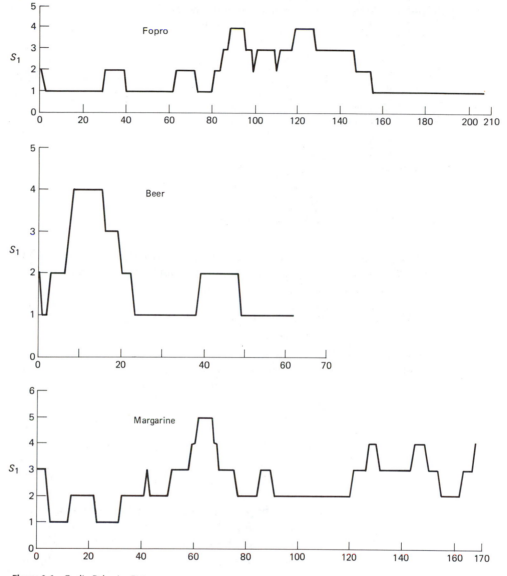

Figure 6-6   Cyclic Behavior Patterns

Source: B. Wierenga, *An Investigation of Brand Choice Processes* (Rotterdam, Holland: University of Rotterdam, 1979), p. 159.

emerges. However, this many-household picture cannot be shown in a two-dimensional diagram as in Figure 6-6. Instead, it must be described by using the *range* of differences between the maximum and minimum value of pool size over all families. The results are shown in Table 6-3. Families that bought only one brand during the two-year period of the data are excluded in an attempt to better show the variation in switching required to conform to the

Table 6-3   Relative Frequency of Range of Values for
Households with More Than One Brand

Variation in Pool Size	Fopro	Beer	Margarine
0	.0269	.1294	.0190
1	.4669	.5055	.3814
2	.3223	.2582	.2975
3	.1147	.0875	.1745
4	.0475	.0241	.0738
$\geqq 5$	.0207	.0044	.0537
Number of households	1.000	1.000	1.000
with $\geqq 2$ brands	484	457	894

SOURCE: B. Wierenga, *An Investigation of Brand Choice Processes*
(Rotterdam, Holland: University of Rotterdam, 1979), p. 170.

search-loyalty cycle. These excluded continuous repeat purchasers, although not shown, constitute roughly a fourth (fopro = 28%, beer = 27%, margarine = 16%) of the total number of families buying all three products.

As you can see in Table 6-3 from the variation in pool size that there were substantial differences in levels of switching activity. In fopro, for example, 2.69% exhibited no variation, while 46.7% showed a variation of 1. That the pool size is not constant but has periods of low values and periods of high values is consistent with the cyclic behavior of Figure 6-5, the familiarity curve.

The study sheds further light on the cyclic pattern by examining panelists' search behavior. It concludes that "the additional brands of the many-brand-households are used more to intensify the *search* during *search periods* . . . than to increase the general level of brand-switching activity."[27] This fact provides greater evidence that the buyer shifts to get information about a brand—not merely to shift in some random way.

Although marketing effort does not appear to cause the shift,[28] it does make a difference to which brands they shift, once they *do* decide to shift. In line with the "boredom" hypothesis set out earlier, boredom causes them to look around, and the marketing effort reduces the boredom.

Finally, and most important of all, the study supports the basic notion of RPS behavior defined at the outset of the chapter and is the subject of the whole chapter. Specifically, those consumers who shifted had formed an evoked set. The evoked sets were never more than seven brands—except in margarine, where the maximum was nine. And the buyers shifted among these brands according to price, availability, and other changes in the market. A fascinating conclusion, however, was that they did not shift *directly* in response to market changes. We can say they were basically motivated to shop around by what we

[27] Ibid, p. 169. This conclusion is based on the linear learning model, and the interested reader is urged to consult the original source.
[28] Ibid, p. 180.

might call an instinctive desire not to miss new opportunities in the market, or put another way, a desire for variety caused by boredom.

7. RECONCILIATION OF THE DIRECT EFFECT AND CYCLIC BEHAVIOR

In this chapter the two types of behavior—a direct response to information that bypasses the thinking process involved in brand image formation and a cyclic response—seem to be in conflict. A buyer can logically behave in either manner, but not in *both*.

The bypassing effect that we were seeing earlier in the chapter applies continuously only to those buyers who do not exhibit cyclic behavior. These consumers made up about 25% in the Dutch study, leaving about 75% of them to exhibit some minimal cyclic behavior. Those exhibiting cyclic behavior presumably experience direct effect mainly during the period of brand loyalty, if at all. It is not possible to give a definitive answer, since the conclusions of direct and cyclic effects each came from a different body of data and different types of analysis were used. However, Johnson and Russo have shown that the RPS consumer (well informed) is an efficient information processor, which is consistent with cyclic behavior where the consumer utilizes available information.[29]

8. RELATION OF RPS TO THE CDM

The foregoing discussion suggests that to model RPS, a slightly modified CDM version is appropriate. This can be accomplished by merely adding the arrow from information (F) directly to intention (I), as was shown in Figure 6-1. But for those buyers who show cyclic behavior, the *total CDM* is necessary: an RPS buyer is temporarily thrown back from RPS into LPS as he reviews the brands in his evoked set as originally stated in Figure 6-5 and so processes information. The correct CDM is seen in Figure 6-7, but recognize that about 75% of the consumers periodically take the information processing route.

In this model, the buyer has well-defined concepts of the brands to control his attention and to exploit fully his perceptual processes. He needs to search only minimally, and when he does, his expectations will guide him. A *phased strategy* of choice is appropriate, because the buyer is confronted with a large number of brands and finds he must limit them to a manageable few, which is his evoked set. The specific rule for choosing products in the first phase may be that the buyer sets a minimum cut-off point and rejects those alternatives that don't meet it. In the second phase, the weighted linear compensatory model is probably appropriate because the buyer is even better informed than in LPS.

[29] Johnson and Russo, "Product Familiarity and Learning New Information."

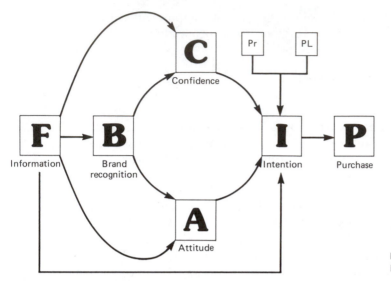

Figure 6-7
Routine Problem-Solving Model

The model described in this way, however, overemphasizes the thinking or information processing that is typical of RPS. As the consumer cycles back into LPS, he does do some thinking. More frequently, however, this thinking is small. The extreme, of course, is the roughly one-fourth in the Dutch study who apparently had a choice tactic, "Buy the same brand," and so continuously exhibited the direct effect of marketing.

9. IMPLICATIONS FOR PRACTICE

The implications of the cyclic model are substantial for marketing managers. The direct effect of information (F) to intention (I) suggests an emphasis upon reminder and motivational advertising, for example, seeing the product in a pleasant setting, instead of informative advertising.[30] Research shows that for low-involvement situations, the celebrity status of the product endorser has a strong effect on consumer attitudes.[31] For high-involvement situations, celebrity status has no effect, and the cogency of information about the product is powerful instead.

The cyclic aspect suggests an easier entry for a new brand into a stable market—the top of the product life cycle—than would otherwise be expected. The cyclic behavior would improve the chances of even an innovation because the innovation that replaces the existing product would likely be judged on some of the same benefits and these would, of course, be familiar to the consumer.

[30] R. B. Zajonc, "Feeling and Thinking," *American Psychologist*, 35, no. 2 (February 1980), 151–75.

[31] Petty, Cacciopo, and Schuman, "Central and Peripheral Routes to Advertising Effectiveness."

It especially encourages product improvements that extend the product life cycle, a policy that Procter & Gamble has used effectively in the past and described earlier in the chapter. Finally, it indicates the need to supplement the reminder advertising with some informative copy on both the most important attributes and the attributes where the marketer has a competitive advantage.

Equally and perhaps even more important are the implications of cyclic behavior for public policy. Without the cyclic notion, there would be a state of equilibrium where the buyer is fully informed. If this were the case, it would be difficult to justify advertising and the required resources—especially to the degree practiced by some packaged goods industries. This has long been a very troublesome point between marketers and economists, since the apparent waste of resources is undesirable from a public policy point of view. The cyclic behavior provides a rationale for some advertising even in a stable market, a point developed further in the discussion of consumerism in Chapter 18. The function of such advertising is not to prompt the switch back to LPS, but to prompt the brand shift once the consumer has decided to cycle back to LPS.

In spite of the cyclic behavior, however, RPS behavior is overall substantially more stable than is LPS. Put another way, customers do learn a pattern of behavior. The evidence for this is seen in Table 6-4. It compares the R^2 for the equations used in modeling an established brand of instant breakfast (Carnation) with those for a new brand (Post) in an established class. The R^2 is a measure of how much the independent variables in the brand identification equation $B = f$ (Information (F), Satisfaction (S), etc.), for example, explain the level of B. Put another way, the higher the R^2, the less the error in the relation. Carnation Instant Breakfast had been in the market about 2 years when General Foods introduced its version, Post Instant Breakfast. When the sums of the R^2s in each of the equations are compared in Table 6-4 you quickly see how much stronger the RPS relations (Carnation) are than the LPS relations (Post). Carnation is far more stable.

As you can see Carnation does much better than Post except in the case of the satisfaction equation ($S = f(P)$). The smaller difference in satisfaction

Table 6-4   Stability of Established Brands versus New Brands

Equation	Carnation R^2s	Post R^2s	Post R^2s as % of Carnation R^2s
$B = f(F, S, \ldots)$	1.0190*	.4856*	48%
$A = f(B, F, \ldots)$	1.0952	.5985	55
$C = f(F, B, \ldots)$	1.0708	.5313	50
$I = f(A, C, \ldots)$	2.7646	.4894	54
$P = f(I)$	.5099	.1308	26
$S = f(P)$	.2466	.2177	88

* Sum of R^2s over waves and groups.

From M. Laroche and J. A. Howard, ''Nonlinear Relations in a Complex Model,'' *Journal of Consumer Research*, 6, no. 4 (March 1980), 381–82.

(S) would be expected because the consumer has more to learn about the quality of Post and therefore satisfaction (S) would be more responsive to purchase (P) and to the consequent consumption experience from that purchase.

10. CONCLUSIONS

The trip through this chapter may at times have seemed tenuous, but a definite pattern of routine problem-solving (RPS) emerges for the frequently purchased item. It is not a simple pattern as we have seen, however, because consumers differ in the amount of variety they need to avoid boredom or missing a good buy. It was possible to modify the CDM as in Figure 6-7 to accommodate this type of behavior.

Also in RPS there is probably more impulse buying than in the other two stages where impulsive buying is defined as "thoughtless actions" instead of the more traditional definition of "unplanned" purchasing. Recent research suggests that "thoughtless buying" is stimulated by emotion or "short-term motivation" as the term was used in Chapter 5. Progress has been made in measuring this motivational state by using cameras and interviews that portray the buyer's facial expression.[32] In sum, this is the nonutilitarian behavior that you have probably been looking for. It also appears in the purchase of certain products such as in the marketing of art events.[33] More about this type of behavior will be found in Chapters 10 and especially 16.

Finally, as documented in Table 6-2, brand loyalty of consumers is not generally declining, contrary to what is often thought.

Questions

1. What is brand loyalty and how common is it?
2. What is meant by the "bypassing" or "direct" effect in LPS?
3. Describe the cyclic pattern of behavior in LPS.
4. What is the role of advertising in cyclic behavior?
5. Is cyclic behavior consistent with the notion of the consumer having an evoked set? Explain.

[32] P. Weinberg and W. Gottwald, "Impulsive Consumer Buying as a Result of Emotions," *Journal of Business Research*, 10, no. 1 (March 1982), 43–57.

[33] E. C. Hirschman, "Aesthetics, Ideologies and the Limits of the Marketing Concept," *Journal of Marketing*, 47, no. 3 (Summer 1983), 45–55.

CHAPTER 7

Comparison of Models

1. INTRODUCTION

You have now seen the overall framework of the three-stage analysis in Chapter 2, the simple six-variable Consumer Decision Model (CDM) in Chapter 3 and the theory supporting the CDM in Chapters 4, 5, and 6 that act as a feedback to information (F) of the CDM as described earlier in Figure 5-2. You may have wondered if there are alternative models of consumer behavior with which you might compare the CDM to obtain a better understanding of the nature of models. Also, you may have wondered if the CDM is a valid model.

There are a number of models. We will discuss two of them to give you a basis of comparison with the CDM. The first is Engel, Kollat, and Blackwell,[1] and the second is Bettman's work.[2] These two models have been the most influential, and each is probably most representative of its particular type, marketing practice or basic research. These two models will be described and then evaluated by using the 10 criteria of a good model from Zaltman and Wallendorf,[3] as shown in Table 7-1, and one other, to guide the design of marketing strategy,

---

[1] J. E. Engel, R. D. Blackwell, and P. W. Miniard, *Consumer Behavior*, 5th ed. (Chicago: Dryden Press, 1986).

[2] J. R. Bettman, *An Information Processing Theory of Consumer Choice* (Reading, Mass.: Addison-Wesley, 1979).

[3] G. Zaltman and M. Wallendorf, *Consumer Behavior: Basic Findings and Management Implications*, 2nd ed. (New York: John Wiley & Sons, 1983), pp. 622–24.

Table 7-1 Desirable Properties of a Model

A model should be:

1. Capable of explanation as well as prediction
2. General
3. High in heuristic power
4. High in unifying power
5. Internally consistent
6. Original
7. Plausible (have face validity)
8. Simple
9. Supported by facts
10. Testable, verifiable

SOURCE: G. Zaltman and M. Wallendorf, *Consumer Behavior: Basic Findings and Management Implications* (New York: John Wiley & Sons, 1983), p. 623.

introduced in Chapter 1 to describe a theory. The two models will then be compared with the CDM.

2. EKB MODEL

2.1 Introduction

The Engel, Kollat, and Blackwell (EKB) book was the pioneering text in 1968. It performed yeoman service in providing almost a generation of teachers with a vehicle to help students understand the significance of many previously unrelated ideas. In succeeding editions they kept up with the flow of new research findings.

2.2 Description of Model

The most recent version of their model is made up of five classes of concepts as you can see in Figure 7-1.[4] First, on the upper left, is the "Input," which refers to information the consumer receives. Second, it contains "Information Processing," which refers to things like the concepts in Chapter 4, 5, and 6 but perhaps not as sharply defined. As you can see, these are familiar terms. Third, "Decision Process" captures more of the outcome of the buying process. Familiar terms abound. Fourth, "Variables Influencing Decision Process" deals largely with motivation and with which you are already familiar. Finally, "Social Influences" are also familiar from Part IV of our text, namely, culture, reference groups, and family. Let us proceed to apply the criteria in Table 7-1.

[4] Engel and others, *Consumer Behavior*, p. 35.

Input	Information Processing	Decision Process	Variables Influencing Decision Process

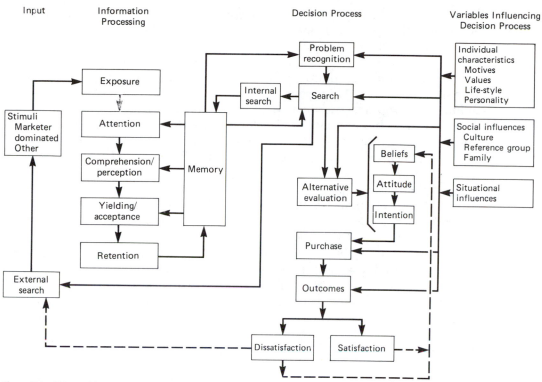

Figure 7-1 EKB Model

Source: J. Engel, R. D. Blackwell, and P. W. Miniard, *Consumer Behavior*, 5th ed. (Chicago: Dryden Press, 1986), p. 35.

2.3 Criteria Applied

Only in a loose way do these processes *explain* how consumers buy and consume. Specifically, they do not explain when particular operational variables will influence others, how this influence occurs, or what the strength of the influence is. They *predict* what consumers will do in a given situation still less well. For example, if you were to operationalize the variables with actual data, run regression equations, and try to predict behavior, the predictions are likely to be highly inaccurate.

One of the advantages of the EKB model, however, is its *generality*. It can be applied to a wide range of situations. But it does not deal with buying by a group or with the interactive relations between a consumer and the selling company. The model is not strong in having the *heuristic* power to encourage you to ask new questions about how consumers buy and consume, and so it does not encourage developing new knowledge. Its lack of sharp definition probably discourages this. Its *unifying* power is substantial in the sense that it brings together a wide range of concepts and propositions. But it does not accomplish this in a systematic way into what could be called a well-formulated theory that provides good prediction.

A common criterion of a good model is that it is *internally consistent* instead of containing contradictions that weaken its usefulness in explaining why consumers buy. There may be inconsistencies, but the looseness could be hiding them. Another criterion is whether the model is *original* and so contributing something new. It was original in developing the information seeking and evaluation process as a textbook 20 years ago. Its strength lies not in its originality but in helping interpret a wide range of research findings in almost any situation in a loose way.

The model is *plausible* in that on the surface it seems to make sense. This quality is essential for the theory to be easily accepted by other people. To use a model one needs to understand it, and for it to be *simple* helps this understanding. The EKB model is not simple as a glance at Figure 7-3 will readily assure you by the very large number of boxes and their interconnections. Imagine trying to work with it as a set of equations.

An essential characteristic of a model is that it be *supported by facts* so that the user can assume its explanations and predictions are true. This model was primarily designed for teaching consumer behavior and when the field was not well developed. As the authors say, "it never was our expectation that the model would be tested in the same manner as the Columbia group has done with the Howard model."[5] The concepts making up the EKB model are not notions that can be operationalized and used as variables for testing or simulation purposes. They are mere categories of things operating, as you see in Figure 7-1.

A model that has not yet been supported by the facts should at least be *testable* and therefore verifiable. Otherwise, the user can have no confidence in it. For it to be tested, it must be quantifiable. This model in its current form is not quantifiable and so not testable as stated in the preceding paragraph.

Finally, a key characteristic of a model used in a professional school is that it should have some relevance for practice. In marketing terminology it should contribute to formulating and implementing marketing strategy. This loose, very complex model shown in the diagram can be useful in a comprehensive textbook approach to consumer behavior discussed in Chapter 1 where the purpose is to impart "what we know" about consumer buying in a very general sense. It can also be helpful with the standard marketing case approach of qualitative analysis by organizing the data. However, it is not useful for modeling consumer behavior and providing the quantitative information that marketing management needs.

---

[5] J. F. Engel and R. D. Blackwell, *Consumer Behavior* (Hinsdale, N.J.: Dryden Press, 1982), p. 686.

3. BETTMAN MODEL

3.1 Introduction

Bettman's work is a milestone in the development of consumer theory.[6] It was not intended as a teaching text or as the basis of practical application but intended as a basic research document to guide the creation of new knowledge of how consumers buy. Yet it is organized in terms of issues that are relevant for management practice. It is a major source that a generation of consumer behavior researchers are drawing upon and has been the most fully developed model available. It is used here to illustrate the contrast between heavily applied research such as the EKB model and Bettman's basic research model. Both types are needed in a business school, one for current practice and the other for developing knowledge for *future* marketing practice. The comments about it in applying the characteristics of a good model are in a sense unfair to the Bettman model, which was designed as the foundation of future research and which is how it has been used. Nevertheless, we need to make clear what remains to be done to make it a full-fledged operating model so that you will value it for what it is. In Chapter 16 we will discuss future developments in consumer behavior theory, and in doing so you will see the crucial role of the Bettman-type model.

3.2 Description

The Bettman model brings to bear specifically on consumer behavior the concepts of how humans process information. This human information-processing view represents one of the major developments in the understanding of human thinking, as Howard Gardner has so enthusiastically described it.[7] This knowledge of how people think and solve their problems, including buying and consuming, largely grew out of the research by the Nobel prize–winner Herbert A. Simon of Carnegie-Mellon University, which was made possible by the development of the computer as a multifaceted research tool.

Previous chapters, especially Chapter 5, of our text drew upon Bettman's model so that the concepts used in Figure 7-2 are almost identical in meaning to the way we used them. Let us examine Figure 7-2. "Processing capacity" has come up again and again such as the limit that the consumer's short-term memory puts on his capacity to take in information and make sense of it discussed in Chapter 5. "Motivation," both short term and long term, has played an integral role in our thinking. "Attention" places severe limits on whether the consumer will take in and be affected by our advertising. "Information acquisition and evaluation," often under the title of "search," is the means by which the consumer finds the information he needs to make a choice among brands.

[6] Bettman, *Information Processing*, p. 17.
[7] H. Gardner, *The Mind's New Science* (New York: Basic Books, 1985).

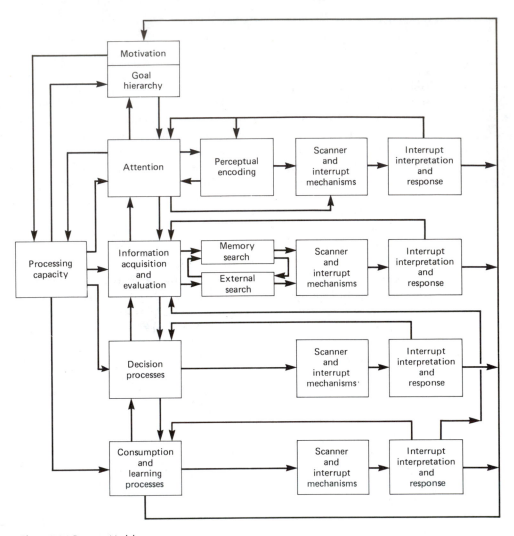

Figure 7-2 Bettman Model

SOURCE: J. R. Bettman, *An Information Processing Theory of Consumer Choice* © 1979, Addison-Wesley Publishing Co., Inc., Reading, MA, p. 17. Reprinted with permission.

Memory is not mentioned here, but it is implied in "Memory search." Memory has, of course, been paramount in shaping our understanding of the consumer, for example, the powerful role of the customer's product hierarchy in facilitating the consumer's thinking in Chapters 4 and 5. "Decision processes" are illustrated by the linear compensatory rule used by consumers in limited problem solving (LPS) as shown when the CDM is applied. Finally, "Consumption and learning processes" were discussed briefly in Chapter 3 where the possibility was mentioned of adding a seventh variable, "Satisfaction," to measure how pleased the consumer is from the experience of consuming the product.

3.3 Criteria Applied

Now let us apply the same criteria to the Bettman model. The model is capable of *explaining* much of consumer behavior. However, it is more process oriented than variable oriented. In most instances, it does not show when particular variables influence others, how this influence occurs, or what the strength of the influence is. Many individual relations would probably *predict* reasonably well as indicated by the basic research from which they were derived but not as a part of the system as described here. Some of the relations *predict* but in a qualitative way.

It is quite *general*, being applicable to a wide range of individual consumer buying. But it does not throw much light on consumers buying as a group or on the interactive relations between a consumer and the selling company. It does have the *heuristic* power to stimulate new ideas about consumers. This is probably its greatest strength. It clearly does serve a *unifying role* of bringing previously unrelated ideas together in a systematic way. It appears to be *internally consistent*.

When the model first appeared, it was quite *original* in bringing information-processing concepts into the context of consumer behavior. Bettman has continued this work. Most consumer behaviorists would agree that it is *plausible*. But it is by no means *simple*, as you can readily see in Figure 7-2 by the large number of boxes and their interconnections. This lack of simplicity hampers its use as an applied system. Many of the individual relations are *supported by the facts* in previous research. But the total system as seen in Figure 7-6 has not been tested as a system. In its current form, it is probably not *testable*. To be testable, it would have to be considerably more specified.

As for its relevance to designing marketing strategy, knowing the Bettman system could be useful to a manager designing *marketing strategy* by stimulating new insights about his consumers. In its current form it can be used qualitatively but not quantitatively to model consumer buying for immediate application.

4. COMPARISON OF EKB AND BETTMAN WITH THE CDM

4.1 Introduction

Two alternative models to the CDM have been presented. One was a principles approach and the other a basic research approach. Let us now compare these with the CDM using the Zaltman and Wallendorf criteria that were earlier presented in Chapter 1 and Table 7-1 along with another criterion. We will not bother to describe the CDM since you are already familiar with it, but its sources will be briefly identified.

The two previous models are "large-system" models as you saw in Figures

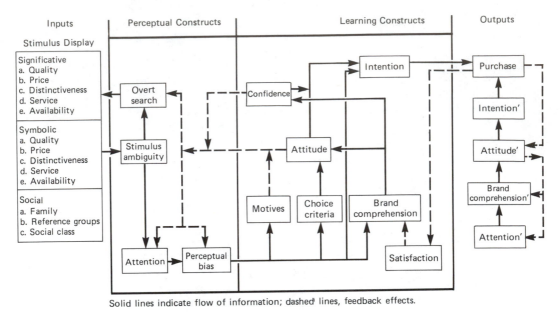

Solid lines indicate flow of information; dashed lines, feedback effects.

Figure 7-3   A Simplified Description of the Theory of Buyer Behavior

Source: J. A. Howard and J. N. Sheth, *The Theory of Buyer Behavior* (New York: John Wiley & Sons, 1969), p. 30.

7-1 and 7-2. The CDM grew out of such a big-system model as shown in Figure 7-3,[8] but first let us briefly trace that development.

The CDM had its earliest beginnings in a Ford Foundation study of the state of knowledge in marketing that appeared in 1963 and concluded that only in consumer behavior was there much immediate potential for development of marketing knowledge.[9] Research built upon this study until 1966, when General Foods generously offered to collect three waves of consumer data from a test market for instant breakfast to test the validity of the theory. This was a major step because, to operationalize the theory so as to be able to write a questionnaire that would provide the data needed to test the theory, required the enormous effort of describing the theory adequately. The analysis of the data then led to further specification of the theory. Finally, to describe the implications of the theory for General Foods marketing strategy required still further specification. The outcome was Figure 7-3.

Another very important step occurred when John Farley in 1968 decided to model the instant breakfast data using econometric techniques applied to the consumer theory.[10] From this and the earlier work just described emerged

[8] J. A. Howard and J. N. Sheth, *The Theory of Buyer Behavior* (New York: John Wiley & Sons, 1969), p. 30.

[9] J. A. Howard, *Marketing: Executive and Buyer Behavior* (New York: Columbia University Press, 1963).

[10] J. U. Farley and L. W. Ring, "An Empirical Test of the Howard-Sheth Model of Buyer Behavior," *Journal of Marketing Research*, VII, no. 4 (November 1970), 427–38.

Table 7-2   Comparison of the Three Models

	EKB	BETTMAN	HOWARD
Explanation	Loosely	Substantial	High
Prediction	Very little	Some	High
Generality	High	High	High
Heuristic power	Fair	High	High
Unify	Somewhat	Substantial	High
Internally consistent	Not known	Seems to be	Yes
Original	Fair	Good	Yes
Plausible	Yes	Yes	Yes
Simple	No	No	Yes
Supported by facts	Not at all	Not as a system	Yes
Testable	Not at all	No	Yes
Serves marketing strategy	Somewhat qualitatively	Qualitatively	Very well, qualitatively and quantitatively

two parallel strands of development that culminated in the CDM. First, the theory was applied in a number of companies as shown in Table 3-1 of Chapter 3. Second, John Farley and Don Lehmann working with others developed their meta-analysis approach, which yielded a number of important findings.[11] With this historical background let us compare the three models and summarize the results in Table 7-2.

4.2 Application of Criteria

The CDM offers an *explanation* of how brand recognition (B), attitude (A), and buying confidence (C) combine to convert information (F) into intention to buy (I). As you have seen, Chapters 4, 5, and 6 provide a much larger system supporting the CDM. This larger system, shown in Figure 5-2, has not yet been tested as a total system, but it is approaching the testable stage. We will refer to it repeatedly as the CDM's "supporting system." It offers much in the way of explanation.

The CDM also *explains* when particular variables influence others, for example, that confidence (C) has a *large* effect or intention (I) when attitude (A) is high. As the consumer bothers to get more information her confidence is thereby increased. This difference would be less in comparison with Bettman than with EKB. As for *prediction* of how consumers will buy, the CDM has been shown to perform substantially better because it has been repeatedly quantified in practice as described in Chapter 3 and used in simulations.

In its simple state, the CDM is not as *general* as either of the other two models. However, with the extensions discussed at the end of Chapter 3 and developed in Chapters 12 through 18, it is more generally applicable. For exam-

---

[11] J. U. Farley and D. R. Lehmann, *Meta-Analysis in Marketing*: *Generalization of Response Models* (Lexington, Mass.: D. C. Heath, 1986).

ple, it systematically incorporates competitive relations, as you will see in Chapter 9. Also, group buying behavior within the formal organization is presented in Chapter 11.

The judgment on *heuristic power* is not easy, but the CDM does have substantial heuristic capacity. To illustrate, in Chapter 3 the analysis of brand recognition stimulated the question of how the trademark and slogan, which probably serve different psychological functions, relate to each other in the Merrill Lynch advertising of its *Cash Management Account*.

The capacity to *unify* strongly characterizes the CDM. The simplicity of the six variables provides a sharp point of focus that serves to integrate and synthesize previously unrelated ideas. Two of those six variables—brand recognition and attitude—are in turn parts of the consumer's product hierarchy, which, in turn, drives search, attention, memory, and choice in regulating information intake. These have not previously been viewed as related.

The CDM appears to be *internally consistent*, and it is sharply enough defined that if it were not internally consistent, this defect would probably be apparent. The CDM as it stands is *original*. The information-attitude-intention-purchase linkage is, of course, not new, these having been the center of attention for more than a decade. Confidence as used here is somewhat new, and brand recognition is quite new. The linkage to product hierarchy in Chapter 4 and its linkage in turn to the information processing variables in Chapter 5 are new. Feedbacks from satisfaction (S) to confidence (C) are new. The Bettman model originally showed new linkages as did the EKB model. All three models are *plausible*.

The CDM receives substantially higher marks for being *simple* than do either of the other two. This is so even though the supporting system combines the CDM, product hierarchy, and information-processing elements.

The CDM itself is known to be *supported by the facts* because it has been tested a number of times as shown in Chapter 3. In addition is the "meta-analysis" by Farley, Lehmann, et al., "which involves quantitatively summarizing several partially comparable studies."[12] As earlier stated the supporting theory has not yet been tested as a total system. It calls heavily upon the Bettman research and other research, and so linkages among particular variables have been tested. The EKB has been little subjected to testing of its conformity to the facts.

The CDM itself is quite *testable* and verifiable as substantial experience cited in Table 3-1, Chapter 3, indicates. The supporting theory is approaching testability. Much of the support for this assertion is contained in the extensions discussed in later chapters. Table 7-2 provides a summary of the ratings that you may find useful, especially before the last one is discussed.

The final criterion of a good model in a course in the marketing depart-

---

[12] J. U. Farley, D. R. Lehmann, and M. J. Ryan, "Patterns in Parameters of Buyer Behavior Models: Generalizing from Sparse Replication," *Marketing Science*, I, no. 2 (Spring 1982), 181–204.

ment of a business school is whether the model contributes to the design of *marketing strategy*. Here is where the EKB and Bettman models come up short. Take about the simplest possible case: the marketing manager is deciding whether to change his level of advertising, either increase or decrease it. How could either of the two models be used in making this decision? Just how would this be done with either EKB or Bettman? From the propositions in either model the manager might feel a little more comfortable, let us say, increasing the advertising, but he would not feel a lot more comfortable.

The CDM, however, can be very useful. First, a choice can be made by a marketing manager as to which paths to pursue. For example, in Figure 7-4 you see the CDM applied to Shearson's Financial Management Account in mid-1985. The numbers on each of the arrows are regression coefficients. The size of the coefficient indicate the strength of each path. For example, on the information (F) to attitude (A) path, ".23" shows that Shearson could increase information by its advertising to the client by 10% and thereby increase the client's attitude toward the product about 2.3%. By calculating these increases for information (F) to brand recognition (B) and information (F) to confidence (C), the manager could decide whether he would be better advised to take the attitude (A) path, the brand recognition (B) path, or the confidence (C) path by providing different advertising copy.

The CDM can also be used for simulating the market. Shearson's marketing manager could multiply the numbers through the system and learn how much increasing information (F) by 10% would increase the client's intention (I) to buy. Notice the number from information (I) to purchase (P) in Figure 7-4 is blank because so few clients change suppliers in this industry that the relation is not significant. Knowing the effect of his advertising upon the client's

Figure 7-4 Consumer Decision Model of Shearson Lehmann Hutton

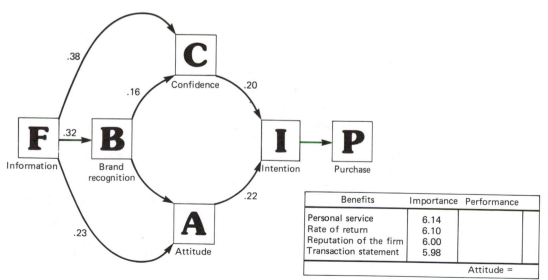

Benefits	Importance	Performance
Personal service	6.14	
Rate of return	6.10	
Reputation of the firm	6.00	
Transaction statement	5.98	
	Attitude =	

intention (I), the marketing manager could decide whether the increased advertising would be justified.

Further, using the CDM analysis in the managed cash account industry as described is at the *brand* level. However, managers often want to apply the CDM at the category level in the client's product hierarchy to determine the strength of preference for the category. Here it provides input for the much longer-term future as Holbrook has implied when he writes, the "across-products perspective appears more central to questions about how people organize the activities that shape their lives."[13]

The CDM can also incorporate competitive behavior, as you will see in Chapter 9. This adds immensely to its contribution to developing marketing strategy.

Finally, one of the great needs today is the specification of the marketing data needed to fill a company's marketing information system. At first, it is astounding how difficult marketing managers find it to identify the information for such a system. On second thought this is not surprising, however, because marketing in contrast to finance based on economics has had almost no formal intellectual foundations. The CDM can serve that role by helping to identify and to specify the nature of those data requirements.

4.3   Conclusions

The CDM compared with the EKB and Bettman models has certain key advantages that make it especially useful for business students.

First, it provides a systematic explanation of the process by which consumers buy, and these specified relations are predictable.

Second is its simplicity. It does not lose generality because it is designed so that by a slight modification it can fit each of the three stages of the PLC. The simplicity gives it immensely greater currency. A novice can quickly grasp its structure. No prior consumer behavior, statistical, computer, or modeling skills are necessary. Because of this simplicity and other characteristics, it brings together an enormous range of hitherto unrelated areas of research and relates them all to practice as you will see in succeeding chapters.

Third, it is well supported by the facts and is eminently testable. It has been directly tested in a number of actual applications. Equally important, building upon some of these applications a number of "meta-analytic" studies have been performed to further validate the model.

Fourth, it was designed for building marketing strategy for buying at both the brand level and the category level. It also deals with competitive behavior. Further, it can serve as a marketing information system.

Finally, Carol Scott in reviewing a number of consumer books in 1981

---

[13] M. B. Holbrook, "O, Consumer, How You've Changed: Some Radical Reflections on the Roots of Consumption," unpublished mimeograph (Columbia University, New York, November 1985), p. 9.

wrote, "Yet no books, with the possible exception of the one by Zaltman and Wallendorf, seem to be written with the MBA student in mind."[14] The CDM, because of its simplicity and the care with which computerized cases and other technical material are made available, can meet the MBA need and still be used by a wide range of students, instructors, and practitioners.

Questions

1. From the description in this chapter, evaluate the EKB model as an aid to a marketing manager.

2. From the description in the text, what would be your evaluation of the Bettman model as an aid to a marketing manager?

3. Would you compare the CDM with the EKB and Bettman models as an aid to the marketing manager?

4. Practitioners in any field are often unsympathetic to discussing theory. If you encounter this skeptical attitude in a marketing manager, how will you answer it?

5. Describe the difference between using a consumer model quantitatively versus using it qualitatively.

---

[14] C. Scott, *Journal of Marketing*, 45, no. 1 (Winter 1981), 160.

CHAPTER 8

Strategy for Extensive Problem Solving

1. BACKGROUND

We know from Chapter 4 that extensive problem solving (EPS) exists when the consumer has no concept of the category of the brand. For example, in the 1970s when the oil crisis hit, many Americans for the first time considered buying a subcompact car because it was not a "gas-guzzler." To do this, they had to develop a new set of recognizing (B) and evaluating (A) criteria in buying a car. However, it was not so difficult because they already knew about compact cars, family cars, luxury cars, and sports cars. Consequently, they could draw upon this knowledge for ideas about the appropriate brand recognition (B) and attitude (A) criteria for recognizing and evaluating subcompacts.

How about the case of a consumer being confronted with a personal computer, as many of us have in the past three or four years? We have had very little familiar experience to draw upon that even hinted about possible criteria. Specifically, most of us had no relevant product hierarchy "to put it in" in our minds. It appeared unrelated to an adding machine or a calculator. We will call the subcompact car case a "normal innovation" and the far less familiar personal computer, a "radical innovation." Fortunately, there aren't many instances of such extreme innovations. Both are often called "new to the world products."

2. STRATEGY

2.1 Introduction

EPS decisions are the least common of all compared with limited problem solving (LPS) and routine problem solving (RPS). Also, they are the most difficult because of the great uncertainty and risk they involve. Finally, they are the most important in the sense of their contribution to the success or failure of the company. The risk is so high in large part because of the difficulty of determining the consumer's needs at the beginning of the product life cycle. Bear in mind that, as discussed in Chapter 4, and later here, EPS involves two levels of choice. First, the consumer is choosing among categories of products. This involves judgments about the long-term future. Second, the consumer is choosing whether to buy this brand, the innovator, within that category. This second choice has shorter-term implications but still is longer than the LPS case.

Because of the importance of the EPS case, it is essential that you take advantage of the framework of Figure 5-2 in Chapter 5 showing how the product hierarchy links the CDM and the supporting information processing that feeds back to information (F) of the CDM. This framework is so useful because in EPS that product hierarchy does not exist for a radical innovation at all as it hasn't for many buyers of the personal computer. Recognizing this will give you a keener appreciation of the magnitude of EPS marketing. A similar "radical innovation" was Merrill Lynch's Cash Management Account in 1977. Not only was it radical, it was horribly complex, with literally about a half-dozen component services for the potential client to consider and somehow develop a set of adjectives by which to evaluate any brand of managed cash account.

The first of these two levels of managing is product category strategy, and the second is brand strategy. These are obviously part and parcel of the same thing, but it is useful to separate them in the discussion.

2.2 Strategy for Product Category

The foundation for product class strategy is technology. Unfortunately, until recently, there has not been much of systematic analysis of technology viewed strategically, with one exception. Abernathy and Utterback did some interesting research in the 1970s.[1] Recently, however, Richard Foster of McKenzie & Co., the large consulting firm, has come forth with a highly useful view that we will use here.[2] He comes at it with a very strong technical background and yet with an excellent feel for strategy:

> In 1947, Procter & Gamble introduced Tide, the first synthetic laundry detergent. It was superior to the conventional natural detergents because it contained phos-

---

[1] W. J. Abernathy and J. M. Utterback, "Patterns of Industrial Innovation," *Technology Review*, 80, no. 7 (June/July 1978), 41–47.

[2] R. N. Foster, *Innovation* (New York: Summit Books, 1986). He uses the term "S curve" to mean essentially the same as "product life cycle."

phate "builders" which improved its cleaning power. At that time P&G's major competitor in detergents was Lever Brothers. But Tide changed all that. Its sales took off, leaving Lever far behind, unable to match P&G's technical achievements. Lever eventually responded with its own synthetic product called Surf, but it was too little too late. P&G had stolen the lead.

In each of these cases and many more like them, companies that were leaders in their field saw their fortunes suddenly disappear. Do leading companies in fact not have the natural advantages they are supposed to or are their natural advantages outweighed by other inherent disadvantages? I think the latter is the case, and that these disadvantages result from technological change. Technological change is the reason why only one company out of three manages to cover its cost of raising money most of the time.

The roots of this failure lie in the assumptions behind the key decisions that all companies have to make. Most of the managers of companies that enjoy transitory success assume that tomorrow will be more or less like today. That significant change is unlikely, is unpredictable, and in any case will come slowly. They have thus focused their efforts on making their operations ever more cost effective. While valuing innovation and espousing the latest theories on entrepreneurship, they still believe it is a highly personalized process that cannot be managed or planned to any significant extent. They believe that innovation is risky, more risky than defending their present business.[3]

Foster uses three ideas as the basis of his strategy: product life cycle (PLC), the attacker's advantage, and discontinuities. The first, the PLC, has been well developed in Chapters 2 and 4.

To discuss the other two elements—attacker's advantage and discontinuities—let us first deal with a related idea of the limits of a technology.

By technology I mean several things. In some cases it is a specific process—say a chemical process—that produces a specific product. In this case, it's hard to distinguish the product from the technology. More broadly, technology can mean a manufacturing process, say continuous casting of steel versus the open-hearth method. Here the technology is distinct from the product: the cash management account (CMA) is another example of a distinct process and product. New information processing technology made the CMA possible.

The point is this: technology even variously defined always has a limit—either the limit of a particular technology, for example, the ultimate density of devices we can get into a silicon chip, or a succession of limits of several technologies that together make up the larger technology or product or way of doing business.[4]

Once the limit of a technology—the top of the PLC—has been reached, it is not possible to make more progress. Further, even in approaching the limits, the cost of making progress increases dramatically. The task of a strategist is to find where the limits of his technology are.

Now let us turn to technological *discontinuities*. These discontinuities refer to the case where one PLC is reaching its limits and another curve, the upper curve, is forming as in Figure 8-1.

[3] Ibid., pp. 28–30.
[4] Ibid., pp. 32–33.

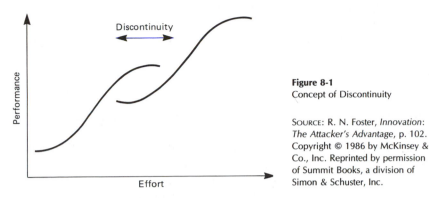

Figure 8-1
Concept of Discontinuity

SOURCE: R. N. Foster, *Innovation:
The Attacker's Advantage*, p. 102.
Copyright © 1986 by McKinsey &
Co., Inc. Reprinted by permission
of Summit Books, a division of
Simon & Schuster, Inc.

Finally, Foster argues that the attacker always has the advantage as the industry moves from one PLC to the next. He further asserts:

> The results of discontinuity are almost always brutal for the defender. The failure to recognize the limits of electro-mechanical cash registers at NCR cost thousands of workers and executives their jobs. It cost NCR's investors millions of dollars as well. For Unilever it meant months spent scrambling to produce their own synthetic detergents all the while losing the lead to P&G.[5]

The attacker's advantage is that he is *prepared* for battle, but the defender, unfortunately, is lulled by *past* successful performance, conventional wisdom that encourages sticking with the product, and a faith in evolutionary change. As Figure 8-1 shows, greater "Performance" is possible on the higher curve, but greater "Effort" will be required.

This is the advantage the attacker has over the defender. The strategist should identify these discontinuities and develop a strategy that moves his organization quickly into the new PLC. A company that is doing reasonably well on the lower curve usually finds it very difficult to move to the new PLC for fear the new product will cannibalize the old product. Foster cites dozens of firms that were unwilling to do so and lost out as a consequence. This strategic advantage was splendidly illustrated by Miller Brewing in 1973 as described in Chapter 1. Regular beer was at the top of its product life cycle. Miller developed an enzyme that could remove the residue of sugar from beer. This process was the basis of its low-calorie Lite beer, representing a new category and the new product life cycle above the existing one for regular beer, as represented in Figure 8-1. As Foster suggests, other beer manufacturers did not believe there was a market for such a low-calorie beer. They ridiculed the possibility. Today, this new category makes up 20% of all beer sales, and Miller with its Lite beer is way ahead with its share of the new category.

An ideal product category strategy is to be sensitive to the limits of the technology of the current product life cycle as Miller was. Before these limits are approached, the strategist needs to have identified a new technology to

[5] Ibid., p. 36.

move his company over the discontinuity to utilize fully the attacker's advantage in doing so and to have the courage to advise his superiors to do so.

2.3   Brand Strategy

Once the dimensions of the brand begin to take shape, the marketer can focus better on the brand strategy.

One of the questions to be answered early in discussing an EPS product is, "How do I know whether my product is in EPS?" A test of this is whether, in constructing the attitude measure for the CDM, weighting the benefits by their importances improves the fit or whether a simple additive unweighted version does as well. If the unweighted version does just as well, you can assume it is an EPS situation.

Our objective here is to design strategy, and we will focus only upon core strategy.[6] It is the formulation of one step of the strategy process, a step that is often called "positioning." It links customer characteristics and strategy design. In this way, you can see how to use consumer theory to design not only core strategy, the heart of total strategy, but also to design both total marketing strategy and the annual marketing plans that flow out of the total strategy.

Core strategy is made up of three elements: the *benefits* that consumers want in the product, a description of the *consumers* who want these product benefits, and a *description of each of the competitors* who can also supply the product. To a nonprofit manager such as one providing health care service it may seem a little strange to think of himself as facing competitors. However, it is safe to say there is no case of a product or service that does not at least have indirect substitutes in meeting the consumer's needs, and these we call "competitors." Let us put these three elements together—consumers, consumer characteristics, and competitor characteristics—to illustrate the concept of a core strategy.

The multiattribute measure used in the CDM as in Table 8-1 and first introduced in Chapter 3 provides an estimate of the attitude of a typical consumer toward a brand of herbicide for his lawn. It illustrates how the manager of that product would go about designing a core strategy for it. First, he must select which benefits will be the key element in his core strategy.

He would tentatively select the "effectiveness" benefit because as Table 8-1 indicates it is important and his brand does well on it. "Cost" is not a possibility because it is not so important and he does poorly on it: his price is too high. He does well on "convenience," but it is not an important benefit to the consumer.

But the actual decision would also depend upon whether this particular consumer is like all other consumers or are there segments of consumers? Let us assume that this customer is representative of the third of the market made

---

[6] J. M. Hulbert, *Marketing: A Strategic Perspective* (Katonah, N.Y.: Impact, 1985), p. 102.

Table 8-1 A Typical Consumer's Attitude

Benefits	Importance	Performance	
Effectiveness	4	4	16
Cost	3	3	9
Convenience	2	4	8
		Attitude = 33	

up of owners of the larger lawns who will usually worry more about effectiveness and less about cost and convenience.

The actual decision would further depend upon the competitors' strengths and weaknesses as measured by the CDM. Let us assume that the products of the other competitors do not measure up nearly as well as he does on "effectiveness." Consequently, in this case core strategy would be described as (1) effectiveness, (2) to this group of consumers, and (3) to position his product against all other competitors because he believes that these three conditions will give him the best competitive advantage.

Having adopted this core strategy, it serves as the foundation upon which to build the complete product strategy. The remaining two parts to be added are, first, the four dimensions of the marketing mix—product, price, promotion, and distribution (place)—often called the four Ps and which are required to complete a marketing plan. The CDM can provide information about how these affect the consumer and therefore how each of them should be designed.

Second, a fifth dimension of marketing strategy is the relations with the other functions in the organization: manufacturing, finance, human resources, and research and development (R&D). Their cooperation is usually essential to the successful implementation of a marketing strategy and plan.

In this way the core strategy facilitates design of marketing strategy by linking the theory to strategy via the CDM. These general ideas about how this is done will be discussed throughout Chapters 8, 9, 10, and 11, but the emphasis will be upon strategy, not upon marketing plans such as quarterly or annual plans.

Designing a core strategy for EPS is substantially more difficult than for LPS. One reason is that customers in EPS lack a goal hierarchy for choosing the brand as described at length in Chapter 5, and so they must proceed to develop it. Once they have fairly firm ideas about how good the brand is on a given set of benefits, they still are quite unsure about the importance weights to attach to these benefits. Second, the manager's planning time horizon is necessarily much longer.

Finally, the major problem in marketing to EPS consumers once the product is designed is supplying an adequate amount of the right kind of information in both form and content and at the right time. Why this is the central problem can be seen in the early attempts to understand how an innovation diffuses through a society.

2.4   Early Diffusion Studies

Rural sociologists have long had a professional interest in how innovations are diffused through society, and this interest deals directly with our evolutionary view of EPS. These scientists working with the U.S. Department of Agriculture were faced with explaining why some innovations in farming practices, such as hybrid seed, succeeded and others did not. Also the length of time required for this new product category to diffuse among farmers was obviously a relevant issue.

By 1975, more than 1,800 studies of the diffusion of an immense variety of products and social practices had been done over the world. The general conclusion was that a logistic curve, as shown in the upper part of Figure 8-2, describes the process quite well.

The lower curve in Figure 8-2 shows how adopters are distributed over the product life cycle. Each category, from innovators to laggards, represents a percentage of people who bought the product at that particular time. For

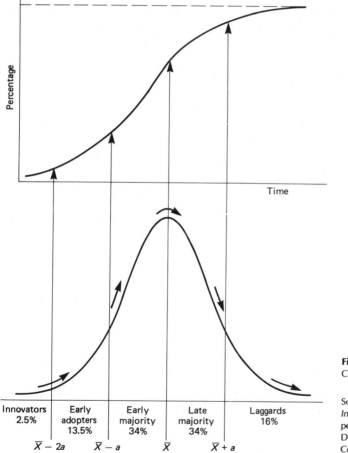

Figure 8-2
Cumulative Distribution of Adopters

SOURCE: E. M. Rogers, *Diffusion of Innovations*, p. 162. Reprinted with permission of The Free Press, a Division of Macmillan, Inc.
Copyright © 1962 by The Free Press.

instance, only 2.5% are innovators, while 81.5% are early and late innovators, and 16% are laggards. Consumers with the following characteristics are more likely to be innovators:

> Higher income
> Higher education
> Younger
> Greater social mobility
> Favorable attitude toward risk
> Greater social participation
> Higher opinion leadership[7]

The upper curve is the logistic curve, which correctly represents the product life cycle, as we learned way back in Chapter 2. It also happens to be a cumulative version of the normal curve shown at the bottom of Figure 8-2. Now you can see from the normal curve that if we put instant coffee on the cumulative curve, 50% had accepted the brand by about 1950, the midpoint, which was 12 years after it was introduced. It began to flatten out about 1960 and then to decline four or five years later.

This example of instant coffee shows how the logistic curve can be used for forecasting an EPS product. Taking a modern example, recently 1 of the 23 companies that had followed Merrill Lynch's pioneering Cash Management Account into the managed cash account market was debating whether to invest heavily to extend its share. There is some evidence that the growth of the managed cash account industry is slowing down. Using the foregoing logic, the company assumed that the industry is at the mean level $\bar{X}$ of the lower portion of Figure 8-2. From this it predicted that since Merrill Lynch entered the market in 1977, which was nine years ago, the industry will cease growing and level off in another nine years, about 1995. By that time the industry could be expected to be twice as large in volume as it is today. Much more refined studies have been done, but the example illustrates the principle.

As you can see, the logistic diffusion curve gives support to the product life-cycle notion, which in turn implies the three stages of the product life cycle and the corresponding three types of consumer decision. A recent study reviews the evidence on product diffusion and extends it to show how the speed of diffusion has substantially increased.[8] Figure 8-3 has the year of introduction on the bottom axis and rate of growth on the vertical axis. As you see, out of the 25 innovations studied, the early ones, for example, those in the 1920s and 1930s, had a much lower growth rate than did those in the 1950s and 1960s. The numbers in the chart refer to specific innovations shown in Table

[7] H. Gatignon and T. S. Robertson, "A Propositional Inventory for New Diffusion Research," *Journal of Consumer Research*, 11, no. 4 (March 1985), 861.

[8] R. W. Olshavsky, "Time and the Rate of Adoption of Innovations," *Journal of Consumer Research*, 6, no. 4 (March 1980), 425-28.

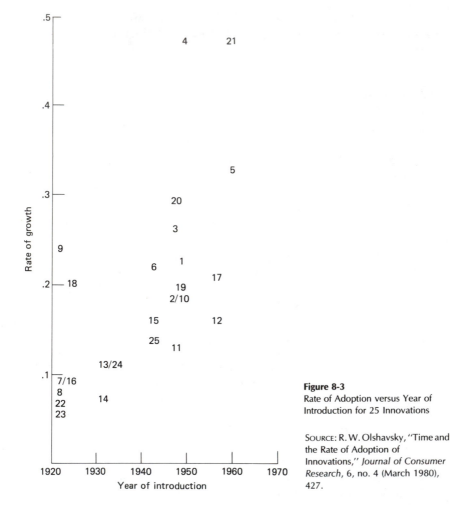

Figure 8-3
Rate of Adoption versus Year of
Introduction for 25 Innovations

SOURCE: R. W. Olshavsky, "Time and
the Rate of Adoption of
Innovations," *Journal of Consumer
Research*, 6, no. 4 (March 1980),
427.

8-2. For example, air conditioners are "1," and you can see in Figure 8-3 that air conditioners were introduced in the 1950s and achieved a growth rate (ϕ_j) of a little over .2, specifically .23, as Table 8-2 shows you. Still greater speed is shown by broilers (.47) and color televisions (.47). This increasing speed causes innovation to be even more difficult and riskier, but the rewards for the successful innovations can be enormous.

The diffusion studies have been extremely useful in giving us evidence for how innovations grow and become diffused throughout a market. This is obviously important because if the product does not diffuse widely, there will be no market. Yet they have contributed little evidence on the nature of the *individual* consumer's psychological *processes* by which that diffusion occurs. Marketers of innovations need this latter knowledge to design their marketing strategy and it is the purpose of this chapter to provide it.

Table 8-2 Rate of Growth for 25 Innovations

Innovation	1_j	$\emptyset_j$	R_j^2
1. Air conditioners	−14.0	.23	.96
2. Bed coverings	−12.0	.19	.99
3. Blenders	−17.0	.26	.92
4. Broilers	−23.8	.47	.87
5. Can openers	−22.0	.33	.99
6. Clothes dryers	−13.8	.22	.94
7. Clothes washers	−3.3	.09	.99
8. Coffee makers	−3.9	.08	.95
9. Dishwashers	−16.3	.24	.95
10. Disposals	−12.4	.19	.91
11. Freezers	−7.8	.13	.91
12. Frypans	−9.3	.16	.93
13. Heating pads	−4.2	.11	.95
14. Hotplates	−2.1	.07	.91
15. Mixers	−9.2	.16	.99
16. Ranges, standard	−5.0	.09	.96
17. Ranges, built-in	−13.1	.21	.99
18. Refrigerators	−8.0	.20	.93
19. Steam irons	−12.0	.20	.99
20. Televisions, black and white	−15.3	.29	.89
21. Televisions, color	−32.6	.47	.98
22. Toasters	−22.9	.07	.90
23. Vacuum cleaners	−2.1	.06	.87
24. Waffle irons	−3.8	.11	.89
25. Water heaters	−7.7	.14	.94

SOURCE: R. W. Olshavsky, "Time and the Rate of Adoption of Innovations," *Journal of Consumer Research*, 6, no. 4 (March 1980), 426.

2.5 Summary of Strategy

The product category strategy deals with the critical concept of technology and thereby provides a foundation for linking it to the competitor and the consumer as a guide to determining EPS strategy for the long-term future. Then, the brand core strategy brings the consumer and the competitor together to develop a competitive advantage for the less distant future. Finally, the diffusion studies show us that there is a systematic pattern to this process by which new product categories are introduced into the market and grow as new competitors enter the category. This growth rate is clearly getting faster. This greater speed presents new opportunities to marketing managers but lays heavier demands upon them to recognize changing markets more quickly and to adapt with more alacrity.

Armed with this information, we will proceed to examine each of the four components of the marketing mix—product design, price, promotion, and distribution—in terms of an EPS product.

3. PRODUCT DESIGN

Although innovations—"new to the world products" as contrasted with "brand extensions"—were found by Booz, Allen & Hamilton, to be, not surprisingly, the most difficult to evaluate in terms of their potential return on investment, they are often quite successful.[9] For example, these and "new lines of products in the company" made up only 30% of the new products, but they accounted for 60% of the most successful new products in terms of profit contribution, sales volume, or return on investment. However, the attacker has the advantage, but it takes courage on the part of the attacker's top management, especially if its current product is now doing reasonably well. Here we see the enormous need the marketer has for a vocabulary to articulate a logic for this venture that will be persuasive to others in the organization needed to support the innovation such as finance, manufacturing, and R & D.

The key practical question is how to find out the relevant benefits that the new product category should provide the customer. The less concrete the design, for example, a product *concept* instead of the actual product in physical form, the more difficult it will be to present the product to focus groups of potential customers, although it can be fruitful. This was found to be so, for example, when IBM was planning the videodisk. More fruitful was to hold very lengthy individual interviews where a design of the product was presented and described at length.

However, only users of an existing product have the experience to be able to make accurate judgments about their response to attributes of a product. But how able are they to make accurate judgments about some new attributes that might be developed in the existing product to make it an innovation? As Von Hippel has pointed out, they are *least* likely to.[10] This is because they have developed a mind-set that militates *against* that consumer performing in the *creative* way required to think of new attributes. He cites evidence to support his conclusion that this is exactly what happens. If this is difficult, imagine what it is like to try to evaluate when you have only a concept of a product that has never existed before.

As two alternative ways of providing these critically essential product judgments, he proposes taking advantage of "lead users" or of "high-benefit users." Lead users are defined as buyers "who have needs which are not now prevalent among users of a given product, but which can be predicted to become general and to constitute a commercially interesting market in the future."[11]

In applying the concept of a lead user, the first step is to identify a *trend* in a given market. We know that markets are continually changing because

[9] "New Products Management for the 1980s," report (Booz, Allen & Hamilton, New York, 1982).

[10] E. Von Hippel, *New Product Concepts from Lead Users: Segmenting Users by Experience*, unpublished working paper, Report No. 84–109, (Marketing Science Institute, Cambridge, Mass., December 1984), Table 1, p. 6.

[11] Ibid., p. 8.

of new product technology, shifting prices, and new consumer needs. For example, the managed cash account as described in Chapter 2 was possible only because of new technology, the computer. However, the market became far larger because of shifting consumer needs: the number of people with adequate funds substantially increased. By examining these three causal factors of product technology, shifting prices and new consumer needs, a trend can often be predicted; for example, lower oil prices will discourage energy-efficient cars.

The second step, after discovering the trend, is to find consumers who are facing those "tomorrow's needs today." In the case of home computers, for example, in the early 1970s, interviewing college students in the major universities would have shown that students using a similar arrangement—time-sharing terminals linked to large university computers—were having a wonderful time playing computer games. "Student bootlegging of expensive computer time was known to despairing college deans nationwide."[12]

The second source of information about new needs is from "high-benefit users." These are defined as those people now using a product but "who have a significantly stronger unmet need for a given novel or familiar product attribute or product concept than does the average user. (Thus, drought-stricken farmers have a high *unmet* need for water and are therefore high-benefit users with respect to products and product attributes bearing on obtaining water, conserving water, and so on. In contrast, rice farmers with a high *met* need for water may be heavy users of water, but they are *not* high-benefit users, in our terminology.)"[13] The idea is that these people will be motivated by their relatively stronger unmet needs to devote effort to understanding and perhaps experimenting with how to solve the need at issue. This has been shown to be true in the case of industrial products where "high benefit" was measured by profit.[14]

Because these "high-benefit users" have thought about the problem and may even have some solutions, they can be a good source for ideas about the need for products that do not yet exist. This logic is spelled out as follows:

> We reason that high-benefit users will be motivated by their relatively strong unmet needs to devote effort to understanding and perhaps experimenting with how to solve the need at issue. From this, they will gain a relatively rich and elaborated real-world understanding of the need, which can be explored by appropriate market research. Possibly, as we will see, the problem-solving activity will produce novel and useful product concepts as well.
>
> The idea of users having useful "solution data" of potential interest to market researchers is currently a somewhat alien one, we find. "Marketing research is about needs, not solutions," we have often been told. Really, however, *all* need statements implicitly or explicitly contain more or less information about possible solutions to the need. Consider the following sequence of need statements, each addressing the same need but each containing more *solution* content than the one preceding:

[12] Ibid., p. 11.
[13] Ibid., p. 12.
[14] Ibid., Table 2, p. 17.

- I am unhappy . . .
- about my children's clothes . . .
- which are often not fully clean even when just washed.
- I find that X type stains on Y type clothes are especially hard to remove.
- If I mix my powdered detergent into a paste and apply it to the stain before washing, I find it helps get things clean.

Note that the later statements have useful solution content, e.g., one could invent liquid detergent on the basis of the last statement. They also suggest the *type* of solution the high-benefit user prefers. Thus, we see that the user is approaching the problem as a "stain removal" problem rather than a "keep the kids away from X staining agent" problem. And, probably, the consumer is ranking this choice after having experimented with both approaches. In essence, this *experience* with the need/problem is what makes high-benefit user data— whether seen as need data or solution data—so valuable to market researchers.[15]

Table 8-3 summarizes what we have been saying. If you read it carefully, you will agree. The key point is that by combining both the "high-benefit" and the "lead user" customers, we can obtain "Tomorrow's product concepts today": the product concepts that we need for developing EPS products.

Once a potential list of the benefits is obtained, there are two general approaches—compositional and decompositional—to designing the EPS product. The compositional approach is implied in the CDM where the benefits are put together into a multiattribute model. Specifically, a sample of consumers in the survey, after being told about the proposed new product, are confronted with the list of possible benefits and asked to rate the importance of these benefits. These data, along with other information collected in the survey, are fed into the CDM as described in Chapter 3 by regression and a mathematical model is derived. The model will reveal which benefits are clearly most essential to what types of consumers. This procedure was followed by IBM in its videodisk study, for example.

An alternative is the decompositional approach of which the most common example is conjoint measurement, although there are other approaches such as multidimensional scaling, discriminant analysis, and factor analysis.[16] To illustrate conjoint measurement, assume that you have a spot remover for carpets and upholstery and that it is conceptualized by the customer on five criteria with levels of importance as indicated by the number: package design (3), brand name (3), price (3), Good Housekeeping seal (2), and money-back guarantee (2). A group of customers are then asked to rate various combinations of these attributes according to how well they like each combination. A carefully drawn experimental design of selected questions ensures a maximum of information with a minimum of customer ratings required. By special computer program, the data are analyzed so that each product concept (combination of attributes) can be located in space and compared with other product concepts. Also, from

---

[15] Ibid., p. 13.

[16] P. E. Green and Y. Wind, "New Way to Measure Consumers' Judgments," *Harvard Business Review*, 53 (July/August 1975), 107–15.

Table 8-3   Marketing Research Data Obtained from "Lead" and "High-Benefit" Experienced User Segments

User Segment	Nature of Their Experience	Data Obtainable
Routine users	Today's needs and products	Minor variations
High-benefit users	High need-related problem-solving	Novel product concepts related to high need dimensions
Lead users	Tomorrow's needs	Tomorrow's need data
High-benefit + lead users	High needs for tomorrow's products	Tomorrow's product concepts

SOURCE: E. Von Hippel, *New Product Concepts from Lead Users: Segmenting Users by Experience*, unpublished working paper, Report No. 84–109 (Marketing Science Institute, Cambridge, Mass., December 1984), 16.

this ranking, it is possible to derive the "utility" of each value of each attribute and thus to estimate consumers' preferences for concepts *not* included in the original ranking. The technique of conjoint measurement has come to be rather widely used.[17]

Fortunately, the two methods, the one used in discussing the CDM and conjoint measurement, can be combined and used in some ways to give us the best of both possible worlds. By drawing on the lens model developed by eminent early psychologist Egon Brunswick, Holbrook combined the two in evaluating the attractiveness of piano concerts.[18] Conjoint measurement was used to elicit the relevant physical attributes and then the compensatory method of the CDM to relate those physical attributes of the music into benefits as viewed by the consumer. The output can be used for a variety of marketing decisions such as designing the product/service, setting promotional strategies, identifying the relevant features, and designing the more microscopic elements of the marketing mix, such as advertising copy (words, pictures, headlines, blank space, color, type size, etc.). The integration of the two methods can be especially useful for dealing with products where esthetic characteristics may be dominant such as in entertainment. These emotional benefits are more difficult to identify than are the more common utilitarian motivations.[19]

To the extent the consumer benefits can be articulated in the technology stage, the manager can move more quickly and effectively into the new PLC. If the product development stage is farther along and approaching the second level of choice, knowing the benefits is essential. The development of a core strategy is impossible without knowing them.

[17] P. Cattin and D. R. Wittink, "Commercial Use of Conjoint Analysis: A Survey," *Journal of Marketing*, 46, no. 3 (Summer 1982), 44–53.

[18] M. B. Holbrook, "Integrating Compositional and Decompositional Analyses to Represent the Integrating Role of Perceptions in Evaluative Judgments," *Journal of Marketing Research*, XVIII (February 1981), 13–28.

[19] Ibid.

Finally, if you are introducing a new product that is a new category, you should ask yourself whether this is a product about which consumer preferences will be ambiguous. There is substantial evidence that in this situation it is possible to become the prototype brand against which succeeding brands will be judged. If it becomes the prototype in the consumer preferences as described in Chapter 4, you can have a continuing advantage that new competitors simply cannot match. This enviable position has been researched and supported by Greg Carpenter and Kent Nakamoto.[20] This is described at some length in Chapter 16.

The farther along the product development, the more price becomes an issue, which we turn to next.

4. PRICE

The EPS consumer appears to be unresponsive to price changes except to those changes of major magnitude.

Current competition is usually not an issue because an innovation, by definition, is first in the market. The product category strategy is the "attacker's advantage." However, potential competition usually is an issue. The question asked is, "Who also has the capacity to produce and market this new thing?" The trade press, trade association meetings, and research associations are a common source of such information.

Also, it is conceivable that future competition may be looked upon not as a potential enemy but as a friend. A competitor can be helpful in the tasks of getting this new thing accepted in the market. For example, Tappan stove delayed the introduction of the electronic range for the home kitchen until it knew that G.E. planned to introduce its version.

The farther along the product is on the product life cycle, the more price becomes an issue. If various prices exist in the market instead of single standard price throughout, a consumer survey can be conducted and the price sensitivity, or in economic terms, the price elasticity of the consumer can be determined by using the CDM. Also, different consumer segments may have different price sensitivities.

Finally, price and promotion effects are often interrelated, and if so, the two should be considered together as will be discussed in Chapter 17.

5. PROMOTION

5.1 Introduction

Once the product is designed and priced, the next major task for EPS consumers is to communicate it. Communication with EPS consumers can be very difficult.

---

[20] G. S. Carpenter and K. Nakamoto, "Market Pioneers, Consumer Learning and Product Perceptions: A Theory of Persistent Competitive Advantage," unpublished paper (Columbia University, New York, November 1986).

At first, their involvement is low, and they have limited capacity to process information because they have little or nothing stored in their memory to aid them. Once some hint gets through to them of the merit of the innovation for their needs, their involvement will increase. But this increased involvement will not remedy their lack of knowledge about the innovation and its uses. Time, great care, and imagination by the marketers in providing the information via promotion will be necessary.

The novelty of the innovation can help get attention and word-of-mouth can be substantial. Also, advertising tends to be effective early in the process and word-of-mouth later.

Beyond these general guidelines, however, communication in EPS is substantially more difficult than in LPS. Without a well-formed product hierarchy and goal hierarchy, the consumer lacks the automatic guidance in attention to and search for relevant information that is provided to LPS customers by their *expectations*. Further, let us distinguish between his involuntary and voluntary attention. The buyer's involuntary attention is different in EPS than in LPS. He is less apt to be involuntarily interrupted by information about a new product in EPS, since lacking any prior knowledge, he will be less likely to *notice* it. In other words, it won't stand out as distinct from his expectations, since he has no expectations.

In EPS, the *voluntary attention* process is also different from LPS. The first stage, "feature analysis," in which the consumer looks at each specific feature of a product, she probably relies more heavily upon brand recognition in EPS than she does in LPS, and brand recognition is more concrete than is the product's benefits. Without a product class image, the EPS buyer who is voluntarily paying attention, just as with involuntary attention, has less previous knowledge to guide her in making a choice between products.

Finally, the figures of speech that are so useful for communicating the EPS usually have heavy cultural overtones as discussed in Chapter 12, which can be devastating in the wrong culture. One of our petroleum companies was advertising the great power of its gasoline by advertising "Put a tiger in your tank." When run in Africa, however, the advertising conjured up a tiger chasing the car, and presumably it encountered similar problems in other countries.

The usual promotion questions must be answered: copy, media, and budget.

5.2 Copy

5.2.1 Introduction. The nature of this new thing can best be communicated by figures of speech: analogies, similes, and metaphors. These will communicate, as described in Chapter 4, the dramatic but imprecise "practical knowledge" the consumer first needs as contrasted with the more precise lexical or word knowledge used later.

An innovation requires the marketer simultaneously to gain acceptance for the new *product category* concept and also for the particular *new brand* that is the innovation, which is the two-level choice problem we discussed in Chapter

4 and described in Figure 4-6. Imagine you are directing the introduction into the U.S. market of the new CD-V (compact disk-video), a joint venture of N. V. Philips of Netherlands and Sony of Japan. It is a concept that was almost unknown until November 1986.[21] You know that building the consumer's motivation process for this new product category is the major task of advertising copy in this clear EPS situation. The CD (compact disk) brought better sound than the VCR (video cassettes), but it lacked the pictures which the CD-V provides. The consumer will also have to buy a CD-V player as well as the disk.

You could use the two-level choice described in Chapter 4 made up of values, norms, and benefit importances. But you know that a more compact way to describe the buyer's motivation process is the goal hierarchy discussed in Chapter 5. The components making up the goal hierarchy are values, norms, and benefit importances. Taking this goal hierarchy approach, the task in EPS is to communicate the benefits of this CD-V and their importances that will characterize the innovation. You can easily learn the benefits used by consumers in evaluating a CD (compact disk, which is sound only, with no video). This could be a starting point. Given that you have developed a reasonable set of benefits, you will want some data on where typical customers will place the CD-V by Philips-Sony on these benefits. This information is needed to guide the development of reasonable copy.

The next question concerns how much and what kind of information to put into the copy. The rule in providing the consumer information when in EPS is to avoid technical information. Also, "presentations should be limited to the attributes most relevant to preference judgments. Additional information, particularly when it is nondiagnostic of product performance, could cause deterioration in the quality of the choice."[22] This recommendation grows out of major studies of consumer behavior. But some kind of language is necessary to describe this new thing, the CD-V.

5.2.2 Language.   "Practical knowledge" tells the consumer that a subcompact car is something he can drive to the station, take his kids to school, or drive to the office or his wife can go shopping but not take a long drive across the country. Figures of speech are very helpful in conveying this practical knowledge.

One of the major difficulties at this stage is that an ordinary vocabulary that the layperson can understand usually has not been developed. The product is too recently out of the laboratory, which is exactly the case of the CD-V. Technical vocabulary still tends to be used to describe it. The marketing manager, by using the theory of consumer behavior and working closely with the laboratory, however, can develop a vocabulary that is reasonably accurate and far better understood by the public. This is why the marketer's choice of brand name can be so helpful when consumers are in EPS. Often, the nature of the brand

---

[21] *The Wall Street Journal* (New York edition), May 4, 1987, p. 35.

[22] E. J. Johnson and J. E. Russo, "Product Familiarity and Learning New Information," *Journal of Consumer Research*, 11, no. 1 (June 1984), 549.

name—the noun used to label the product innovation—is a clue to how an innovation is supposed to be used. Contrast the following brand names for four different product classes: cosmetics, cleaners, deodorants, and dog foods. Which of them best imply how each brand is intended to be used?

Arbitrary	Descriptive	Positioning/Imagery
Almay	Chapstick	Cover Girl
Ajax	Janitor in a Drum	Mr. Clean
Mitchum	Light 'n Dry	Sure
Alpo	Moist 'n Chunky	Fit 'n Trim

SOURCE: Kathryn Feakins, "What's in a Name," *The Research File* (Ogilvy and Mather), 17 (March 1980), 1.

Once the category of product is beginning to be understood, the consumer will try to formulate the *brand* concept. Here lexical or word knowledge is needed. The identity of the brand (B) is important in itself, but, also as you will recall, it serves as a foundation, a "chunk," upon which the other two elements of the brand concept—attitude (A) and confidence (C)—can build. A picture—the familiar Merrill Lynch bull—may be effective in conveying the brand recognition (B) if the slogan relates the bull to managed cash accounts.

Because of the difficulty the consumer has in handling information without the guidance of a well-developed product hierarchy and goal hierarchy, the lexical language used should be chosen with care. Where appropriate, polar adjectives as described in Chapter 4 will help to communicate brand recognition (B) and product benefits (A). Kernel sentences, which are simple, declarative, active, and affirmative sentences, as contrasted with their opposite—complex, negative, passive, and interrogative—can also make it easier for the consumer to interpret the ad copy and to store it in memory. Contrast, "The Escort goes very fast," a kernel sentence with, "Is it that the car that does not go slow is an Escort?" a complex, negative, passive, and interrogative sentence. Which form do you think can best convey the message?

5.2.3 Timing of Information.
Implicit in this discussion of getting information to the consumer so far is the necessity to pay attention to the timing of that information. This is fairly obvious, but let us be explicit about it. The development of practical knowledge is first the product category concept. Then within lexical information, brand recognition is first, then attitude, and finally confidence.

The timing is not well studied. It is illustrated by Don Armstrong who was the J. Walter Thompson account executive for the Ford account a number of years ago. He explained that he had long tried to persuade the Ford Motor Co. when introducing a new model to show only the car for the first three months of advertising, then begin to describe the nice things the car would do for you. He was intuitively thinking of first building brand recognition (B).

5.3 Media

Media should be carefully selected to ensure that potential customers are exposed to the ad; put technically, it is necessary to ensure that the ad has adequate reach and frequency. Again, EPS customers lack the guidance in attention and search that a well-defined product hierarchy and goal hierarchy would provide in the form of "expectations."

The information overload problem also is relevant to media selection, "suppose a marketer believes that the sponsored brand is, overall, the best if a detailed comparative analysis is made of all brands. Rather than present such an analysis in a 30-second TV commercial and cause information overload, the commercial may merely state that the sponsored brand is best on an overall basis and encourage the consumers to go through the detailed comparative analysis presented in newspaper advertisements and/or in-store displays."[23]

5.4 Budget

The budget should be very large in EPS. The usual rule indicated by substantial research, that a third exposure contributes little to the consumers' information, probably does not apply to EPS. However, evidence to support this generalization is not available. It is a relatively unresearched area.

For some time, media have been becoming more specialized. Magazines on very narrow topics have tended to replace "family" magazines like *American*, *Saturday Evening Post*, and *Life*. Too, we seem to be on the verge of a literal revolution in electronic media that will supplement the three television networks. Cable TV, satellites, and videodisks will greatly increase the available channels. The networks are considering more specialized audiences, speaking in terms of "narrowcasting" instead of "broadcasting."

Take cable, for example. Its total penetration is 25%, and by 1990 it is expected to have a major market share and be an important medium for the consumer and advertiser alike. Substantially longer ads are expected to appear on it as an upscale medium. This could make it an especially effective medium for EPS products where much more information needs to be imparted. Also, it could encourage imaginative and entertaining ads.[24]

In a recent study, cable channels presented 5- to 10-minute informational ads continually throughout the day.[25] The study tentatively indicates that people are interested in learning more from ads and will tune in to watch an hour or two of this continuous advertising. Also, in a recent CABLE SHOP study in which "informercials" of 5 to 6 minutes in length with extensive demonstrations

---

[23] N. K. Malhotra, "Information and Sensory Overload," *Psychology and Marketing*, I, no. 3/4 (Fall/Winter 1984), 17.

[24] "Key Viewers Cool to Cable Fare," *Advertising Age*, (September 29, 1980), 1 and 16.

[25] S. Yuspeh and G. Hallberg, "The Radical Potential of Cable Advertising," *Journal of Advertising Research*, 23, no. 4 (August/September 1983), 51–54.

were run continuously on three channels or the viewer could call in and request a certain ad. Of the viewers, 85% found them useful, 80% found them about the right length, and two-thirds reported they viewed them only once. Whether cable saturation will ultimately offset this strong favorable response remains to be seen.

5.5   Personal Selling

The use of sales representatives may sometimes be the most effective way to reach consumers in EPS, even though far more expensive per contact. This can be seen in consumers buying life insurance, as a study of this product indicates.[26] "Total cost" was the single strong evaluation criterion. The insurer was chosen on recommendation from others. The salesperson was the principal source of recommendation, but some of these respondents turned to parents, friends, relatives, and professional sources in the form of accountants and bank officers. Other than this, there was little if any search for information.

Well-trained salespersons can be more flexible in serving the particular type of information needs of a variety of customers and quantities of information. Further, the margins of innovative products are often large enough to accommodate the high cost of personal selling. Finally, the producer of an innovation probably knows little about the market, and so salespersons, again if well trained, can at least partially compensate for this lack of knowledge by meeting the customer's information needs directly, and also providing feedback to the company about needed product redesign and so on. This complex interaction process in EPS is illustrated well with a salesperson introducing Philips-Sony CD-V to the retail market as discussed earlier. The retailers are not enthusiastic about having to stock up on regular $600 players or the $1,200 player that will play both regular compact disks and larger-type videodisks. Also, at this point, it is not definite that the public will fully appreciate the improved tonal and picture qualities. The retailers wonder whether the manufacturer will invest in the necessary product improvements. Finally, the salesperson is not only persuading the retailer but at the same time is guiding him in how to market this new product category.

The sales situation involving the Philips-Sony sales force and the retailer is truly an *interactive* process. The salesperson says something and the retailer responds, then the salesperson responds to the retailer, and so on. Thus, there is continuous feedback. Recent basic research has begun to throw light on the nature of this exceedingly complex relation and so lays a foundation on which to begin to build guidelines for selecting and training a salesforce, as will be illustrated in the following paragraphs.

A description of this interactive process and some of its consequences

---

[26] R. A. Formasino, R. W. Olshavsky, and S. Tap, "Choice Strategy in a Difficult Task Environment," *Journal of Consumer Research*, 8, no. 4 (March 1982), 474–79.

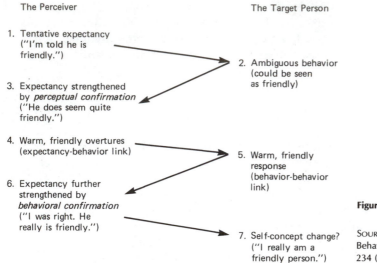

The Perceiver   The Target Person

1. Tentative expectancy
   ("I'm told he is
   friendly.")

                                                 2. Ambiguous behavior
                                                    (could be seen
                                                    as friendly)

3. Expectancy strengthened
   by *perceptual confirmation*
   ("He does seem quite
   friendly.")

4. Warm, friendly overtures
   (expectancy-behavior link)

                                                 5. Warm, friendly
                                                    response
                                                    (behavior-behavior
                                                    link)

6. Expectancy further
   strengthened by
   behavioral confirmation
   ("I was right. He
   really is friendly.")

Figure 8-4   A Typical Social Interaction Sequence

                                                 7. Self-concept change?
                                                    ("I really am a
                                                    friendly person.")

SOURCE: E. E. Jones, "Interpreting Interpersonal Behavior: The Effects of Expectancies," *Science*, 234 (October 3, 1986), 43.

are pictured in Figure 8-4. The basic principle is that "To an important extent we create our own social reality by influencing the behavior we observe in others."[27] The basis of this principle is seen later in Table 9-1, where the CDM is applied to interaction in car buying. It finds that personal reinforcement (PR) of the customer by the salesperson increases the customer's attitude toward the brand. Other research on sales representatives supports this conclusion as well.

There can be, and often is, an element of self-fulfilling prophecy in this interactive behavior, which can mislead the salesperson. Let us use Figure 8-4 to describe how this confusion happens. The "perceiver" in Figure 8-4 on the left, we will assume, is the CD-V salesperson and the "target person" on the right is the retailer.

Let us now describe the process of Figure 8-4 but in terms of the CD-V salesperson who is making his first call on this retailer. What the retailer thinks depends partly upon what he believes the salesperson really knows about the supplying industry, the technical nature of the product, its characteristics relevant to the consumer, and the market. If the salesperson does know these things, the customer wonders whether he will tell the truth.

Correspondingly, the salesperson wonders whether this retailer knows the supplying industry and market, whether he is a nice person or a crabby bastard, and how badly the salesperson needs this retailer as a customer and so be willing to put up with the customer.

In step 1 of Figure 8-4, the salesperson believes that the retailer is a

---

[27] E. E. Jones, "Interpreting Interpersonal Behavior: The Effects of Expectancies," *Science*, 234 (October 3, 1986), 41.

"friendly person." The retailer's behavior is ambiguous since he wants to get as much information as he can from the salesperson but not appear to be a sucker. In step 2, the retailer's behavior is ambiguous but can be interpreted as being friendly, for example, he gives the salesperson a wan smile, a feedback. The existence of the feedback is emphasized because in Chapter 3 you were told that the simple six-variable CDM does not allow for dealing with feedbacks. However, in Chapter 16 you will see how these feedbacks, which are important here, can be incorporated into the CDM.

In step 3, this conclusion about the retailer's behavior being friendly is thus interpreted ("perceptually confirmed") by the salesperson, which adds to the strength of the salesperson's original beliefs about the retailer, another feedback. Consequently, the salesperson exhibits warm friendly overtures, which is the "expectancy-behavior link."

In step 5, the retailer, seeing the salesperson's favorable behavior, becomes really friendly in his behavior, which is a "behavior-behavior link."

In step 6, the salesperson in seeing this warm response by the retailer has his expectancy from step 4 further strengthened. This is "behavioral confirmation." Step 6 is the key. This "behavioral confirmation" of the retailer's friendliness could have been a valid conclusion on the salesperson's part. However, it need not be, since it really occurred because the salesperson originally triggered it and concluded it was true, but he did this without adequate evidence.

In step 7, the customer could really undergo a fundamental "self-concept change" by concluding that he, the retailer, actually is a friendly person and so actually becomes a truly friendly person, in fact. But even if he doesn't, the self-fulfilling process has taken place.

The important conclusion from this discussion of interactive behavior is that a major aspect of training the salesperson should be directed at this subtle self-fulfilling prophecy. He should be taught to avoid it and its consequent confusion for him about what the customer is probably thinking. Unless our CD-V salesperson properly diagnoses the retailer's thinking, he will inadequately carry out the selling strategy for that retailer.

Evidence indicates that the salesperson's type of training for EPS needs to be different.[28] Customers value four characteristics in a salesperson: expertness, trustworthiness, problem identification, and understanding. To an EPS buyer, expertness is more important than is trustworthiness. Also, he values problem identification more highly. The salesperson can help him identify his problem and so come to a conclusion about whether the attributes (benefits) of this new thing are appropriate in solving that problem. A good salesperson can be very effective in helping him to articulate those needs that he often feels only intuitively but cannot articulate.

---

[28] D. T. Wilson, "A Decision Process Model of Organizational Buying," in A. G. Woodside, J. N. Sheth, and P. D. Bennett, eds., *Consumer and Industrial Buying Behavior* (New York: North-Holland, 1977), pp. 355–65.

6. DISTRIBUTION

6.1 Introduction

An example of how consumer behavior changes over the PLC is seen in a study of German mothers with their first baby. They shifted from specialty stores to discount stores in buying baby fruit as they came to know the product and brands and became accustomed to buying it for the child.[29] Even more striking is how the distribution of women's panty hose has tended to shift as mentioned earlier—from specialty stores, then to department stores, and finally to supermarkets as the category moved up the product life cycle. This example suggests the kind of store through which an innovation should be first distributed.

6.2 Use of Specialty Stores

Using the diagrammatic analysis of Figure 8-5, the high information needs of EPS customer suggest he will tend to use specialty goods stores.

In the left column, Figure 8-5 lists two extreme sets of product characteristics, and across the top, it shows two extreme sets of consumer characteristics. In this four-celled table, you see four different types of products—specialty goods, preference goods, convenience goods, and shopping goods—each of which is sold in different kinds of stores. Thus, Figure 8-5 brings together the three key elements of the marketing decision of choosing the type of retail stores to market a product: characteristics of products, characteristics of customers, and characteristics of stores.

"Specialty goods," such as consumer package goods and appliances, are frequently sold in *specialty stores*. The clerks tend to be well informed, but such stores are not conveniently located, and the retailer's margin is high—perhaps 43%.

"Preference goods," including convenience foods, are sold in *department stores*. There are several brands to compare, and stores are well located. However, the clerks know substantially less about the products and the margin is lower—perhaps 39%.

"Convenience goods," including fresh produce, are frequently purchased and sold in *supermarkets* and *discount stores*. Clerks are few and know almost nothing about the product. However, brand comparison is possible and the margin is still lower—perhaps 25–30%.

Finally, "shopping goods" are things like furniture—big-ticket items, sold in department stores by clerks who are fairly well informed. In this category, the product is easily compared, but the consumer must imagine how the product will appear in his home. He must compare items in terms of room layout and

[29] K. P. Kaas, "Consumer Habit Forming Information Acquisition and Buying Behavior," *Journal of Business Research*, 10 (1982), 3–15.

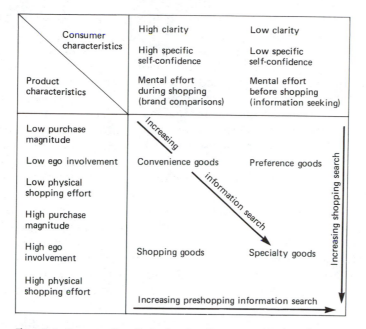

Consumer characteristics	High clarity	Low clarity
	High specific self-confidence	Low specific self-confidence
Product characteristics	Mental effort during shopping (brand comparisons)	Mental effort before shopping (information seeking)

Figure 8-5   Consumer Store Choice Based on Consumer and Product Characteristics

SOURCE: M. B. Holbrook and J. A. Howard, "Frequently Purchased Nondurable Goods and Services," in R. Ferber, ed., *Selected Aspects of Consumer Behavior* (Washington, D.C.: U.S. Supt. of Documents National Science Foundation, 1976), p. 215.

color schemes. Here the margin tends to be the highest of all—perhaps as much as 50%.

The logic of Figure 8-5 for the EPS shopper should now be clear. The consumer often uses a specialty shop in buying an innovation because she needs a great amount of information for the purchase, which is shown by the arrow sloping to the right. She can obtain much of that information by reading ads before she goes to the store. In other words, she does a considerable amount of "preshopping information seeking," then gets more information in the store, where she physically compares brands with the aid of a well-informed clerk, which is "shopping search." Consequently, she is willing to pay the higher margin that specialty stores charge for this extra service.

6.3   Direct Marketing

Recently the evolution in forward integration by manufacturing has appeared in a new form called "direct marketing," and in some products it is having a great effect. A major requirement is a high margin to support the cost. It is by no means confined to EPS products, however. *Direct marketing* has a number of characteristics. Basically, it usually involves the manufacturer selling direct to the ultimate consumer. The product is then delivered by mail. A second characteristic most always exists: a computerized *data base* is maintained that includes information about each individual customer, and usually includes the names of potential customers.

New technology of computer storage of both masses of names and the associated characteristics of the individuals involved and the capacity to group these names for mailing purposes, and so on, is leading to many versions of this major new development. For example, the Ford Motor Co. is selling a luxury car, the Lincoln, by putting the names of all recent Mercedes buyers on the computer and sending each one a questionnaire to obtain demographics and other data that then become a part of a permanent record on each person. This can then be extended to other people of similar characteristics but who are not now owners. A series of ads matched to each recipient or type of recipient can then be sent along with a questionnaire. Rather quickly, then, a series of experiments using different advertising can be carried out, the results are stored in the computer for analysis, and the conclusions can be used in designing future strategies and plans in marketing to these selected customers.

Direct marketing is well illustrated with General Foods new coffee, *Gevalia Kaffe*. General Foods recently bought a Swedish high-quality coffee company. Gevalia Kaffe is the first of its products introduced into the U.S. specialty coffee market, and it is sold by mail. It sells for as much as $7.00 or $8.00 per pound in the United States. The coffee is shipped to each customer on a regular schedule. There is a vast amount to learn in developing this kind of marketing program.

Strictly empirical analysis of such a mass of data can be highly useful as you can readily imagine. But as we have learned throughout the book, a theory-based analysis such as guided by the CDM can be infinitely more useful. Further, this new trend seems to be occurring only in the brands that carry the higher prices. Consequently, the payoff for good analysis is especially high.

Also, some products by their nature are difficult to sell through a retail store. Consequently, some sales are made directly to the consumer by the manufacturer. Procter & Gamble recently announced its intention to sell Attends diapers for incontinent adults through direct marketing channels. This follows closely Kimberly-Clark's effort to market a competing product, called Depend. Obviously a buyer would be sensitive about purchasing such products from a store clerk, and so buying direct is a way of avoiding personal embarrassment. The CDM model can be applied simply and straightforwardly in this situation. But in obtaining the input data, the researcher may have to avoid direct questioning because of the sensitivity of the product and instead ask what the respondent thinks that *other* people think of the product. This type of marketing will probably be increasingly important as names are tied into computerized information networks.

7. SUMMARY

The profitability of product innovation has been emphasized, but the risk deterrent to a company innovating becomes apparent when strategy is considered. The innovation process, especially the product category level, is lengthy and loaded with risks. Yet the "attacker's advantage" places this risk in much better perspective and suggests that "risk avoidance," protecting the status quo, is probably the riskier strategy. Further, the increasing speed of the product life cycle is favoring a still greater emphasis on the technology.

The design of the product is fraught with uncertainty. However, the "lead user" and "high-benefit user" concepts combined offer hope of finding "Tomorrow's product concepts" today because markets tend to be highly dynamic. The core strategy concept requires a better understanding of the consumer benefits.

Once the product concept is available, promotion becomes the number one task. Copy is a complex issue such as illustrated in the necessity to build the consumer's product hierarchy and goal hierarchy. Further the task is complicated by the danger of overloading the customer with information. Next are the issues of language. Figures of speech are needed first, followed by the more precise brand concept word description, where the form of language is critical. Thus, timing is essential. The salesperson's role can be important, but it is subject to the interpersonal dynamics of Figure 8-4.

In this picture the specialty store is seen in its role as a purveyor of information about innovations. Finally, vertical channel issues, for example, whether to use a wholesaler, were not discussed in Chapter 8. Such buyers tend to be formal organizations, not individual consumers, and so the discussion is delayed until Chapter 11.

Questions

1. Foster of McKenzie & Co. has advanced the attacker's advantage and technological discontinuities as a way of approaching an EPS situation. Explain these two ideas and how they relate to each other in setting strategy.

2. What can you conclude from the diffusion studies that is relevant to EPS marketing?

3. In the chapter it was said that "by combining both the 'high-benefit' and the 'lead user' customers we can obtain 'Tomorrow's product concepts today.'" Please explain the meaning and relevance of this assertion.

4. What guidelines can you offer for designing advertising copy and sales presentations in EPS?

5. In what kind of a store would you consider placing a new consumer product and why?

CHAPTER 9

Strategy for
Limited Problem Solving

1. INTRODUCTION

In discussing strategy for extensive problem solving (EPS) in Chapter 8, the foundation was laid for designing limited problem-solving (LPS) strategy. The core strategy concept alone will, of course, suffice for LPS because we can assume that the buyer has a category concept already in her memory, making the problem of strategy design substantially easier. The buying task is easier and faster for the LPS consumer. It is also much more frequent than is the EPS decision. Consequently, it will be possible to apply more consumer behavior theory in this chapter.

Core strategy as used in Chapter 8 is often called "positioning" a brand and is made up of three elements that will be briefly reviewed: the benefits that consumers want in the product, a description of the consumers who want these product benefits, and a description of the competitors.

The remaining parts to supplement the core strategy are the four dimensions of the marketing strategy: product, price, promotion, and distribution, which are the foundation of marketing plans. Finally, a fifth dimension of marketing strategy is the relations with the other functions in the organization: manufacturing, finance, human resources, and research and development (R & D). Their cooperation is usually essential to the successful implementation of the marketing strategy and plans. In this way the core strategy facilitates the design of marketing strategy by linking the theory to strategy via the CDM.

With this brief review, let us turn to each of the four elements of strategy: product design, pricing, promotion, and distribution.

2. PRODUCT DESIGN

2.1 Introduction

A recent *Wall Street Journal* headline illustrates the crucial role of product design in a leading company. "Faced with more competition P & G sees new products as crucial to earnings growth."[1] The company reported the other side of the coin, however, "sizeable investments in research and development, start up of new manufacturing capacity and introducing marketing expenditures (will have) a negative effect on earnings." Going further, "P & G has unveiled 11 test products since mid 1982, and at one point earlier this year had 22 products in testing." As illustrated by this quote, this section deals with the heart of a company's future.[2]

Most important, once both the target audience and target competitors for the core strategy have been selected, designing products for LPS consumers can be sharply focused, because LPS consumers have a well-defined product category image. Consequently, the relevant benefits are well established as we learned in Chapter 5, and the consumers have well-formed expectations to guide their search for information about a new brand in that category.

But how important is product design?

2.2 Importance of Product Design

It's generally agreed that product design is probably the most important general factor in ensuring success of an LPS new product. The product must meet customer needs. The remarkable ability of the LPS customer to process information effectively as we saw in Chapter 5 drives home this message. Let us examine some of the evidence.

Introducing a new (and better) product continues to be a major way of gaining share and improving profits. This is confirmed by the consulting firm of Booz, Allen & Hamilton, Inc., which recently made a study of new products, similar to the classic study it did 20 years ago.[3] Booz, Allen found that the failure rate on new products is about the same as it was 20 years ago. The study, however, does find some differences between the two time periods.

---

[1] *The Wall Street Journal* (New York edition), September 13, 1983, p. 37.

[2] For a general text, see G. L. Urban and J. R. Hauser, *Design and Marketing of New Products* (Englewood Cliffs, N.J.: Prentice Hall, 1980).

[3] "New Products Management for the 1980s," report (Booz, Allen & Hamilton, New York, 1982).

First, a greater emphasis on segmentation was found, leading to smaller markets for each new product.

Second, fewer ideas are required to generate a new product. Third, some companies do much better today keeping new products afloat; some even have a 99% success rate. The successful companies conduct far more analyses, up front, in specifying and designing the product and defining its market, but Booz, Allen does not pretend that in-depth research is the key to successful new product management. The director of the study, in fact, believes that too much emphasis on the research approach "has the danger of managing your way out of risk-taking."

There is other evidence to support the notion that product design is crucial. In a systematic study of industrial product introduction, the following were the key factors in success:

> Product uniqueness and superiority (product design)
> Market knowledge and marketing proficiency
> Technical/production synergy and proficiency[4]

It is no coincidence that both studies support the notion that knowledge of the market is a major ingredient in a successful product introduction. "Knowing your market" here refers primarily to knowing the buyer's needs and benefits where needs are general requirements ("practical knowledge"), and benefits are the specific attitude components. Knowing these enables the marketer to select those customers where a carefully designed product can meet the customer's requirements—but with a differential advantage over competitors.

The Strategic Planning Institute has been collecting data for a number of years from a wide variety of companies. Product quality has been one item of information being collected.[5] As these data are being carefully mined, a picture of the powerful role of product quality is emerging.[6] Sometimes in practice it is not obvious that product quality is playing such a powerful role. Management may think, for example, that it is the advertising that is creating the differential advantage. To separate the effect of advertising from that of product quality is an important role for the Consumer Decision Model (CDM) as will be discussed in Chapter 16, where extension to feedbacks in the model is dealt with.

2.3 Physical Product Versus a Service

The term "product" usually implies a physical product, but it can just as well be used to include a service or an idea as we have been doing throughout the

---

[4] R. G. Cooper, "The Dimensions of Industrial New Product Success and Failure," *Journal of Marketing*, 43, no. 3 (Summer 1979), 100–101.

[5] "Study Product Quality/Profit Relationship to Firms Can Leapfrog over Foreign Competitors," *Marketing News*, January 21, 1983, pp. 4–5.

[6] G. Carpenter, "Product Quality, General Promotion and Profitability," unpublished working paper (U.C.L.A., Center for Marketing Studies, Los Angeles, 1983).

text and as Murphy and Enis believe should be the standard practice.[7] However, the design of a service is quite different from the design of a physical product.

The one characteristic that is generally agreed to distinguish a service from a physical product is tangibility.[8] The service is usually intangible and, therefore, provides no brand recognition (B). Repeatedly in the previous chapters we have referred to the significance of this characteristic of brand recognition (B). In addition to this primary difference is the fact that the product cannot be stored. This exaggerates the problem of matching product supply from the plant with the demand in the market. Also, most of the "workers in the plant" producing a service such as an airline, tellers in a bank, waitresses in a restaurant, and so on are in direct contact with the customer. Consequently, they become a part of the product. They must be managed to achieve efficiency and yet at least not detract from and preferably add to the quality of the product.

Finally, "managing quality control is particularly difficult for intangible services, especially when the service is delivered in real time by failure–prone human beings."[9]

2.4   Elements of Product Design

Four elements can be said to make up design. The foremost are the dimensions of the product itself. Then, there are other dimensions of the offer: branding, packaging, and service. The dimensions of the product often sum to "quality" in the customer's mind.

2.4.1 Product Dimensions.   Let us first examine the nature of product dimensions and then discuss how to identify them. There are two kinds of product dimensions, as we know. First, there are form or physical dimensions of color, size, and shape used to identify the product.[10] We have seen evidence in earlier chapters of their importance. In the Vega study for General Motors, for example, four measures were made of brand recognition: gas economy, horsepower, selling price, and body styles. It was found that only the last one, body styles, actually functioned in a brand identifying role, which is what would be expected.

This brand recognition element is illustrated by the trademark of Shearson's Financial Management Account in Figure 9-1, which competes very strongly with Merrill Lynch's Cash Management Account. Trademarks are effective for creating brand identification. As Dorothy Cohen writes, "Marketers have the

---

[7] P. E. Murphy and B. M. Enis, "Classifying Products Strategically," *Journal of Marketing*, 50, no. 3 (July 1986), 24–42.

[8] K. L. Bernhardt and G. L. Shostalk, "Comments on Christian Gronroos' *Strategic Management and Marketing in the Service Sector*," unpublished report, Report No. 83–1045 (Marketing Science Institute, Cambridge, Mass., May 1983).

[9] *The Wall Street Journal* (New York edition), February 10, 1984, p. 20.

[10] C. B. Mervis and E. H. Rosch, "Categorization of Natural Objects," *Annual Review of Psychology*, 32 (1981), 107–8.

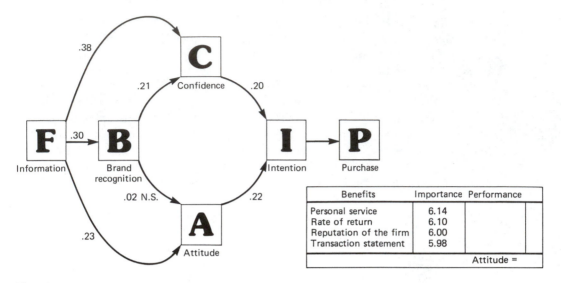

Figure 9-1   Customer Decision Model of Shearson's Financial Management Account

opportunity to develop a strategic orientation for top management decision making by devising an effective trademark strategy."[11]

The second kind of product dimension is the functional or evaluative attributes or benefits. The design engineer obviously must think in terms of physical dimensions if he is designing a tangible product instead of a service. This is the way products come. However, the customer is not buying the physical product, but the service that it will render him as one well-known cosmetic producer put it, "In the factory we make cosmetics and in the drugstore we sell hope!"

The benefits are presented in Figure 9-1 by the attitude (A) for Shearson's Financial Management Account. The specific dimensions are listed in the box below the diagram. These are Personal service, Rate of return, Reputation (of company) and (quality of the monthly) Transaction (statement). The average importance ratings of the benefits for the sample as a whole are shown. However, the performance ratings are not included because they vary from consumer to consumer in the sample.

It is helpful to know just how the customer uses these benefits. As he becomes familiar with them as he does in EPS, he merges them together as a part of his product hierarchy to simplify his choice. For example, if you will look at Figure 9-2 you will see this for the Ford Escort. Importantly, there is a middle point on this scale in his mind, and it is called the prototype, as discussed in Chapter 4. Customers will surprisingly agree on where that prototype is. Further, a new product on the market is more easily and quickly understood the nearer it is to that prototype. Also, by using this prototype, she compares

[11] D. Cohen, "Trademark Strategy," *Journal of Marketing*, 50, no. 1 (January 1986), 61.

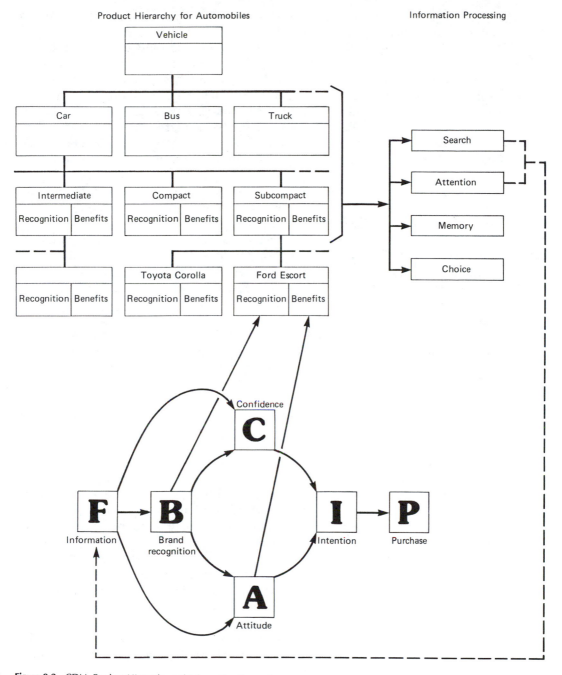

Figure 9-2   CDM, Product Hierarchy and Information Processing

any new product with existing products. Thus she avoids mentally rehearsing all their individual product benefits.

The distinction between the physical product and its contribution to the customer is so obvious that it would seem to be unnecessary to emphasize it. However, it cannot be emphasized too much. It is so much easier to talk and think about the physical product than about what the customer gets from it. To provide a vocabulary about the customer's view of a product is a major contribution of the CDM. The core of this vocabulary is the benefits, where the customer thinks in terms of your and competing brands as being located on these benefits and the importances of those benefits as summarized in Figure 9-2.

For a framework to think about these two types of product dimensions, refer to Figure 9-2, which was earlier shown as Figure 5-2 in Chapter 5. As you see in Figure 9-2, the two dimensions—brand recognition and attitude— link the CDM to the consumer's product hierarchy in the upper left. The product hierarchy aids in the process by guiding the consumer's information processing as shown by the upper right of Figure 9-2, which, in turn, feeds back into the consumer's information (F). Figure 9-2 shows the integrating and synthesizing process that operates and that will be developed in still more detail in Chapter 10.

The vocabulary used for describing benefits must be emotional and subtle in dealing with certain products and services like musical recordings, singers, fashion designs, architectural styles, paintings, museum exhibitions, novels, concerts, performing arts series, and associated patterns of leisure activity.[12] Up to now in this book, the usual verbal descriptions of benefits that are closely related to the physical product, for example, calories, fluoride, and miles per gallon, have been emphasized, and for many products this conventional utilitarian information processing approach is adequate as discussed in Chapter 5. But for the products just mentioned, for example, musical recordings, the verbal descriptions that apply to utilitarian, work mentality, and economic criteria may not be adequate. Instead, esthetic, play mentality, and psychosocial criteria may be needed to supplement the regular criteria. Another way to make the contrast is to distinguish between the relatively simple problem-solving approach that we have been emphasizing and a more hedonic response. The motivation aspects are discussed at length in Chapter 10 since it is probably much more relevant in routine problem solving (RPS). For most products the conventional utilitarian information processing approach, however, probably captures most buying behavior.

Let us now focus on identifying the relevant product attributes. The procedure for determining what the appropriate attributes or benefits are is a serious issue for any approach to customer behavior including the CDM. There

---

[12] M. B. Holbrook and E. C. Hirschman, "The Experiential Aspects of Consumption: Consumer Fantasies, Feelings and Fun," *Journal of Consumer Research*, 9, no. 2 (September 1982), p. 134.

are two general approaches—compositional and decompositional—to obtaining the essential input of relevant benefits.

The compositional approach is implied in discussing the CDM so far and is described earlier in Chapter 8. The alternative is the decompositional approach, of which the most common example is conjoint measurement, although there are other approaches such as multidimensional scaling, discriminant analysis, and factor analysis.[13] The two methods, the one used in discussing the CDM and conjoint measurement, can be combined and used together to get the advantages of both, as also discussed in Chapter 8.[14]

2.4.2 Branding.

Another issue in product design is the decision of *whether* to brand. The brand name serves an identifying role and can be a part of the brand recognition (B) variable in the CDM. A brand name influence can be strong such as said about the Japanese, "Flush with cash and unsure of their tastes, the Japanese behave the way we might expect the newly rich to behave: they worship names. Brand names are the perfect solution in a society where individual preference is muted."[15] A similar phenomenon in the United States is the very popular designer clothing discussed shortly.

In everything we've said up to this point, we have assumed that your product is branded. This is not necessarily true. "Commodity" products—also called unbranded products—are common in some industries, such as steel and forest products. But in these industries, the whole marketing strategy is different, so we won't discuss industrial commodity products further.

Recently, though, there have sprung up "commodity" consumer products, called "generic" products. Jewel Food Stores initiated them in the Chicago area in February 1977. A can of tomatoes, for instance, was simply labeled "Tomatoes." A bottle of syrup, just "Syrup," with no other identifying information on the label. Shoppers were told they could save 10% to 35% by switching from comparable national brand items.[16]

There has been an expansion of another type of labeling: designer clothing, furniture, and so on. For example, "Halston" is now designing for J. C. Penney.[17] The marketer hopes that quality is implied in the designer's name and the designer hopes his name won't be ruined!

2.4.3 Packaging.

Packaging can, in some cases, influence the consumer's perception of the product's quality so that it too can be an important aspect of

---

[13] P. E. Green and Y. Wind, "New Way to Measure Consumers' Judgments," *Harvard Business Review*, July–August 1975, 107–15.

[14] M. B. Holbrook, "Integrating Compositional and Decompositional Analyses to Represent the Integrating Role of Perceptions in Evaluative Judgments," *Journal of Marketing Research*, XVIII (February 1981), 13–28.

[15] J. Taylor, *Shadows of the Rising Sun* (New York: William Morrow, 1983), pp. 103–4.

[16] Venitia Hands, "Generic Products' Volume Gains Could Be a Serious Threat to National Brands," *The Research File* (Ogilvy and Mather), no. 13, January 1979, 1.

[17] "Penney Licensing a Big Leap for Halston," *Advertising Age*, October 4, 1982, p. 30.

product design. For these products, packaging becomes an important decision. Preventing decay is a common function of a package. For example, Tetra Pak, a type of paper container, will keep milk, fruit juice, and a long list of other liquids for up to a year at room temperature.[18] In ordinary paper containers, milk spoils and becomes inedible in a matter of hours at room temperature.

Convenience is another characteristic that packaging can contribute to a product. Quaker State Oil Refining Corp. is expected to be distributing all its oil in plastic containers.[19] The current fiber foil containers are cheaper and can be stacked; the plastic containers are preferred because they do not have to be punched with special spouts, and the customer can use only a part of a bottle today and the balance next week. Also, Campbell Soup Co. is replacing its tin cans with aseptic boxes because these do not require an opener, mixing the soup with water, or cleaning the utensil used in heating it.[20] The microwave oven may be exerting an influence, too, but this was not discussed.

In its simplest form, a package has several practical functions. It prevents spoiling, helps the buyer carry the product easily, and explains what is inside. The latter function has been receiving growing attention. In other cases, however, the role of packaging is to aid in identifying the product. We learned in Chapter 3 that the consumer's brand recognition (B), which may be the packaging, can have a strong influence upon his response. The value of packaging as an identifier of contents has long been known by the marketing community intuitively, but the actual theory has not guided many decisions involving packaging.

International Paper recently bucked that trend, running full-page ads to explain how it had helped Knowlton Dairy in San Antonio, Texas, with its packaging problem. One ad read, in part, "Like most other dairies, Knowlton's yielded long ago to supermarket requests for milk in plastic gallons. But by using those plain plastic jugs, Knowlton's had to watch their *brand identification* fade in dairy cases and in consumers' minds." To counter that perceived problem, International Paper developed a 2-Pak carrying handle that holds two half-gallon cartons. This innovative use of paperboard cartons not only provides Knowlton with brand recognition (B) for its product, but saves it more than 2 cents on each gallon, since plastic is a more expensive container. Packaging also serves a "symbolic" function such as "cleanliness."

2.4.4 Product Service.   If we define "product" broadly to mean everything about a product that the customer is exposed to, then product servicing should also be included. For many products, particularly consumer durables, servicing is crucial. Recognizing this, General Electric recently announced a Quick Fix System to help solve the customer's repair service problems and delays.[21] Under this

---

[18] *Christian Science Monitor* (Boston edition), March 25, 1982, p. 11.

[19] *The Wall Street Journal* (New York edition), May 2, 1984, p. 33.

[20] *The Wall Street Journal* (New York edition), March 27, 1984, p. 35.

[21] "Making Service a Potent Marketing Tool," *Business Week*, June 11, 1984, p. 165.

arrangement, franchised dealers sell repair parts to customers, along with manuals that explain how to use those parts to repair broken G.E. appliances. The rest is up to the customer. No longer will he wait days for and spend significant sums on a repairperson.

In industrial products, IBM is a classic case of a company whose reputation and size have been largely built upon servicing its product. As we all know, from firsthand experience or the grapevine, it has been unbelievably successful in this respect.

However, today many companies are just beginning to learn the value of customer service. Historically, customers have been dubious that complaining to the manufacturer would get results. In a White House–sponsored study, "fewer than one in six complained to the manufacturer; they believed their complaints would not be satisfied. And 90% of the disgruntled buyers did not repurchase from the offending company. This contrasts sharply with the 54% who remained loyal when their complaints were satisfactorily handled."[22]

3. PRICING

Even when customers are in LPS—the growth stage of the product—they are sensitive to price. This is illustrated in pocket calculators. First, the price was $250 and up, and bought by engineers. As the price came down to $100, MBA students, among others, began to buy them in numbers. Later, when they were down to $10.00 and $15.00, homemakers bought them to help with their shopping. However, price sensitivity is usually much less for LPS than it is for RPS. Consequently, pricing will be discussed at length in Chapter 10.

One point to bear in mind is that the entry of a new brand does not much change the slope of the relations in a CDM of a competing brand.[23] Its effect is to move customers on the attitude scale instead of changing the slope of the relation between attitude and intention. An illustration here can make this subtle but important point more obvious. Figure 9-3 shows the relation between attitude (A) and intention (I). The impact of a new competitor typically is to push the customer to the left on the A axis but not change the shape of the relation. The *shape* of the relation, you will recall, as in Figure 9-1, the CDM of Shearson's Financial Management Account, determines how strongly attitude (A) affects intention (I). This is typically unaffected by competitive entry.

Having discussed price, let us move on to the equally important strategy problem of promotion.

---

[22] Ibid.

[23] J. U. Farley, D. R. Lehmann, R. S. Winer, and J. P. Katz, "Parameter Stability and 'Carry-over Effects' in a Consumer Decision-Process Model," *Journal of Consumer Research*, 8, no. 4 (March 1982), 465–71.

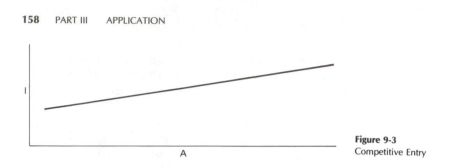

Figure 9-3
Competitive Entry

4. PROMOTION

The objective here is to understand how best to communicate with a consumer in LPS. Some of the communication problem was implicit in the earlier discussion of product design, but here we will go much more deeply into this very important issue of how the consumer receives the information she uses to buy. Further, the consumer tends to have a higher degree of involvement in LPS than in EPS and much more than in RPS. Also, the consumer has a high capacity to process information because her product and goal hierarchies are formed and so her expectations are well formed.

The two most common means of communicating with her are advertising and retail salespersons in implementing the competitive advantage developed in an effective core strategy.

4.1 Advertising

When using advertising, three major questions arise: what to say (copy), how to reach the consumer (media), and how much to say and how frequently (budget).

4.1.1 Copy. Having designed a core strategy and consequent differential advantage for an overall marketing strategy, the first items on the advertiser's agenda are *what* to say to this audience and *how* to say it to build the ABCs of marketing. "What" is concerned with the function of that content, the meaning of the message. "How" is defined in terms of the form in which that content is presented such as sentence structure and vocabulary.

We will refer many times to the "creative" task of converting ideas about the product into effective copy. Woody Carlsen, a creative individual, brings this process down to earth.[24] He uses the form-versus-function distinction effectively in his "funnel approach" to aid creativity. He refers to the "what" as the function, the meaning of the copy, the brand's unique consumer benefit. The "how" is the form in which that meaning is transmitted.

Figure 9-4 describes that "funnel approach" to creativity.

---

[24] *Advertising Age*, September 13, 1984, p. 34.

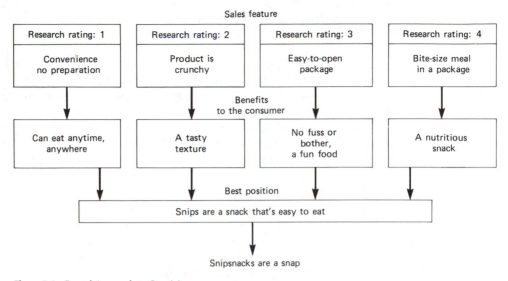

Figure 9-4 Funnel Approach to Creativity

Let's look at a hypothetical example of how the model might work for a new food product called Snips.

Focus group testing indicates that the new product has four major sales features, in order of importance: 1. Convenience, no preparation required; 2. product is crunchy; 3. unique, easy-to-open package; 4. bite-size meal in a package.

These sales features translate, respectively, into the following consumer benefits: 1. Can eat anytime, anywhere; 2. tasty texture; 3. no fuss or bother, a fun food; 4. nutritious snack.

The snack concept wins on two points—convenience and the fact that focus group members called it a bite-size meal in a package. Snips' unique packaging stands out, too. The package breaks open when the product is broken in half. The snapping noise the product makes when broken implies crunchiness. Nutrition pulled the lowest rating, so that component should be a major copy point and not incorporated into the theme itself. You know what they say about messages that try to please everyone.

If we look long enough and hard enough here, it's likely that we'll come up with an initial idea along these lines: Snips are a snack that's easy to eat. This is *what* we want to say. But *how* it is said is not necessarily going to bowl 'em over in Peoria. If you stop here, you've only won half the battle. Your next step is to *try* to make this line as memorable, catchy, clever, interruptive and street-wise.

How about "Snipsnacks are a snap"?

Monosyllabic and alliterative, it's easy to understand and remember. It's catchy and sounds like fun. What else? The snap aspect points up crunchiness, convenience and the unique easy-to-open packaging at once. And the physical act of snapping the package reinforces the verbal concept. Changing the name of the product is an obvious improvement. We can go a step further creatively and write a jingle of "Snipsnacks are a snap" with '50s music and finger-snapping in the background to enhance recall.[25]

Even this more systematic view does not hide the fact that doing advertising is largely an art that some people do better than others but are able neither to explain nor to teach others how. This is, of course, not unique to advertising but true of all creative work.

Content is the central issue of copy. In terms of the CDM, copy should contain content that favorably influences the customer's brand identification (B), attitude (A), and confidence (C). Using Woody Carlsen's distinction of function versus form, the function ("what") of advertising is to change the "ABCs of marketing" and the form is "how" the message accomplishes it.

Much research has been done on consumer attitudes, and it shows us that advertising can without question affect attitude. However, the effect is in shifting their performance ratings of a brand on the relevant benefits. It does not tend to change the importance of those benefits.[26] Some research also indicated it can affect brand recognition and confidence.

Recent research has also found, however, that advertising can have other effects. These other impacts that advertising can have upon the buyer is seen in one of the few very carefully designed experiments of advertising effect.[27] The experimenters conclude that advertising can have either of two paths of effect: central or peripheral.

If the situation is involving or important to the buyer such as pertaining to an important product that she believes she will be buying, she will think about the purchase and the central path will be operative. "[T]he cogency of the information about the product contained in the ad was a powerful determinant of product evaluations."[28] This implies that the buyer has both the motivation to consider carefully and the ability to process the information. The information was specific and unambiguous. Both of these are consistent with Chapter 5. But the celebrity status of the endorser of the product in the ad had no effect on attitudes.

On the other hand, if it was not an involving situation for the buyer when she saw the ad, such as when she did not believe she would be buying the brand, the results were quite different. The celebrity status of the brand endorser in the ad was "a very potent determinant of attitudes about the product."[29]

---

[25] Ibid.

[26] R. J. Lutz, "Changing Brand Attitudes Through Modification of Cognitive Structure," *Journal of Consumer Research*, 1, no. 4 (March 1975), 49–59.

[27] R. E. Petty, J. T. Cacioppo, and D. Schuman, "Central and Peripheral Routes to Advertising Effectiveness: The Moderating Role of Involvement," *Journal of Consumer Research*, 10, no. 2 (September 1983), 135–46.

[28] Ibid., p. 143.

[29] Ibid.

The important general conclusion from the experiment is

The critical feature of the central route to persuasion is that an attitude change is based on a diligent consideration of information that a person feels is central to the true merits of an issue or product. This information may be conveyed visually, verbally or in source or message characteristics. In the peripheral route, attitude changes because of the presence of simple positive or negative cues, or because of the invocation of simple decision rules which obviate the need for thinking about issue-relevant cues or that invoke simple decision rules may be presented visually or verbally, or may be part of the source or message characteristics.[30]

Now let us use our theory from previous chapters as guidelines in design-ing ad copy. To convey "useful news," the copy will use language and maybe pictures and even music to transmit the desired meaning. Assuming that the new brand does have some advantages over existing brands, the customer's interest can usually be attracted by a straightforward statement to this effect such as follows.

A picture of the product and a few words, words that "frame" or tie that picture to the product and indicate that the product pictured has certain benefits, will serve to place the brand in the correct product class in his mind.[31] It is in this sense that the product hierarchy guides an LPS consumer in his search: it causes him to find a place "to put it" in his memory and so identify what kind of a thing (what product class) this new brand is. This, in turn, triggers his appropriate goal hierarchy.

With the brand placed in the right category of his product hierarchy, he will now be stimulated by his product hierarchy as Punj and Staelin find to compare this new brand with other brands on the benefits (A) used for this category and to search for information that will facilitate this comparison.[32] The intensity of the search will depend upon the importance of the product to him. Also, the product hierarchy will guide his attention to sources that from his memory and experience are likely to pay off with information about this kind of product. If the copy is in a medium that the viewer has come to associate with this type of product, he will more likely perceive the copy.

To build on this foundation chunk of brand recognition, the consumer needs information about the benefits of the product conveyed by words. Some words are better than others for doing this as discussed in Chapter 4. First, the consumer needs a noun labeling the brand that conveys what the brand is and does. Second, adjectives are needed to label the benefits the product offers. Here polar adjectives that describe the extremes of the benefits such as slow-

[30] Ibid., p. 144.

[31] J. A. Edell and P. Staelin, "The Information Processing of Pictures in Print Ads," *Journal of Consumer Research*, 10, no. 1 (June 1983), 59.

[32] G. N. Punj and R. Staelin, "A Model of Consumer Information Search Behavior for New Automobiles," *Journal of Consumer Research*, 9, no. 4 (March 1983), 366–80.

fast, sweet-sour, and so on will best convey the meaning. As stated in Chapter 4, these are the 39 polar adjectives that do most of our work for us. Also, the consumer needs meaningful adverbs to give numerosity to the adjectives. The pickle is "very sour" or "slightly sour" and so on. Finally, all these words have to be put into sentences and the sentences into paragraphs sharply describing an idea.

Brand recognition (B) will also provide a foundation on which to build confidence (C). This, of course, requires that he is getting other information from the copy that tells him that the brand is distinct and that his peers think highly of it, too. Also, this information must be consistent in the meaning that it imparts because contradictory information will be highly damaging to his confidence (C) rather than supportive.

As he now focuses his attention upon the verbal content of the advertising, he proceeds in two stages: "feature analysis" and "active synthesis." First, he separates out the key features of the ad, and the copy can be designed to facilitate identifying these features. He then proceeds to relate these in his thinking (from short-term memory to existing "chunks" in his long-term memory such as the brand recognition (B)).

This latter part is the "active synthesis," where he is putting together the pieces of information in such a way as to make sense of—to form the meaning of—the new brand. To the extent the ad copy facilitates this process, the ad will be more effective, for example, the Procter & Gamble "slice-of-life" ads with their familiar, homey setting. This meaning adds to his expectations as to what information he will find, which simplifies immensely his attention effort; he pays sharp attention only to the unexpected. Further, he is guided by looking for information about the more important benefits.

He probably will not work with more than three or four benefits at most because of the five-chunk limit on his short-term memory. This includes his brand recognition component(s) as well. To include excess benefits in the copy will only limit the effectiveness of the ad.

To the extent that our advertising takes advantage of the form aspects of the copy content by using kernel sentences, polar adjectives, and so on, he can handle the information more effectively. Also, to the extent that he already has closely related information such as about similar and familiar brands in his memory, he can more easily call it up from long-term memory and put it to work in short-term memory in making sense of this new brand. Further, if the brand happens to be stocked in a convenient supermarket, he will compare it with existing brands and derive further information to facilitate his choice.

His thoughts about the nature of the advertising per se and the benefits as he views them will have a corresponding positive or negative effect upon his evaluation of the advertising content and thus influence his attitude toward the brand. But it may not affect his brand recognition or confidence.

In addition to content of copy, there is the issue of context. The *context* in which the customer receives the ad copy can influence the customer as well as does the message. There are three types of context effects.[33] Let us use television to illustrate. First is the environment of the message, which is the type of program. The attractiveness of the star can increase the message effect. There is good evidence that the television program can operate here. For example, as McGuire has pointed out, photographs of women are rated significantly less attractive by men who have just watched *Charlie's Angels*. This kind of context effect may be very useful in explaining advertising results.

A second context effect is within the ad itself. Evidence is good, for example, that the credibility of the speaker in an ad is influenced by nonverbal cues of the speaker such as facial expressions, postures and gestures, voice qualities, and so on, often called "body language." To be specific, speakers are more likely to be considered deceptive to the extent that they avoid eye contact, smile less, shift their posture more often, speak at a slower rate, and so on.

A third type of context is that within which the ad is viewed. "There is evidence that an ad's impact on attitude is affected by the viewer's emotional context when it is received."[34] The impact is greater, for example, if the person is in a mellow mood such as having a snack while watching the ad. The studies in this area have come to be called the "peanuts and Pepsi" studies.

These examples are used merely to convey the general notion that the context of an ad may have an independent and unexpected effect. We would expect, however, that these may be largely captured by whether the consumer likes the ads as discussed earlier.

4.1.2 Advertising Media.

For an ad to be effective, it must be placed in a medium that members of the target audience will be exposed to. Without exposure, obviously, there can be no effect. Hence, a major task in selecting media is to find a medium that will expose the target consumers to the ad. The media to which a customer will be exposed is, of course, heavily influenced by her tendency to search. The determinants of both, where she searches and how much, were discussed in Chapter 5.

But the nature of the relationship between the advertising and the consumer can be quite different among types of media. For example, how much the consumer searches when exposed to the medium is very different depending on whether it is television or print. These two forms have been systematically compared by Carl Hixon and John Fiedler.[35] They find the consumer has little control over the TV. The advertising appears in a predetermined sequence and at a certain time. Further, it doesn't much differentiate among viewers,

---

[33] W. J. McGuire, "New Developments in Psychology as They Bear on Context Effects in Advertising," unpublished paper, delivered at Advertising Research Foundation Conference, New York, 1982), p. 6.

[34] Ibid.

[35] C. Hixon and J. Fiedler, "Print: The Message, the Medium, the Environment," in J. Bighmey, ed., *Attitude Research Under the Sun*" (Chicago: American Marketing Association, 1979), pp. 198–215.

their needs, or how they relate to various products. The viewer's role is passive.

Contrast print. "It is a number of media, not a single one. The audiences for these media are created by the editorial style and content of specific vehicles. Even within magazines . . . there is far more diversity than watching television." Print is active and involving. You have to concentrate and pay attention. You have to do something physically with your hands. The reader's role is active.

For some time, media have been becoming more specialized. Magazines on very narrow topics, for example, backpackers, have tended to replace "family" magazines like *American*, *Saturday Evening Post*, and *Life*. Too, we seem to be on the verge of a literal revolution in electronic media that will supplement the three television networks with cable TV, satellites, and videodisks and greatly increase the available channels. And the networks are considering more specialized audiences, speaking in terms of "narrowcasting" instead of "broadcasting."

Take cable, for example. Its total penetration is 25%, and by 1990 it is expected to have a major market share and be an important medium for the consumer and advertiser alike. "I expect to see much longer commercials on cable," says one media buyer. "With two or three minutes of time to explain the attributes of a product, a commercial on cable could be imaginative and entertaining as well as informative."[36]

In addition to the sheer ability to expose a target audience to the message, media have other characteristics. Some media come to be known by the reader for containing certain kinds of information. Consequently, two media offering the same exposure may give different results for an ad.

Exposure value is a measure of the medium's effectiveness that is relatively easy to apply: the measure is cost per thousand viewers, or CPM. But nonexposure value—the degree to which the buyer pays attention to a particular medium to which he is exposed—is more difficult to test. One way of testing it is to use feedback analysis in the CDM discussed in Chapter 16, but it requires that the same ad be run in different media to "wash out" the effect of the copy.

4.1.3 Advertising Budget.   How much should be spent on advertising for a product? Since the nature of the copy will heavily influence the kind of media, the kind of media will largely determine the cost of the ad campaign. Cost is determined partly by the ad's "reach," which is the proportion of people that recall the ad from the population that you wish to reach.

Once the ad's reach has been determined, the ad's "frequency" of exposure is set. Frequency is defined as the average number of times that a person, who has been reached by a medium, is exposed to that medium. For a careful, critical review of the validity of the reach and frequency measures, see Kenneth Longman.[37] Figure 9-5 indicates the common finding that increasing frequency quickly leads to leveling off of the effect on attitude. Figure 9-5 also indicates,

---

[36] "Key Viewers Cool to Cable Fare," *Advertising Age*, 51 (September 29, 1980), 1 and 16.

[37] K. Longman, *Advertising* (New York: Harcourt Brace Jovanovich, 1961), Chapter 17.

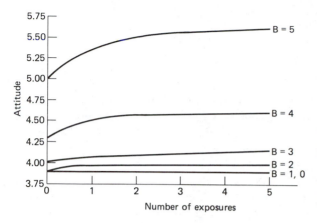

Figure 9-5
Advertising Effects and Levels of
Brand Identification

Source: M. Laroche and J. A. Howard, "Nonlinear Relations
in a Complex Model of Buyer Behavior," *Journal of Consumer
Research* 6, no. 4 (March 1980), 384.

however, that by increasing the customer's brand recognition (B), this tendency for the curve to drop off can be offset. The sample here was broken up into subsamples of different levels of B. This leveling-off tendency is less for involving and complex products. The CDM can test out the gain in effect on attitude from increasing brand recognition as will be discussed in Chapter 17.

Finally, by means of simulation, the CDM offers substantial guidance for setting the budget. This is especially true if the decision is whether to change the size of the budget with given copy and media.

4.2   Personal Selling

Salespersons are supposed to influence the buyer. There is some evidence that the degree of this influence arises from the salesperson's job satisfaction, her motivation, ability, role clarity, and other attributes peculiar to her biographical or psychological profile.[38]

Substantial evidence also supports the idea that the salesperson's face-to-face relationship can influence the customer. In an early study, 180 life insurance prospects (90 sold and 90 unsold) were compared in terms of the role congruence of the salesperson and prospect.[39] Role congruence describes the extent to which each party in the salesperson-prospect dyad *conformed* to what the other *expected* of her. Specifically, each party to the dyad, the salesperson and the client, had certain expectations about how the other would behave. From the customer's standpoint, she expects either a patient or an impatient sales demeanor, fast talking or normal speech, high pressure or soft sell. When the two groups of prospects—sold and unsold—were compared, the extent of role congruence clearly distinguished the sold from the unsold. Also, agents, sold prospects, and unsold prospects were compared on questions pertaining to attitude about life insurance agents, life insurance as a product, purchasing

[38] E. A. Riordan, R. L. Oliver, and J. H. Donnelly, "The Unsold Prospect: Dyadic and Attitudinal Determinants," *Journal of Marketing Research*, XIV (November 1977), 530–37.
[39] Ibid.

life insurance, and the particular insurance company involved. The differences in these attitudes were significant among all three groups but greatest between the salesperson and the unsold prospects.

A more recent study brings out the interesting conclusion that if the salesperson is what the consumer expects her to be, the consumer responds quite differently than if she is different.[40] Specifically, if the salesperson is viewed as "typical," her arguments about the benefits have significantly less effect and the consumer tends to recall fewer of the product features. If she is "atypical," her cogent arguments will affect the consumer attitude and the consumer will recall more of the product's benefits.

The nature of the process by which the dyadic effect between salesperson and client occurs has been well described by David Wilson.[41] The process can be analyzed if the CDM information (F) is operationally defined to include the effect of the salesperson upon the buyer as seen in Table 9-1. The salesperson's behavior and the customer's evaluation of her influences how much weight her information will carry with the customer.

To incorporate this new element—the evaluation of the salesperson—into the CDM, we can use the same format the customer uses in evaluating a brand. With the salesperson, however, he is obviously looking for different benefits than when he evaluates the brand. He wants service, delivery, and advice in using the product. He also wants information, but he wants that information to be from a certain kind of source. First, that source must be credible. Put another way, the salesperson must be an *expert* in the area of the product and its use. Second, she must be *trustworthy*. She must be deemed not only able to tell the truth, but willing to do so. This quality is sometimes related to "similarity." If the salesperson is like me, I can trust her. With this information on the source, it is possible to begin to construct a "salesperson effectiveness" measure (see Table 9-1).

This evaluation measure can be put into the CDM—as an input to brand recognition, attitude, and confidence. Again, the interplay among the components of the model will give more insights than have previously been possible. When the buyer is in LPS, the salesperson is less essential, since the customer now knows the relevant benefits of the product. But now he needs information about where the brand stands on the product benefits, and *trustworthiness* becomes the important benefit.

Madge Lyman has recently done a study that shows how salesperson effects can be linked to the CDM.[42] Her purpose was mainly to capture and

[40] M. Sujan, J. R. Bettman, and H. Sujan, "Effects of Consumer Expectations on Information Processing in Selling Encounters," *Journal of Marketing Research*, XXIII (November 1986), 346–53.

[41] D. T. Wilson, "Dyadic Interaction" in A. G. Woodside, J. N. Sheth, and P. D. Bennett, eds., *Consumer and Industrial Buying Behavior* (New York: North-Holland, 1977), pp. 355–65.

[42] M. M. Lyman, "Sales Interaction and Buyer Behavior Model: An Extension of the Howard Model of Buyer Behavior to Include the Salesperson Interaction," unpublished doctoral dissertation (Columbia University, New York, 1984).

Table 9-1   Salesperson Effectiveness Measure

Benefit	Importance	Rating	Contribution
Expertness			
Trustworthiness			
Problem identification			
Understanding			
	Salesperson Effectiveness		

measure the interaction *process* that goes on between the salesperson and the client on the sales floor in an automobile dealership. She did this by having a third person observe the interview and record both the salesperson's and the client's responses as the sales interview took place. Few studies have attempted to get at this vital sales interaction process of who says what to whom and with what effects which is so essential in practice. This lack of understanding of the sales process is true even though a massive number of studies have been made of sales effort.

Her results are shown in Figure 9-6. PR is "personal reinforcement" that the salesperson gives the customer such as by agreeing with the customer's statements. "NB" is the salesperson's statements about the "number of benefits" of the car. A is "attitude," the sum of the customer's ratings of the most important benefits. B is "brand recognition," the customer's ability to recognize correctly drawings of each car. C is our familiar scale of the customer's confidence in his ability to judge the quality of the car. I is the familiar "intention to buy," and P is whether they "purchased." CAS is "customer attitude toward the salesperson," and SC is "sensitivity to the customer." The number above each line is the regression coefficient for that relation, while the number below the line is the significance level of that coefficient. "NS" is "nonsignificant."

I to P, as you see, was not significant, presumably because the recession sharply increased unemployment in the area and suddenly changed customers' plans to buy. The results of confidence (C) having a greater effect than attitude (A) on intention (I)—.47 versus .41—are consistent with the experience of the General Motors' Vega. Brand identification (B) is operative but not strong.

Salespersons appeared not to be very persuasive as indicated by the low and nonsignificant effect of NB, but a car is an expensive and important purchase to most people. However, personal reinforcement (PR) was significant and reasonably strong as indicated by the regression coefficient on attitude (A) of .24. Also, the salesperson's sensitivity to the customer (SC) was significant in affecting the "customer's attitude toward the salesperson" (CAS), but, as you see, this did not carry through to influence the "customer's attitude toward the brand." However, the incomplete effect probably is largely due to the lack of feedbacks in the model. As you learned in Chapter 8, feedbacks play an important role in interaction. In Chapter 16 you will learn how feedbacks can be incorporated into the CDM.

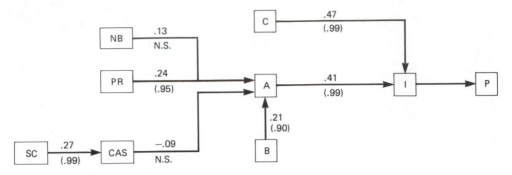

Figure 9-6   Salesman-Customer Interaction Process

Source: M. M. Lyman, "Sales Interaction and Buyer Behavior Model: An Extension of the Howard Model of Buyer Behavior to Include the Salesperson Interaction," unpublished doctoral dissertation (Columbia University, New York, 1984), Chapter 7.

That personal reinforcement can be effective is shown in a study of why people give blood that included a "labeling" alternative.[43] That is, the salesperson told the consumer, for example, that she was "a charitable person." The result was that those so "labeled" were much more inclined to act charitably. This is the theory of attribution that has received considerable attention in psychology, namely, that being so labeled causes the person to see himself in a new light, and actually attribute the quality to himself. The results of labeling in this study were surprisingly strong. In fact, the customer still exhibited the effects of being so labeled two weeks after the labeling treatment. The authors of the study concluded that "Labeling (telling the customer she has good qualities) can be a creative tool for every salesman, and will increase in effect as discounting (questioning the truth of the label) opportunities are minimized and sincerity and directness are maximized."[44]

In discussing the salesperson we have up to now been implicitly assuming that your salesperson is an "outside salesperson." An outside salesperson is one who calls upon the customer in person. In recent years there appears to have been a substantial shift to "inside salespeople" where the salesperson contacts the customer typically via telephone.[45] Some companies have gone so far in this direction as to eliminate their outside salespeople. Most companies, however, have increased the number of inside salespeople while continuing some of their outside salespeople. The telephone is cheaper because the salesperson can reach substantially more customers during a given period of time.

Videodisk players and compact portable computers are being used to

[43] W. K. Swinyard and M. L. Ray, "Advertising-Selling Interactions: An Attribution Theory Experiment," *Journal of Marketing Research*, XIV (November 1977), 509–16.

[44] Ibid., p. 515.

[45] "Rebirth of a Salesman: Willy Loman Goes Electronic," *Business Week*, February 27, 1984, pp. 103–4.

some extent to aid the salespeople. However, their major role appears to be in training salespeople.

By adding the salesperson effectiveness measure to the CDM, you can evaluate how well your salespeople are doing and what the size of your sales budget should be.

5. DISTRIBUTING TO YOUR MARKET

5.1   Introduction

The final area of strategy is choosing distribution channels for your product, which can be a highly strategic decision. This is supported by Murphy and Enis who have recently formulated a more systematic way of classifying products that can facilitate developing strategy.[46] The key point here is to implement that competitive advantage that was built into the core strategy when it was first designed.

First, obtaining distribution, such as space on the retailer's shelf, can be difficult. The retailer has to be persuaded it will be profitable for him. Second, it can be vital to the success of a product. For example, Sweda, the Swedish maker of cash registers bought by Litton a few years ago, is using 200 retail stores to reach the small-business person. Among the manufacturers of small computers, for example, IBM, this route has been viewed skeptically. IBM has argued that it is better to use a direct sales force. But some customers agree with Sweda. More recently, IBM shifted its position on this issue, and its decision has generally been regarded as one of the reasons for its great success with the personal computer, which is now accepted as a classic in successful innovation.

Finally, the distribution channel is one of the major elements of the customer's environment, and one of the most complex features to discuss. It can be simplified somewhat if it is divided into horizontal and vertical distribution relationships. Horizontal relationships running across channels concern buyer choice among several intermediate sellers, for example, retailers. Vertical relationships run upward and downward, from seller to customer. We often speak of a company "integrating forward," which, for example, means a manufacturer takes over, from, say, a wholesaler, the next stage of the distribution channel from seller to end user.

The distribution component of strategy will be more fully developed here than it was in EPS, where distribution often plays a secondary role. We will discuss only horizontal relationships, however, and simplify these by dealing only with the retail level. Vertical channel issues, such as whether to use a wholesaler, will be discussed in Chapter 11 since such middlemen buyers tend to be formal organizations, not individual consumers.

---

[46] Murphy and Enis, "Classifying Products Strategically." For a recent review of the issues, see W. T. Ross, "Managing Marketing Channel Relationships," unpublished working paper, Report No. 85–106 (Marketing Science Institute, Cambridge, Mass., July 1985).

5.2   Consumer Selects Store

The core strategy concept should focus your thinking.[47] The three key dimensions of a retail store are the *convenience* of its location, the *price* at which it sells its products, and the *information* it provides about the product. In fact, just as we have used the CDM to describe choice of a brand, so can we use it to describe the consumers' choice of a retail store.[48] In short, the buyer forms an image of the store just as he does the brand.[49] However, the consumer may describe the benefits of one store over another in different terms than we're using here. For instance, he might say, "quality of service" instead of "information" but mean much the same thing. To simplify the discussion, we will use the terms "convenience," "price," and "information" as the benefits in the consumer's image of the store. These become the benefits in the store manager's core strategy and are his marketing variables.

5.3   Role of CDM

"Information" from the channel (retail store) acts as a part of information (F) in the CDM, for it describes the consumer's image of the *brand*. The thinking processes the consumer uses in building her store and brand images are shown in Figure 9-7. In LPS the consumer's judgment of "availability" of the brand is thought to be contained in her attitude (A). Consequently, "Type of store" is an external influence capable of affecting B, A, and C. To the extent it does affect all three, the channel is playing a strong role. In Figure 9-7, the shopper in the store receives information about the PC and the store from both outside the store and inside the store. Let us use it to illustrate this subtle point implied in Figure 9-7.

What happened in Figure 9-7 is that the customer's image of the PC is the merger of the elements of these two interacting objects, the PC and the store. The PC was, in effect, a different product in the customer's view in one specialty store than it was in another specialty store with a different combination of convenience, information, and price. Thus, conditions in the retail store become an intimate part of customer X's image of the brand.

Finally, the channel also makes the product available in varying degrees: the extent to which a customer's regular store stocks the brand, "availability" as a benefit dimension of attitude can be used to describe this condition. The feasibility of the approach is supported by James Bettman in his study of consumer

---

[47] For a report on market research techniques useful for the retail store, written for managers, see E. A. Pessemier, "Retail Patronage Behavior," Report No. 80–112 (Marketing Science Institute, Cambridge, Mass., December 1980).

[48] W. Baumol, "Calculation of Optimal Product and Retailer Characteristics: The Abstract Product Approach," *Journal of Political Economy*, 75, no. 5 (October 1967), 450–61.

[49] E. G. May, "Management Applications of Retail Image Research," Report No. 73–109 (Marketing Science Institute, Cambridge, Mass., 1973).

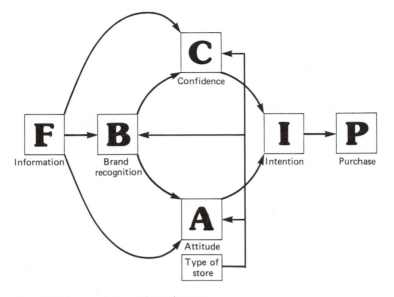

Figure 9-7   Integrated Store and Brand Images

information processing.[50] He points out that a consumer does use the store to obtain information and thus reduces her risk or, perhaps alternatively, increases her confidence in her ability to judge the quality of the brand. In one study, for example, the customer reported using the store to reduce her risks: "Any product carried by a reliable store must be of acceptable quality" was her rationale. In fact, in another study of consumers' store images, it was found that, just as there is sometimes a price-quality association so is there a store–product quality association that consumers make and that can influence their purchasing.

There are other specific features of the retail store environment that can influence customer behavior. One issue that has had heated discussion is whether the price should be placed on each specific item. It has occurred especially with the development of "scanners" at the checkout counter, which have become increasingly common and which require the price be included in the scanner code. However, customers want item pricing. To provide this item pricing service is costly for the retailer who wants to avoid putting the price on the store shelf and on the item. In one study, 20% of the shoppers who were familiar with scanners but who were interviewed in a nonscanner store reported that they would shift to another nonscanner store if their current store installed them.[51] In an experiment, when item pricing was used, customers reduced the average prices paid by 1%. When an organized list of unit prices was also made available

[50] J. R. Bettman, *An Information Processing Theory of Consumer Choice* (Reading, Mass.: Addison-Wesley, 1979), pp. 340–41.

[51] B. F. Harris and M. K. Mills "Retail Headache: Consumers Still Distrust Scanning," *Marketing News*, 15, no. 5 (September 4, 1981), 1.

Table 9-2 Comparison of Department and Grocery Stores on Store Benefits

Department Store	Grocery Store
1. Dependable products	1. Dependable products
2. Fair on adjustments	2. Store is clean
3. High value for money	3. Easy to find items you want
4. High value for money	4. Fast checkout
5. Easy to find items you want	5. High-quality products
6. Fast check out	6. High value for the money
7. Helpful personnel	7. Fully stocked
8. Easy-to-return purchases	8. Helpful store personnel
9. Easy-to-exchange purchases	9. Easy to move through store
10. Store is clean	10. Adequate number of store personnel

SOURCE: R. A. Hansen and T. Deutscher, "An Empirical Investigation of Attribute Importance in Retail Store Selection," *Journal of Retailing*, 53, no. 4 (Winter 1977–1978), 59–72 and 95.

to the consumers, the average price paid was reduced another 2%.[52] This latter finding indicates that customers do effectively use the price information in deciding which brand to buy.

The benefits that customers actually use in evaluating retail stores will add realism. These can be contrasted with the simplified picture given in connection with Figure 9-7 of "convenience," "price," and "information." When 485 people in Columbus, Ohio, were asked to rate department stores and grocery stores on the relative importance of 41 attributes, the results listed in the order of their importance in Table 9-2 were obtained.[53] These were the top 10 attributes for each type of store, department versus grocery. As you can see, there is substantial similarity between the two types of stores. However, there are also significant differences, for example, "clean" as might be expected is no. 2 for grocery stores but no. 10 for department stores. These questions of the content of the attributes and their precise names have to be determined for each particular product.

5.4 Types of Stores Patronized

Figure 9-8, also appearing in the previous chapter as Figure 8-5, allows the marketer to focus her thinking more sharply on the issue of how the consumer chooses a retail store.[54]

[52] J. E. Russo, "The Value of Unit Price Information," *Journal of Marketing Research*, XIV, no. 2 (May 1977).

[53] R. A. Hansen and T. Deutscher, "An Empirical Investigation of Attribute Importance in Retail Store Selection," *Journal of Retailing*, 53, no. 4 (Winter 1977–78), 59–72 and 95.

[54] M. B. Holbrook and J. A. Howard, "Frequently Purchased Nondurable Goods and Services," in R. Ferber, ed., *Selected Aspects of Consumer Behavior* (Washington, D.C.: U.S. Supt. of Documents, National Science Foundation, 1976), pp. 189–222.

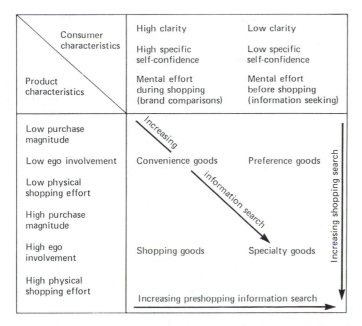

Figure 9-8   Consumer Store Choice Based on Consumer and Product Characteristics

SOURCE: M. B. Holbrook and J. A. Howard, "Frequently Purchased Nondurable Goods and Services," in R. Ferber, ed., *Selected Aspects of Consumer Behavior* (Washington, D.C.: U.S. Supt. of Documents, National Science Foundation, 1976), p. 215.

The logic of Figure 9-8 should now be clear. The consumer uses a specialty shop whenever she needs a great amount of information before she goes to the store. In other words, she does a considerable amount of preshopping information seeking, then gets more information in the store, where she physically compares brands with the aid of a well-informed clerk. She is willing to pay the higher margin that specialty stores charge for this extra service.

She uses a preference goods store such as a department store when the product is less important and she needs less information. This store has the advantage of a lower margin over the specialty store. Here she will use substantial information from preshopping information seeking and the manufacturer has to build package identity and brand name to provide that information.

She uses a convenience goods store such as a supermarket if she knows the product well, the product is not important, and she values convenience. She can choose it without a clerk providing information. As with fresh fruits and produce, she can examine it and tell whether it is good.

She will use a shopping goods store such as a furniture or department store for furniture and clothing without much preshopping information seeking. She gets considerable information in the store—mainly by seeing the furniture there in a setting analogous to her home, which enables her to make physical comparisons. Turnover in such stores is very low and the margin is high.

Finally, there is an important dynamic element that applies to LPS.

An LPS brand is likely to be on the growth stage of the PLC and is still being distributed in a specialty shop. A good opportunity may exist for this new brand, especially if the category is approaching the top of the PLC to be placed in a preference or convenience goods shop. This may require substantial package design and other promotional approaches. It can pay off handsomely, however. Hanes' L'Eggs panty hose was a classic case in how to make the transition from a specialty shop to the supermarket. It was carefully planned, well executed, and eminently successful in acquiring almost a third of the market.

6. SUMMARY

This chapter has been confined to how to apply the relevant theory to designing a core strategy for a new product within an established category that will give that new product a competitive advantage.

Market selection can play a primary role if real intercustomer differences in buying exist and you can serve some of these better than your competitors can. But be sure these two conditions are met. Product design is the most basic element of all. Brand differences tend to be declining. Unless you have a better product than your competitors, you are forced to rely upon a cost advantage or superior marketing skills, both of which are usually less dependable than is product quality.

Pricing can be important especially in the upper reaches of the growth stage as brand differences decline and as customer segments emerge. Promotion of some kind is required to convey that superior product quality. Advertising is the most common. The task is fairly straightforward, communicating the brand image elements: brand recognition, benefit performance, and confidence.

Appropriate horizontal channel relations are also essential. The new brand must be made accessible to the selected consumers. To do this can be a complex problem.

Questions

1. What is meant by a "prototypical brand," and what is the relevance of it in designing LPS strategy?
2. Describe the role of product packaging as part of an effective marketing plan in LPS.
3. It has been found that advertising can operate through either of two effects: central or peripheral. When is the central impact likely to occur, and when the peripheral impact?
4. What advice have you to offer in designing a personal selling strategy in LPS?
5. In what type of retail outlet would you expect an LPS product to be distributed? Explain your conclusion.

CHAPTER 10

Strategy for
Routine Problem Solving

1. INTRODUCTION

The core strategy concept is still the point of focus as it was in Chapters 8 and 9. However, it becomes more complicated in routine problem solving (RPS) as we see in Figure 10-1, where the Consumer Decision Model (CDM) has to be modified by including a bypass of the thinking process. The causal relation is direct from information (F) to intention (I) to explain at least some routine buying. Second, price (Pr) and availability (Pl) tend to become separated from attitude. They operate as independent influences upon intention (I) instead of as a part of attitude (A), which will be discussed later in connection with pricing.

Price and availability obviously can change the nature of the marketing problem in RPS. Also, consumers in RPS are less involved in the process of buying, and this probably is an important factor in their behavior. They pay less attention to and search less for information. Other factors can influence the level of the consumer's involvement, such as the cost of the product, interest in the category, perceived risk, situation of product use, and social visibility of the product. But being in RPS is one of the major influences. Low-involvement buying in the study of the influence of advertising has been called the "peripheral route" and high-involvement, the "central route,"[1] as discussed in Chapter 9.

[1] R. E. Petty, J. T. Cacioppo, and D. Schumann, "Central and Peripheral Routes to Advertising Effectiveness: The Moderating Role of Involvement," *Journal of Consumer Research*, 10, no. 2 (September 1983), 135–46.

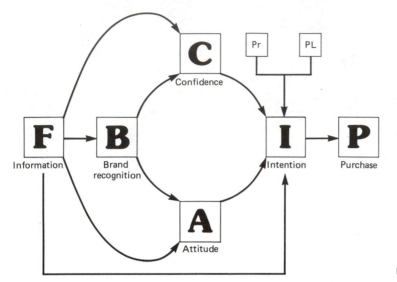

Figure 10-1   Routine Buying Model

Consequently we can think of RPS influence process as a peripheral route compared to LPS. In a sense, the bypass is the extreme case: they buy it, try it, and *then* change their attitude accordingly. In Chapter 16 you will see how effective trying it can be in changing attitude.

We must be careful not to conclude, however, that most of the customers are not responsive to relevant information. They are more likely to respond to relevant information than are LPS consumers because, knowing much about the brands in their evoked set, they have well-developed expectations about what information to expect, which guides them. Also, with this background of knowledge, they can easily handle information. You will recall that at the end of Chapter 6, in Table 6-3, it was shown how much stronger the relations in the CDM were for Carnation Instant Breakfast, a routine buying situation, than for Post Instant Breakfast, a newly introduced brand in the same category. In a nutshell, if they get relevant information, they respond to it. Also, we saw in Chapter 6 in the Dutch study, roughly a fourth of the consumers of beer, margarine, and powdered milk bought the same brand each time. However, the preponderance of consumers occasionally shifted brands within their evoked set of acceptable brands. This willingness to shift brands periodically is obviously important for the marketer who is considering whether to improve the quality of his brand as a way of gaining a competitive advantage.

Repeatedly we have referred here and earlier to consumers choosing from within their evoked sets of typically not more than three or four brands. In RPS we seem to find the two-stage choice process that Johnson and Russo and others have found.[2] First is a choice task of choosing from within an evoked set. Second is a judgment task as the CDM portrays.

---

[2] E. J. Johnson and J. E. Russo, "Product Familiarity and Learning New Information," *Journal of Consumer Research*, 11, no. 1 (June 1984), 542–50.

Table 10-1   Mean Attitude, Intention, Confidence, Information for Evoked, Hold, Foggy, Reject Sets

	Evoked	Reject	Hold	Foggy
Attitude	7.020	3.950	5.480	4.709
(Std. Error)	(.092)	(.182)	(.158)	(.198)
Information	6.391	4.315	5.367	4.152
	(.110)	(.199)	(.162)	(.212)
Intention	3.643	2.788	3.053	2.421
	(.128)	(.184)	(.164)	(.169)
Confidence	6.176	4.467	5.372	4.312
	(.118)	(.198)	(.168)	(.208)

SOURCE: M. Laroche, J. A. Rosenblatt, Friedhalm Bliemel, and R. K. Ransom, "The Economic Impact of Price Quality Evaluations on Brand Categorization: The Examination of the Microcomputer Market," working paper series (Concordia University, Montreal, January 1986), p. 18.

The general idea of an evoked set is useful, but it can be refined and made still more useful for designing strategy. In 1983–84, 205 people in Montreal and Toronto, Canada, were interviewed about their views on 14 of the leading brands of minicomputers in terms of their evoked sets.[3] The results are shown in Table 10-1. The average evoked set responses are shown in column 1. They were also asked those brands that they definitely would not consider (Reject, col. 2), those they could not say whether they would consider even though they had an opinion (Hold, col. 3), and those for which they had not formed an opinion (Foggy, col. 4).

The number in each cell of Table 10-1 is the average value for one of the four variables in the CDM. The results even for microcomputers are consistent. The values are strongest for the brands in their evoked sets, the weakest are in their reject sets, the next strongest to the evoked sets are the hold sets, and then the foggy sets. Table 10-1 thus gives you a good picture of what the market out there is like now. If your brand is in their evoked sets, your marketing task is obviously going to be radically different than if it is in their reject sets. If your brand is in their hold sets, the task would appear to be mainly a communication job with considerable uncertainty as to which way they may go once they become adequately informed. The outcome of those with foggy sets is most uncertain and would suggest substantially more analyses of the existing data such as of their attitude ratios, and probably additional data should be collected before proceeding.

With this background to draw upon, let us proceed to examine the relevance of consumer theory for designing core strategy for each of the four key components of marketing strategy—product, price, promotion, and distribution—in terms of securing a competitive advantage in RPS.

[3] M. Laroche, J. A. Rosenblatt, F. Bliemel, and R. K. Ransom, "The Economic Impact of Price-Quality Evaluations on Brand Categorization: The Examination of the Microcomputer Market," working papers series (Concordia University, Montreal, January 1986).

2. PRODUCT DESIGN

Product design in RPS can be more effective in developing strategy than it might appear. Lack of technology is likely to prevent a major change, but a small change directed to modifying the product to conform more closely to the customers' needs can substantially strengthen a product. For example, P&G has historically shown remarkable skill in identifying the potential for small but significant changes in RPS products. Chairman Harness illustrated this with Ivory Soap, Crisco, Tide, Crest, and Pampers. In reporting on these five leading products, he said, "their combined age is 220 years, and their average age is 44 years. The oldest of these brands is 97 and the youngest is 10 years old."[4] The five products and their ages were Ivory (97), Crisco (64), Tide (29), Crest (20), and Pampers (10). He reported that continual product improvement is the major reason for this performance. Recently, however, P&G has found that competitors are catching up with it in being able to gauge the customer's needs.[5]

3. PRICING

3.1 Introduction

The high sensitivity of RPS consumers to the price of competing brands implied in the introduction to the chapter encourages our attention to price. However, the customer in RPS is usually price inelastic, and the total market is not much affected by price changes. Consequently, extensive use of price can be a risky game in which all competitors end up selling at a lower price with lower dollar sales and no gain in share. Therefore, because of the competitive sensitivity to price, we need to introduce the general idea of competition.

It may seem inappropriate to discuss competition in a buyer behavior text. But price is usually one of the major market variables to a consumer in RPS and to discuss the consumer's response to price, ignoring competition, is highly unrealistic. Also, competition conditions the effect of other marketing variables upon buyer behavior as well. How your advertising affects the consumer depends, in part, on your competitor's advertising as shown by the competitive vulnerability model later in the chapter. Further, in Figure 10-2 we see how the consumer determines the nature of competition. Here, however, we are recognizing that the product hierarchy not only guides the consumer's information processing but, very important, also describes competition. At the bottom level of the product hierarchy *direct* competition is being shown. Specifically, Toyota Corolla and Ford Escort compete directly with each other. At the next level, the competition is *indirect*, and farther up in the hierarchy, it is still more indirect.

[4] E. G. Harness, "Some Basic Beliefs About Marketing," speech to the Conference Board (New York, October 21, 1976), p. 1.
[5] *The Wall Street Journal* (New York edition), May 1, 1985, p. 35.

Product Hierarchy for Automobiles

Information Processing

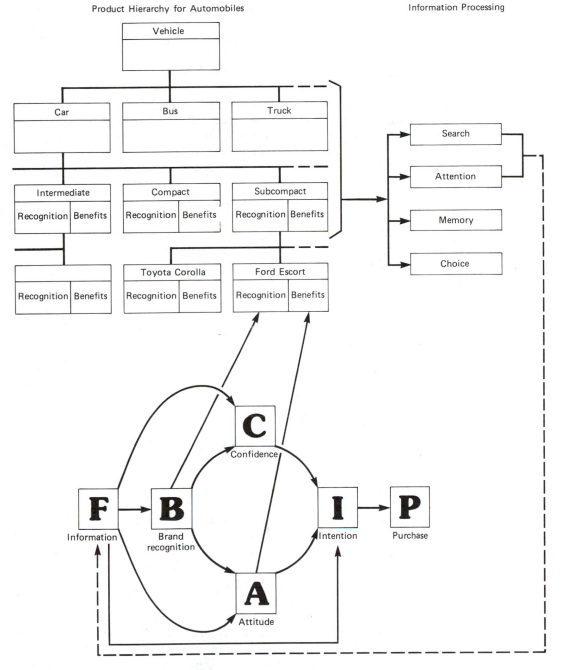

Figure 10-2   Theory of Consumer Behavior

Earlier in Chapter 9 we learned from a study by Greg Carpenter that the consumer has a greater effect on company profits than does competition, contrary to what managers usually think.[6] More recently we have learned that Figure 10-2 is a valid way of thinking about the way consumers behave as shown by Mita Sujan's finding that the consumer's product hierarchy does guide the consumer's information processing as discussed in Chapter 5.[7] This fact opens up a number of strategic possibilities; for example, we can now use the concept of prototypicality of a brand as discussed in Chapter 4. In designing or otherwise positioning a brand, the optimum position is the "most typical" or middlemost in the consumer's prototype for that product category. But this goes much beyond our needs here, and let us return to the specific issue of pricing.

To a customer, the price he pays for a product is much more than a number. It has at least two major symbolic roles. First, it can indicate forgone pleasure—money spent in buying one product is no longer available to spend for anything else he desires. As such, it's a symbol of *sacrifice*. Second, price can be a symbol of product *quality*: the higher the price, the better the quality, or so he believes. This second symbolic role may sound absurd, but if a consumer doesn't know much about a brand, the rule of a price-quality association is a logical one to follow. Third, the absolute price level also serves a *motivational* role: the higher the price, the more important the product, other things being equal; thus price can stimulate the consumer's search for information.

Although very important, price is only one dimension of a company's marketing strategy. Other elements of that strategy, such as the customer's expectations of cost, can influence his response to price. For example, because of this possibility, Texas Instruments for some time followed the practice of "forward pricing" its semiconductors. That is, it lowered the price in anticipation of a greater volume of sales—and thus lower costs. Recently, however, it appears to have dropped the practice.

3.2   Where Price Impacts

One of the first questions to be answered in using the CDM to deal with pricing problems is where price impacts on the model. That point of impact depends upon the particular situation. First, let us deal with buyers in RPS. In RPS, as discussed in Chapter 6, price has become separated from the brand image in the buyer's mind and is operating independently of that image. If in this situation the customer knows the price of the brand *before* she goes to buy, the price will probably impact the buyer's intention to buy, as Pr in Figure 10-1. If, on the other hand, the buyer only learns the price when she goes to buy in the store, price will probably impact purchase instead of intention. Finally, it is believed that buyers in EPS and LPS usually perceive price as a dimension of

[6] G. Carpenter, "Product Quality, General Promotion and Profitability," unpublished working paper (Center for Marketing Studies, U.C.L.A., Los Angeles, 1983).
[7] M. Sujan, "Consumer Knowledge: Effects on Evaluation Strategies Mediating Consumer Judgments," *Journal of Consumer Research*, 12, no. 1 (June 1985), 31–46.

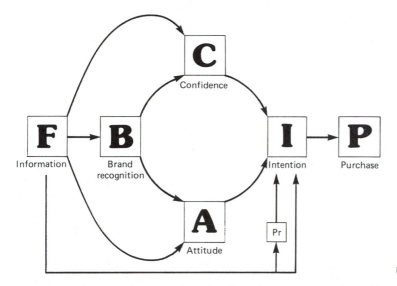

Figure 10-3   Impact of Price on CDM

the product, and so in those two cases, price affects attitude. To simplify the discussion here, we will refer only to the price-intention relationship and *omit* the availability (distribution)–intention relation as shown in Figure 10-3.

How much the price impacts intention (I) depends upon the particular conditions. Two conditions that matter most in pricing are the responsiveness of the customer and the nature of competition.

3.3   Customer Response to Price

Following are a variety of aspects of the customer's response to price. Knowing these can be helpful in interpreting the measure of price effects using the CDM.

3.3.1 Amount of Effect.   Does price really make a difference in whether a consumer purchases our product? And does it have a large effect or a small effect upon the quantity he intends to purchase? In reviewing a number of econometric studies, Bass concludes that price has a much stronger effect than does advertising.[8] But, in addition to studying the size of this relationship, we must also look at the direction of the relationship.

3.3.2 Direction of Relationship.   Normally, you expect a negative relationship between price and intention: the higher the price, the lower the intention to buy. This is the case where the customer uses price as a symbol of sacrifice.[9]

---

[8] F. M. Bass, "Some Case Histories of Econometric Modeling in Marketing: What Really Happened?" *Interfaces*, 10, no. 1 (February 1980), 86–91.

[9] G. E. Eskin and P. H. Baron, "Effects of Price and Advertising in Test Market Experiments," *Journal of Marketing Research*, XIV (November 1977), 499–508. For a behavior review of price effects, see J. C. Olson, "Price as an Informational Cue: Effects on Product Evaluations," in A. G. Woodside, J. N. Sheth, and P. D. Bennett, eds., *Consumer and Industrial Buying Behavior* (New York: North-Holland, 1977), pp. 267–86.

But, as mentioned, price can also be a symbol of product quality: the customer believes that the higher the price, the higher the product quality. For example, Nabisco had been selling Fleischman's gin at $4.50 for 750 milliliter bottles and losing share. Over two years ago, it raised the price to $5.50. Ferdie Falk, in charge of Nabisco's beverages, reports: "The strategy helped incredibly. Sales were deteriorating; now they are coming up. Sales are considerably above last year."[10]

This second role that price plays can occur when the customer is not well informed about the quality of the product and/or the product has social-status implications. The latter is probably true of the Fleischman's gin example. Evidence shows that a price-quality association is usually formed when price is the only information that is given the customer.[11] However, when information other than price ("other cues") is also given the customer, the findings do not clearly support the notion that customers make a price-quality association.[12]

3.3.3 Psychological Pricing. It is generally believed by practitioners that whether the price is "odd" or "even"—$.99 instead of $1.00—can make a substantial difference in the customer's response. This may or may not be true, but it is fair to say, as one marketing researcher puts it, that "many other factors are probably more important than odd-even pricing."[13]

3.3.4 Product Line Pricing. Setting prices for different brands in a product line—recognizing that they may be interdependent on either or both the cost and demand side—is a common marketing problem, and yet it raises new challenges for the manager. If the brands are substitutes for each other, and so interdependent on the demand side, they can cannibalize each other. Or they can complement and support one another—as razor blades do with razors and cameras with film.

Product line pricing is further complicated by the issue of range of prices. The low-end price is most often remembered and therefore can be a traffic builder. However, the high-end price is more visible than are intermediate and low-end prices, and if buyers associate the higher-price product with quality, purchase may be inhibited by a low price.

In sum, these are some of the elements that should be incorporated into the CDM to obtain and interpret the data the marketer needs to make his price decisions.

3.3.5 Price Structure Decisions. The marketer also often must make a variety of price discount or structure decisions. Price structure involves determining

---

[10] *The Wall Street Journal* (New York edition), November 25, 1981, p. 29.

[11] D. M. Gardner, The Role of Price in Consumer Choice," in R. Ferber, ed., *Selected Aspects of Consumer Behavior* (Washington, D.C.: U.S. Supt. of Documents, National Science Foundation, 1976), p. 424.

[12] Ibid., pp. 424–26, 428.

[13] Ibid., p. 419.

such things as (1) the time and conditions of payment, (2) the nature of discounts to be allowed the customer, and (3) where and when the customer is to take title to the goods. Two very common types of discounts are (1) cash discounts (lower price if sale is for cash instead of credit) and (2) quantity discounts (price is lower for larger volume of sales). Trade (distributors), quantity, and cash discounts are the most common, and, of these, the cash discount is probably the most common.[14]

Although we typically think of total satisfaction as the criterion for choosing price in the case of cash discounts, we should use marginal satisfaction. When these discounts are given, it generally indicates that consumers' marginal satisfaction is likely to be declining—meaning they aren't as apt to buy additional units of a brand at the same price. Hence, although the customer may not be willing to pay the full price for an additional unit, he will be willing to buy it if he can pay something less for it. By adjusting price through a quantity or cash discount, the marketer may be able to sell substantially more units over the entire market of all customers, providing he has a market that is protected from competition; that is, there is an unusually strong preference for his brand.

Let us be more specific about marginal pricing. In all of the discussion up to now, *total* satisfaction as captured in the satisfaction variable of the CDM described in Chapter 3 was the issue. The buyer acts according to the total satisfaction that he receives. However, when it comes to how much the buyer will spend on a product—that is, how many units he will purchase—economists have long argued that it is the anticipated *marginal* satisfaction that is the determining variable, not the anticipated total satisfaction.[15] The central issue is how much satisfaction he gets from buying the *additional* unit. In technical terms, the marginal satisfaction is a derivative of total satisfaction, as shown in Figure 10-4. It is the slope of the curve instead of the absolute level of it.

If we are deciding whether to increase the volume of sales in a protected market, then we look at the satisfaction the buyer gets from purchasing additional units as a guide to setting not only the price but the entire marketing mix. However, the marketer can price according to marginal satisfaction only if his product has a differential advantage, that is, if he controls the marginal unit as Reynolds did with aluminum wrap especially after Alcoa and Kaiser withdrew from the market. This marginal satisfaction approach can be carried out by fitting a straight line tangent to the total revenue relation in Figure 10-4 and parallel to the total cost. The optimum sales volume is 750,000 units.

3.4 Competitive Vulnerability

3.4.1 Introduction. Several times in this discussion of pricing we have referred to the effect of competitors. The first step is to identify your competitors. This

[14] K. B. Monroe and A. J. Della Bitta, "Models for Pricing Decisions," *Journal of Marketing Research*, XV (August 1978), pp. 422–25.

[15] R. G. Lipsey and P. O. Steiner, *Economics*, 6th ed. (New York: Harper & Row, 1981), pp. 243–44.

Figure 10-4 Total Revenue and Total Cost for Post Instant Breakfast

is the role of the product hierarchy, which, you will recall from Chapter 4, also guides the thinking of customers. The measurement of product hierarchy is now possible.[16]

Second, the marketer is probably not equally vulnerable to all of them, and he would like to know specifically to which competitor he is most vulnerable and by how much. This question can be answered by the CDM discussed next.

3.4.2 Measurement of Competitive Vulnerability. Competition as a factor influencing the performance of your product in the market has not been dealt with quantitatively up to now. But like Banquo's ghost in *Macbeth*, it has hovered in the background of all our discussion of the CDM. In fact, most current strategic planning is focused primarily upon the competition and secondarily upon the customer whereas we reverse the roles here. How can we tie competition into the CDM more systematically and thus greatly enhance the understanding of the market that the CDM can give us? We have already seen how to do it analytically in Figure 10-3. Now you will see it done empirically.

Computing the cross-elasticity measures for our product and each of the key competing products as discussed in economics is difficult if not impossible. A far easier and much more meaningful way to integrate competitive effects into the CDM directly, however, is by obtaining measures of competitive vulnerability, as shown in Table 10-2.

Table 10-2 represents the details of a study of the beer market in Quebec by Laroche and Brisoux in 1980.[17] Here each of the brands is from the 11-

[16] S. Sattath and A. Tversky, "Additive Similarity Trees," *Psychometrika*, 42, no. 3 (September 1977), 319–45.

[17] M. Laroche and J. E. Brisoux, "A Test of the Competitive Effects in the Relationship Among Attitudes and Intentions," in K. Bernhardt and others, eds., *The Changing Marketing Environment: New Theories and Applications* (Chicago: American Marketing Association, 1981), pp. 213–16.

Table 10-2 Vulnerability Model*

Attitudes

Intention (Attitude)	Laurentide	Labatt 50	Molson Export	O'Keefe	Labatt Blue	Brador	Carlsberg	Black Label	Dow	Canadian	Heidelberg	Constant	R-Square Adjusted
Laurentide 2.79	.4495† (141)	−.1969† (27)	−.1071† (7.1)	−.1234† (11)	−.0924‡ (4.7)				−.1439‡ (3.8)			2.478† (35)	.3520† (35)
Labatt 50 2.60	−.1568‡ (20)	.4840† (179)	−.1245† (12)	−.0884‡ (6.5)		−.0795§ (2.9)	−.1083§ (3.6)				−.2197† (4.2)	2.209† (31)	.4332† (44)
Molson Export 1.80		−.1012† (9.5)	.4431† (178)		−.0630§ (3.2)							.7212† (6.8)	.3839† (79)
O'Keefe 1.37	−.0836† (9.0)		−.0480§ (2.9)	.3242‡ (139)								.7207† (8.8)	.3062† (56)
Labatt Blue .49	−.0435‡ (5.8)	−.0173† (6.8)	−.0512† (7.8)		.1896† (86)						.0948§ (3.3)	.7113† (15)	.2326† (21)
Brador .40	−.0472† (12)					.2443† (171)	−.0516§ (5.8)		−.9488§ (3.11)			.3730† (14)	.3223† (46)
Carlsberg .28		−.0253‡ (4.1)	−.0433‡ (12)		−.0513† (1.1)		.2604† (174)				.1098† (8.4)	.3934† (13)	.3980† (50)
Black Label .12	−.0203‡ (7.0)		−.0251† (11)	−.0188‡ (6.1)				.2515‡ (237)				.2806† (18)	.4044† (65)
Dow .11	−.0123‡ (4.2)	−.0169† (8.2)		−.0133‡ (5.2)	−.0117§ (3.0)	−.0165‡ (4.3)			.1425‡ (139)	−.0300‡ (5.0)		.2995† (24)	.2398† (23)
Canadian .04	−.0071§ (3.2)	−.0092‡ (5.3)	−.0111† (7.3)	−.0084‡ (4.8)						.0639† (54)		.1631† (16)	.1363† (13)
Heidelberg .03	−.0070‡ (4.1)						.0101§ (3.3)				.0649† (38)	.0378 (0)	.1252† (19)

*Members in parentheses are F-tests.

†Significant at $p < .01$.

‡Significant at $p < .05$.

§Significant at $p < .10$.

SOURCE: M. Laroche and J. E. Brisoux, "A Test of the Competitive Effects in the Relationship Among Attitudes and Intentions," in K. Bernhardt and others, eds. *The Changing Marketing Environment: New Theories and Applications* (Chicago: American Marketing Association, 1981), p. 215.

brand beer market. Previous research, such as the Dutch study, has shown that beer tends to be RPS. Typically, however, the CDM would be applied only to your key competitors instead of the entire market as is done here.

In fact, the only difference between the data from the beer market and that which we have been thinking about in discussing the CDM up to now is the intention to buy (I) measure. The intention (I) measure used here is a *"constant sum scale."* The customer is given 100 points as a "constant sum" and is asked to allocate these points according to his intention to buy each of the 11 brands. This measure of intention (I) causes the customer to rate his intention to buy each brand more carefully in relation to his intention to buy each of the competing brands. Hence, it provides a more accurate measure than the simple intention scale presented in Chapter 3.

You should work carefully through Table 10-2 to understand the process of analysis and what the numbers mean. But, first let us concentrate on the upper left-hand cell. There consumers' attitudes toward Laurentide are related to consumers' intentions to buy Laurentide. As you see, the highly significant regression coefficient is +.4495 with an F value of 141 (where 4 is a significance level of about .99). Also, the mean intention for Laurentide is the highest of all, 2.79. These are all strong relations.

Now, knowing the meaning of the numbers in the upper left corner cell of Table 10-2, let us explain the other numbers in the table. The column descriptors are "Attitudes" and the row descriptors are "Intentions." In each cell is a regression coefficient relating the attitude (A) toward that brand in the column to the intention (I) to buy the beer shown in the row. In this way each row becomes a series of regression coefficients as you see in the following example from Table 10-2 relating attitude (A) toward a given beer to the intention (I) to buy another beer, except on the diagonal, which is our familiar situation.

$$I_{Lau} = 2.478 + .4495A_{Lau} - .1969A_{Lab} - .1071A_{Mol} - .1234A_{OK} - .0924A_{LB} - .1439_{Dow}$$

Only the first A in row 1 is the coefficient positive. The other A coefficients, with a slight exception of five missing coefficients, are negative, which is what you would expect. The more favorably a customer is disposed to one brand, the lower will be his intention to buy another brand. The missing coefficients were not significant.

Thus, as in Figure 10-1 we are modeling each brand but using only attitude (A) and intention (I), the heart of the CDM as shown in Figure 10-5. However, this analysis can incorporate the total model. In this way, it is possible to *analyze* and *predict* not only how customers will respond to a brand, but how vulnerable it will be to the competitive effects of key competitors such as when they change customers' attitudes toward their brands. For example, if Labatt 50 succeeds in improving the attitudes toward its beer, the negative effect upon Laurentide's sales will become greater.

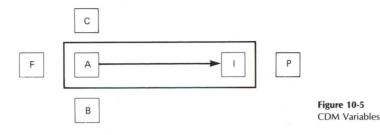

Figure 10-5
CDM Variables

3.4.3 Significance of the Measurement.

Now, let us be specific. As you can see, the *best* predictor of intention (I) for each of the 11 brands of beer in Quebec in 1980 is the customers' attitude (A) toward that respective beer. We know this by the fact that the coefficients on the diagonal are far larger than are those elsewhere in the diagram and are positive. Check this. The coefficients of attitudes toward other brands, which is the measure of *competitive vulnerability*, are much smaller, as you see.

Let us discuss these measures of competitive vulnerability. If a line is drawn through the diagonal cells, there are 41 off-diagonal relations. These are significant competitive effects operating in that market out of a possible 110 effects: $(11 \times 11) - 11$ diagonal cells $= 110$ effects. Note in Table 10-2 that F is being used in parentheses instead of t values, that is, $t^2 = $ F; for example, $2^2 = 4$.

Further, 38 of the 41 *off*-diagonal relations are negative, which is what you would expect, and therefore this gives you greater confidence in the validity of the approach to measuring competitive effects. Is the "negativity" surprising to you? The more you like one brand, the less you are likely to intend to buy another brand? If you think about it, you will not find it surprising.

Out of the three off-diagonal relations that are not negative, only one (Heidelberg → Carlsberg) is significant. The other two (Heidelberg → Labatt Blue, Carlsberg → Heidelberg) are not significant. You will recall from basic economics that the Heidelberg-Carlsberg relations represents *complementary products* instead of the usual substitute products that we think of when dealing with competition. Is there a reason why Heidelberg and Carlsberg should be complementary brands, which means that if you like one you also intend to buy more of the other? An example of complementary products could be butter and bread. Someone familiar with this particular beer market could probably answer this question.

Further, out of the 41 competitive effects, only 18 represent reciprocal effects: one brand is affecting a second brand and the second brand is also affecting the first brand. What is the meaning of this reciprocal effect? When the effects are reciprocal, each one is battling the other directly; the familiar "head-on competition," as it is called. Where these reciprocal effects are strong, we can probably assume that they represent oligopoly cases, which in economic terminology are called "interdependence recognized." Reciprocal effects are used as a measure of the competitive strength of each company. For some of these

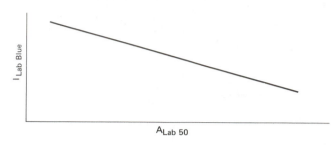

Figure 10-6
Intention for Lab Blue Related to
Attitude for Lab 50

reciprocal relations, the coefficients are fairly similar. What are some examples? What does it mean? It means that the competitive strengths are about the same.

The remaining 24 significant relations are not reciprocal. What is the meaning of this lack of "reciprocity"? It means that brand A is vulnerable to competitive promotional effects of brand B but B is not vulnerable to A. For example, a campaign designed to inspire customers' attitude toward Labatt 50 would lead to an increase in intention (I) toward it and a decrease in $I_{Lab\ Blue}$ as shown in Figure 10-6. At the same time an increase in $A_{Lab\ Blue}$ would have no effect on the intention toward Lab 50 as seen in Figure 10-7.

3.4.4 Predictive Power of Measurements. Having interpreted the relations in terms of their explanatory power, what can we say about their *predictive* power? First, this model, which incorporates the effects of competitors, can be compared with our usual CDM where previously until this chapter competitive effects have not been included. We find that by incorporating competitive effects, the R^2 for every brand was improved somewhat at a significance level of .95 or better, which gives us confidence in the results. Thus, the competitive effects model will improve your estimates of change in intentions (and so of changes in market share) following competitive actions and counteractions.

Second, it also allows the marketer to identify the strength of particular competitors in competition with a specific brand and so enable her to sharpen her marketing strategy. Finally, she can use it to trace the effects of an advertising campaign. She can first check changes in the customer's attitude due to advertising by using the regular CDM. Then through the multiple effects version of the CDM shown in Table 10-2 she can determine how this will increase their increased intentions toward her brand due to the increase in attitude toward her brand and how much it will decrease their intention toward which particular competing brands. This gives her a much fuller and more precise picture of the consequences of her advertising.

3.4.5 Conclusions on Competitive Vulnerability. When studying customer behavior, it is no longer necessary for competition to hover in the background like Banquo's ghost. Using the CDM, it has now been brought into the open to permit a complete view of the market that incorporates *both* customers *and* competitors. This more complete, integrated view provides a much better foundation upon which to build strategy.

Figure 10-7
Intention for Lab 50 Related to
Attitude for Lab Blue

One point to bear in mind is that the entry of a new brand as discussed in Chapter 3 does not much change the slope of the relations in a CDM of a competing brand.[18] Its effect is to move customers on the intention scale instead of changing the slope of the relation between attitude and intention. Thus, the measure of vulnerability is dependable.

Finally, by knowing the output of the vulnerability model from customers and competitors, a manager is in a far better position to design an effective core strategy that will give him a competitive advantage. This knowledge can also be the foundation for designing a promotion strategy, which we turn to next.

4. PROMOTION

The notion of cyclic behavior that characterizes routine buying is obviously highly relevant for promotion decisions as we saw in Chapter 6. Let us focus upon advertising alone to simplify. Economists earlier believed that advertising is not socially justified in an RPS market because consumers are well informed as will be discussed in Chapter 18. Cyclic behavior, however, indicates there is indeed a role for advertising for roughly three-fourths of the consumer population. The other one-fourth will be discussed in the paragraphs that follow.

These cyclic buyers are apparently not well informed about all the brands in their evoked sets. While they are in one of their periodic "shopping-around stages" as described at length in Chapter 6, they are open to information about these lesser brands in their evoked set of satisfactory brands. Also, they find it easy to process information because they are well informed about these brands and have well-developed expectations about information to guide them. Thus, they are likely to take in substantial information even though they are in a state of low involvement.

4.1 Copy

Just what the copy content should be is an important consideration. We would expect the brand recognition to be fairly well established. Krugman has empha-

---

[18] J. U. Farley, D. R. Lehmann, R. S. Winer, and J. P. Katz, "Parameter Stability and 'Carry-Over Effects' in a Consumer Decision-Process Model," *Journal of Consumer Research*, 8, no. 4 (March 1982), 465–71.

sized that in "low-interest, low-involvement, repeat-purchase products"—the typical RPS case—in an Advertising Research Foundation study of 1956 showed that recognition (of pictures) was much stronger and more enduring than was recall (of words).[19] It did not specify the recognition, however, to be *brand* recognition, as it is defined here. It could have been pictures in the ad that did not show the product. Nevertheless, Krugman phrased it as follows, "[This situation] is best described as an audience that recognizes the pictures and images but cannot recall the words. We are all like the person who claims, 'I don't remember your name, but I never forget a face.' "[20]

Copy should be specifically tailored to the relevant benefits, and generally, the more important benefits. These would probably also be the ads that will cause the consumer to think when he encounters them. Information about benefits and cognitive responses to the ads appear to account for about 40–60% of the effect of advertising.[21]

Another possible copy strategy in RPS is that of confidence building. As we saw back in Chapter 6, Figure 6-2, the effect of confidence on intention was strengthened by a stronger attitude; however, this approach requires building attitude. Further, it appears that attitude builds earlier. Consequently, copy that builds confidence may be especially effective in RPS where attitude is likely to already be substantial.

Still another copy strategy is to design ads that customers like. In fact, liking the ad explains most of the effect beyond benefits and cognitive responses.[22] It may well be that where interbrand differences are not large as in RPS, entertaining ads are more effective in shifting consumers from one brand to another. Entertainment has become a substantially greater proportion of television ad copy.[23] One reason is to decrease the viewer's tendency to use his technologically increased capacity to "zap" ads. But there is also a belief that entertainment is more effective than previously thought. According to Video Storyboard, a TV ratings concern, Pepsico's ad was the top ranking TV ad in 1985. It was "a sly commercial in which archeology students in another century find a relic nobody can identify: a Coca-Cola bottle."[24] Also, a former advertising tenet was to mention the brand name 4 to 10 times early in a commercial. Now, only at the end is it more likely to be found.

In specifying the benefits to stress in promotion up to now, we have omitted a type of benefit that probably is often an important influence in RPS. This type of benefit is emotional; for example, Gucci perfume recently distributed

[19] H. E. Krugman, "Point of View: Measuring Memory—An Industry Dilemma," *Journal of Advertising Research*, 25, no. 4 (August–September 1985), 49–51.

[20] Ibid., p. 51.

[21] A. A. Mitchell, "Cognitive Processes Indicated by Advertising," in R. J. Harris, ed., *Information Processing Research in Advertising* (Hillsdale, N.J.: Lawrence Erlbaum Associates, 1983), pp. 26–27.

[22] Ibid., p. 37.

[23] For an extensive review see *The New York Times*, September 1, 1985, p. F7.

[24] *The Wall Street Journal* (New York edition), March 13, 1986, p. 33.

a brochure in which it referred to Gucci No. 3 as "Elegant. Indefinably sophisticated. Confidently contemporary." Does this sound like our usual, utilitarian benefits? The utilitarian type of benefit for most products is probably dominant. But in RPS, the brands tend to be alike, and managers search for distinguishing characteristics of the brand. Also, the brand is probably being used, and usage may involve emotional experiences as has been emphasized. Hence, emotion may well provide that distinguishing characteristic. This is not a well-studied area, but substantial attention is now being devoted to it. A recent article by *Advertising Age* illustrates it:

> Advertisers and their ad agencies have found new ways to tug on consumers' heartstrings and tickle their funny bones with animals. Today, it's a man and his dog—and his Cutty Sark. A woman and her two cats—and her Kodak disc camera. A group of poker players and their four-footed, Stroh's-loving bartender, Alex.[25]

Joseph T. Plummer, a professional psychologist and executive vice president of Young & Rubicam is an advocate of emotional advertising and is quoted as saying

> all great selling ideas establish a vital emotional bond with their prospects. Some examples include:
> - Avis tapping inherent sympathy for the underdog;
> - Clairol relieving anxiety by promising no woman on earth will know when you dye your hair;
> - Miller Lite assuring you that the boys won't think you're a sissy for drinking a light beer;
> - Perrier giving you permission not to drink alcohol if you don't want to; and
> - American Express promising that even "achievers" won't go unnoticed when travelling.[26]

Holbrook and O'Shaughnessy have recently reviewed the evidence and developed a way of describing the complex emotional process but in a familiar framework shown in Figure 10-8.[27] On the left you see information input, "Message, object, or event." It leads to the formation of "Cognitive beliefs," which are the utilitarian benefits the category offers. From this emerges an "Evaluation" of the brand to which "Personal values" give importances to the "Cognitive beliefs." This leads to "Desires," which in turn stimulates "Expressive behavior." This is all pretty much familiar.

Now to emotion. Holbrook and O'Shaughnessy conclude that for that evaluation stage to be a part of an emotion, the evaluation must prompt some

---

[25] J. L. Erickson, "Ads' Animal Magnetism Has Deep Roots," *Advertising Age*, February 10, 1986, p. 45.

[26] "Emotions Important for Successful Advertising," *Marketing News*, April 12, 1985, p. 18.

[27] M. B. Holbrook and J. O'Shaughnessy, "The Role of Emotion in Advertising," *Psychology and Marketing*, 1, no. 2 (Summer 1984), 45–64.

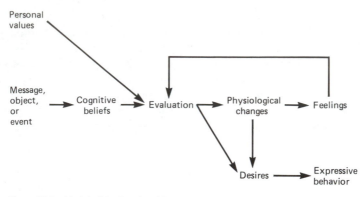

Figure 10-8 Model of the Emotional Process

SOURCE: M. B. Holbrook and J. O'Shaughnessy, "The Role of Emotion in Advertising," *Psychology and Marketing*, 1, no. 2 (Summer 1984), 50.

physiological changes such as pulse rate, sweat glands, muscles, hormones, or brain waves. These physiological responses when experienced result in "Feelings," that is, emotion. These feelings, in turn, feedback to aid evaluation of the product as shown in Figure 10-8.

Having reviewed the process of emotion, can we be more specific? We can. In Table 10-3 on the left you will notice the three broad categories of emotion: pleasure (P), arousal (A), and dominance (D). This is the PAD typology of emotions. PAD represents more specific emotions that are to the right and represent the extremes, that is, joy and sadness. These are emotions that might be used in advertising.

An illustration of each of the three PAD categories of emotions can help you see their relevance. For pleasure we could think of a direct experience of sensuous gratification, physical comfort, or social intimacy. Sexy imagery of perfume might evoke such feelings. Then, later, seeing the brand on the retailer's shelf probably comes to trigger a favorable response. Arousal can be illustrated by an ad about Pepsi where the drinkers are gathered on a beach with some

Table 10-3 A Typology of Emotional Content

	Positive	*Negative*
Pleasure	Joy	Sadness
	Friendliness	Loneliness
Arousal	Vitality	Sluggishness
	Liveliness	Overstimulation
Dominance	Competence	Futility
	Self-fulfillment	Ennui

SOURCE: M. B. Holbrook and J. O'Shaughnessy, "The Role of Emotion in Advertising," *Psychology and Marketing*, 1, no. 2 (Summer 1984), 54.

satisfactory level of activity, enough to be enjoyable but not so much as to be extremely physical. Finally, feelings of dominance could be generated by emotional appeals related to the motivating effect of competence. The associated feelings of mastery and self-fulfillment can be viewed as desirable for their own sake.

Having explained the nature of the emotion process, it must be emphasized that in product maturity (RPS), cognitively recognizable differences among brands are sometimes competed away until the brands are much alike. In these circumstances, emotion can be used to add a dimension of difference and so provide a brand with a competitive advantage.

4.2 Media

The media used to convey this copy should be convenient to the consumer. He would not be expected to search as extensively in RPS as in LPS especially if competitive advertising can also meet those needs.

Nothing so far has been said about differences among consumers that are often essential in allocating the budget. These are obviously important in RPS in the form of the roughly one-fourth, at least in food items, who buy the same brand repeatedly but can be relevant for all consumers.

4.3 Budget

The advertising budget should probably be substantially smaller than for LPS. One caution is that though high budgets appear more common for RPS products than this recommendation suggests, you must bear in mind that they appear larger because the markets are typically larger for mature (RRB) products. Assael has reviewed substantial evidence on the characteristics of people who are brand loyal.[28] He cites such characteristics as being more influenced by reference groups, being more self-confident, perceiving a higher level of needs in the purchase, and being store loyal. Individual differences will be dealt with at length in Part IV.

4.4 Conclusion on Promotion

Nothing is said here about salespeople, because for products where RPS is the typical case, salespeople are usually too expensive as a means of communicating directly with the consumer. True, "telemarketing," the use of the telephone, has modified this conclusion somewhat, but not a lot.

Advertising is essential to most consumers in RPS and so is usually a key feature of an RPS strategy. Important benefits and confidence building should be the focus of copy. Liking the ad is also relevant. Emotional benefits, illustrated by the P (pleasure), A (arousal), D (dominance) typology, are more

---

[28] H. Assael, *Consumer Behavior and Marketing Action* (Boston: Kent, 1981), pp. 69–70.

likely to be important than in LPS or EPS because differences among brands are usually less in RPS.

Media should be carefully chosen because RPS customers are not inclined to search. Segmenting variables are often essential.

The budget can be substantially smaller than in LPS and much less than in EPS.

5. DISTRIBUTION

One element of strategy for RPS buyers can be to reduce costs of distribution. An avenue for accomplishing the cost reduction is to route the brand through a lower-margin channel. A way to aid your thinking in this direction is to use Figure 8-5, "Consumer Store Choice Based on Consumer Product Characteristics." This diagram is repeated in Figure 10-9 but is used dynamically here. Here we look at the possibility of shifting to convenience good retail stores where the margins are perhaps 25–30% as compared with department store margins of about 39%, specialty store margins of about 43%, and shopping stores of 50%.

Figure 10-9 Consumer Store Choice Based on Consumer and Product Characteristics

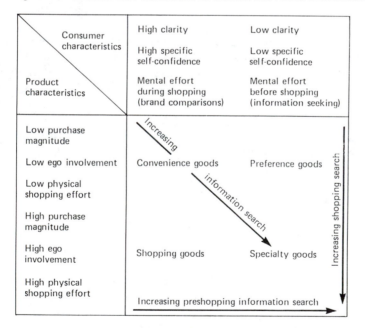

SOURCE: M. B. Holbrook and J. A. Howard, "Frequently Purchased Nondurable Goods and Services," in R. Ferber, ed., National Science Foundation, *Selected Aspects of Consumer Behavior* (Washington, D.C.: U.S. Supt. of Documents, 1976), p. 215.

As the diagram indicates, it is a case where the consumer has a clear picture in her mind of the product, is confident of her ability to judge it, and carries out much search for information while shopping. Also, this is most likely where the product is characterized by low value, low involvement, and low shopping effort. The movement toward RPS will itself bring about some of these last three characteristics.

One example of how consumers change over the PLC is seen in a study of German mothers with their first baby. They shifted from specialty stores to discount stores in buying baby fruit as they came to know the product and brands and became accustomed to buying it for the child.[29] Even more striking is how the distribution of women's panty hose has tended to shift as mentioned earlier—from specialty stores then to department stores and finally to supermarkets as the category moved up the product life cycle.

The CDM can guide the marketing manager of an RPS product in deciding where a product is on the PLC and therefore which of the three types of stores is appropriate for his product.

6. CONCLUSIONS

The RPS case is the most common situation that you will encounter. The major problem is to develop a core strategy that provides a differential advantage for the product.

In RPS, price typically is a major aspect of strategy and is separated from attitude (A) in the CDM and impacts upon intention (I). But the nature of the relationship is complex.

One of the most critical aspects in pricing in RPS is making judgments about how your competitors will respond to your price decision and how that response will affect you. For example, a competitor may respond to your price cut by upping his advertising. There is now an effective way of measuring your vulnerability to particular competitors as described in the chapter.

Promotion is usually an integral part of an RPS strategy. Benefits are an important part of copy, but the nature of these benefits can be different from those with LPS or EPS. Liking the ad and emotional benefits are relatively more important. Media should be carefully chosen and often requires market segmentation. A smaller budget is typically enough.

In distribution there is usually a drive to move toward lower-cost retail outlets, but this must be done with care.

Finally, the tendency of a large proportion of RPS consumers to be looking around for something new suggests opportunity for the strategist. He should be looking for new technology to initiate a new PLC that will give him the "attacker's advantage" described in Chapter 8.

[29] K. P. Kaas, "Consumer Habit Forming Information Acquisition, and Buying Behavior," *Journal of Business Research*, 10 (1982), 3–15.

Questions

1. How can the concept of an evoked set of brands be useful in designing marketing strategy?
2. It is said that price can be either a symbol of sacrifice or a symbol of quality to a consumer. Explain the difference between these two roles of price.
3. How can you use a measure of competitive vulnerability in designing core strategy?
4. How would you describe and illustrate emotion as an element of advertising copy?
5. What are the consumer and product characteristics most relevant in selecting retail stores for an RPS product?

CHAPTER 11

Strategy for Organizational Buying*

1. INTRODUCTION

The objective in this chapter is to describe the effect of the *formal* organization upon the behavior of those people buying for that organization. The formal organization is a type of social group like the family and other *informal* groups of great variety discussed later in Part IV. In the formal organization, however, the group relations are much more fixed and highly influential in shaping its buying behavior. This is reflected in the concept of the "buying center" as the group of people making the purchase decision instead of one person. It will be developed in the paragraphs that follow.

The need to think of the organization in marketing is especially critical in the health area that has become so conspicuous in marketing within the last decade. This need arises because marketing health to individual consumers is fairly new and so the need is obvious. The need is even greater, however, for the health organizations themselves that will be marketing to and buying from other organizations. This marketing interaction between two organizations is especially complex, as you will see in the following pages.

The strong need is also seen in the legal area where large organizations are even more recent than in health. "The megafirms—the half dozen or so with more than 500 lawyers—are opening branches in major cities and aggres-

---

* H. O. Bender co-authored this chapter.

sively wooing business from local rivals."[1] These large law firms illustrate the need to market to or buy from large organization such as when they are obtaining public relations services and advertising services. For example, a legal firm was described as follows by the account executive from its public relations firm:

> They wanted press and a lot of it. But working with them was a nightmare. Some partners refused to talk to me because they were so opposed to PR. But then if partner X got in the paper, partner Y got jealous and mad. I tried to tell them to get the firm's name in the paper, but the partners were more interested in getting their own names in.[2]

This interactive marketing relation can be difficult, and the following pages throw light on it.

Consequently, that your "consumer" is a formal organization can make a profound difference in your marketing task whether it is profit or nonprofit. The principles of individual consumer behavior developed in the earlier chapters are just as applicable though they sometimes have to be applied in a somewhat different way. But, in the design of marketing strategy, the principle of core strategy is applied in precisely the same way as with the consumer in Chapters 8, 9, and 10. Finally, since middlemen buyers almost always represent formal organizations we have delayed discussing vertical distribution issues to be able to deal more effectively with such problems as promotional discounts to retailers. In this chapter, attention will focus first on the type of formal organization that has predominated in our economy—the manufacturing firm—because it is more concrete and easily understood. However, what is discussed here applies equally to the service organization, such as distributive, financial, and health maintenance.

The purpose here is to show how the organization influences the actual individual buying decision (just as we have done for the consumer in earlier chapters) and then to show how it is relevant to someone marketing to that buying decision maker.

In some cases, such as extensive problem-solving situations (EPS), the formal organization can greatly complicate the buying decision. Several people usually get brought into the decision each coming from a different function of the company—marketing, manufacturing, finance, research & development (R & D), and purchasing—each with a different orientation and specifically a different set of needs that they feel must be satisfied. Such a group has come to be called a "buying center," which is a highly useful term to convey the complexity of the behavior, and it will be used henceforth.

How to apply the Consumer Decision Model (CDM) to the buying center can be much more complicated: how do you aggregate (add up) three or four

---

[1] *The Wall Street Journal* (New York edition), January 30, 1987, p. 25.
[2] Ibid.

buyers into a single decision? In selling to them you might sometimes feel that these functional representatives because of their differences in objectives, instead of cooperating with each other in buying are a set of warring factions at each other's throats; for example, finance wants it cheap but manufacturing wants to be sure it works. As with the legal firm cited a few paragraphs back, the hassle was among the lawyers wanting to get their individual names in the newspaper and not worrying about the promotion of the firm's name. Also, at what level in the organization do you market—to the assistant purchasing agent or, at the other extreme, to the CEO? When the CDM was applied to Emery Air Freight referred to in Chapter 3, for example, it was found that Emery sales representatives were calling on the lowest level when they should have been calling on the vice president level.

In limited problem-solving (LPS) situations, fewer people usually make up the buying center than in EPS. In a routine problem-solving (RPS) situation, the formal organization usually simplifies the buying decision by giving one person—the industrial purchasing agent—purchasing responsibility, and so he alone performs the role of the buying center. He is provided with a set of procedures to use and benefits to pursue in making the decision. Even here, if a new supplier is involved, the purchasing agent may consult others in the company so that, in effect, a buying center evolves. This routine buying may occur early in the life of a product category if it is not an important product, such as minor supplies.

Because of the possible complexity, we shall have to scrutinize the total manufacuring organization buying process, namely, *the process by which product and service inputs are purchased and converted into benefits to customers.*[3] This may at first seem roundabout, but later you will find this foundation very useful in understanding the greater complexity of organizational buying.

Our discussion will begin with a brief examination of the scope of organizational buying and its major differences from the consumer buyer: focus on organizations, derived demand, goal orientation, group decision processes, explicit choice criteria captured in standardized languages, experts making decisions in their area of specialization, and buyer-seller interdependence. We shall then define industrial products as arrays of technical, economic, service, and social variables and shall observe that organizational buying tends to be thorough, stable, and slow to change.

Discussion will then turn to the theory of organizational buying, the Industrial Conversion Framework (ICF), which is the structure within which the CDM is applied to organizational buyers.[4] This framework will be demonstrated to provide a complete representation of the *purchase and resource conversion*

---

[3] We use the term "organizational marketing" to connote a firm's buying *and* marketing activities.

[4] H. O. Bender, "Industrial Conversion Framework. A Theory of Organizational Marketing," unpublished doctoral dissertation (Columbia University, New York, 1983).

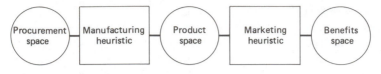

Figure 11-1   Unit Industrial Conversion Framework

processes within a *single* unitary firm, then between *two* firms (seller and buyer are referred to as "dyadic"), and finally, the special case of these operating in the marketing channel where a manufacturer sells to a wholesaler, for example.

Starting with the decision processes in a single firm (unit ICF), we shall explore the five key constructs of the framework. Three of the constructs are procurement space, product space, and benefits space. Manufacturing processes connect procurement and product spaces, whereas marketing processes connect product and benefits spaces.

These connections are shown in Figure 11-1. These three "spaces" are the three different ways of conceptualizing the product within the organization—buying, manufacturing, and selling—that must be reconciled for the firm to operate effectively. Further, two of the three spaces relate intimately to the CDM. The dimensions of procurement space are the identifying and evaluative dimensions of the CDM when it is applied by someone selling to this organization. At the other end, the dimensions of the benefits space are the identifying and evaluative dimensions that the marketing company believes its customers use in buying from marketing, and so are those respective dimensions of marketing's CDM. In this way, the organization's influence is exerted upon the CDM. Now you can see as said at the outset that the organization (the ICF) provides a framework for applying the CDM.

The ICF framework will later be extended to the transaction *between* the selling and buying firm (dyadic ICF). This shall lead us to examine the product and information dynamics between the two parties to the exchange. There we will examine the individual learning mechanisms that operate in the system, and their relationship to the EPS, LPS, and RPS modes of processing of information discussed in Chapters 4 to 6.

In much of the chapter, we will make extensive use of an example to demonstrate the features of the ICF framework and to illustrate how it can be used to assist managers in their decision making.[5] We will conclude by expanding the ICF to the complete chain, including the ultimate consumer, whom we will represent in LPS; the resulting model will provide a complete representation of those complex decision processes in the marketing channel.

---

[5] The example is taken from R. Karl Van Leer, "Industrial Marketing with a Flair," *Harvard Business Review* (November/December 1976), pp. 117–24.

2. ORGANIZATIONAL BUYING: IMPORTANCE AND CHARACTERISTICS

2.1 Introduction

Organizational buying can be characterized as the decision-making process by which companies and other formal organizations such as health and educational institutions (1) establish the need for purchasing products and services and (2) identify, evaluate, and choose among alternative offerings and suppliers relative to the products or services that (3) they, in turn, market to their customers.[6] Organizational buying thus includes all transactions in the marketing channel down to, but not including, the household level. Organizational buying is different from consumer behavior on a number of dimensions, the most important of which we shall now discuss.

2.2 Derived Demand

Demand for industrial products and services is derived demand instead of the direct demand represented by consumers: it depends on the level of economic activity of the selling firm's actual and potential customers. It is, of course, ultimately driven by the aggregate of consumer spending as medical firms are now finding, that is, by the consumer buyer.

2.3 Goal Orientation

Organizational buying can be understood as the management of "outside manufacturing." Specifically, antecedent to each procurement activity is the "make or buy decision"—the explicit or implicit assessment that it is more advantageous to the company to purchase the good in question, rather than to manufacture it. This distinction is not as academic as it may appear: firms capable of manufacturing a good that they presently purchase have greater bargaining power over a supplier.[7]

Given the decision to rely on outside sources, the buying process can be expected to be targeted toward "buying the *right* items in the *right* quantity

---

[6] See, for example, F. E. Webster and Y. Wind, *Organizational Buying Behavior* (Englewood Cliffs, N.J.: Prentice-Hall, 1972); J. N. Sheth, "A Model of Industrial Buying Behavior," *Journal of Marketing*, 37, no. 4 (October 1973), 50–56; J. N. Sheth, "Recent Developments in Organizational Buying Behavior," in A. G. Woodside, J. N. Sheth, and P. D. Bennett, eds., *Consumer and Industrial Buying Behavior* (New York: North-Holland, 1978), pp. 17–34; Y. Wind, "Organizational Buying Behavior," in G. Zaltman and T. V. Bonoma, eds., *Review of Marketing 1978* (Chicago: American Marketing Association, 1978), pp. 160–93; and K. Moller, *Industrial Buying Behavior of Production Materials: A Conceptual Model and Analysis* (Helsinki: The Helsinki School of Economics, Publications Series B-54, 1981).

[7] L. Lee and D. W. Doebler, *Purchasing and Materials Management* (New York: McGraw-Hill, 1977).

at the *right* price for delivery at the *right* time and place."[8] Decision processes in organizational buying are thus different from consumer behavior, as Ames and Hlavacek observe:

> Industrial products are not sold because someone really wants to buy them. Industrial customers have economic needs, not wants. Unlike consumer products, they don't make anyone look or feel better and they don't have any particular aesthetic value. Industrial products are bought only to help the user to manufacture, distribute, or sell more effectively so that he can improve his economic and competitive position. For this reason, the industrial firms emphasize price/quality checks and balances in company procurement roles which are often non-existent in many household purchase situations.[9]

2.4 Group Decisions Guided by Explicit Choice Criteria

In examining organizational buying decisions of the LPS type, we cannot simply focus on the purchasing agent. In fact, the decision as to what exactly constitutes "right" with respect to quality, volume, price, services, delivery, and so on in all but the most routine decision (RPS) situations, is likely to be the outcome of deliberations among experts from procurement, manufacturing, engineering, and R & D, in a "buying center" as defined earlier.

Let us elaborate on this important idea of the buying center. A key dimension of it is its size, the number of buyers making it up. As mentioned earlier the number of participants in the buying decision appears to vary directly with the product's stage of its product life cycle. The earlier in the cycle, the greater the number of buyers. Also, the extent of its importance varies from situation to situation. Jagdish Sheth has summarized the conditions where it is likely to be important:

1. There is a high perceived risk.
2. It is a capital expenditure rather than a routine purchase.
3. Time pressure is low.
4. The organization is large.
5. The organization is decentralized.[10]

Within the buying center, we can make a number of distinctions: between *users*, who actually use the product or service; *influencers*, who impact the buying decision; *buyers*, who have the formal authority to place the order; *deciders*, who have the formal or informal power to select the final supplier; and *gatekeepers*, who are in a position to control the flow of information to other members of the center.[11] Needless to say, there may be complex power-dependence relationships between these individuals that can influence the outcome of the decision.

---

[8] F. E. Webster, *Industrial Marketing Strategy* (New York: John Wiley & Sons, 1979).

[9] See B. C. Ames and J. D. Hlavacek, *Managing Marketing for Industrial Firms* (New York: Random House, 1984), p. 22.

[10] Sheth, "A Model of Industrial Buyer Behavior," p. 51.

[11] Webster and Wind, *Organizational Buyer Behavior*.

However, while knowledge about these relationships often helps greatly in getting the product adopted, they are often difficult to identify, given their political nature.[12] Just how much impact each of these individuals has on the decision at hand may be difficult to determine, but we can expect them to have rather explicit opinions as to what constitutes "quality," for example. Quality to these experts will mean compliance with technical specifications, such as "total solids," "pH," "residual styrene," and so on as examples. These quality dimensions then constitute one important set of choice criteria or benefits for the buying and marketing center and for the CDM that describes that buying center. Other choice criteria will refer to cost or selling price, and still others to service attributes.

Yet the principle of core strategy developed in Chapter 8 is just as appropriate here as there. In designing marketing strategy, the nature of overall organization objectives and customer benefits will be different, but they should be put together in exactly the same format as in marketing to consumers. The CDM can be applied as you will see in examples presented later in the chapter.

2.5   Expert Buyers and Use of Standardized Languages

As consumer buyers, we are laypersons in our consumption decisions, and we continue to remain laypersons even after having resorted to *Consumer Reports* or after having consulted with an expert—better informed laypersons perhaps, but still laypersons. The professional who sells us a durable good in a department store—such as a video recorder, stereo set, or refrigerator—is likely to be better informed than we are. This is hardly surprising as he does it to earn a living, day in, day out.

This principle of information asymmetry (the seller is better informed than the buyer)[13] is much less severe in business marketing, where we are likely to encounter specialists with their technical, scientific languages making decisions in their areas of expertise: professionals with years of training and experience in procurement, engineering, finance, chemistry, physics, and so on. Decision making by those experts is enhanced by "hard" measures—measures that are objectively verifiable, such as technical and accounting standards—and by company resources, such as laboratories, pilot plants, decision support systems, and so on. It would be difficult indeed to "sell" these experts; rather, they will have to be convinced that the offering will do the job, that price is fair, and that service is provided at the desired level. Buying center actors may ask for blueprints, technical specifications, and a sample, which they will carefully scrutinize.

Given their different backgrounds and areas of specialization, their pursuit of hard measures, and their employment of standardized languages (technical terminology, for example, chemical), experts in the buying center—users, influencers, buyers, deciders, and gatekeepers—can be expected to employ different

---

[12] A. M. Pettigrew, "The Industrial Purchasing Decision as a Political Process," *European Journal of Marketing*, 9, no. 1 (1975), 4–19.

[13] G. A. Akerloff, "The Market for 'Lemons': Quality Uncertainty and the Market Mechanism," *Quarterly Journal of Economics*, LXXXIV, no. 3 (August 1970), 488–500.

choice criteria in examining an offering and to employ different importance weights on these criteria to judge products.[14] They consequently have different information processing requirements, a phenomenon that needs to be addressed by the selling firm in formulating account strategy to inform the buying center members.[15]

2.6   Interdependence Between Selling and Buying Firms

Industrial products are bought to help the user to manufacture, distribute, or sell more effectively. On-time delivery in the agreed on quality then is highly important in the firm's conduct of business operations, with serious implications if this flow of goods gets disrupted. Detroit's eleventh commandment—"Thou shall not close down the assembly line!"—is a reflection of the more than $100,000 cost per hour of downtime and their dependence on outside suppliers for raw materials, processed materials, and so on. Failure to deliver on time or to meet specifications indeed may result in total loss of business to the vendor.

One other example of buyer-seller interdependence is Johnson & Johnson's crash effort to supply Tylenol in tamperproof containers, in which it relied on no less than 12 suppliers, and which it was able to assemble within three months. Seller-buyer interdependence is manifest in elaborate safeguards against disruptions in supply, such as maintenance of multiple sources, vendor rating, insistence on safety stocks, and purchase contracts. However, it also leads to continuity in supplier-customer relationships and thus greater dependability, with many firms conducting business with each other over decades.

Business organizations are slow to change suppliers for numerous reasons. First, the incumbent supplier, all other things being equal, is perceived to be the low-risk supplier.[16] Second, examining other brands is costly; it requires physical and work force resources. Third, seller-buyer interdependence leads to the accumulation of goodwill and to the establishment of social relationships between members of the selling and buying firm, who come to know and trust each other. These are relationships that are difficult to overcome for outsiders. Seller-buyer interdependence thus leads to source loyalty and to stability in industrial marketing exchanges.

2.7   Industrial Products Defined

Industrial products encompass a broad array of tangible and intangible goods. Industrial products include construction, light and heavy equipment, raw and

---

[14] J. E. Scott and P. Wright, "Modeling an Organizational Buyer's Product Evaluation Strategy: Validity and Procedural Considerations," *Journal of Marketing Research*, XIII (August 1976), 211–14.

[15] A. K. Chakrabarti, S. Feinman, and W. Fuentevilla, "Targeting Technical Information to Organizational Positions," *Industrial Marketing Management*, 11, no. 3 (1982), 195–203.

[16] P. J. Robinson, C. W. Faris, and Y. Wind, *Industrial Buying and Creative Marketing* (Boston: Allyn & Bacon, 1967).

processed materials, components and subassemblies, maintenance, repair and operating supplies, and services. Industrial products are usually described in terms of a set of core technical and economic attributes, like performance on technical specifications, selling price, and terms of delivery. These technical and economic choice criteria are augmented by services, such as provision of technical assistance and postinstallation service.[17] However, to arrive at a complete understanding of industrial products, we must also take into consideration past and present relationships between the members of the selling and buying firms as discussed earlier or the accumulation of goodwill and social relationships. Thus, *industrial products* are defined as arrays of technical, economic, service, and social variables, not just the physical product alone.[18]

2.8 Organizational Buying Characteristics: Thorough, Stable, and Slow to Change

The joint assessment of the preceding phenomena leads us to conclude that organizational buying tends to be thorough, stable, and slow to change—thorough, because of its goal orientation and the stakes involved, because of the existence of explicit choice criteria, and because of experts doing the buying; stable and slow to change, because of buying center decision processes characteristic of organizational buying, because of seller-buyer interdependence in the form of shared interests, because of mutual economic dependencies and accumulated trust, and because of a mutual understanding of each other's business problems. However, not all organizational buying fits this pattern. It can be quite simple, such as in RPS.

Up to this point, we have done little more than describe organizational buying within the ICF framework. It is now time to use the ICF framework to integrate these phenomena and foster explanation and prediction of buying behavior.

3. UNIT INDUSTRIAL CONVERSION FRAMEWORK

3.1 Introduction

The unit Industrial Conversion Framework (unit ICF, Figure 11-2), which is our model of the organizational buying activities of a *single* firm, is quite simple. It provides a representation of the ways in which companies purchase goods to manufacture, market, and distribute their offerings to make a profit. It has the great virtue for our purposes of enabling us to think simultaneously about a company buying and a company selling.

---

[17] T. Levitt, *The Marketing Mode* (New York: McGraw-Hill, 1969).
[18] F. E. Webster, "Management Science in Industrial Marketing," *Journal of Marketing*, 42, no. 1 (January 1978), 21–27.

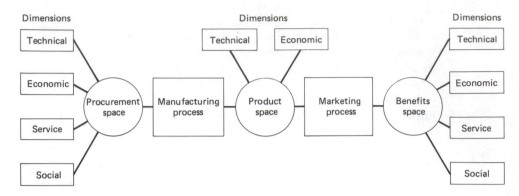

Figure 11-2 Unit Industrial Conversion Framework

The unit ICF describes an organization as a resource conversion system and is based on the notion that companies purchase products as arrays of technical, economic, service, and social benefits. Via the manufacturing process, these are then converted into products and viewed under a technical orientation as physical entities with defined technical and economic properties. The marketing process then conceptualizes and describes these physical entities as benefits to customers.

As discussed earlier, the unit Industrial Conversion Framework is formed by *three* multidimensional spaces—procurement, product, and benefits space—which are connected via *two* types of transformation mechanisms, the manufacturing and marketing processes. These will now be briefly defined.

3.2 Procurement Space

Procurement space is defined by the choice criteria (benefits) established by the buying center defined and described earlier. In correspondence with our definition of industrial products as arrays of technical, economic, service, and social variables—it consists of just these dimensions. They are formed in roughly the same way as are the identifying and evaluative characteristics used by consumers as described in Chapters 4 through 6. Procurement space, in the most simple case, RPS, represents just the purchasing agent's view of the offering. Position in procurement space, if weighted by the importance attributed to each dimension, is designed to provide a quantitative measure of preference for the offering for each member of the buying center.[19] This is our familiar multidimensional attitude measure of the CDM as presented in Chapter 3.

3.3 Product Space

Product space is defined as those physical (technical) and economic dimensions that the company uses in its quality assessment and cost accounting procedures

---

[19] Via the multiattribute model; see, for example, P. E. Green and V. Srinivasan, "Conjoint Analysis in Consumer Research: Issues and Outlook," *Journal of Consumer Research*, 5, no. 2 (September 1978), 103–23.

to examine the product that the company manufactures. The technical dimensions reflect a scientist's or engineer's view of the product, and the economic dimensions are those characteristic of managerial accounting.

3.4 Benefits Space

Benefits space is defined as those technical, economic, service, and social dimensions that the firm's marketing people perceive to be wanted by their customers. Benefits space thus becomes the selling firm's estimate of the buying firm's procurement space. Somewhat simplified, it represents a marketing manager's view of benefits provided and customer needs demanded. Notice that this definition is again consistent with our previous characterization of industrial products. As before, product position in benefits space, weighted by the importance of those benefits, is an indicator of the overall "goodness" of the offering just as in the CDM discussed in Chapter 3 and used throughout the book.

The number of benefits *spaces* associated with a single product is usually the same as the number of markets toward which it is aimed. This implies the possibility of market segmentation. This concept of different benefits spaces for the same physical product then derives its justification from the existence of segmented markets. It takes into explicit consideration the fact that different groups of industrial customers (segments) will often seek slightly different benefits from the product they are purchasing. Their manufacturing processes may be different, or their customer needs are different.

3.5 Manufacturing and Marketing Procedures

It should be clear by now the procurement, product, and benefits spaces do not exist in isolation from each other but that they are closely related. The conversion between procurement and product space is called *manufacturing* process. It portrays the firm's investment in plant and equipment that transforms the purchased good(s) into the company's own product, and its setting of the manufacturing parameters.

Then, the transformation mechanism between product and benefits space is called *marketing* process. It denotes the company's setting of the usual marketing parameters—product, place, promotion, and price parameters—and the degree to which products are augmented segment specifically, as indicated. This interrelatedness of the parts of the company explains why the concept of the buying center is so important.

3.6 Example of Unit Industrial Conversion Framework: Polylatex

The ICF models Polylatex as a resource conversion system: resources are input in the form of physical products, converted via manufacturing, and then marketed (Figure 11-3). Specifically, we assume that the company purchases styrene and butadiene monomer, surfactants, catalysts, modifiers, and inhibitors to manufac-

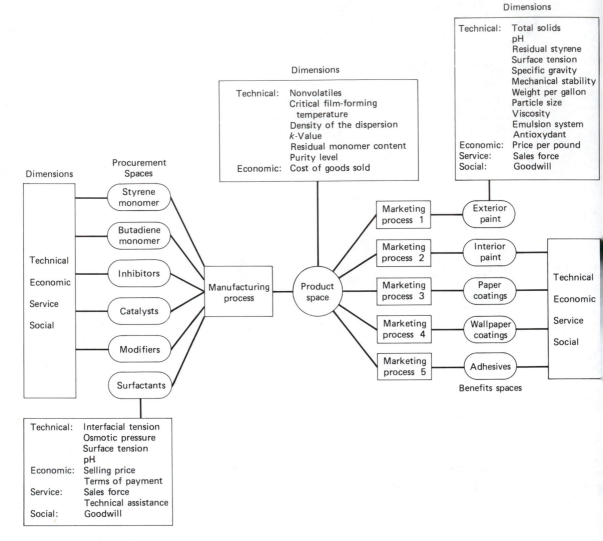

Dimensions

Technical: Total solids
pH
Residual styrene
Surface tension
Specific gravity
Mechanical stability
Weight per gallon
Particle size
Viscosity
Emulsion system
Antioxydant
Economic: Price per pound
Service: Sales force
Social: Goodwill

Dimensions

Technical: Nonvolatiles
Critical film-forming
temperature
Density of the dispersion
k-Value
Residual monomer content
Purity level
Economic: Cost of goods sold

Technical: Interfacial tension
Osmotic pressure
Surface tension
pH
Economic: Selling price
Terms of payment
Service: Sales force
Technical assistance
Social: Goodwill

Figure 11-3 ICF for Polylatex

ture its latex, which it then markets in the form of six products serving five different market segments: exterior and interior paint, paper coatings, wallpaper coatings, and adhesives. Consequently, we encounter six procurement spaces and five marketing processes with the corresponding benefits spaces as seen in Figure 11-3.

In exploring the *procurement spaces*, we note that these materials are purchased for an explicit technical reason and not to satisfy some latent need. Surfactant, for example, is bought to bring about the following to the products:

Solubilization (monomers and catalysts dissolve and react in surfactant micelles)
Emulsification of monomers
Stabilization of latexes

Surfactant space, defined on the choice criteria of the buying center, might thus encompass *technical measures*, such as interfacial tension, osmotic pressure, surface tension, and pH; *economic measures*, such as price and terms of sale; *services*, such as sales force and technical assistance; and *social relationships*, expressed as goodwill.

In examining these benefits or choice criteria, you will note that they are "hard," or standardized, measures: the technical measures are derived from the natural sciences and are likely to be expressed in terms of performance on standardized tests, such as ASTM (*American Society for Testing and Materials*), which are objectively verifiable by design. There is also nothing ambiguous about the economic criteria, which are price and terms of sale. We thus conclude that the members of the buying center are likely to be in agreement about product position on at least these "hard" technical and economic attributes.[20] However, just as in consumer buying these several attributes tend to be grouped into a few dimensions. There are limits to the number of dimensions the human mind can handle. This is true of all three spaces.

Procurement space was based on the characteristics of each material input that manufacturing believed to be essential. *Product space* was defined on those physical (technical) and economic dimensions that Polylatex uses in its quality assessment and cost accounting procedures to examine the product it manufactures. *Benefits space* was said to be based on those attributes that the Polylatex marketing people perceive to be pursued by their customer groups. Acme Paint, a Polylatex customer that sells exterior paint to dealers, displayed an analogous set of benefits for each of its four spaces seen in Figure 11-3.

3.7   Unit ICF: Summary

The unit Industrial Conversion Framework, our model of the organizational marketing activities of a single company, provides a representation of the ways in which companies purchase materials to manufacture products, which they then market to segments to meet their customers' needs, and are the value added by the firm. In exploring the spaces and processes in the unit framework, we saw that a company's purchases are largely governed by technical and service considerations relative to a profit contribution motive.

Profit contribution is monitored via the economic indicators of these spaces, with the procurement spaces monitoring raw materials costs, product

---

[20] Note that many choice criteria in consumer decisionmaking are inherently "soft"; that is, not objectively verifiable (such as "style," "comfort," "freshness," "taste," "sex appeal," etc.).

space monitoring cost of goods sold, and benefits space monitoring the selling prices to the respective segments. The difference between the sum of raw material costs and cost of goods sold provides manufacturing costs, difference between cost of goods sold and selling price provides gross contribution, and difference between the sum of raw materials costs and selling price provides value added. We also note that decision making in this framework takes the form of experts processing information in their area of specialization and that such information processing makes extensive use of standardized measures.

However, in reviewing the unit framework, we must also observe that the company is constrained in its ability to provide benefits to customers. First, there are financial and manpower constraints, which denote limitations in the company's financial and human resource base. Second, there are technical constraints. Quality and price of raw materials will impact quality and price of the good manufactured and marketed. Moreover, the manufacturing process facilitates and constrains the company's benefits generating capability. This is because, once a firm has decided to employ a specific manufacturing technology and has made the investment into plant and equipment, it is committed in the long term: significant improvements in performance may not be feasible because of limitations in the manufacturing process and manufacturing costs may be largely a function of capacity utilization.

Finally, the company's market information base facilitates (or constrains) its ability to procure and market goods and services effectively. However, attainment of market information may be largely under control of the company's actual and potential suppliers and customers. To understand the important marketing problem of these supplier/customer information dynamics and to see how improvements in quality, price, and services can actually be diagnosed in the system, the unit ICF needs to be expanded to the *dyad*—the two-unit relationship—between the selling firm and the buying firm.

This description of the manufacturing firm may first appear totally unrelated to the marketing problems of health and legal firms, for example. However, legal firms have serious organization problems as we have already seen earlier in the chapter.

4. DYADIC INDUSTRIAL CONVERSION FRAMEWORK

4.1 Introduction

The unit ICF of Figure 11-2 approaches organizational buying as goal-oriented group decision processes aimed at providing benefits to customer segments at a profit, and governed by explicit technical, economic, and service criteria. However, it does not capture seller-buyer interdependence and social interaction between firms. To account for this seller-buyer interdependence and to show how the framework can be used to analyze the industrial marketing exchange, we need to expand the framework to the *two firms* making up the dyad and

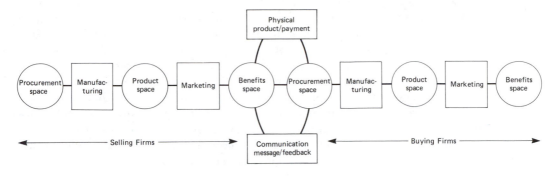

Figure 11-4 Dyadic Industrial Conversion Framework

each of which are party to this transaction. The resulting dyadic ICF (Figure 11-4) now provides a model of both the activities within and between these two organizations, including the marketing and buying activities. Let us assume that Polylatex is on the left of Figure 11-4 and Acme is on the right.

Intraorganizationally, the companies are viewed under the unit perspective discussed in Section 3 as converting resources via the procurement to benefits space through a series of transformations. Interorganizationally, as you see in Figure 11-4, focus is on the exchange process between the two firms: physical (product/payment) and communication (message/feedback). The dyadic ICF thus is consistent with the often-discussed notion of marketing as exchange processes[21] and with the suggestion from research studies that a dyadic perspective be used in the study of organizational buying.[22] Given two unit ICFs and the focus on both the physical and communication dynamics between the two firms as in Figure 11-4, the dyadic framework can serve as a diagnostic tool of seller-buyer product and communication exchanges. It is this depth of understanding that can be so helpful in designing marketing strategy in selling to a firm.

4.2   Product Dynamics in the Dyadic ICF

Product dynamics are recorded in the dyadic framework via the indicators of each firm's procurement, product, and benefits space. For example, a price change will affect the cost of goods sold according to the degree to which a purchased good enters the produced good. Also, a change in the technical attributes of a purchased good will get recorded via the technical indicators of procurement space. This alteration may then affect the technical properties of the product that the company, in turn, produces, in which case product position on the technical product space indicators will change. This shift in product

[21] R. P. Bagozzi, "Marketing as Exchange," *Journal of Marketing*, 39, no. 4 (October 1975), 32–39.

[22] T. V. Bonoma, G. Zaltman, and W. J. Johnston, "Industrial Buying Behavior," Report No. 77–117 (Cambridge, Mass.: Marketing Science Institute, 1977).

space may then get mapped into any or all of the benefits spaces; that is, there may be a change in the marketing department's perceptions about the provision of benefits to these market segments.

The actual provision of benefits finally gets monitored in the customer organization's ICF via the same recording mechanism. For example, an alteration in the technical attributes of a purchased good may enable the company to produce more effectively, in which case position on the cost of goods sold indicators in product space will change. Finally, a change in the manufacturing process may cause a shift on the technical and/or economic indicators of product space, and may affect position in any or all of the benefits spaces.

4.3   Change in Manufacturing Process

A change in the manufacturing process may cause a shift in position in product space: changes in manufacturing costs will be captured by the economic dimensions and in the physical attributes by the technical product space indicators. For a change in technical attributes to constitute an improvement, it must get mapped into the customer's ICF.

4.4   Price Change

A decrease in selling price will get recorded via the economic dimensions of Polylatex' benefits space and Acme's procurement and product space. Needless to say that a price reduction, with all other product attributes remaining unchanged, will be considered favorably by Acme, which now faces the following options:

1. To pass the savings on to their customers in the form of a lower selling price (position in benefits space changes)
2. Not to pass them on and to enjoy a higher margin (position in benefits space remains unchanged)

4.5   Improvements in Services

Confronted with an undifferentiated core product and the threat of competitive retaliation to price reductions, Polylatex' marketing manager decides to augment his offering through a unique service, the paint scrubber, which is aimed at demonstrating equivalent or superior durability in a point-of-purchase display to the dealer segment, that is, to educate both dealers and the ultimate user. Mr. Brown's marketing strategy affects all members of the marketing channel and can be recorded via a series of three levels of ICFs: those of Polylatex, Acme, and the paint dealers.

1. Provision of the paint scrubber and booklets get recorded on the service dimensions of Polylatex' benefits space.

2. Paint scrubber and booklet not only affect the service dimensions of Acme's procurement, but also of benefits space, as they are designed to be passed on to the dealer segment.
3. Procurement and benefits space of dealers are similarly affected, for the paint scrubber provides them with a tool geared to attract and educate their customers, the ultimate users.

The examples provide some indication of the value of the ICF as a diagnostic tool. Actually, the dyadic ICF is useful in examining the entire array of product and process innovations, such as demand-pull and technology-push, as well as evolutionary versus revolutionary product developments. It also aids in identifying the two major types of new product failure: it doesn't get adopted at all or it gets adopted by a few but is not diffused throughout the market.[23] The following are the major features of the dyadic ICF in the diagnosis of seller-buyer product dynamics:

> The distinction between physical product characteristics and customer benefits forces the user to differentiate between attributes that are merely physical product descriptors and those that actually provide customer value.
>
> The framework explicitly models the differential provision of benefits to segments from the same physical product.
>
> The focus in the dyadic framework is not only on the customer organization's purchase needs (in procurement space) but on its manufacturing process and the benefits provided to its customers and alerts the user to opportunities that may not be stated explicitly by members of the buying center.
>
> This same focus permits use of the dyadic ICF in sensitivity analysis, that is, of mental or, if quantified, computer experiments that explore the impact of product modifications upon the provision of customer value (via assessment of the customer organization's ICF).

5. APPLICATION TO OTHER FORMAL ORGANIZATIONS

To provide an understanding of the manufacturing organization, a great amount of detail has been presented. Other types of organizations behave in similar ways. Health organizations face similar problems of intracompany interdependencies. Their customers tend to be somewhat different, as Bill O'Neill, president of International Clinical Laboratories, has found.[24] He provides laboratory services to hospitals. For example, hospital administrators are found to be concerned about saving money "but not if it means he's going to annoy the staff or lose some admittances." Some of the administrators want to keep their own testing equipment, even though it will be redundant. But these are types of constraints that any organization may face. Earlier in the chapter, we saw how legal firms were confronting serious organization problems.

---

[23] See Bender, *Industrial Conversion Framework*.

[24] G. Smith, "Tricky Technology: Man for All Seasons," *Forbes*, May 19, 1986, pp. 102–5.

Gary Lillien and Tony Wong did a study of buying in the metalworking industry and found it was possible to model the buying centers in this industry.[25] The people in those centers seemed to conform to the three stages of the product life cycle because the differences could be largely explained in terms of degree of "product complexity." Lillien and Wong also found that as the company became bigger, the chances of an employee being involved in a buying center became smaller. This implies that the task of buying became more specialized.

6. INDIVIDUAL LEARNING IN THE DYADIC ICF

6.1 Introduction

Learning in the dyadic framework over time may occur in any or all of the spaces and processes and—as in consumer behavior—can be expected to evolve from EPS through LPS to RPS, as suggested by the Lillien and Wong study. With the introduction of learning, the information processing concepts can be applied here in a straightforward manner.

According to our previous definition, the individual, who is now likely to be an expert, is in EPS when learning about the dimensionality of the space, be it about procurement, product, or benefits space; he is in LPS when utilizing the full set of dimensions to judge an offering; and he is in RPS when utilizing a subset of benefits. The definitions of EPS, LPS, and RPS are unequivocal as they apply to the individual. LPS, and especially EPS, organizational buying decisions are typically group processes, however. Also, different buying center members may be in different psychological states at any given point in time, but this happens among consumers in a family, too.

6.2 Extensive Problem Solving

Polylatex, our previous example, allows us to highlight this point that EPS buying is typically group processes and to explore organizational learning in some greater detail by incorporating individual learning that occurs through processing information. Assume that Acme had decided to manufacture its own latex (which represents extensive problem solving for a multitude of actors in R & D, engineering, production, and finance, because a plant needs to be built and run) and that a buying center had been formed and assigned the task to purchase surfactant. This signifies product category concept learning at least for technical specialists of the buying center. The buying decision might well proceed as follows:

1. The purchasing agent identifies potential suppliers and invites them to provide product literature and price quotations that he distributes to other members

[25] G. L. Lillien and M. A. Wong, "An Exploratory Investigation of the Structure of the Buying Center in the Metalworking Industry," *Journal of Marketing Research*, XXI (February 1984), 1–11.

of the buying center. This is a fairly routine assignment for the purchasing agent, which for him will be in the LPS mode.

2. A chemist examines candidate surfactants by scrutinizing the technical literature, through obtaining advice from the vendors' sales and technical personnel, and by screening samples in the laboratory with the help of a quality control technician. That is, the chemist learns about space structure and then positions candidate offerings. This process typifies EPS for the chemist and LPS for the technician.

3. After having narrowed down the set of candidate products, the chemist can be expected to recommend that a trial order be placed for one or several surfactants. These surfactants will then be subjected to trials in the pilot plant, and, eventually, in full-fledged manufacturing. The locus of extensive problem solving thus moves from the chemist to, say, the plant manager.

4. The members of the buying center will eventually have to choose a surfactant.[26] This decision may well be based upon product performance in the trial stage, but is likely to be mediated by price, terms, reputation of the supplier, and so on. Buying center actors may disagree as to which surfactant should be adopted. This may be because of "hidden agendas," such as striving to dominate the decision process,[27] or because of differences in preference. For example, purchasing agents and engineers were shown to differ systematically in the importance they attribute to choice criteria.[28] Prediction of the group decision is difficult in such instances.

6.2.1 Business Decision Making in EPS: A Factory Automation Example.

To give our description of EPS buying the precise content needed to guide the design of marketing strategy, we incorporate more of the theory of individual buying presented earlier in Chapters 3 through 6 to supplement the description of organizational buying. Let us use an example of buying factory automation consulting service.

In April 1982, General Electric announced its entry into the factory automation market. A part of G.E.'s effort was the formation of a consulting service to provide critical information to companies thinking of automating their manufacturing facilities. G.E. expected this decision of whether and how to automate to be an unusually difficult EPS choice for any manufacturing company and especially for the vice president of operations charged with this responsibility (just as General Motors is finding today as it attempts to carry out complete automation)![29]

Modern automation has profound implications throughout the manufacturing operation. Usually, in a typical EPS situation, a vice president of manufacturing would consult some knowledgeable and trusted person down in the plant to obtain information about the technical features of the problem and to get recommendations for action. However, in the case of modern factory automa-

---

[26] See J. M. Choffray and G. L. Lillien, *Market Planning for New Industrial Products* (New York: John Wiley & Sons, 1980), for models of aggregating individual into group scores.

[27] G. Strauss, "Tactics of Lateral Relationships: The Purchasing Agent," *Administrative Science Quarterly*, 7, no. 2 (September 1962), 161–86.

[28] Scott and Wright, "Modeling an Organizational Buyer's Product Evaluation Strategy."

[29] *The Wall Street Journal* (New York edition), July 9, 1984, pp. 1 and 10.

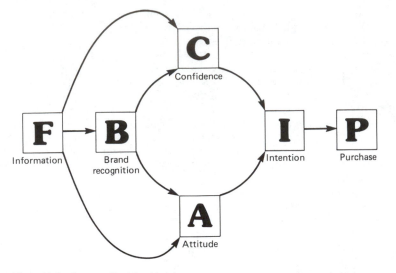

Figure 11-5 Customer Decision Model

tion—computer-aided design, operations management systems, computer-aided manufacturing, and intelligent warehouse systems—this was not likely to be a feasible course of action, as nobody in the plant could be expected to understand the effect of this radical innovation over the whole plant. Consequently, the usual operating procedure for this kind of decision could be expected to "break down." The vice president of manufacturing would be forced to handle the problem largely by himself. G.E. consequently envisioned a real need for a consulting service like the one they were prepared to offer.

How the VP of manufacturing was able to handle this problem within the limits of his own *individual* thinking processes is shown by applying the Customer Decision Model to his situation. From the discussion that follows, you can now see how the Vice President of manufacturing forms his decision process for this product class, but subject to the limits of his decisions capacities as set by search, attention, memory, and choice as described in Chapters 3 and 4. You will recall the CDM as pictured in Figure 11-5.

In the first place, the "product" here was a consulting *service*, which is intangible and provides no basis for a brand identification measure (B) unless it is contrived, for example, a trademark or workers' uniform. Thus, B was missing. Also, the information measure (F) was not adequate, which is not surprising. The service was exceedingly complex, requiring an enormous amount of information to understand it, especially with no brand identifying chunk upon which to build that understanding. The confidence measure (C) did not contribute much, but again remember the enormity of the information load required. However, attitude toward the service (A) was effective. You will recall A is made up of two to four of the most important benefits that become the foundation of the customer's goal hierarchy. The customer rates (evaluates) the service against these benefits. This evaluation then drives intention to buy (I) as you will recall from Chapter 3. Figure 11-6 portrays the results of the A input.

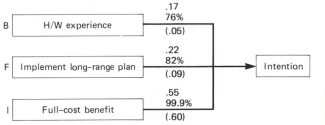

Figure 11-6
Benefit-Intention Relations for High
Potential Automaters

These data were obtained as follows. In a lengthy personal interview 29 vice presidents had been asked to rate the importance of 10 different benefits that were thought to be relevant. The most important of these 10 were the following, as shown in Figure 11-6.

1. Experience with factory automation hardware
2. Ability to develop and implement a long-range automation plan
3. Likelihood of getting full-cost benefit

Let us explore the significance of Figure 11-6. The first benefit is abbreviated as "H/W experience." The top number to the right, .17, is the standardized regression coefficient relating that benefit to the customer's intention to buy (I). This indicates that if you were to increase the customers' evaluation of the G.E. consulting service on this benefit decision through your marketing effort by 10%, such as through advertising, personal selling, and so on, you would increase the customers' intention to purchase (I) by 1.7%. The "76%" is a measure of statistical significance and "(.05)" the proportion of variance in (I) explained by the H/W experience variable. You can see from the three numbers that the H/W experience is not a strong buying influence.

However, let us go to full-cost benefit, where quite a different picture emerges. The regression coefficient of .55 indicates that if the vice presidents' evaluation were raised by 10% on this dimension, their intention to purchase would increase by 5.5%. The 99.9% figure indicates that this measure is highly significant, and the (.60) that the full-cost benefit's variable explains a very high proportion of the variance, 60%, in the intention-to-purchase measure. From your review of the most important benefits, what should be the key element of G.E.'s marketing strategy for its factory automation consulting service?[30] Full-cost benefit!

Finally, Figure 11-7 describes the product hierarchy that was thought by the interviewers to exist in the minds of most of the respondents in the study. Specifically, there were two types of consulting service being offered. One offered advice but no equipment (Booz, Allen), and the other offered both consulting service and at least one piece of the equipment required in automating.

---

[30] For a thorough and creative analysis of the complete set of data, see J. U. Farley, B. Kahn, D. R. Lehmann, and W. L. Moore, "Modeling the Choice to Automate," *Sloan Management Review*, 28, no. 2 (Winter 1987), 5–15.

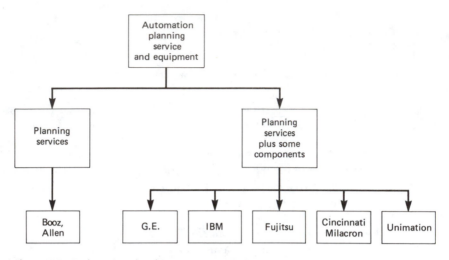

Figure 11-7   Product Hierarchy of Factory Automation Customer

6.3   Limited Problem Solving

For LPS let us now return to our original example used in the chapter. When considering purchase of an alternate surfactant—say, with the same chemical composition, but from a different supplier—we face a situation where procurement space structure is already established and where candidate products may have previously been identified and tested. Still, the purchasing agent and the quality control technician can be expected to scrutinize the supplier's offering carefully (LPS for both of them), with the chemist and the plant manager providing little, if any, assistance (RPS).

Here the individual buying process described in Chapter 5 applies. These people have to form a concept of the new supplier, but from their product hierarchy and goal hierarchy, they are armed with a set of identifying characteristics and benefits acquired from previous experience with other brands (such as performance on quality standards, cost and service features, etc.). And the same limitations in their thinking we found in Chapter 5 apply just as well as they do to the consumer. For example, to the extent that advertising is not presented in familiar vocabulary and simple sentences, the customer will have difficulty in absorbing the information about the new brand's identifying characteristics and benefits.

6.4   Routine Problem Solving

In the process of repurchasing the surfactant, only the purchasing agent and a quality control technician are likely to be involved. The purchasing agent will place the order on a routine basis by merely specifying price and delivery from some supplier in his evoked set. The technician will run quality control tests of the shipment to ascertain compliance with standards on a reduced set of dimensions that are perceived to be indicators of overall quality, such as density, pH, and surface tension. This situation is characteristic of RPS, where buying centers are smaller or nonexistent and where organizational actors use only a subset of choice criteria in decision making.

A key question is whether these RPS buyers—the purchasing agent and quality control technician—exhibit the cyclic behavior of consumer buyers discussed in Chapter 6. You will recall that cyclic behavior—periodically in and out of the market—enables a large proportion of consumer buyers to keep up with market changes. The equivalent to this cyclic behavior in business markets is a policy of maintaining multiple sources of supply (routinely buying from two or more vendors). It is supported by the establishment of an information network—one of the key responsibilities of the purchasing agent—and the continuous monitoring of the price-quality-service performance of actual and potential offerings (a practice called "vendor rating"). In consumer terms, this is the way the buyer maintains his evoked set.

6.5   Conclusions on Individual Learning

When examining the modes of learning in the ICF, we need to distinguish between intra- and interorganizational learning. Companies learn about

1. Procurement space largely through interaction with and product literature from actual and potential suppliers, that is, interorganizationally
2. Product space predominantly through R & D and production (learning by doing), that is, intraorganizationally
3. Benefits space primarily through market intelligence and research, that is, again interorganizationally

Given the intraorganizational mode of product space learning—through R & D and production—acquisition of knowledge about product space is largely at the discretion of the company via allocation of funds. This is not true for procurement and benefits space learning, which are highly dependent upon feedback from outside sources. It turns out that this feedback may be opportunistic and biased.[31]

> *The seller's communication*, because it might not be in the interest of the selling firm to communicate potentially disadvantageous product attributes to the buying center. Consequently, there might be attempts to omit or distort information on these attributes.
>
> *The buyer's communication*, because the members of the buying center might realize that unequivocal feedback about positive product attributes might lead to increases in selling price and to an updating of the seller's message. This, in turn, could result in the faster adoption of the seller's product by the buyer's competitors.

[31] O. E. Williamson, *Markets and Hierarchies: Analysis and Antitrust Implications* (New York: The Free Press, 1975), pp. 32–33.

Both parties thus recognize that their counterpart's communication may to some degree be distorted, which adds uncertainty to both procurement and benefits space learning.

However, as you have seen previously, possession of accurate knowledge about procurement space (and benefits space, for that matter) is critically important if the company is to get the most out of its purchasing (marketing) dollars. The people in the buying center then are well advised to recognize the importance of reliable and valid market information and to be aware of the potential of receiving distorted information.

The Industrial Conversion Framework is useful in establishing such a management decision support system: it helps to identify the information that is collected through purchasing, via market research, through the sales and technical force, and through analyzing published data. This information then can be classified according to the framework into procurement, manufacturing, and marketing data. The decision support system should entail facts and evidence about functional and generic substitutes, that is, about all competitive offerings that the company's suppliers and customers could actually and potentially purchase and market.

The role of market research can always be useful, but in some industrial situations it can be absolutely essential. Let us explain. Throughout the discussion in this chapter, it has been assumed that the selling company is the source of new technology in a product. But in at least two industries—scientific instruments and semiconductor and electronic subassembly manufacturing equipment—the *buying* company was the source of the new technology.[32] To many this has been a surprising discovery. How to exploit this possibility was discussed at length in Chapter 8. To the extent the buyer is the source of the technology, the burden on market research to find out about it in a particular industry is far greater. Also, the market researcher is wise to distinguish in the buying process between "users" of the product (production and engineering personnel) and related managers. The user is typically involved first and then managers later according to Lillien and Wong in their study of the buying center in the metalworking industry.[33]

7. VERTICAL DISTRIBUTION CHANNELS

Extension of the dyadic ICF to the entire marketing channel is straightforward: the dynamic framework is simply extended according to the degree that there are channel members. Figure 11-8 depicts such a channel framework. It consists of three unit ICFs, those of companies A, B, and C (e.g., Polylatex, Acme, and the paint dealers), and of the ultimate customer, whose information processing is represented via the Customer Decision Model. Figure 11-8 thus makes it

[32] E. Von Hippel, "Users as Innovators," *Technology Review*, 80, no. 3 (January 1978), 2–11.

[33] Lillien and Wong, "An Exploratory Investigation of the Structure of the Buying Center."

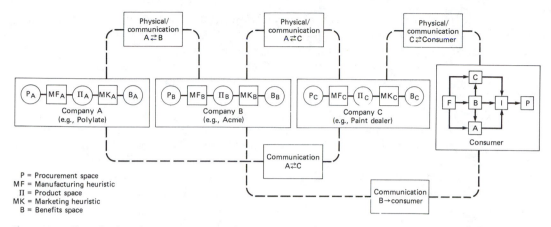

Figure 11-8   Channel Industrial Conversion Framework

P = Procurement space
MF = Manufacturing heuristic
Π = Product space
MK = Marketing heuristic
B = Benefits space

clear that the channel ICF ought to include the companies in the distribution system, such as wholesalers and retailers, as these firms also add value to the product (they warehouse, break bulk, make the product available, etc.).

Figure 11-8 then permits an analysis of the complex product and information flows. First, each unit ICF provides a description of the organizational manufacturing and marketing activities of the three firms. Second, each firm's addition of value to the product is captured by the economic indicators of the respective procurement, product, and benefits spaces. Overall value added in the consumption chain then is the sum of value added by the individual channel members. Finally, the market transactions between adjacent firms are captured via the physical/communication flows representation (product/payment and message/feedback) of the dyadic ICF. Figure 11-8 thus provides a framework for thinking about the typical case of vertical channels where the members are formal organizations.

Promotional discounts to buyers in retail establishments is a key problem. Recently, manufacturers have begun to realize how costly expenditures to middlemen happen to be; for example, they are often becoming larger than consumer advertising budgets. Historically, little research has been devoted to them.[34] These incentives provided by the manufacturer to the middleman at each level, particularly to the retailer, are varied. The most basic one is the margin. But in addition there is a gamut of incentives usually called "trade promotions." "Consumer promotions" are the corresponding items direct to the consumer of which coupons are probably the most common. Here we will confine the discussion to "trade promotion." Some of the items included are displays, trade shows, exhibitions, demonstrations, motion picture, and videotape films. In gen-

---

[34] However, see R. Barger, *Distribution's Place in the American Economy Since 1869*, National Bureau of Economic Research (Princeton, N.J.: Princeton University Press, 1955). For a more recent attempt to conceptualize it, see L. W. Stern and T. Reve, "Distribution Channels as Political Economies: A Framework for Comparative Analysis," *Journal of Marketing*, 44, no. 3 (Summer 1980), 52–64.

eral, their purpose has been (1) to communicate, (2) to convince, and (3) so to compete. Each type of promotion probably has to be handled separately in attempting to understand and evaluate its impact.

That the CDM is appropriate for a study of retailer response to promotional discounts is suggested by two studies of new product acceptance among Canadian supermarket buyers.[35] The purpose was primarily to devise a way of reducing the time that these retail buyers devote to evaluating new products. New products, if successful, are the most profitable to supermarkets, and yet each store typically has only limited shelf space for the additional products. Sixty-seven choices of new product decisions by supermarkets were investigated. Three different models—linear compensatory, conjunctive, and disjunctive—were fitted to the data. The linear compensatory model, which you recall from Chapter 3 that the CDM is, was clearly much better than either of the other two. The benefits used in it, with their respective standardized regression coefficients, are shown in Table 11-1. The powerful role of manufacturer advertising in gaining access to the supermarket shelf is obvious in the foregoing results.

Later, 124 new products proposed to three Boston supermarket buyers were investigated with a quite different approach called a "gatekeeping" model.[36] Price was relevant in both studies. Supplier advertising ranks high in both.

Table 11-1   Supermarket Buyers' Benefits

Supplier advertising	.655
Time discount on payables	.231
Number of competing items stocked	−.151
Gross profit percentage	.050

SOURCE: R. M. Heeler, M. J. Kearney, and B. J. Mehaffey, "Modeling Supermarket Product Selection," *Journal of Marketing Research*, X, no. 1 (February 1973), 36. Published by the American Marketing Association.

8. CONCLUSIONS

The Industrial Conversion Framework of this chapter represents a model of the complex product and information dynamics in the organizational marketplace, and it relates the CDM to this type of market.

It explores the physical and communication exchanges within and between firms and provides a representation of value added in the channel. By systematically relating properties of purchased materials and/or changes in the manufacturing process to the provision of benefits to customer segments, it serves to demonstrate how business, health, legal, and other organizations can

[35] R. M. Heeler, M. J. Kearney, and B. J. Mehaffey, "Modeling Supermarket Product Selection," *Journal of Marketing Research*, X, no. 1 (February 1973), 34–37.

[36] D. B. Montgomery, "New Product Distribution—An Analysis of Supermarket Buyer Decisions," *Journal of Marketing Research*, XII, no. 3 (August 1975), 255–64.

meet their customer needs by helping them to manufacture, distribute, and market more effectively. The ICF is useful as a conceptual framework and as a vehicle to guide market research.

> *As a conceptual framework*, the ICF forces the user to distinguish between product attributes (in product space) and customer benefits (in benefits space), and to be aware of limitations imposed upon this provision of benefits by quality, technological, and price constraints. Moreover, the ICF signals the value of accurate market information to the user and helps guide new product development and market communications strategy.
>
> *As a research tool*, the ICF can be used to develop and estimate operational models of information integration in the value-added chain such as the CDM. Furthermore, the ICF can be employed in establishing market decision support and competitive intelligence systems.

Clearly the ICF can be useful in designing strategies and plans for industrial marketing in a general sense, such as in telling you roughly the nature of the customers' interests and how to reach them. But the CDM is needed to tell you much more about what to say, how to say it, how much to say, and when to say it. For example, you will recall the G.E. example of Figure 11-7. It suggests that G.E. should probably focus upon telling the specific customers identified by the ICF all about *full-cost benefit*, how to phrase that content, how frequently to say it, and just when to tell them about it. That it should is shown by the enormous problems the American car manufacturers are now undergoing in attempting to automate.[37]

ICF theory, particularly in combination with the CDM designed for RPS, LPS, and EPS, respectively, represents a useful tool for marketing managers and researchers in organizational markets.

Questions

1. What is a "buying center" and what is its relevance to marketing?
2. How does the purchasing agent, who is ostensibly responsible for buying for an organization, fit into the "buying center"? In what ways will his role likely be different in RPS than in EPS?
3. What is the relation between the ICF and the CDM? Describe this as carefully as you can.
4. If you were designing G.E. marketing strategy and you had access to Figure 11-6, how would this influence your strategy?
5. If you were the marketing manager for a manufacturing firm selling to large retailers, how could you use the dyadic ICF in designing strategy to reduce "trade promotion" costs?

---

[37] *The Wall Street Journal* (New York edition), May 13, 1986, pp. 1 and 10.

CHAPTER 12

Culture and Subcultures

1. INTRODUCTION

Up to now we have simplified the consumer behavior discussion by assuming that all consumers are alike. Yet we know intuitively that one consumer may be quite different from another in his or her innate characteristics such as culture or buying situation. As a consequence, they might buy differently. This possibility is, of course, what market segmentation is all about: finding these differences and catering to them as a way of obtaining competitive advantage. In fact, positioning our product in terms of consumers is the most fundamental element of marketing strategy, as we saw in Chapters 8 through 11.

Culture has much more relevance than just segmentation. For international, or cross-cultural marketing, culture may provide an almost complete orientation toward your total marketing problem because culture is so pervasive in its effect upon human behavior.

2. CULTURE

2.1 Introduction

The broadest and most general characteristic of a consumer is her culture. A culture area usually coincides with nationality but is more restrictive than race. *Culture* can be defined as the material and behavioral arrangements whereby a society achieves greater satisfaction for its members. Values, language, and beliefs are perhaps the more significant of these arrangements.

The fundamental role of values in marketing has been discussed in Chapter 4. Language, also discussed in Chapter 4, has been emphasized as a central feature of marketing. Consequently, we can assume that language may play a subtle role in marketing across cultures. For example, if you are introducing an innovation and need figures of speech to convey it, these are often different across cultures. "The Saudis' interest in expensive perfume (the sixth biggest fragrance market in the world) has more to do with history. . . . Perfume has been a part of their commercial culture since ancient times. Perfume has also been one of the few sensuous luxuries allowed by a very austere and religious society that bans alcohol and formerly prohibited tobacco."[1]

Beliefs have to do with what a people think the world is like. As you saw in Chapter 3, beliefs about anything can have dimensions. One is the recognition dimension: how people recognize a thing when they see it. But beliefs also can have a second dimension, the evaluative or attitudinal: how good it is. The need for a marketer to be sensitive to cross-cultural differences and have well-developed beliefs has become sharper in recent years, as managers in the American economy have focused more upon the multinational market.

Robertson et al. nicely describe three dimensions of world culture—demographic, organizational, and normative—that can help us structure our thinking in this complex area.[2] Not only are the issues complex but they are subtle: we often don't recognize the characteristics of our own culture. Outsiders are much more likely to do so. The demographic dimensions are not only important but are more concrete and easily understood. A review of Table 12-1 shows how important these demographic differences can be, for example, literacy rates, and how population can be studied.

The organizational dimension is relevant for understanding the consumer as well as the industrial buyer. We focused upon its role in industrial buying and dealt with it in Chapter 11, Strategy for Organizational Buying. But here the term "organizational" is used in a broader sense to refer types of societies, for example, folk society versus an industrial society, and the participation patterns associated with them.

The normative dimension is made up of the culturally approved attitudes and behaviors. We need to distinguish culturally relevant values and *norms*. We are already familiar with the distinction but not exactly in these terms. Values were emphasized earlier in Chapter 4 as the source of the benefits that a consumer uses in buying.

Norms are the *weighted* benefits used in buying. In our society today high-calorie foods are considered undesirable. In 1973 when Miller introduced

---

[1] M. Field, "Fragrance Marketers Sniff Out Rich Aroma," *Advertising Age*, January 30, 1986, p. 10.

[2] T. S. Robertson, J. Zielinski, and S. Ward, *Consumer Behavior* (Glenview, Ill.: Scott, Foresman, 1984), p. 556.

Table 12-1 Demographic Variables in Selected Countries

	India	Chile	Ghana	Japan	Iraq	Switzer-land	United States
Population (thousands)*	643,000	10,880	10,650	114,850	12,350	6,310	203,235
Population density†							
(per square mile)	506.6	37.2	115.6	799.0	73.5	395.8	57.5
Population growth‡ (%)	2.2	1.9	2.8	1.3	3.4	0.3	0.8
Urbanization§							
(% in urban areas)	20.0	76.0	32.0	72.0	51.0	55.0	74.0
Life expectancy (years)							
(male-female)	41.9–40.5	60.5–66.0	41.9–45.1	72.1–77.3	57.6–57.4	70.3–76.2	68.7–76.5
Infant mortality							
(per 1,000 births)	122	55.6	156	9.3	108.1	10.7	15.1
Literacy (% of adults)	33.4	88.1	30.2	97.8	24.2	99.0	99.0
Per capital income‖	$150	$1,050	$580	$4,910	$1,390	$8,880	$7,890

* Est. 1978, except U.S., 1970.

† Est. 1978, except U.S., 1970.

‡ Annual rate of increase, 1970–77.

§ Figures for 1970. These are not strictly comparable, because the countries define urban areas differently.

‖ In U.S. dollars (1976).

Sources: Harold H. Kassarjian and Thomas S. Robertson (1981), *Perspectives in Consumer Behavior*, 3rd ed. (Glenview, Ill.: Scott, Foresman), p. 481. Data from *Information Please Almanac* (1979), 33rd ed. (New York: Viking); *The Statesman's Year Book—1979/1980* (1978), 115th ed. (New York: St. Martin's); *Statistical Yearbook, 1977* (1978) (Paris: UNESCO); *Demographic Yearbook* (1978) 29th ed. (New York: United Nations); and *World Tables—1976* (1976) (Baltimore: International Bank for Reconstruction and Development/World Bank).

Source: T. S. Robertson, J. Zielinski, and S. Ward, *Consumer Behavior* (Glenview, Ill.: Scott, Foresman, 1984), p. 557. © 1984 by Scott, Foresman and Company. Reprinted by permission.

Lite beer, competitors ridiculed it as being "for sissies," but today that market has become a major source of revenue and competitors have followed suit. This happened because "low calories" as a benefit have become weighted more heavily by many Americans.[3] However, cultural norms apply not only to buying but to all behavior. Nevertheless, the principle is the same: they are the *action implications* of a *person's values*. A society may place a strong value on achievement versus other societies and consequently a norm in that society could be that all children will complete high school. Obviously a marketer needs to be sensitive to these norms as Miller was with its Lite beer, identifying the relevant ones and not violating any of them with your marketing.

Having briefly examined the nature of culture and something of its relevance, we might ask, "In what specific ways is it really significant?" and, therefore, "Where does it impinge on the CDM?"

[3] Monci Jo Williams, "Betting on a Beer Without a Buzz," *Fortune*, 109, no. 13 (June 25, 1984), 76.

2.2   Cross-cultural Standardization

A long-running debate among marketing people is the extent to which a company's marketing program should be different across cultures to be successful. If culture is a matter of values and values differ across cultures, there would seem to be no question but that different marketing programs may be necessary since values are the sources of benefit importance weightings that drive consumer behavior.

But a recent quote from *The Wall Street Journal* asserts that

> If advertising agencies had their way, multinational companies would all be racing to develop "world brands" that would be marketed the same around the globe. "As you expand brands across continents, you keep getting bigger economies of scale and more power," says John O'Toole, chairman, Foote, Cone & Belding Communications, Inc.[4]

Some evidence is provided by Al Boote who in 1978, surveyed British, French, and German women in their homes and compared their values.[5]

The differences are seen particularly in Table 12-2, where the values are grouped in four categories. These categories can then be compared across countries. The differences are great. For the "Spontaneous" grouping, which refers to the relevance of "inside interests," the French clearly dominate. As for the "Contemporary homemaker" the British dominate, but most strongly for "Appearance conscious," the German women stand out. These findings leave little doubt that major differences exist.

It is not surprising, then, to find in *The Wall Street Journal*:

> At Unilever PLC, the Anglo Dutch food and detergent company, executives say it takes patience to cash in on a gradual merging of national tastes. Standard preferences are more common in detergents and soaps than in foods, they add, Unilever's Jif brand liquid soap sells well across Europe, but its margarine had different names and styles in each country. And Unilever says its Italian-style ice cream had to be modified for France even though sales were good elsewhere in Europe. The reason: a French belief that if it wasn't French, it wasn't worth eating.[6]

In summary, there is undoubtedly a trend toward standardization of tastes. Improved communication technology, for example, satellites, and cable TV, would be expected to have an effect especially in changing the belief element of culture. Values and language will probably be much slower to change. Further, if we find such differences across such well-developed countries as seen in Table

---

[4] *The Wall Street Journal* (New York edition), June 14, 1984, p. 33.

[5] A. S. Boote, "Psychographic Segmentation in Europe," *Journal of Advertising Research*, 22, no. 6 (December 1982/January 1983), 21.

[6] *The Wall Street Journal* (New York edition), June 14, 1984, p. 33.

Table 12-2 Composite European Segments by Country

	SEGMENTS DEFINED BY VALUES ORIENTATIONS (%)			
Countries	Traditional Homemaker	Spontaneous	Contemporary Homemaker	Appearance Conscious
United Kingdom	37	29	53	16
France	36	66	23	3
Germany	27	5	24	81

SOURCE: A. S. Boote, "Psychographic Segmentation in Europe," *Journal of Advertising Research*, 22, no. 6 (December 1982/January 1983), 25.

12-2, imagine what those differences must be across a wider world including the Third World countries. The need is for sharper tools such as the CDM to tell us what these differences are and what their significance is in terms of the relationships among the variables. Clearly these cultural differences will impinge upon the recognition variable (B) and upon the attitude (A) variable in the CDM via the benefit weightings. They will also probably impinge more broadly upon the consumers' intention (I); that is, perceptual differences as well will occur. There will also be times when it would be advisable to separate the information (F) input according to culture because their perception of the ad can be influenced by their culture.

Let us now return to the characteristics of culture that makes it so profoundly relevant and that we should be fully aware of in planning marketing strategy in cross-cultural settings.

2.3 Key Characteristics of Culture

Robertson and others nicely list four aspects of culture.[7]

1. Culture is *symbolic*. Words, objects, products, and actions are not neutral but often have very important emotional meanings.
2. Culture is *pervasive*. It permeates every aspect of life. It is often very difficult to identify cultural influences, because we are so surrounded by and absorbed in them.
3. Cultural values and norms are transmitted from *generation to generation*. Values and norms define numerous aspects of accepted behavior.
4. Culture and language are integrally *connected*. Language is not only a tool that we use for expression, but also a dynamic force that can sometimes shape reality.

The symbolic characteristic of culture is a subtle notion, as are all symbols. For example, take a country's flag. It is in physical terms merely a piece of cloth that is brightly colored. But when a loyal citizen sees that flag, particularly such as standing at attention at evening retreat in the military, he *perceives*

---

[7] Robertson and others, *Consumer Behavior*, pp. 561–62.

something far more symbolic and entirely different from the physical description. Tears may flow, especially if the person is in a foreign country and his nation is at war. A more marketing-relevant example is probably the Merrill Lynch bull discussed at length in the outset of Chapter 2. In our culture, the "bellowing bull," for many of us, probably conjures up the image of strength, power, and the "machismo."

We are now beginning to consider the *signs* that these physical objects like the flag emit for some people and the symbolic meaning that the physical object conveys for them. Some American advertisers are beginning to study and use the sign concept. In fact, there are two schools, the American and the Continental European. Morris Holbrook has described and distinguished them well.[8] The American version, called *semiotics*, is older and better developed. Jay Houghton, a former advertising man and new manager of marketing for Audi of America, writes

> I believe it (semiotics) can provide a conceptual framework for decoding the pictures, symbols and signs of today's culture, which include advertising as well as products.[9]

The Continental European version is called *semiology*, is newer and not as well developed but may ultimately be even more useful.

A marketer must be able to identify and understand these expressive symbols, which can connote something highly influential in shaping buying behavior. The *referential* symbols—those that label, represent, and indicate tangible objects—are essential to know. But it is an *expressive* symbol on which you can really stub your toe in designing marketing strategy cross-culturally. This danger was implied in Chapter 10 in discussing the extension of the CDM with its emphasis upon utilitarian benefits to nonutilitarian products and services. These expressive symbols probably often connote those nonutilitarian benefits that are dominant in buying works of art, musical programs, and other items of this type. Tools for dealing with these expressive symbols are now being forged by Holbrook and others. Holbrook and Grayson, for example, show the subtle meanings that can be found when the tools are applied to the movie *Out of Africa*.[10] The study indicates how these expressive symbols can be applied to communicating subtle cultural characteristics to consumers.

The need for these tools is great because of the second characteristic of culture, its pervasiveness. It pervades almost every aspect of one's life, and yet it is difficult for members of that culture to identify these effects because

[8] M. B. Holbrook, "The Study of Signs in Consumer Esthetics: An Egocentric View," unpublished working paper Eighth Annual Summer Institute for Semiotic and Structural Studies (Northwestern University, Evanston, Ill., July 10–12, 1986).

[9] J. C. Houghton, "Semantics on the Assembly Line," *Advertising Age*, March 16, 1987, p. 18.

[10] M. B. Holbrook and M. W. Grayson, "The Semiology of Cinematic Consumption: Symbolic Consumer Behavior in *Out of Africa*," *Journal of Consumer Research*, 13 (December 1986), 374–81.

they are so surrounded by and absorbed in them. It is much easier for an outsider to identify them. Once marketers begin to use those tools and rely less upon their intuition, they will begin to be able to sense these cultural effects and to describe them to themselves and to communicate them to others.

Related to this is that most of us believe our own culture is best: we are *egocentric*. This has been seen in many Americans in the past decade or so with regard to Japanese cars. It has been very difficult for them to accept the fact that small Japanese cars may be better than small American cars as we have all observed. This fact has violated our basic beliefs.

The third characteristic of a culture is that its values and norms are transmitted from generation to another generation. But in the past its implications for buying products were not clear. With the CDM, however, those implications are fairly obvious: the weightings attached to benefits can be passed down from generation to generation. These norms, however, may be secondary because they are more subject to change. It is the values that are the more permanent.

But marketers can benefit from knowing more than just these norms (product benefits) even though the norms are the foundation of marketing strategy. The marketer has to design advertising, a distribution system, and so on, and in doing this he can run afoul of norms that he never dreamed of in designing a cross-cultural marketing program. Back in the "States," a seminude young lady may draw favorable attention to an ad and the product, but in Saudi Arabia this may draw attention that the advertiser may wish he never had. In Pakistan, for example, when the local womens' club wish to hold a fashion show and model Western styles, they cannot use a native but must use a Western woman.[11]

The final characteristic of culture is that it is so integrally connected to *language* and can be another place to stub your toe. Most of marketing is communication, and most of communication is by language. The disasters of advertising being translated into another language are legion. Why the cultural content should be so important is seen in the following example:

> In one of the Motilone dialects of Colombia, the single word *eto kapa* means to hatch out eggs, to commit suicide and to make corncakes. For speakers of this language, three meanings that seem unrelated to us are thought of as three different ways of using the same word. In that society, a corpse is wrapped in a fetal position before burial, so a person who commits suicide is thought of as making himself into an egg-shaped object. And in making corncakes, the corn is molded into egg-shaped lumps. Without a thorough knowledge of the Motilone culture, it would not be possible for us to deduce a single coherent concept from the English translations of the word eto kapa.[12]

Imagine the mistake that a copywriter could make in advertising corncakes in that culture. Unfortunately, most of us live our daily lives without encountering

---

[11] D. Kline, "How Islam Collides with Advertising," *Advertising Age*, August 2, 1982, p. M-3.

[12] G. A. Miller, *Language and Speech* (San Francisco: W. H. Freeman, 1981), p. 101.

any of these translation problems and hence seldom notice the cultural presuppositions underlying our own words. Do our dictionaries tell us anything about the cultural presuppositions of our words that can aid us? Unfortunately not.

3. SUBCULTURES

Obviously not everyone within a given culture is always like everyone else in that culture. They may merely share some very important similarities, as we have indicated in the foregoing paragraphs. It is often convenient to work with subcultures within a culture in attempting to find meaningful market niches or segments. A *subculture* is defined as "a category of people who share a sense of identification that is distinguishable from that of the total culture."[13] Notice that they share most of the overall values but differ on some.

Should the Yuppies—young urban professionals—be viewed as a subculture? An SRI International study defines them as young (between 25 and 40), well paid (over $40,000 a year), and holding managerial jobs: "they smoke far less and jog far more than the average American adult. They are three times as apt to travel abroad, and nearly twice as apt to go to the movies. And they are heavy users of credit cards. . . . To find a chunk of the population whose priority is not in finding a bargain but in paying for quality—not in getting by, getting *style*—is to find an ideal target for consumer goods."[14] But do they share a sense of identification that would suggest even more values and norms held in common? Talking with them often suggests they do.

Three of the major subcultures in the United States are blacks, Hispanics, and whites and are compared in Table 12-3. We emphasize them because they are "built-in" segments waiting to be served. Blacks and Hispanics represent important markets, especially in the metropolitan areas. Hispanics are the strongest of the three. It is interesting that Hispanics have a significantly higher income than do blacks, but both are substantially lower than whites. These characteristics have obvious implications for marketing, for example, the number of consumers, where they are located, and how much they are likely to buy if their buying behavior is really different.

That Hispanics, for example, respond differently to advertising than do Anglos is indicated in Table 12-4. As you can see, Hispanics respond in general more favorably. This caused Ogilvy and Mather to conclude that

> With Hispanics responding less critically to advertising that is primarily designed to reach Anglos, it is little wonder that marketers who understand how to address them directly are finding out just how rewarding this market can be.[15]

[13] Robertson and others, *Consumer Behavior*, p. 528.
[14] *Christian Science Monitor* (Boston edition), January 28, 1985, p. 21.
[15] *Listening Post* (Ogilvy and Mather), no. 58 (June 1984), p. 1.

Table 12-3 Demographic Profiles of Major Subcultures in the United States, 1980 Census

Characteristics	*SUBCULTURE*		
	Blacks	*Hispanics**	*Whites*
Population[†]	26.5 million	14.6 million	188.3 million
Population, percent, 1980	11.7%	6.4%	83.1%
Projected population, percent, 1990[‡]	12.2%	7.0%	80.8%
Median age[†]	24.9 years	23.2 years	31.3 years
Average family size[§]	3.8	3.9	3.3
% of Population in metropolitan areas[‖]	75.1%	85.3%	65.0%
Median education[¶] (years of school completed by those 18 and over)	12.1	11.3	12.5
Median family income**	$12,618	$14,711	$20,840

* Hispanics in the 1980 Census are those who classified themselves in one of the Spanish-origin categories—*Mexican, Puerto Rican, Cuban,* or *Other Spanish/Hispanic.* Hispanics in the 1970 Census classified themselves as *white* in 93 percent of cases, but in the 1980 Census, only 56 percent reported their race as *white* and 40 percent reported *other.*

[†] Total U.S. population for 1980 is reported at 226.5 million. Totals here are larger since Hispanics are also included in *white* and *black* categories. U.S. Bureau of the Census (1981), *1980 Census of Population, Supplementary Reports,* PC 80-S1-1 "Age, Sex, Race, and Spanish Origin of the Population by Regions, Divisions, and States: 1980" (Washington, D.C.: GPO), p. 3.

[‡] Reid T. Reynolds, Bryant Robey, and Cheryl Russell (1980), "Demographics of the 1980s," *American Demographics,* 2 (Jan.), pp. 16–17.

[§] U.S. Bureau of the Census (1979), *Current Population Reports,* Series P-20, No. 340, "Household and Family Characteristics: *March 1978*" (Washington, D.C.: GPO), pp. 10–13.

[‖] U.S. Bureau of the Census (1979), pp. 53–59.

[¶] U.S. Bureau of the Census (1980), *Current Population Reports,* Series P-20, No. 356, "Educational Attainment in the United States: March 1978 and 1979 (Washington, D.C.: GPO), pp. 24–27.

** U.S. Bureau of the Census (1980), *Provisional Estimates of Social, Economic and Housing Characteristics: 1980,* PHC80-S1-1 (Washington, D.C.: GPO), p. 36.

Source: T. S. Robertson, J. Zielinski, and S. Ward, *Consumer Behavior* (Glenview, Ill.: Scott, Foresman, 1984), p. 537. © 1984 by Scott, Foresman and Company. Reprinted by permission.

That Anglos consider advertising a less helpful source of new products may seem surprising. However, Hispanics, being mainly in an unfamiliar culture, probably use word-of-mouth from peers to verify information received from advertising.

In examining a subculture for determining whether it offers market segmentation possibilities, you should go much deeper. As in the case of blacks, for example, there has been much discussion about the black subculture. Blacks received particular attention a decade ago after David Caplovitz wrote his challenging book, *The Poor Pay More.*[16] Andreasen has nicely summarized the point of view that emerged in that book:

[16] David Caplovitz, *The Poor Pay More* (New York: The Free Press, 1963).

Basically, Caplovitz saw the marketing system in the ghetto as "a deviant one in which unethical and illegal practices abound" (p. 180). In a mass consumption economy, the poor are likely to want much of what the non-poor have, some of them to compensate for inabilities to spend for other status symbols (educating, housing, etc.).[17]

Caplovitz had observed but had no systematic data to support his general thesis that blacks paid more than whites in the city.

Table 12-4   Attitude Toward Advertising

	AGREE	
	Hispanics	Anglos
Advertising helps to inform people about new products.	78%	92%
Advertising presents an honest picture of products.	41	22
Advertising gives a good idea about a product by showing the kinds of people who use it.	41	20
The way to an average family as shown on TV commercials is true to life.	27	12

Source: *Listening Post* (Ogilvy and Mather), no. 58, (June 1984), p. 1.

As other researchers dug into providing an answer to the important question that Caplovitz had raised, differences were found but apparently not to the extent expected. The question became much more sharply focused on why such differences existed, if they did. One of the most thorough pieces of work was done by Don Sexton. He concluded that part of the reason that blacks pay more was that they shop more in independent stores, and these tend to charge higher prices than chain stores.[18] This conclusion coincided with a study by Goodman.[19] A key question was whether black people were victims of price discrimination. Neither Sexton nor the Federal Trade Commission could support an affirmative answer here.[20]

Blacks have improved their situation. If you look at Table 12-5, which compares blacks in Chicago in 1971 versus five years earlier, you notice their income has improved. To illustrate, those with over $15,000 family income went from 3% of the sample to 12%.

[17] A. Andreasen, "The Ghetto Marketing Life Cycle: A Case of Underachievement," *Journal of Marketing Research*, XV (February 1978), 20.

[18] D. E. Sexton, Jr., "Comparing the Cost of Food to Blacks and to Whites," *Journal of Marketing*, 35, no. 3 (July 1971), 45.

[19] C. S. Goodman, "Do the Poor Pay More?" *Journal of Marketing*, 32, no. 1 (January 1968), 18–24.

[20] Sexton, "Comparing the Cost of Food," 46.

Table 12-5   Family Income Before Taxes for Selected Black Households

Income Range (Annual)	HOUSEHOLDS	
	1971	1966
Under $3,000	3%	18%
$3,000–4,999	10	25
$5,000–7,999	20	28
$8,000–9,999	24	15
$10,000–14,999	28	11
$15,000 and over	12	3
No answer	3	—

SOURCE: C. M. Larson and H. G. Wales, "Brand Preferences of Chicago Blacks," *Journal of Advertising Research*, 13, no. 4 (August 1973), 17.

Table 12-6   Jewish Ethnicity and Buying Characteristics

	Students	Adults
Childhood information exposure		
Correlation*	.22	.21
Significance	.001	.001
Adult information seeking		
Correlation	.30	.34
Significance	.0001	.0001
Consumption innovativeness		
Correlation	.23	.27
Significance	.001	.0001
Consumption information transfer		
Correlation	.21	.40
Significance	.001	.0001
Active memory capacity		
Correlation	.23	—
Significance	.001	—
Divergent processing		
Correlation	—	.21
Significance	—	.001
$n = 298$ students, 363 adult consumers.		

* Regression coefficients are uncorrected for attenuation due to unreliability of the measures. Hence the reported coefficients should be viewed as conservative estimates of the relationship between the predictor and criterion variables. Correcting the coefficients for attenuation would not substantially affect the magnitude of the reported correlations, however, as reliability of the measures employed was generally quite high ($> .75$) (Greene and Carmines, 1980).

SOURCE: E. Hirschman, "American Jewish Ethnicity: Its Relationship to Some Selected Aspects of Consumer Behavior," *Journal of Marketing*, 45, no. 3 (Summer 1981), 108. Published by the American Marketing Association.

Religious groups also make up subcultures, for example, the Amish, Mormons, and Jews. Elizabeth Hirschman did a carefully controlled study of Jews versus non-Jews,[21] specifically, computing regression coefficients for both Jews and non-Jews against a number of marketing-related characteristics (see Table 12-6). For three of the characteristics—information seeking from mass media, innovativeness, and transfer of information to others about new products—the greater the Jewish ethnicity the more likely they were to exhibit these three buying characteristics. These relations suggest that both students and adults of Jewish background are more likely than non-Jews to engage in these three activities.

As you can see in Table 12-6, clear indications of the potential role of subculture for marketing emerged. From this study and the information-processing theory of earlier chapters, we can begin to draw inferences about innovation diffusion and information transmission among Jewish as distinct from other subcultures. Innovativeness is probably greater among Jews and a faster product life cycle may occur, particularly because Jews are more inclined to be "opinion leaders" as the term has been used in the diffusion literature or, more accurately, "information givers."

Finally, the data in Table 12-6 combined with the theory of earlier chapters permits us to conclude that subculture may *cause* consumption patterns, not merely "be associated with them." This conclusion deepens our understanding of subcultural influences in buying.

4. CONCLUSION

The key elements of culture—values, language, and beliefs—especially if they are related back to the CDM variables—give you a set of tools to recognize, compare, and evaluate cultures for marketing purposes. As you readily see, cultures and subcultures can bring marketing opportunities. Specifically, each culture will tend to have its own product hierarchies coded in terms of the language of that culture.[22] Thus, you can easily see why these cultural and subcultural differences may cause consumers to buy different products. This is especially true of products bought on a nonutilitarian basis such as artistic events (e.g., music, drama, perfumes).

But not only are different products bought depending upon the culture but also different communication copy and media are often necessary, as we saw in the case of the Hispanics earlier in the chapter, for example. A good way to conceptualize the significance of culture, to remember it and to communicate it to others in the company, is in terms of core strategy used in Chapters

---

[21] E. C. Hirschman, "American Jewish Ethnicity: Its Relationship to Some Selected Aspects of Consumer Behavior," *Journal of Marketing*, 45 (Summer 1981), 102–10.

[22] E. Rosch, "Principles of Categorization," in E. Rosch and B. B. Lloyd, eds., *Cognition and Categorization* (Hillsdale, N.J.: Lawrence Erlbaum Associates, 1978), p. 28.

8 through 11. Specifically, the impact of culture is heavily on benefits used by consumers and their weighting of those benefits so as to give you a competitive advantage by segments. These benefits are the centerpiece, the attitude (A) of the CDM. The cultural variable can also be fed into the intention (I) variable to capture other cultural influences. Finally, the same measures are taken of a few key competitors.

These important and complex differences among consumers are dealt with more systematically and critically in Chapter 15.

This additional precision of the CDM can be exceedingly useful as a company explores and attempts to serve widely different cultures. This precision becomes especially important in decisions at the corporate level. If marketers have difficulty communicating cross-cultural differences to each other, imagine the difficulty of communicating those same ideas to finance, manufacturing, R & D, and human resources people at the higher levels in the organization whose cooperation is always essential to effective marketing.

Questions

1. What is culture and its elements?
2. What evidence can you provide of differences across cultures?
3. What is a subculture and what are the major subcultures in the United States?
4. What are the demographic dimensions of world culture?
5. Describe the normative dimensions of world culture and their role that influences the use of the CDM.

CHAPTER 13

Social Class and Reference Groups

1. INTRODUCTION

Having examined the two broad social groupings of culture and subcultures, let us turn to two additional social groupings: social class and reference groups. These are two more dimensions on which consumers can differ and therefore offer both market segmenting possibilities and further understanding of the consumer.

2. SOCIAL CLASS

2.1 Introduction

Social class can be defined as an aggregate of individuals in the society who occupy a broadly similar position on the scale of *prestige*. Most everyone would agree that a social structure exists in the United States that reflects variation in the prestige of its members. Therefore, we have different social classes that probably buy somewhat differently according to class. AT&T's market research, for example, shows that social class makes a substantial difference in how people respond to types of telephones. As you note in Table 13-1 where all relations are significant at the 5% level, upper classes are much more likely to prefer telephones that improve the decorative style of a room, that are modern in design, and that offer a variety of telephone styles. This is less true of lower classes.

Table 13-1   Consumer's Socioeconomic Status and Telephone Preferences

Style/Color Statements	Lower-Class Agreement (%) (n = 25)	Lower-Middle-Class Agreement (%) (n = 108)	Upper-Middle-Class Agreement (%) (n =202)	Upper-Class Agreement (%) (n =105)
Phones should come in patterns and designs as well as colors.	60%	80%	63%	58%
A telephone should improve the decorative style of a room.	47	82	73	77
Telephones should be modern in design.	58	85	83	89
A home should have a variety of telephone styles.	8	46	39	51
You can keep all those special phones. All I want is a phone that works.	83	67	68	56
The style of a telephone is unimportant to me.	86	54	58	51

SOURCE: A. M. Roscoe, Jr., A. LeClaire, Jr., and L. G. Schiffman, "Theory and Management Applications of Demographics in Buyer Behavior," in A. G. Woodside, J. N. Sheth, and P. D. Bennett, eds., *Consumer and Industrial Buying Behavior* (New York: North-Holland, 1977), p. 74. Reprinted by permission of the publisher. Copyright 1977 by Elsevier Science Publishing Co., Inc.

But social class is a slippery concept as one of the pioneer researchers, Richard Coleman, indicates:

> There are no two ways about it: social class is a difficult idea. Sociologists, in whose discipline the concept emerged, are not of one mind about its value and validity. Consumer researchers, to whose field its use has spread, display confusion about when and how to apply it. The American public is noticeably uncomfortable with the realities about life that it reflects. All who try to measure it have trouble. Studying it rigorously and imaginatively can be monstrously expensive. Yet, all these difficulties notwithtanding, the proposition still holds: social class is worth troubling over for the insights it offers on the marketplace behavior of the nation's consumers.[1]

Americans with their heavy value on democracy have difficulty accepting the inequality implied in social class as Coleman indicated. Consequently emotion is often encountered in discussing the topic.

2.2   Origins of Social Class Concept

Much research has been done on the concept, beginning with W. Lloyd Warner's Yankee City Series at the University of Chicago in the 1940s. His basic idea was that people interacting "in the social systems of a community evaluate the participation of those around them, that the place where an individual participates is evaluated, and that the members of the community are explicitly or implicitly

---

[1] R. P. Coleman, "The Continuing Significance of Social Class to Marketing," *Journal of Consumer Research*, 10, no. 3 (December 1983), 265.

Table 13-2 Measuring a Person's Status

Status Characteristic	Rating		Weight		Weighted Ruling
Occupation	2	×	4	=	8
Source of income	3	×	3	=	9
House type	2	×	3	=	6
Dwelling area	3	×	2	=	6
				Weighted total =	29

SOURCE: W. L. Warner, M. Meeker, and K. Eells, *Social Class in America* (Chicago: Science Research Associates, 1949), p. 41; Torchbooks, Harper & Row Publishers, Inc.

aware of the ranking and translate their evaluations of such social participation into social-class ratings that can be communicated to the investigator."[2] Warner developed interviewing and rating techniques that showed this to be essentially true. The ratings and weights are on scales of 1 to 7. The weightings were developed by Warner's group. Table 13-2 indicates how such measures can be taken. Warner's work was indeed an exciting piece of research, and in the 1950s it began to receive considerable attention as a market research tool. Lloyd Warner was often called upon to speak before marketing groups.

But as implied in the quotation from Richard Coleman, another of the pioneers, not a lot of progress has been made to sharpen conceptualizing the idea and rendering it more precisely measurable. Coleman maintains that this is because the results that have been obtained have "remained the private property of research houses and their clients."[3] Coleman's views deserve serious consideration because the weights illustrated in Table 13-2 have probably changed in our society since Warner did the pioneering work in the 1940s.

2.3   New Look at Social Class

Recently two new views of social class have emerged. In a sense they are quite different. One, Dennis Gilbert and Joseph Kahl, *The American Class Structure: A New Synthesis* (1982),[4] took the orientation of "occupational role, income level, living conditions, and identification with a possibly disadvantaged ethnic/racial group."[5] Or as they say, "We pay more attention to capitalist ownership and the occupational division of labor as the defining variables.". . .[6] As you can see in the left side of Table 13-3 from their description of social classes, their emphasis is on the economic, political aspects.

The second approach was by Richard Coleman, Lee Rainwater, and

[2] W. L. Warner, M. Meeker, and K. Eells, *Social Class in America* (Chicago: Science Research Associates, 1949), p. 41.

[3] Coleman, "Continuing Significance of Social Class," p. 270.

[4] D. Gilbert and J. Kahl, *The American Class Structure: A New Synthesis* (Homewood, Ill: Dorsey Press, 1982).

[5] Coleman, "Continuing Significance of Social Class," p. 266.

[6] Ibid.

Table 13-3   Two Recent Views of the American Status Structure

The Gilbert-Kahl New Synthesis Class Structure:* A Situations Model from Political Theory and Sociological Analysis	The Coleman-Rainwater Social Standing Class Hierarchy:† A Reputational, Behavioral View in the Community Study Tradition
Upper Americans The Capitalist Class (1%)—Their investment decisions shape the national economy; income mostly from assets, earned/inherited; prestige university connections. Upper Middle Class (14%)—Upper managers, professionals, medium businessmen; college educated; family income ideally runs nearly twice the national average.	Upper Americans Upper-Upper (0.3%)—The "capital S society" world of inherited wealth, aristocratic names. Lower-Upper (1.2%)—The newer social elite, drawn from current professional, corporate leadership. Upper-Middle (12.5%)—The rest of college graduate managers and professionals; life-style centers on private clubs, causes, and the arts.
Middle Americans Middle Class (33%)—Middle-level white-collar, top-level blue-collar; education past high school typical; income somewhat above the national average. Working Class (32%)—Middle-level blue-collar; lower-level white-collar; income runs slightly below the national average; education is also slightly below.	Middle Americans Middle Class (32%)—Average pay white-collar workers and their blue-collar friends; live on "the better side of town," try to "do the proper things." Working Class (38%)—Average pay blue-collar workers; lead "working class life-style" whatever the income, school background, and job.
Marginal and Lower Americans The Working Poor (11–12%)—Below mainstream America in living standard, but above the poverty line; low-paid service workers, operatives; some high school education. The Underclass (8–9%)—Depend primarily on welfare system for sustenance; living standard below poverty line; not regularly employed; lack schooling.	Lower Americans "A lower group of people but not the lowest" (9%)—Working, not on welfare; living standard is just above poverty; behavior judged "crude," "trashy." "Real Lower-Lower" (7%)—On welfare, visibly poverty-stricken, usually out of work (or have "the dirtiest jobs"); "bums," "common criminals."

* Abstracted by Coleman from Dennis Gilbert and Joseph A. Kahl (1962), "The American Class Structure: A Synthesis," Chapter 11 in *The American Class Structure: A New Synthesis*. Homewood, Ill.: The Dorsey Press.

† This condensation of the Coleman-Rainwater view is drawn from Chapters 8, 9, and 10 of Richard P. Coleman and Lee P. Rainwater, with Kent A. McClelland (1978). *Social Standing in America: New Dimensions of Class*, New York: Basic Books.

Source: R. P. Coleman, "The Continuing Significance of Social Class to Marketing," *Journal of Consumer Research*, 10, no. 3 (December 1983), 267.

Kurt McClelland, *Social Standing in America: New Dimensions of Class* (1978).[7] It was more in line with the view of Lloyd Warner, the founder of social class research. You can see this in the right side of Table 13-3.

Although different the interesting aspect was that both came out with essentially the same structure as you see by comparing the two sides of Table 13-3. This commonality is encouraging for the belief that social class may be a meaningful concept for marketers to consider in trying to classify consumers for strategy purposes.

[7] R. Coleman and L. Rainwater, with K. McClelland, *Social Standing in America: New Dimensions of Class* (New York: Basic Books, 1978).

To serve marketing needs, Coleman suggests that we view social class in the United States as made up of upper Americans, middle-class, working-class and lower Americans. You can see how these are formed from Table 13-3. But he warns that "it must always be kept in mind that a diversity of family situations and a nearly unbelievable range in income totals are contained within each class."[8]

A "prototype" household of middle-class Middle American status has as its head a man employed in some lower management office job, earning between $24,000 and $29,999 a year (1983 urban average dollars), whose wife isn't working, so that is all the family income. Almost as likely to be middle class is a divorcee with two years of college as an educational credential, who is trying to support two children on a legal secretary's salary of as little as $13,500—and who may be best friend and frequent bridge-playing chum to the wife in the first case. Another middle-class home will contain a working couple, both in office jobs, earning in combined total $42,000 or even $45,000 a year. A fourth might have as its head the owner of a bowling alley and restaurant whose wife may or may not be helping to run it. Or the owner could be a widow, divorcee, or never-married woman. In any case, the living standard projected by house, car(s), and clothes suggests an income of $60,000 or $70,000 a year. Yet the social status is still middle class because, through lack of mobility aspirations and/or social skills, no upper-class American connections and acceptance have been established.

2.4   Social Class and Motivation

The value of social class to marketers is that the motivations of each of these four groupings are different; what they value and want are different. They differ greatly, for example, in how much they are tied to their community and existing friends and in the cars they tend to buy. The lower classes are more tied to their community. It is this emphasis on *motivation* that largely distinguishes the two more recent views of social class from earlier views.

2.5   Social Class versus Income

In the 1970s, the belief among market researchers developed that personal income is in general a better predictor of purchase than is social class. Two recent, very thorough studies show that for some products, this is so.[9] For major appliances, soft drinks, mixers, and alcoholic beverages, it was true. Social class alone was better for segmenting food, nonsoft drink/nonalcoholic beverages, as well as shopping behavior and evening television viewing. Both social class and income combined were superior for make-up, clothing, automobiles, and

---

[8] Coleman, "Continuing Significance of Social Class," p. 268.

[9] C. M. Schaninger, "Social Class versus Income Revisited: An Empirical Investigation," *Journal of Marketing Research,* XVIII (May 1981), 192–208.

television. Although the study does not discuss this, we would expect that social class data would be substantially better for guiding and stimulating advertising people to write creative advertising because social class probably captures more of the subculture than does income alone.

It happens that income and social class are not closely correlated as Coleman indicated. Social status derives more from occupational differentiation than from income. It has been pointed out that in twentieth-century America, "blue collar workers can outearn both white collar workers and salaried professionals, yet they still do not rise above either in social class,"[10] Also, income varies markedly according to the earner's position in the age cycle. Finally, there is great family variation in the number and sex of earners. "As more families at all social levels have experienced divorce, leading to households headed by a female earner, household incomes far below class averages have been added to the picture in larger portions."[11]

The question should be asked: "How does social class affect the use of income, when, why, and to what extent?" Income is the obvious first-order segmenting variable whenever expenditure decisions are studied; income and outflow both involve dollars, so a correlation of sorts is inevitable. It makes perfect sense to assume that in a major number of marketplace transactions, income will govern how much can be spent (and hence will be). Yet we always have to use other variables—age, perhaps, or sex, family composition, life-style, self-image, and social class—to understand why income has sometimes operated quite well as a predictor and other times rather poorly. As often as not, the reason will be found in social class, which may be acting all by itself or possibly in concert with one or more other social-psychological or demographic variables.[12]

2.6   Measurement of Social Class

If you are interested in using social class quantitatively, Coleman recommends that how you do it depends upon how systematic you wish to be. For example, "For the consumer researcher who is seeking nothing more than suggestive evidence of a class impact in a product area, it is recommended that a simplified, proxy (substitute) measure be accepted."[13] For this he recommends using Figure 13-1. The scores would run somewhat as follows:

Upper American	37 to 53
Middle class	24 to 36
Working class	13 to 23
Lower American	4 to 12

---

[10] Coleman, "Continuing Significance of Social Class," p. 273.
[11] Ibid., p. 273.
[12] Ibid., pp. 274–75.
[13] Ibid., p. 276.

EXAMPLE OF A COMPUTERIZED STATUS INDEX (CSI)

Interviewer circles code numbers (for the computer) which in his/her judgment best fit the respondent and family. Interviewer asks for detail on occupation, then makes rating. Interviewer often asks the respondent to describe neighborhood in own words. Interviewer asks respondent to specify income—a card is presented the respondent showing the eight brackets—and records R's response. If interviewer feels this is over-statement or under, a "better-judgment" estimate should be given, along with explanation.

EDUCATION:	Respondent	Respondent's Spouse
Grammar school (8 yrs or less)	– 1 R's age: ___	– 1 Spouse's age: ___
Some high school (9 to 11 yrs)	– 2	– 2
Graduated high school (12 yrs)	– 3	– 3
Some post high school (business, nursing, technical, 1 yr college)	– 4	– 4
Two, three years of college—possibly Associate of Arts degree	– 5	– 5
Graduated four-year college (B.A./B.S.)	– 7	– 7
Master's or five-year professional degree	– 8	– 8
Ph.D. or six/seven-year professional degree	– 9	– 9

OCCUPATION PRESTIGE LEVEL OF HOUSEHOLD HEAD: Interviewer's judgment of how head-of-household rates in **occupational status.**

(Respondent's description—ask for previous occupation if retired, or if R. is widow, ask husband's: _____)

Chronically unemployed—"day" laborers, unskilled; on welfare	– 0
Steadily employed but in marginal semi-skilled jobs; custodians, minimum-pay factory help, service workers (gas attendants, etc.)	– 1
Average-skill assembly-line workers, bus and truck drivers, police and firefighters, route deliverymen, carpenters, brickmasons	– 2
Skilled craftsmen (electricians), small contractors, factory foremen, low-pay salesclerks, office workers, postal employees	– 3
Owners of very small firms (2–4 employees), technicians, salespeople, office workers, civil servants with average level salaries	– 4
Middle management, teachers, social workers, lesser professionals	– 5
Lesser corporate officials, owners of middle-sized businesses (10–20 employees), moderate-success professionals (dentists, engineers, etc.)	– 7
Top corporate executives, "big successes" in the professional world (leading doctors and lawyers), "rich" business owners	– 9

AREA OF RESIDENCE: Interviewer's impressions of the immediate neighborhood in terms of its reputation in the eyes of **the community.**

Slum area; people on relief, common laborers	– 1
Strictly working class; not slummy but some very poor housing	– 2
Predominantly blue-collar with some office workers	– 3
Predominantly white-collar with some well-paid blue-collar	– 4
Better white-collar area; not many executives, but hardly any blue-collar either	– 5
Excellent area: professionals and well-paid managers	– 7
"Wealthy" or "society"-type neighborhood	– 9

TOTAL FAMILY INCOME PER YEAR:

TOTAL SCORE _____

Under $5,000	– 1	$20,000 to $24,999	– 5
$5,000 to $9,999	– 2	$25,000 to $34,999	– 6
$10,000 to $14,999	– 3	$35,000 to $49,999	– 7
$15,000 to $19,999	– 4	$50,000 and over	– 8

Estimated Status _____

(Interviewer's estimate: _____ and explanation: _____)

R's MARITAL STATUS: Married ___ Divorced/Separated ___ Widowed ___ Single ___ (CODE: ___)

Figure 13-1 A Computerized Status Index

SOURCE: R. P. Coleman, "The Continuing Significance of Social Class to Marketing," *Journal of Consumer Research*, 10, no. 3 (December 1983), 277.

These social class values would be entered into the intention (I) variable of the CDM and the continuous score method of measuring helps immensely in applying the social class variable to the CDM.

On the other hand, "When the research objective is an in-depth study of the relationship between social class and consumption choice, assignment of sample cases to class groupings should be rendered in qualitative fashion by 'expert' judgment."[14] This "expert" judgment is necessary for proper balancing of the variables and weighting their impact according to the ages involved, household composition, and locale. This second approach, though more accurate, is probably not appropriate for a company market research department to take on but requires a research institute of some type.

Finally, any use of social class now requires a greater emphasis upon the role of the wife in the family's social status. In the past, the husband's characteristics have been viewed as the sole determinant of family status. Increasingly this has become less valid as the woman's position has changed.[15]

Another direction of development in using social class is "geo-demographic clustering." One research firm, for example, has sorted U.S. zip codes into 40 areas, each relatively homogeneous with respect to social class.[16] How it works can be seen in Figure 13-2, where 5 of the 40 areas are listed across the top and labeled so as to indicate their relative social status, for example, Blue-Chip Blues (upper class). The purpose of the research firm is to help one of its clients (brand A) "develop and implement a coupon promotion plan to lure away buyers of its major competitor (brand B) and attract Heavy Category Buyers at the same time."[17] The size of the blocks indicate the number of Heavy Category Buyers, and as you see by its size, Blue-Chip Blues contain more of the Heavy Category Buyers than do either of the other four social statuses.

The solid and broken lines on each block represent a volume index that as you see at the bottom of the diagram is the ratio of the percentage of volume represented by the zip cluster to the percentage of population in the zip cluster. For example, in the Blue-Chip Blues, the index for brand B is 200, which means that the percentage of volume of brand B in this zip cluster of Blue-Chip Blues is twice as much as the percentage of the population in the Blue-Chip Blues. Thus, brand B is very strong in this cluster. As you see, though, the zip cluster of Emergent Minorities has lots of Heavy Category Buyers, both brands A and B are weak in that cluster. One tactic for brand A could be a direct-mail coupon delivered to Blue-Chip Blues neighborhoods. In this way

[14] Ibid.

[15] T. A. Shimp and J. T. Yokum, "Extensions of the Basic Social Class Model Employed in Consumer Research," in Kent Monroe, ed., *Advances in Consumer Research* (Ann Arbor, Mich.: Association for Consumer Research, October 1980), vol. VIII, 702–7.

[16] "Effective Targeting with NPD/PRIZM Interlock," *Insights* (NPD Research), no. 14 (March 1983).

[17] Ibid.

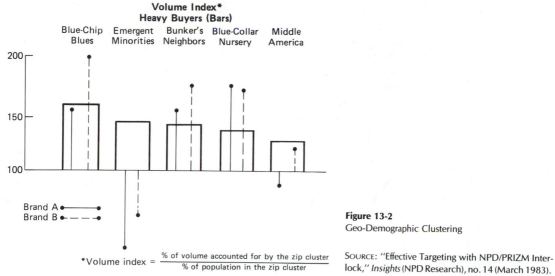

Figure 13-2
Geo-Demographic Clustering

$$\text{*Volume index} = \frac{\text{\% of volume accounted for by the zip cluster}}{\text{\% of population in the zip cluster}}$$

SOURCE: "Effective Targeting with NPD/PRIZM Interlock," *Insights* (NPD Research), no. 14 (March 1983).

it is likely to reach Heavy Buyers and will reach brand B buyers versus brand A buyers at a 4-to-3 ratio.

2.7 Implications for Marketing

Social class has a number of implications for marketing. The discussion has been in terms of its role in segmenting markets. For example, Table 13-1 presented evidence on how different social classes had different preferences for telephones in a study by AT&T.

But social class is relevant for other areas of marketing. Advertising can benefit substantially from using it. It can shape the language and symbols used in advertising copy. Henry Assael points out, for example, based on a study by Martineau how advertising for infants clothing would differ:

> advertisements for infant clothing directed to middle and upper class markets may attempt associations with care and love while advertisements directed to lower class mothers may emphasize ease of cleaning and durability.[18]

Media should be affected because some magazines, for example, clearly are read by upper classes and others by lower classes.

Distribution can be influenced. For example, lower-class people are more likely to buy clothing in local stores and upper-class in specialty-style shops. Product design, too, should sometimes be different. You saw this in the analysis of telephone preferences in Table 13-1.

[18] H. Assael, *Consumer Behavior and Marketing Action* (Boston: Kent, 1981), p. 296.

2.8   Conclusions on Social Class

Social class is a phenomenon that almost any socially sensitive person intuitively senses but has great difficulty being precise about what it is. The fact that consumer motivations are its foundations make it relevant for marketing.

It is very useful as a qualitative tool for conceptualizing a consumer market. Its dimensions, which are related to motivations, can stimulate new thoughts about how a market should be structured as an early step in formulating strategy especially for product innovations.

A more quantitative application becomes a little more demanding. AT&T describes a preliminary but highly constructive application illustrated in Table 13-1. Unfortunately, applications are seldom published. However, if you are using the measure discussed in the preceding section, application of the CDM should not pose serious problems.

3.   REFERENCE GROUPS

3.1   Introduction

Much of the influence that operates on consumers in these large social groupings—culture, subcultures, and social class—occurs via the consumer's reference group. It is important that we understand this because in our marketing we may be able to take advantage of this understanding and enhance our effectiveness in communicating with consumers especially since we can now have extensive computer-accessible customer databases to use. Let us now be more explicit about how this influence operates.

For purposes of understanding social influence, a *group* is defined as a number of people who have common goals, that interact with each other, over a period of time. It is useful to separate them into formal and informal groups. A formal group is one in which the organizational structure and functions for which it exists are specified. Earlier in Chapter 11 we discussed at length a particular formal group, namely, buyers for a company. Our interest here is in the informal group where the structure and functions are less explicit and these characterize most consumer buying. More specifically, our interest is in the informal *reference group*, and we define it as the group that influences a consumer's choice behavior.

3.2   Social Diffusion of Innovations

Earlier in Chapter 8, evidence on the diffusion of an innovation was used to support the evolutionary view of consumer behavior described in Chapter 2, but nothing was said about social influence in shaping the upper curve of Figure 8-2. Let us discuss the role of social influence in that diffusion process now that we have a background in the principles of social influence.

The *diffusion process* is defined as the process by which innovations spread to members of a social system. Knowing this process can be useful even for LPS products because it influences the sales volumes of such products. However, it is crucial to understand and predict how an EPS product will develop as discussed in Chapter 8 on the appropriate strategy for an EPS product.

You can readily imagine how culture, subcultures, social class, and small groups might operate to shape this diffusion process, especially when talking together in small groups. And you have probably been wondering just how the group concept operates in this role. The concepts of strong and weak ties have been designed to clarify the role. *Strong ties* are those associations a person has with her peers in a group. These are her reference group members. These relations clearly operate. In fact, most of the influence operates by strong ties. Before going on to weak ties, let us examine "opinion leaders," within a group as an example of strong ties.

Not all group members are equally influential. The more influential are referred to as "opinion leaders," those to whom others in the group turn to for advice. We need to be careful, however, not to exaggerate their "power" as sometimes in the past has been implied in the marketing literature. A key point to bear in mind is that a person tends to be an opinion leader within a group for a particular product, not for many products. Most helpful in obtaining a sense of the leadership process is the description of opinion leader characteristics developed by Robertson et al. drawing heavily upon Everett Rogers's research:

1. Opinion leaders have greater exposure to external communication. This suggests more exposure to *relevant* mass media (for example, fashion opinion leaders are more exposed to fashion magazines) and a more cosmopolitan (worldly) orientation than for followers.
2. Opinion leaders have greater social participation than followers. This seems to increase the opportunities for personal influence.
3. Opinion leaders have "somewhat" higher social status than do followers. Influence is still transmitted at the peer-group level, however.
4. Opinion leaders are "more innovative" than their followers, but they are not the "innovators"; that is, they adopt new products early but not first.

To these generalizations we could add two others:

5. Opinion leaders have more expertise than their followers.
6. There are separate opinion leaders by product category.[19]

You can readily see from this description the difficulty of taking advantage of these opinion leaders in marketing an innovation. However, some companies have done it. In Table 13-4 Robertson et al. offer a splendid illustration of such effort by Yamaha, the Japanese motorcycle manufacturer. As you read

---

[19] T. S. Robertson and others, *Consumer Behavior* (Glenview, Ill.: Scott, Foresman, 1984), p. 406.

Table 13-4   Yamaha Motor Corporation: Personal Influence in Motorcycle Brand Decisions

Findings	Marketing Implications
Importance of Personal Influence	
1. Personal influence the dominant information source for new buyers	Strategies should build on personal influence processes.
2. Dealers the second most important source of information for most new buyers	Dealers should be provided with maximum support and educated as to their vital role as information givers.
Characteristics of Influentials	
3. Likely to be someone who can work skillfully on his motorcycle	Most influence is transmitted by people who are good at working on their bikes but not by "experts." The person is much like the person being influenced, but has product experience.
Information Sought	
4. New buyers most interested in information on reliability and dependability	Personal influence provides a reality test to a potential buyer through the experience of a previous buyer.
Ownership Characteristics of High Information Seekers	
5. Most likely to be first-time buyers and reported to know less about motorcycling	This is consistent with generally high information needs of new product buyers in any product category.
Topics Discussed by High Information Seekers	
6. More likely to seek brand advice and less likely to seek advice on features or characteristics	New buyers are unsure of their ability to evaluate product features and are likely to rely on a strong brand name.
Personal Characteristics of High Information Seekers	
7. Likely to be younger and to be students	Younger people have less experience and are more in contact with a relevant peer group.
Influence Behavior of New Buyers	
8. New Yamaha buyers highly influential in inducing further purchases of Yamaha	65% talked to other people about their motorcycle. 35% felt they may have influenced one or more persons to buy a Yamaha. 25% are sure they influenced at least one person to buy a Yamaha.

SOURCE: T. S. Robertson and others, *Consumer Behavior* (Glenview, Ill.: Scott, Foresman, 1984), p. 411. Copyright 1984 by Scott, Foresman and Company. Reprinted by permission.

through the descriptions of the people involved, you will readily grasp how social class is applied.

This brings us to weak ties, which are those influence processes operating *across* groups. Specifically, a *weak tie* is defined as one where the individual consumer exerts an influence upon someone in *another* group, not her reference group. It is believed, and there is some evidence to support it, that the greatest influence on accepting an innovation is within the group. However, the key relation in an innovation's success is across groups, which is the weak tie operating. This is a profoundly important point, because the cross-group influence is the means by which the first person in a group often first learns about an innovation.

Everett Rogers, who for many years has been the leading researcher in social diffusion, has summarized the nature of the people who innovate at each stage of the diffusion processing according to adopter categories and their associated characteristics:[20]

Innovators—venturesome
Early adopters—respectable
Early majority—deliberate
Late majority—skeptical
Laggards—traditional

3.3 Types of Social Influence

As has been found in social research, reference groups can exert any one or more of the following different types of influence:[21]

Informational influence—the group members provide credible information
Utilitarian influence—the influence is to conform to get along with the group
Value-expressive influence—the member conforms because it bolsters his/her ego, or he/she likes the members of the group.

The logic of these three criteria is fairly obvious. The credibility of the information a consumer obtains from members of a reference group will depend heavily upon whether he wishes to conform and that conformity gives him satisfaction of values, status, and/or social satisfaction. But this omits expertise in a product area, and this is typically more important.

Some evidence comparing students with housewives in terms of their susceptibility to reference group influence on specific products will give more meaning to these ideas. The results of these three types of influence are shown in Table 13-5. First off, students were overall much more subject to reference group influence than were housewives, as you can see by comparing the size of the scores for students with housewives. For both students and housewives, the informational effects were greater than the utilitarian, and the utilitarian were greater than the value-expressive influences.

3.4 Social Influences and Types of Products

Group influence is also expected to vary across types of products. Earlier research had suggested that if products are divided into four types according to whether they are used publicly or privately and whether they are a necessity or a luxury, as in Figure 13-3, that group influence will be strong for luxuries and publicly used products but weak for necessities and privately used products.

[20] E. M. Rogers, *Diffusion of Innovations*, 3rd ed. (New York: The Free Press, 1983), pp. 248–50.
[21] C. W. Park and V. P. Lessig, "Students and Housewives: Differences in Susceptibility to Reference Group Influence," *Journal of Consumer Research*, 4, no. 2 (September 1977), 105.

Table 13-5 Comparison of Reference Group Influence Scores

Product	INFORMATIONAL		UTILITARIAN		VALUE-EXPRESSIVE	
	Students*	Housewives†	Students*	Housewives†	Students*	Housewives†
Headache remedy	3.69	3.38‡	3.32	2.98‡	2.73	2.42
Beer	2.78	2.50‡	3.68	3.08‡	3.57	2.71‡
Color television	3.94	3.84‡	3.65	3.51	3.69	3.43‡
Clothing	3.43	3.45	3.87	3.59‡	3.93	3.61‡
Laundry soap	3.16	2.99	2.75	2.53	2.47	2.42
Hamburger substitute	2.96	2.58‡	2.89	2.33‡	2.27	1.93‡
Automobile	3.94	3.85	3.92	3.70‡	3.97	3.65‡
Furniture	3.44	3.51	3.60	3.59	3.68	3.52
Facial soap	3.06	2.89‡	2.89	2.94	3.17	2.35‡
Air conditioner	3.78	3.75	3.17	3.21	3.21	3.14
Insurance	3.81	3.71	3.41	3.38	3.23	3.08
Mouthwash	3.05	2.92	3.24	3.02	3.27	2.57‡
Coffee	3.08	2.88	3.64	3.28	2.72	2.58
Refrigerator	3.57	3.70	3.16	3.23	3.16	3.14
Physician selection	3.89	3.72‡	3.67	3.50	3.28	3.18
Canned peaches	2.47	2.49	2.71	2.54	1.97	1.99
Radio	3.34	3.16	2.94	2.79	2.85	2.54
Detergent	2.98	2.88	2.43	2.35	2.47	2.17
Books or magazines	3.18	3.00	3.45	3.36	3.44	3.08‡
Cigarettes	3.00	2.49‡	3.14	2.68‡	3.33	2.51‡

* This score is based upon examination of the *entire* student sample.

† This score is based upon examination of the 100 housewives sample.

‡ *t* test is significant at the .05 level.

SOURCE: C. W. Park and V. P. Lessig, "Students and Housewives: Differences in Susceptibility to Reference Group Influence," *Journal of Consumer Research,* 4, no. 2 (September 1977), 108.

The logic of Figure 13-3 was that in buying *products* that are *luxuries*, reference group influence would be operating because luxuries are exclusive, not everybody has them. Further, if the brand is used in *public*, then reference group influence would operate in buying the *brand*. These two conditions are true as you will note for the upper right-hand box of Figure 13-3 and that influence is said to be strong for both product and brand where the products are golf clubs, snow skis, and sailboats. In the lower left, the products are mattresses, floor lamps, and refrigerators for which influence would *not* be expected in the purchase of either the product or the brand. The products in the other two boxes can be interpreted accordingly. In a carefully designed study of 16 products, of which 12 are shown in Figure 13-3, these relations were tested and found to be true.[22]

Further, whether the influence was informational, value-expressive, or utilitarian, as described in Table 13-5, was also included in this study. The

[22] W. O. Bearden and M. J. Etzel, "Reference Group Influence on Product and Brand Purchase Decisions," *Journal of Consumer Research*, 9, no. 2 (September 1982), 183–94.

Public

	Weak reference group influence (+)	Strong reference group influence (−)
Strong reference group influence (+)	*Public necessities* Influence: Weak product and strong brand Examples: Wristwatch, automobile, man's suit	*Public luxuries* Influence: Strong product and brand Examples: Golf clubs, snow skis, sailboat
Weak reference group influence (−)	*Private necessities* Influence: Weak product and brand Examples: Mattress, floor lamp, refrigerator	*Private luxuries* Influence: Strong product and weak brand Examples: TV game, trash compactor, icemaker

Necessity ———————————————————————— Luxury

Private

Figure 13-3 Combining Public–Private and Luxury–Necessity Dimensions with Product and Brand Purchase Decisions

SOURCE: W. D. Bearden and M. J. Etzel, "Reference Group Influence on Product and Brand Purchase Decisions," *Journal of Consumer Research*, 9, no. 2 (September 1982), 185.

conclusions were the following. First, informational effects were much stronger than were value-expressive or utilitarian effects. Second, all three types of influence operated much more in choosing among brands than among categories. This suggests that personal influence can be used more for LPS and RPS situations than for EPS situations. Third, value-expressive and utilitarian influences varied over products. Fourth, and as implied in Table 13-5, personal influence did vary across products.

3.5   Speed of Diffusion

We have found in this chapter that the process of social influence, which is heavily the basis of social diffusion, to be complex indeed. Can we say anything about the speed of the process? A. C. Nielson, the ratings firm, presented some evidence suggesting that the product life cycle is becoming shorter, that the diffusion process is speeding up. Also, in 1964, R. B. Young of the Stanford Research Institute showed persuasive evidence that the cycle is speeding up. You will recall, however, a more thorough analysis by Richard Olshavsky of the University of Indiana presented in Chapter 10.[23]

[23] R. W. Olshavsky, "Time and the Rate of Adoption of Innovations," *Journal of Consumer Research*, 6, no. 4 (March 1980), 425–28.

The adoption rates of the 25 consumer durables were estimated by Olshavsky using the logistic curve. He found that the more recent innovations from the 1940s through the 1970s have shown, on the average, substantially greater growth rates than have the older innovations. The average of 1960 is about .4, whereas for 1920 it was about .1. Thus, in 1960, an innovation on the average only required about one-fourth as long to reach the top of the product life cycle as in 1920.

This speeding up of the product life cycle has profound implications for management. It promises that the payoff for an innovation can be much faster and presumably also for a new brand in a familiar product class. Nevertheless, management's speed of adaptation has to be correspondingly much faster in light of this speed-up. Going up the product life cycle requires innovation in management procedures—initiating planning and cost control devices and especially in making a major shift in marketing orientation. Many companies will find this speed difficult to deal with.

3.6   Marketing Implications of Reference Groups

Other people, "reference groups," can clearly influence a consumer's choice, but knowing who will influence a particular product and how is much less clear. Thus "who," "when," and "how" are obviously vital pieces of information if the concept of interpersonal influence is to be used in designing marketing strategy.

However, some progress has been made. The Yamaha motorcycle findings in Table 13-4 are an example of its actual use by a company. Also there is Table 13-1, AT&T's telephone study. There has been substantial use but little of it published, as Richard Coleman, one of the leading experts in the field, has complained. Further, the need for companies to use it has become greater as the speed of diffusion has increased.

One of the first questions a practitioner should ask is, "Is my product likely to be one where the purchase is influenced by others?" The more it is used publicly and is a luxury, the more likely it is to be so influenced. This is shown in Figure 13-3. The purchase of an innovation, a new brand in a new product category (EPS), is likely to be influenced by others and there is a great amount of evidence for this from the diffusion literature.

The second question is, "Who are the likely influencers?" You have to know them to be able to take advantage of the concept of personal influence. It was suggested earlier they tend to be exposed to external communication, to have more social participation, and to have higher social status than do followers; they are more innovative themselves and therefore are users, but they are not the first adopters; they have more expertise; and they vary from product to product.

Knowing who they are likely to be, you can think about how to reach them to get them to adopt it early. Also, you can study them to determine the type of influence they are likely to use: informational (merely to get information), utilitarian (conformity to get along with the group), or value expressive (it is consistent with his values). As you saw in Table 13-5, informational effects are the greatest, with utilitarian effects second, leaving value-expressive influence as the third. From this you can begin to infer the kind of advertising and sales messages that can be used to persuade the mass of buyers to consider the brand.

4. CONCLUSIONS

Much of social class influence is exerted through the values of its members, but here we look upon the reference group as the vehicle for transmitting information about specific products as well. This information can be informational, utilitarian, and/or value expressive, but all three can shape the consumer's purchasing behavior. This influence is especially significant for innovations. In using the CDM, you can collect information from the consumers on whom they talked with about the product and thus get a measure of the power of "other people" for this product. If it is a strong effect, the marketing manager is wise to use more general advertising and promotion to reach a wider public than if the "other people" effect is weak.

Finally, the speed of product innovation was examined and found to have increased substantially since 1920. This increased speed obviously raises important issues for marketing such as a greater need for knowing the role of "weak ties" in the product's acceptance.

Questions

1. Coleman says "social class" is a slippery concept. How do you define it?
2. To what extent do social class and income coincide as descriptors of consumers?
3. Coleman suggests that two quite different ways of measuring social class can be used. What are they and when do you use one and when the other?
4. What are the marketing implications of social class?
5. Describe how each of the three types of social influence might operate.

CHAPTER 14

Family

1. INTRODUCTION

An obviously important type of social group for anyone interested in consumer behavior for marketing purposes is the family. The family unit helps to shape the *values* of its members and causes them to weight some benefits heavier than others in evaluating products. In addition, one member may *buy for others* such as a mother buying clothing for her children. Also, members of the family pool their *information* about products. Finally, for many products the family is a *buying unit* that is defined as a situation where the decision is a joint decision made by two or more family members, for example, in buying a new car.

2. DEFINITION OF FAMILY

But we have to be careful about what is meant by "family." The historical definition has been that a family is a husband and wife, often with children. In many cases this is obviously true. However, we are undergoing a period of fantastic change in the nature of the family. It is not at all clear how to bring order out of this chaos by using the family concept to aid in designing core strategy for a product by providing market segment information.

A brief summary of some of these changes provides some evidence of the dimensions of the problem that we face in designing strategy.[1]

> The number of U.S. households increased by 25 percent during the 1970s while population increased by only 9 percent. This increase was fueled by rising divorce rates and by a greatly increased propensity for the baby boom generation to set up single-person households. It has resulted in a decrease in the proportion of husband-and-wife households from 70.5 percent in 1970 to 59.8 percent in all households in 1981. The traditional household of husband, wife, and one or more children now represents just 43 percent of total households; thus, the proportion of childless husband-and-wife households has increased also.

Much, much more evidence of change could be cited, but to do so would not serve the needs here.[2]

Single-parent families have increased. Larger divorce rates exist, but most divorced people marry again. "Singles" have increased substantially. In thinking about "family" you can soon be reduced to equating it with "household," which is *a live-in consuming unit with no other restrictions.* This is about the best that we can do currently. Research has yet by no means caught up with the new picture, but progress is being made as you will see. The family life cycle is one way of trying to order this chaos.

3.   FAMILY LIFE CYCLE

We all have some idea that families exhibit different purchasing patterns at different points in time. For example, newlyweds will find furniture expenditures are a major part of their budget, but as children come along, expenditures will shift to doctor and hospital bills, children's clothing, and so on. This changing pattern of expenditures as the family matures is called the family life cycle. Like the product life cycle, it is a rough concept, but it is useful to trigger and guide our thinking about the marketing of different products and a particular product to different people.

Table 14-1 presents two family life-cycle descriptions.[3] The one on the right was developed before 1966 and therefore does not show recent trends toward higher divorce rates and smaller families. The cycle on the left, however, appeared in the 1970s and incorporates some of these changes. The numbers and proportions on the left were developed from the 1973 U.S. Census data.

[1] M. L. Roberts and L. H. Wortzell, "Introduction," in M. L. Roberts and L. H. Wortzell, eds. *Marketing to the Changing Household* (Cambridge, Mass.: Ballinger, 1984), p. xvi.

[2] P. E. Murphy, "Family and Household Changes: Developments and Implications," in M. L. Roberts and L. H. Wortzell, eds., *Marketing to the Changing Household*, (Cambridge, Mass.: Ballinger, 1984), pp. 3–23.

[3] P. E. Murphy and W. A. Staples, "A Modernized Family Life Cycle," *Journal of Consumer Research*, 6, no. 1 (June 1979), 16.

Table 14-1 Comparison of Population Distributions across the Stages of Two Family Life Cycles, 1970[*]

	MURPHY AND STAPLES			WELLS AND GUBAR	
Stage	No. Individuals or Families (000s)	% Total U.S. Population[†]	Stage	No. Individuals or Families (000s)	% Total U.S. Population[†]
1. Young single	16,626	8.2%	1. Bachelor	16,626	8.2%
2. Young married without children	2,958	2.9	2. Newly married couples	2,958	2.9
3. Other young					
a. Young divorced without children	277	0.1			
b. Young married with children Infant[‡] Young (4–12 years old)[‡] Adolescent[‡]	8,082	17.1	3. Full nest I	11,433	24.2
c. Young divorced with children Infant Young (4–12 years old) Adolescent	1,144	1.9	4. Full nest II	6,547	13.2
4. Middle-aged					
a. Middle-aged married without children	4,815	4.7			
b. Middle-aged divorced without children	593	0.3			
c. Middle-aged married with children Young Adolescent	15,574	33.0	5. Full nest III	6,955	14.7
d. Middle-aged divorced with children Young Adolescent	1,080	1.8			
e. Middle-aged married without dependent children	5,627	5.5	6. Empty nest I	5,627	5.5
f. Middle-aged divorced without dependent children	284	0.1			
5. Older					
a. Older married	5,318	5.2	7. Empty nest II	5,318	5.2
b. Older unmarried Divorced Widowed	3,510	2.0	8. Solitary survivor— in labor force	428	0.2
			9. Solitary survivor— retired	3,510	2.0
All other[§]	34,952	17.2	All other[§]	46,738	23.3
	203,210[‖]			203,210[‖]	

[*] Figures for this table were taken or derived from U.S. Bureau of the Census 1973, Tables 2 and 9.

[†] As there are single and divorced individuals in some of the stages, the numbers were calculated as a percentage of the entire population, not just the number of families. Also, the percentages of the total for families were determined by multiplying the number of families by 2.3 (average number of children per family in 1970) and adding the parents (or parent, in divorced instances) to the number. For example, the 17.1 percent in the young married with children was computed as follows:

$$\frac{8,082 \ (2.3 \ \text{children}) + 16,164 \ (\text{parents})}{203,210} = 17.1\%.$$

[‡] As many families have children at more than one of these age levels, it is not meaningful to compute the numbers for each of these ages independently.

[§] Includes all adults and children not accounted for by the family life cycle stages.

[‖] The numbers do not add to this total because of the calculations explained in Footnote [†].

Source: P. E. Murphy and W. A. Staples, "A Modernized Family Life Cycle," *Journal of Consumer Research*, 6, no. 1 (June 1979), 16; from U.S. Bureau of the Census 1970.

The two columns are not closely comparable. On the left, "Young" are less than 35 years of age and "Middle aged" are 35 to 64. On the right, "Full nest I" refers to families where the youngest child is less than 6, "Full nest II" the youngest is older than 6, and "Full nest III" is older couples with dependent children. In "Empty nest I" the head is employed, and in "Empty nest II" the head has retired. It is known that "Young married with children" (3b) have increased considerably, but that the "Young divorced" (3c) show a much larger increase. On the other hand, "Middle-aged married with children" has been more than cut in half. Thus, you can see that the left column provides a more up-to-date picture than does the one on the right.

The researchers who developed the new representation in the left column of Table 14-1 suggest from it a number of conclusions about purchasing behavior. The declining family size will reduce the market for large-family products and services (e.g., station wagons, several-bedroom homes, and large-size packages). The longer empty nest stage may allow couples to save for vacations, better furniture, and maybe a different home. The following are further extensions of these conclusions.

> The young divorced stage might be a promising segment for marketers of small appliances rather than large ones, because the individual may view this stage as temporary. Within the service area, personal enhancement services, such as health spas and tennis clubs, would seem to be in demand by the more affluent in this group. Also, life insurance marketers may find the divorced woman interested in buying insurance for herself and possibly the children. Moreover, most divorced women with children from middle and lower social classes would probably be seeking inexpensive clothing for herself and the children.
>
> In the middle-aged categories of the revised FLC, those who remain childless may represent a good market for luxury goods, e.g., expensive restaurants, extended vacation packages, high quality furniture. Divorced individuals who hold good jobs and have no dependents may also be classified as part of this same market. Middle-aged divorced parents, on the other hand, would seem to be seeking more low-priced and functional products, such as used cars, inexpensive furniture, and fast food restaurants.[4]

Perhaps the most useful information is that which will stimulate thinking about the problem. Pat Murphy has carefully developed a picture of the market for products in Table 14-2, which recognizes his conclusions about the implications of these great changes in the family. Row 1 refers to stages of the family life cycle and row 2 to the extent these life-cycle groupings will change. Row 3 is the life-style likely to be represented by life-cycle category. The type of decision making for each category is described in row 4. Finally, beginning with row 5 are Murphy's judgments of the marketing implications of each category.

It will be worth the reader's time first to review these categories of family life cycle before considering the marketing implications. The intermediate rows 2, 3, and 4 will add substantial meaning, especially row 3, as to expected change in the size of the category. Perhaps most important of all is the effect

---

[4] Ibid., p. 20.

Table 14-2 Implications of Family Life-Cycle Stages

FAMILY LIFE-CYCLE STAGES

	Single		Cohabiting	Couples		Married With Children	Divorced		Older	
Implications	Young	Mature		Married Without Children	Childless		Without Children	With Children	Married	Unmarried
3 Growth	Decrease until 1995	Increase	Increase slightly	Stable	Increase	Decrease slightly	Increase	Stable	Increase	Increase
4 Life-style	Transitional	Patterned	Impermanent	Hedonistic	Carefree	Child-centered	Self-centered	Constrained	Active if healthy and not poor	Sedentary
5 Consumer decision making	Individual	Individual	Independent	Joint	Joint	Complementary	Individual	Joint	Complementary	Individual/family
6 Marketing products Durable	Basic furniture, automobile	Condominiums, high-quality home furnishings	Low-cost furniture	Sensible furniture, insurance	Smaller homes, sports cars	Toys, larger homes	Fashionable furniture, apartments or condominiums	Inexpensive furniture, low-cost housing	Retirement homes, jewelry	Apartment
7 Nondurables	Records, fashion-oriented clothing	Individual-size servings, home maintenance		Career clothing	Small packages, convenience foods	Family-size packages, functional clothing	Small packages, small appliances	Inexpensive clothing, discount foods, toys	Cosmetics, sports equipment	Salt-free products
8 Services	Travel, restaurants	Better restaurants, financial planning investments	Lowest budget travel, individual financial services	Movies, travel, restaurants	Theater tickets, house cleaning service, luxury travel	Family or fast-food restaurants, discount entertainment	Dating service, travel, clubs	Fast-food restaurants	Travel, brokerage services	Cruises, home delivery services, mass transportation
9 Promotion Message	Special interest me-oriented	Quality appeals	Buy-now appeal	Appeal to both spouses	Quality, luxury	Family oriented	Me-oriented appeals	Low-price appeals	Owe yourself appeals	Enjoyment and comfort appeals
10 Media	Magazines, radio	Personal selling	Mass media	Mass media	Special interest	Women's magazines, mass media	Mood magazines	Mass media especially TV	TV and newspapers	TV

Source: Adapted partially from Wells and Gubar (1966). Pebley and Bloom (1982). Stampfl (1978, 1979), Allan (1981a). Murphy and Staples (1979), and Gilly and Enis (1982).

Source: P. E. Murphy, "Family and Household Changes: Developments and Implications," in M. L. Roberts and L. H. Wortzel, eds., *Marketing to the Changing Household* (Cambridge, Mass.: Ballinger, 1984), p. 4.

upon types of products purchased, which is shown in row 6 for durables. As you see, there is a great difference across the rows in products bought at different stages of the family life cycle. Correspondingly, rows 9 and 10 exhibit wide differences in promotion message and media.

You may be asking just how useful the family life-cycle concept is as a representation of buying behavior. Not a great amount of evidence is available. However, in one study, the traditional description on the left predicted more consistency between husbands' and wives' attitudes toward automobiles than did length of marriage.[5] Similarly, family life cycle correlated better with use of several entertainment activities than did age or social class.[6] A more recent study, however, concludes that "As compared to income, or to income in conjunction with other socioeconomic and demographic variables, sets of family life cycle variables are of limited value in predicting clothing expenditures."[7] However, given the complexity of the problem, this is not surprising.

Having reviewed the family life-cycle analysis, the reader is probably asking if there are better ways of analyzing the family unit. In a sense, there are better ways. However, one has to accept a simpler view and recognize that the results of any study may well soon be outmoded by the currently dynamic nature of the family unit.

4. BUYING UNIT

4.1 Introduction

The third feature of the family group as a buying unit beyond the definition and the family life cycle is the question of who makes what decisions in the family. Just as we saw in Chapter 11 in discussing buying in the formal organization, we also find that in the informal organization represented by the family, different family members serve different buying roles. For example, in buying a house, children may be the *initiators* and to some extent even *influence* the decision, but the *deciders* are probably mama and papa. Obviously many of the family decisions are joint decisions such as buying a house. The issue then becomes one of relative influence.

4.2 Husband-Wife Unit

The key question as to who makes what decisions in the family relates to the husband and wife. Later we will discuss the role of children in shaping the

---

[5] E. P. Cox III, "Family Purchase Decision Making and the Process of Adjustment," *Journal of Marketing Research*, XII (May 1975), 194.

[6] R. D. Hisrich and M. P. Peters, "Selecting the Superior Segmentation Correlate," *Journal of Marketing*, 38, no. 3 (July 1974), 60–63.

[7] J. Wagner and S. Hanna, "The Effectiveness of Family Life Cycle Variables in Consumer Expenditure Research," *Journal of Consumer Research*, 10, no. 3 (December 1983), 291.

Table 14-3 Couple's Relative Influence Responses on Dimensions

Dimension	AGREEMENT*			Disagreement†	Don't Know Response‡
	Husband Influence	Wife Influence	Subtotal		
Age of home	2	7	(9)	3	16
Attractiveness	1	11	(12)	4	10
Central air conditioning	4	3	(7)	0	18
Basement	9	5	(14)	3	13
Builder's reputation	1	0	(1)	1	4
Fireplace	4	4	(8)	1	18
Fenced yard	3	4	(7)	2	10
Humidifier	0	0	(0)	0	1
Insulation	11	3	(14)	1	10
Interior design	0	13	(13)	6	8
Landscaping	3	1	(4)	1	13
Location	3	13	(16)	7	19
Neighborhood	2	6	(8)	4	18
Bedroom	3	9	(12)	7	26
Bathroom	3	5	(8)	2	17
Garage	10	1	(11)	0	20
Patio	0	0	(0)	0	7
Price	17	3	(20)	8	16
Recreation facilities	1	1	(2)	0	3
Resale value	13	2	(15)	2	7
Size of home	1	8	(9)	7	9
Style of home	2	11	(13)	1	10
Tax amount	7	0	(7)	3	10
Wet bar	0	0	(0)	0	0

* A dyad's response reveals an agreement about who influenced more on the dimension.

† A dyad's response reveals a disagreement about who influenced more on the dimension (i.e., each spouse indicated that s/he influenced the other more).

‡ Either one or both of a dyad revealed a "don't know" response about who influenced more on the dimension.

SOURCE: C. W. Park, "Joint Decisions in Home Purchasing: A Muddling-Through Process," *Journal of Consumer Research*, 9, no. 2 (September 1982), 160.

family decision. The husband-wife relationship is especially relevant. It typically involves important issues such as buying a house and making other investments. Investment decisions have been increasingly common in many households. Also, as the wife has come to play a greater and greater role in the family decision, the marketers need to know who is making the decision and in terms of what dimensions has become increasingly sharp. Finally, it is a difficult buying decision to research as you well imagine. This is illustrated in a study of family homebuying decision by 48 families in a moderate-sized Midwestern university town in 1977.[8]

The basic idea guiding the study was that the husband and wife make the decision in such a way as to limit the amount of conflict engendered between

[8] C. W. Park, "Joint Decisions in Home Purchasing: A Muddling-Through Process," *Journal of Consumer Research*, 9, no. 2 (September 1982), 151–62.

the husband and wife. Table 14-3 gives a highly useful picture of the choice process that took place in the 48 families. As you can see, there were six major dimensions in terms of husband's influence: basement, insulation, garage, price, resale value, and tax amount. In terms of wife's influence, there were five: attractiveness, interior design, location, size of home, and style of home. The greatest conflict occurred in location, bedroom, price, and size of home. Finally, there were many "Don't Know Response," as you see in the extreme right.

The purpose of the study was much more fundamental: to see if the decision could be described as "a muddling-through process, characterized by limited knowledge and awareness of each spouse's decision strategies. However, by relying on conflict-avoiding heuristics, the dyad (husband-wife) was hypothesized to reach a choice effectively." The author agreed that this was a good description of what actually took place. We do not examine this purpose further because it is a complex study design. Anyone wishing to know more about this purpose and/or to use this design in a market research project should consult the original study.

Now we turn to a Belgian study to give you another view of this important husband-wife choice process. For the husband-wife unit, Davis and Rigaux studied the buyer behavior of 103 Belgian families, interviewing both husband and wife.[9] In Figure 14-1, you will notice that the right-hand or vertical axis is "Relative influence of husband and wife." If all families had reported for a product that its purchase was dominated by the husband, it would receive a "1." If all reported that it was dominated by the wife, it would receive a "3." You can readily see in Figure 14-1 how greatly products varied over this scale.

The second or horizontal axis, "Extent of role specialization," was measured by the percentage of families reporting that a decision is jointly made. Consequently, if the proportion where it was made jointly was *greater than 50%*, the decision was said to be *syncratic*. If it were less than 50% and either wife or husband was likely to be dominant, it was said to be an *autonomic decision*. A scale value greater than 2.5 indicated wife dominant and a value less than 1.5, husband dominant. The husband-dominant and wife-dominant decisions are also autonomic.

With this two-way analysis you can quickly see how products vary and in what particular way. Obviously, knowing where your product is located in this diagram could strongly influence to whom your marketing effort is directed and the nature of that marketing effort. As a manager you might also like to know whether the husband-wife roles changed over the course of the buying decision process. To capture this the researchers divided the decision process into three stages: "problem recognition," "search for information," and "final decision."

Table 14-4 takes the husband-wife decisions by relative influence—husband dominant, autonomic, and so on—in the left stub and analyzes them by

[9] H. L. Davis and B. P. Rigaux, "Perception of Marital Roles in Decision Processes," *Journal of Consumer Research*, 1, no. 1 (June 1974), 51–62.

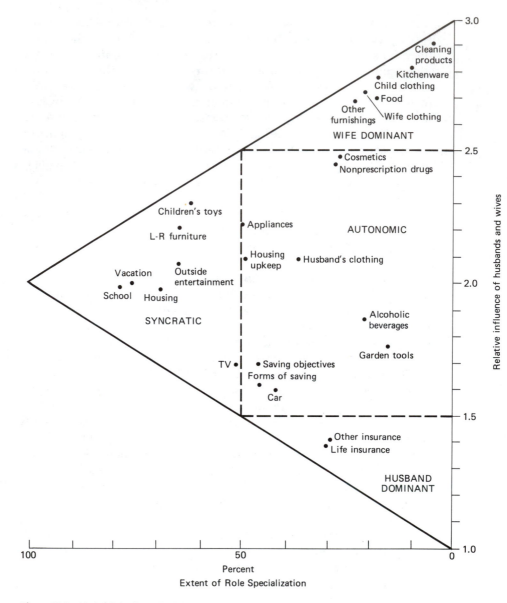

Figure 14-1 Marital Roles in 25 Decisions

SOURCE: H. L. Davis and B. P. Rigaux, "Perception of Marital Roles in Decision Processes," *Journal of Consumer Research*, 1, no. 1 (June 1974), 54.

changes in the phase of decision—problem recognition, search, and final decision—at the top. You will recall from Figure 14-1 that there were two "husband-dominant" decisions: life insurance and other insurance. This was true in problem recognition, but in search, three were husband dominant, and in the final decision two were again husband dominant. As you now see, Table 14-4 gives you more detail of the process by which the husband and wife made these decisions. If you look at the search phase for autonomic, you see again a little more detail. However, when you compare the second and third phases, you see substantially more information. The number that are autonomous are cut in half in the third phase. Similarly, with syncratic decisions, you see that the third phase is doubled. Wife dominant is fairly constant.

These important changes that we have been seeing in Table 14-3 are seen much more sharply in Figure 14-2 and still more sharply in Figure 14-3 because it gives you even more detail of this complex analysis. Figure 14-2 displays the change that resulted when the decision stage moved from problem recognition to search. For example, for a car the husband was more likely to be dominant in the search process than in the recognition of the problem of needing a car.

Analogously, in Figure 14-3 you see that as the decision moves from search to actual decision, the car moves in the other direction, for example. It becomes more of a joint decision.

Finally, an important question is the extent to which husband and wife agree. This is answered in the case of our sample families by Table 14-5. Take the purchase of housing, for instance, which is the first item, 81% agree on the problem recognition stage, 60% on search and 82% in final decision. But how about the cases of lack of agreement? The researchers use the term "Modesty" where one partner overestimated the other partner's influence or underestimated his own. "Vanity" indicates the opposite. Generalizations are difficult to make here, but the data could be very helpful in marketing a particular product.

4.3 Influence of Children on Buying Unit

Going beyond the husband-wife relations are those involving the children and their mothers. The Ward and Wackman study of 109 mothers casts some light on the extent that mothers "gave in" (yielded) to children's requests by product

Table 14-4 Patterns of Influence at Three Stages of the Decision Process

	PHASE		
	Problem Recognition	Search for Information	Final Decision
Husband dominant	2	3	2
Autonomic	10	9	5
Syncratic	7	6	13
Wife dominant	6	7	5

SOURCE: H. L. Davis and B. P. Rigaux, "Perception of Marital Roles in Decision Processes," *Journal of Consumer Research*, 1, no. 1 (June 1974), 55.

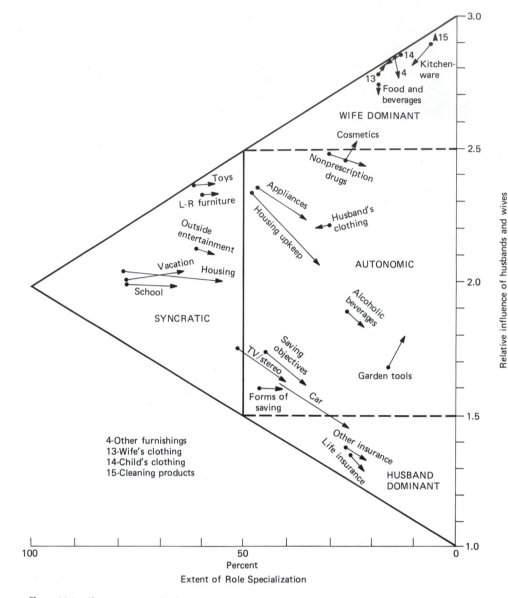

Figure 14-2   Changes in Marital Roles Between Phase 1 and Phase 2

SOURCE: H. L. Davis and B. P. Rigaux, "Perception of Marital Roles in Decision Processes," *Journal of Consumer Research*, 1, no. 1 (June 1974), 56.

and by child's age.[10] As you see in Table 14-6, yielding was high with cereals, but this did not vary much by age of child.

Another study dealt with junior and senior high school student prefer-

[10] S. Ward and H. B. Wackman, "Children's Purchase Influence and Parental Yielding," *Journal of Marketing Research*, IX (August 1972), 316–19.

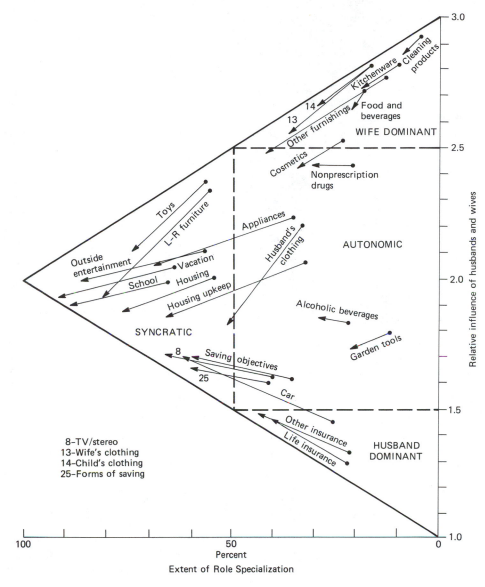

Figure 14-3 Changes in Marital Roles Between Phase 2 and Phase 3

SOURCE: H. L. Davis and B. P. Rigaux, "Perception of Marital Roles in Decision Processes," *Journal of Consumer Research*, 1, no. 1 (June 1974), 57.

ences for sources of information in buying eight products.[11] The results are summarized in Table 14-7. One or both parents were preferred as the source of information for wristwatches, dress shoes, pocket calculators, and hair dryers. This proportion dropped very much for the other four products, however.

[11] G. P. Moschis and R. L. Moore, "Decision Making Among the Young: A Socialization Perspective," *Journal of Consumer Research*, 6, no. 2 (September 1979), 101–12.

Table 14-5   Extent of Husband-Wife Agreement About Roles in 25 Decisions (in percentages)

	PROBLEM RECOGNITION			SEARCH FOR INFORMATION			FINAL DECISION		
	Mod-esty	Con-sensus	Vanity	Mod-esty	Con-sensus	Vanity	Mod-esty	Con-sensus	Vanity
1. Housing (location, purchase price or rent)	7%	81%	12%	20%	60%	20%	11%	82%	7%
2. Housing upkeep (repairs, improvements)	20	63	17	17	59	24	24	62	14
3. Living-room furniture	24	57	19	17	69	14	14	80	6
4. Other furnishings (rugs, drapes)	8	80	12	9	82	9	28	49	23
5. Kitchenware	9	86	5	7	83	10	14	72	14
6. Household appliances, excluding TV	27	55	18	22	54	24	16	63	21
7. Garden tools	10	74	16	9	71	20	17	61	22
8. TV, hi-fi, tape recorder	17	59	24	17	62	21	18	59	23
9. Car	24	53	23	18	58	24	19	64	17
10. Food and nonalcoholic beverages	14	71	15	15	68	17	14	67	19
11. Alcoholic beverages	11	55	34	14	62	24	15	63	22
12. Husband's clothes	22	64	14	25	52	23	24	54	22
13. Wife's clothes	15	70	15	9	74	17	14	72	14
14. Child(ren)'s clothes	7	86	7	10	83	7	17	63	20
15. Household cleaning products	5	91	4	2	90	8	5	82	13
16. Cosmetics and toiletries	15	60	25	10	61	29	17	59	24
17. Child(ren)'s toys for birthdays and holidays	15	70	15	22	59	19	18	60	22
18. Life insurance	8	79	13	5	81	14	18	68	14
19. Other insurance	9	72	19	7	80	13	18	60	22
20. Nonprescription drugs and first-aid items	13	64	23	4	70	26	9	68	23
21. Child(ren)'s school and program of study	8	72	20	7	70	23	7	83	10
22. Concerts, movies, theater	21	58	21	17	56	27	14	76	10
23. Family vacation	18	64	18	14	61	25	5	88	7
24. Saving objectives	16	64	20	15	60	25	9	69	22
25. Forms of saving (stocks, saving accounts, bonds)	10	73	17	16	64	20	11	70	19
Average	14	69	17	13	68	19	15	68	17

SOURCE: H. L. Davis and B. P. Rigaux, "Perception of Marital Roles in Decision Processes," *Journal of Consumer Research*, 1, no. 1 (June 1974), 58.

Table 14-6   Frequency of Children's Attempts to Influence Purchases, and Percentage of Mothers "Usually" Yielding

Products	FREQUENCY OF REQUESTS*				PERCENTAGE OF YIELDING			
	5–7 Years	8–10 Years	11–12 Years	Total†	5–7 Years	8–10 Years	11–12 Years	Total†
Relevant foods								
Breakfast cereal	1.26	1.59	1.97	1.59	88%	91%	83%	87%
Snack foods	1.71	2.00	1.71	1.80	52	62	77	63
Candy	1.60	2.09	2.17	1.93	40	28	57	42
Soft drinks	2.00	2.03	2.00	2.01	38	47	54	46
Jell-o	2.54	2.94	2.97	2.80	40	41	26	36
Overall mean	1.82	2.13	2.16	2.03				
Overall percentage					51.6	53.8	59.4	54.8
Less relevant foods								
Bread	3.12	2.91	3.43	3.16	14	28	17	19
Coffee	3.93	3.91	3.97	3.94	2	0	0	1
Pet food	3.29	3.59	3.24	3.36	7	3	11	7
Overall mean	3.45	3.47	3.49	3.49				
Overall percentage					7.6	10.3	9.3	9.0
Durables, for child's use								
Game, toy	1.24	1.63	2.17	1.65	57	59	46	54
Clothing	2.76	2.47	2.29	2.52	21	34	57	37
Bicycle	2.48	2.59	2.77	2.61	7	9	9	8
Hot wheels	2.43	2.41	3.20	2.67	29	19	17	22
Record album	3.36	2.63	2.23	2.78	12	16	46	24
Camera	3.91	3.75	3.71	3.80	2	3	0	2
Overall mean	2.70	2.58	2.73	2.67				
Overall percentage					25.6	28.0	35.0	29.4
Notions, toiletries								
Toothpaste	2.29	2.31	2.60	2.39	36	44	40	39
Bath soap	3.10	2.97	3.46	3.17	9	9	9	9
Shampoo	3.48	3.31	3.03	3.28	17	6	23	16
Aspirin	3.64	3.78	3.97	3.79	5	6	0	4
Overall mean	3.13	3.09	3.26	3.16				
Overall percentage					16.8	16.3	18.0	17.0
Other products								
Automobile	3.55	3.66	3.51	3.57	2	0	0	12
Gasoline brand	3.64	3.63	3.83	3.70	2	0	3	2
Laundry soap	3.69	3.75	3.71	3.72	2	0	3	2
Household cleaner	3.71	3.84	3.74	3.76	2	3	0	2
Overall mean	3.65	3.72	3.70	3.69				
Overall percentage					2.0	.75	1.50	1.75

* On a scale from 1 = often to 4 = never.

† 5–7 years, $n = 43$; 8–10 years, $n = 32$; 11–12 years, $n = 34$; $N = 109$.

Source: S. Ward and H. B. Wackman, "Children's Purchase Influence and Parental Yielding," *Journal of Marketing Research*, IX (August 1972), 317. Reprinted from *Journal of Marketing Research*, published by the American Marketing Association.

Table 14-7 Percentage of Adolescents Preferring Various Sources of Information in Purchasing Selected Products*

Product	Friends	TV Ads	Consumer Reports	One or Both Parents	Newspaper or Magazine Ads
Wristwatch	27.1%	15.7%	20.6%	74.7%	15.7%
Pair of dress shoes	38.4	13.9	6.0	63.9	19.1
Pocket calculator	19.3	20.6	27.7	58.9	20.2
Hair dryer (blower)	29.2	29.3	17.7	49.9	20.6
Sunglasses	45.4	28.6	8.0	28.6	23.4
Wallet	39.2	15.8	7.8	45.6	24.1
Flash cubes	14.3	32.4	15.1	41.4	25.6
Household batteries	12.5	35.1	16.5	44.6	21.7
Average percent	28.2	23.9	14.9	51.0	21.3

*N = 722. Percentages do not sum to 100.0 for each product because of multiple responses.

SOURCE: G. P. Moschis and R. L. Moore, "Decision Making Among the Young: A Socialization Perspective," *Journal of Consumer Research*, 6, no. 2 (September 1979), 106.

5. CONCLUSIONS

We have seen evidence that the family can strongly influence the buying decision of many products. Hence, if these influences are taken into account, you can much better understand your consumers and more accurately predict what they will do in response to your marketing. These inputs can be used by a manager either intuitively or as input to the CDM.

Here we have focused more upon the actual decision instead of the details of the process leading to a decision, but we have also examined the underlying "why" of decisions by using the family life-cycle concept. Also, the decision was broken into stages of the decision: recognition of the problem, search for information, and actual decision. Further, in the case of children, we studied their response to sources of information.

Most attention was devoted to husband-wife influence in the decision. Knowing the results of these studies of the husband-wife relation in buying decision can clearly aid in designing the product, advertising copy, media, and budget and thus can be the foundation of the marketing strategy and plans.

The fact that one of the husband-wife studies was of couples from another culture, namely, Belgium, may weaken its validity for application in the culture that you are concerned with as a manager. However, knowing the results of the Belgian study can be highly useful for you in designing a study that will get you the information that you want from the particular culture you are serving. Also, above all, we must recognize that any study done today in the United States may soon be outdated.

6. SUMMARY

Part IV has dealt entirely with individual differences among consumers as the basis for segmenting a market. You have seen substantial differences documented and several of those differences were reflected in differences in buying behavior that is essential if they are to be useful for segmenting.

To incorporate these into the CDM will make the CDM much more useful, and this can easily be done usually via the intention (I) variable.

These individual differences are, of course, highly relevant for the discussion of application to practice as you saw in Part III and, specifically, in the design of core strategy. The differences will be fed in as we discuss examples in Chapter 15, where they will be more systematically examined in terms of using them for market segmentation.

Questions

1. Why is it difficult to define such a common term as "family"?
2. What can you infer from Table 14-3 that would be useful to someone in a real estate firm who is responsible for designing marketing strategy and plans for that firm?
3. What are some of the most useful conclusions that you can derive from the Belgian study of husband-wife decision?
4. In what way is it important to know the role of children in buying if you were marketing bicycles?
5. The last three chapters have dealt with differences among consumers in their buying. Where would you expect these differences to impact upon the CDM and why is it important to know this?

CHAPTER 15

Individual Differences among Customers

1. INTRODUCTION

Market segmentation often is one of the most important features of a marketing strategy as suggested by the definition of core strategy or "positioning" as introduced in Chapter 8. Students intuitively and easily grasp its significance. Also, it is probably one of the few areas where marketing has contributed to the sciences as has been pointed out by a physicist.

However, segmentation is a very subtle concept. There is no doubt that differences among consumers in their buying behavior do exist, as we have seen in the three chapters making up the sociocultural environment. But what is not at all obvious is that finding differences among consumers and relating those differences to the elements of marketing required to take advantage of those differences is an entirely different matter. The subtlety of this point is not at all obvious, and only by introducing two new key concepts and doing it illustratively will this subtlety be understood. Further, a part of this subtlety is the question of the source of those individual differences. Knowing this alone will reduce the subtlety considerably. Consequently, the purpose of this chapter is to set out an illustrative framework for introducing both the two new concepts and how these differences among consumers fit into the general theory of consumer behavior.

We have already seen how the Consumer Decision Model (CDM) can be used both qualitatively and quantitatively, both for explanation and prediction as well as being adapted to the extremes of the product life cycle. Here we extend the CDM by incorporating systematically the practical problems of individual differences among customers beyond the discussion in Chapters 12, 13, and 14, and especially those differences that are useful for market segmentation. This is the first of four major extensions of the CDM.

The purpose of this chapter is to present a framework to aid in thinking systematically about the very complex problem of segmenting consumers. You will recall from Chapter 8 that possible segmentation is a key element of core strategy. In the following pages, first, an example of Southwest Airlines is developed at length to sharpen the issues of segmentation and to establish a vocabulary for discussing segmentation in more useful terms. Second, a point of view, a theory, about the source of these segmentable differences among consumers is described. Third, how to take advantage of these segments in developing strategy is discussed. Finally, two other important implications of these differences among consumers when using the CDM, namely, noise reduction and feedback analysis, are explained.

Although the simple CDM assumes all customers are alike, it was presumed from the beginning of the book that readers already knew that differences existed among customers. Some customers are tall and skinny, for example; others are short and fat. But the initial discussion was probably overly simplistic. For example, do tall and skinny people *buy* differently than short and fat people? For most products, the answer is no. These readily observable differences among customers often tell us nothing about buying behavior. Nevertheless, we have to say categorically that individual differences in *buying* behavior *do* exist, as we have seen in Chapters 12, 13, and 14.

An example of clear differences in buying behavior was seen in Chapter 6, in beer, margarine, and a coffee cream (fopro), where roughly 20% of the 2,000 Dutch consumers who bought these products over a two-year period bought the *same* brand again and again. But the remaining roughly 80% exhibited

Table 15-1   Relative Frequency of Range of Values for Households with More than One Brand

RANGPLZ	Fopro	Beer	Margarine
0	.0269	.1249	.0190
1	.4669	.5055	.3814
2	.3223	.2582	.2975
3	.1147	.0875	.1745
4	.0475	.0241	.0738
≧ 5	.0207	.0044	.0537
Number of households	1.000	1.000	1.000
with ≧ 2 brands	484	457	894

SOURCE: B. Wierenga, *An Investigation of Brand Choice Processes* (Rotterdam, Holland: University of Rotterdam, 1974), p. 170.

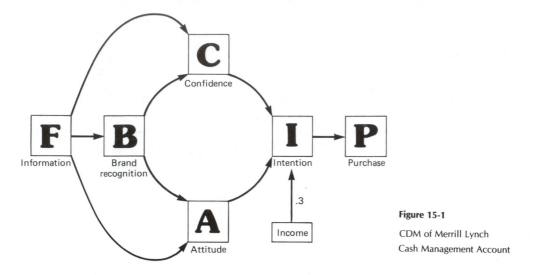

Figure 15-1

CDM of Merrill Lynch
Cash Management Account

quite different brand-switching patterns (see Table 15-1, which repeats Table 6-3). The column RANGPLZ is the range in variation of number of brands purchased over the last ten purchases of the product. Most of them varied by two brands or less, but as you can see on the bottom line, a large number bought two brands or more. Some were even greater than five—a large amount of brand switching. In this sample, we are left with no doubt about the great differences among customers in their brand-purchasing behavior.

Although the evidence is undebatable that these differences do occur, this statement is not very helpful to a manager. When he encounters differences in cultures, he is merely warned to be on the lookout for differences in buying behavior. But this tells him little about just what these differences will be, so that he can take advantage of them. He needs to know these differences in terms of some continuous variable that can be introduced into the CDM when applied to a particular product. For example, in Merrill Lynch's Cash Management Account, the level of the consumer's income was a clear segmenting variable, as shown in Figure 15-1, with a coefficient of .3. This indicates that if the average level of income is increased by 10%, the intention to buy (I) would increase by 3%. Given this key piece of information and cost data of what the expenditure would have to be to exploit these different levels, the manager is in a position to calculate which level of customer income will give the greatest payoff.

Lacking this kind of systematic information represented in the CDM, one of the first steps to applying it should be to learn if there is any opportunity to segment our market. Perhaps there are no segments. If so, to go fishing for segments is a waste of time. Fortunately, Greg Carpenter, John Farley, and Yoshi Sugito have developed a tool to tell us whether individual differences exist among the particular consumers and how great these differences are without having to know specifically what they are.[1] With such information the manager can decide whether it is worth the trouble to search for the segmenting variables and how much.

2. USE OF INDIVIDUAL DIFFERENCE DATA FOR SEGMENTATION

2.1 Introduction

The most common reason for knowing about individual differences among consumers in marketing is to define market segments.

2.2 An Illustration of the Need for Segmentation

This example will be the groundwork for taking a critical and systematic look at this important but complex problem. Jerry Wind notes "Surprisingly, despite thousands of academic and commercial studies by marketing and consumer researchers, one can draw very few generalizations as to which variables would have what effects under what conditions."[2] Although written a decade ago, Wind's statement is still generally valid. One of the consequences of this lack of knowledge is that segmentation studies are often questioned. For example, an established New York marketing consultant, after describing the history of increased use of segmentation, recently asserted

> yet segmentation studies have come under increasing fire, and are considered worthless by some marketing people.[3]

Southwest Airlines (SWA) was attempting to break into the triangular airline market of Dallas-Fort Worth, Houston, and San Antonio in the early 1970s. A special plum was the heavily trafficked Dallas-to-Houston leg of that triangle. To grab a piece of this market, Mr. Muse, chief executive of SWA, was attempting to offer optimal service. He took into consideration a number of attributes of his offering that might appeal to different people, including

1. Size of plane (twin jets versus single engine)
2. Fast ticketing
3. Price of ticket
4. Glamorous hostesses, "go-go girls"

[1] G. Carpenter, J. U. Farley, and Yoshi Sugito, "Detecting and Estimating Structural Parameter Differences over Data Subsets in Simultaneous Equation Models," unpublished paper (Columbia University, New York, 1986).

[2] Y. Wind, "Issues and Advances in Segmentation Research," *Journal of Marketing Research,* XV (August 1978), 320.

[3] M. Amoroso, "Segmentation: The Marketing Concept vs. The Research Technique," *Marketing Review,* 39, no. 7 (March/April 1984), 21.

5. Holiday spirit (e.g., party in flight)
6. Inexpensive drinks
7. Frequency of service
8. Reliability of meeting schedules
9. Airport location (close in or out)
10. Safety

The challenge was heightened by the stiff competition: Braniff, an international line, and Texas Air International, a small local line, which also flew that triangle. Moreover, these two lines had colluded in trying to prevent SWA from entering this lucrative market, which, had recently been further enhanced with the opening of a splendid resort area in south Texas. For three years, they had blocked Mr. Muse from receiving a state license to fly each of the three main routes, making up the triangle.

But Braniff, as a huge international carrier, did not have the flexibility to change its marketing strategy and tactics to take advantage of different segments the way SWA did. As for Texas Air, it had merely followed Braniff's actions without taking any initiative of its own.

Muse was a creative and highly flexible marketer. He proceeded to try various combinations of service, price, and safety tactics. Some appeared to be the cause for an increased average plane load; others didn't. But there seemed to be neither rhyme nor reason to the pattern of success and failure. Unfortunately, Muse saw his planeload of customers only as a mass of people instead of perceiving systematic differences in buying behavior among individual passengers.

Let's consider what marketing objective he might have employed in segmenting his market. This objective is crucial because the manager's objective of how to meet the consumer's needs is one of the *two* key features of all segmentation analysis.

The first feature is the *basis for segmentation*.[4] It has to do with their buying behavior, that is, what it is the consumer likes or intends to buy. His objective could have been to please his existing customers even more. The implication here, of course, is that all the passengers, no matter into what segment they fell, wanted to fly SWA over its competitors. But Muse could also have had another objective, which was to attract new customers to flying instead of using other forms of transportation—and by using tactics that might lead to their flying SWA. Either way he had to find differences in why they used one airline instead of another.

The second feature is that he did *not* but should have tried to find a relationship among the differences, for example, amount of plane travel, in customers' basis for flying by which he could *identify* them as being in some grouping—and their readily observable demographic characteristics such as age,

---

[4] Wind, "Issues and Advances," pp. 317–37.

sex, occupation, and income. These would be the relevant *descriptors of the segments.*[5]

The basis for segmentation is the dependent variable (Intention) in the CDM and the possible descriptor (Income) is the independent variable as seen in Figure 15-1. Intention (I) was the dependent variable or basis of segmentation, but it is the reflection of attitude (A) or confidence (C) such as time of travel. Consumer income was the independent or descriptor variable.

It is essential that you bear in mind the two underlined definitions—basis differences and descriptor differences—when you read further. Ideally, these two different aspects of segments would be the same. For example, if fat buyers buy more frequently than do skinny buyers, weight would be both a differentiating variable and a segment descriptor. Usually in practice, however, they are not the same. People who like sweet foods will buy different brands than will people who do not have a strong preference for sweetness. Preference for sweetness is the basis for segmenting in this case, but it is not observable and so cannot serve as descriptor as do age, income, location, and other demographics. In summary, the two key elements of any segmentation problem are the two concepts: basis of segmentation and descriptors of segments.

In the Southwest Airline case there were some signals of customer differences that could have served to identify segments but Muse failed to catch them:

1. When $10 flights *after 9:00 P.M.*—a reduction from $29—were made available daily instead of just Friday, sharply higher load factors resulted.
2. Another time, when *daytime flights* were raised from $20 to $26 (regular fare), there was some decline in passengers but revenues increased substantially, indicating an inelastic demand on the part of most of these daytime flyers.
3. At still another time, when the prices of weekend flights were cut in half from $26 to $13, there was substantial increase in traffic.

The key point is that there were at least two major market segments as indicated by their buying behavior and whose descriptors could have been "businessmen" and "vacationers." Note in Table 15-2 that each group rated the importance of the benefits differently. Note, too, how customers conceptualize "time" and "reliability" as "schedule"; "cheap drinks," "go-go girls," and "parties" as "entertainment"; and "airport location" and "ease of ticketing" as "convenience."

Later, after leaving SWA, Muse was to say publicly that his greatest single mistake in attempting to enter the Texas market was his failure to recognize that he was serving two quite different markets. The descriptors were specific: businessmen versus vacationers. The bases for segmenting were clear. The crucial point is that business travelers wanted a convenient and comfortable flight on time; prices were largely irrelevant because the company paid the bill. The vacationing customers, more price conscious, didn't worry much about whether the airline kept to its schedule; they simply wanted a cheap, good time. Unfortu-

[5] Ibid.

Table 15-2 Hypothetical Businessman's and Vacationer's Ratings

Businessman's Ratings			Vacationer's Ratings		
Benefit	Importance		Benefit	Importance	
Schedule time and reliability	5		Schedule time and reliability	3	
Price	3		Price	5	
Entertainment	2		Entertainment Cheap drinks "Go-go" girls "Parties"	4	
Convenience	4		Convenience Airport location Ease of ticketing	2	

nately Mr. Muse did not observe the relevant differences. If he had, he could have analyzed them further and probably found substantial differences in income and readership habits, for example, which could have guided him in selecting his advertising media for each market. Parties could have been eliminated except in evenings and weekends. These are a few of the several possible implications.

An important point can be made with the SWA example. For segmenting purposes, ideally measurable individual basis differences among customers are essential. Crucial, however, is that the descriptors must readily identify members of the customer segment so that the proper appeal can be made to the responsive segment. In the SWA case the descriptor distinction between businessmen and vacationers was not at all obvious to Muse and his staff. In most cases, it will not be. Once identified, however, these descriptors could have been very useful to Mr. Muse.

Later on, we'll look at how a marketer can assess a customer's values for segmenting purposes. We'll learn how to identify a customer with one set of characteristics (bases) and to recognize him with another set (descriptors) to direct advertising to him. Ideally, descriptors should make the target customers easily identifiable—by some demographic or other characteristic.

Although segmenting is an age-old challenge, in direct marketing there appears to be a new and growing need for segmenting theory and techniques. To learn more about a consumer's values, the manufacturer can go directly to the ultimate consumer and thus bypass the wholesaler or retailer. While this concept is not new, what *is* new is the use of the computer to aid in ascertaining the consumer's buying-related characteristics: differences that can serve as bases and those that can serve as descriptors.

Consider this recent example: General Foods has purchased a Swedish coffee producer and is introducing the expensive product by direct mail into the United States. The company is directing the coffee at the "Achievers" segment of the SRI's VALS system. An essential feature of the GF marketing campaign are the names of the target audience that it has stored in the computer. GF is applying a variety of promotional efforts to different subgroups within the segment; it even stores in the computer the responses to questionnaires sent to each respondent in the computer. By identifying the characteristics of each person, GF is able to refine further its understanding of them. Thus, the study represents an unusually powerful example of segmenting in designing a marketing strategy in a direct marketing context.

On the other hand, it has been argued that segmentable differences are becoming less pronounced internationally and that greater emphasis should be placed on standardized products and services. This belief holds, for example, that washing machines, soft drinks, and so on, should all be simple, standardized, inexpensive, and of high quality.[6] The validity of this belief probably varies across products and countries.

3. THEORETICAL FOUNDATION OF SEGMENTATION BASES

3.1 Introduction

Now that we have a more precise terminology to exploit when trying to use differences among customers for segmentation purposes, we will describe these differences more formally for additional insight into them as to when they serve as bases and when the differences are merely descriptors.

Practically, purchase is usually the basis for segmenting. The manager will argue that purchase is what the whole consumer behavior problem is about. In one sense this is true. However, it is a limited answer because purchases are the result of a number of influences, for example, price, availability, and so on, as well as how well they like the brand. Benefit importance weights focus specifically on the foundation of why they like the brand. Consequently, to simplify we will focus upon the most central influence, these importance weights. This focus is needed because as Jerry Wind indicated earlier we lack any generalizations as to which variables would have what effects under what conditions.

3.2 Differences in Information Processing Capacity

Some research has been devoted to identifying differences among customers in their ability to process information and these could affect their buying behavior. Clearly, there are differences among people in the way they process information.

---

[6] T. Levitt, "The Globalization of Markets," *Harvard Business Review,* 61, no. 3 (May/June 1983), 92–102.

For example, in one study differences in the way in which they combined variables were strong and differences in the way they isolated variables were less strong.[7]

Also, in another study, people well informed about the product ("experts") made decisions differently than did the less well informed ("novices").[8] For example, the well-informed persons focused *more* sharply upon the important attributes, and they used similarity and difference information more fully, which, of course, is consistent with the evolutionary view of buyer behavior—EPS, LPS, and RPS—as first presented in Chapter 2. How much this type of intercustomer difference that occurs over the product life cycle explains the great differences that we observe in purchasing behavior remains to be seen.

Demographic characteristics, such as age, sex, and income, are useful in creating segments and most widely used, because they are good descriptor variables but are usually not good bases for segmenting. Customers are easily identified by these characteristics, and marketing activity such as advertising can be directed to them because it too is identified by demographics. But such characteristics have failed to explain very much of buying behavior, and consequently in their place, marketers have turned to psychographics.

Psychographics are often called "AIOs" (general attitudes, interests, and opinions). Yet, while psychographics explains more of the customers' behavior, they are not a lot better, and they are not good segment descriptors. They don't permit us to recognize easily the customers as targets for marketing purposes. So market researchers turned to attempting to combine demographics and psychographics as SRI VALS do—and, it is hoped, end up with the best of both possible worlds. Stanford Research Institute with its VALS, which are essentially psychographics, solved this problem some years ago by joining with a magazine research firm called Simmons Market Research Bureau that does studies of magazine readership. This firm had its magazine readers fill out a form from which it was possible to decide what their VALS characteristics were.[9] Thus, VALS and demographics were joined.

3.3   The Foundation of Individual Differences

3.3.1 Nature of Individual Differences.   We will now be more specific about the fundamental nature and sources of the basic individual difference variables because we have seen in the previous pages that this is a very complex but highly important strategic problem.

[7] N. Capon and R. Davis, "Basic Cognitive Ability Measures as Predictors of Consumer Information Strategies," *Journal of Consumer Research*, 11, no. 1 (June 1984), 551–63.

[8] A. E. Beattie, "Effects of Product Knowledge on Comparison Memory, Evaluation and Choice," in A. Mitchell, ed., *Advances in Consumer Research* (Ann Arbor, Mich.: Association for Consumer Research, 1982), Vol. IX, 336–41; A. E. Beattie, "Product Expertise and Advertising Persuasiveness," in R. Bagozzi and A. Tybout, eds., *Advances in Consumer Research, Advances in Consumer Behavior* (Ann Arbor, Mich.: Association for Consumer Research, 1983), Vol X, 581–84.

[9] R. H. Holman, "A Values and Lifestyles Perspectives on Human Behavior," in R. E. Pitts and A. G. Woodside, eds., *Personal Values and Consumer Psychology* (Lexington, Mass.: Lexington Books, 1984), pp. 35–37.

It is now known that a customer's concept of a brand can be decomposed into two sets of dimensions as has been done throughout this book—recognizing (B) and evaluating (A).[10] Traditionally, psychologists have considered only the perceptual or recognition dimensions while marketers have considered only the functional or evaluative. It is now clear as seen in the CDM, however, that both are essential to an understanding of consumer behavior.

Presumably, while the customer judges the recognition attributes of a brand less than perfectly, his judgments, we believe, tend not to contain systematic error. Similarly, his judgments of where a brand is located on the evaluative scale are not subject to systematic error, but with one exception. The more important benefits will likely be more dependable because evidence indicates that the customer pays more attention to information about them than about less important benefits.[11]

This leaves only the *importance* ratings of the benefits as the systematic source of relevant individual differences in buying behavior. We use "relevant" here in the sense of serving as the bases of segmentation. Consequently, we hypothesize that it is these importance ratings, as illustrated earlier in the SWA example, that best represent individual differences. This identity between importance ratings and individual differences was asserted a few years ago[12] as a step toward meeting Jerry Wind's primary requirement for improved segmentation. In his careful review of segmentation, he stated that one of the greatest needs in improving segmentation was for a "new conceptualization of the segmentation problem."[13]

Essential, of course, is the ability to distinguish importance and performance ratings empirically. For a careful study of this, see David Curry and Michael Menasco's work, which concludes that this distinction can be made with substantial precision.[14]

If it is true that benefit importance ratings can be the foundation of segmentation, it implies that EPS buyers do not exhibit individual differences since at that stage they haven't yet adequately formed their importance ratings of the new product class. Still, the manager can estimate from other information

---

[10] J. A. Howard and J. N. Sheth, *The Theory of Buyer Behavior* (New York: John Wiley & Sons, 1969); G. A. Miller and P. N. Johnson-Laird, *Language and Perception* (Cambridge, Mass.: Harvard University Press, 1976); C. B. Mervis and E. Rosch, "Categorization of Natural Objects," *Annual Review of Psychology*, 32 (1981), 89–115; E. Rosch and B. B. Lloyd, *Cognition and Categorization* (Hillsdale, N.J.: Lawrence Erlbaum Associates, 1978), p. 214.

[11] M. B. Holbrook, D. A. Velez, and D. G. Tabouret, "Attitude Structure and Search: An Integrative Model of Importance-Directed Information Processing," in K. B. Monroe, ed., *Advances in Consumer Research* (Ann Arbor, Mich.: Association for Consumer Research, 1980), Vol. VIII, pp. 35–41.

[12] J. A. Howard, *Consumer Behavior: Application of Theory* (New York: McGraw-Hill, 1977), p. 172.

[13] Wind, "Issues and Advances," p. 334.

[14] D. J. Curry and M. B. Menasco, "On the Separability of Weights and Brand Values: Issues and Empirical Results," *Journal of Consumer Research*, 10, no. 1 (June 1983), 83–95.

what the importance ratings will likely become. Then, once the product category is fully formed in the customer's mind, the manager can correct his estimates by comparing the predicted with the actual differences.

But are the importance ratings stable, which they must be if they are to be useful? If they are not stable and change frequently, they cannot serve the purpose of segmenting consumers. They have been found to be particularly stable in the banking services industry.[15] Also, John Farley and his colleagues found with a number of products that the coefficients of exogenous variables—including segmentation variables—were stable.[16]

3.3.2 *Values as Source of Importance Weights.*
But what is the source of importance ratings? Earlier, in Chapter 4, we distinguished as psychologists generally do, between two aspects of buying behavior—direction and intensity. Direction is the brand being bought and intensity is the push or motivation to buy it. The importance ratings can be thought of as the motivation element of customer behavior as discussed in Chapter 4. The stability mentioned in the preceding paragraph indicates that we are dealing largely with long-term motives that are cultivated, for example, insatiable desires the customer learns in his cultural development called values. However, in the case of industrial buying, it is the organization values that are relevant, not those of the individual "buyer" per se.[17] Also, values were seen in Chapter 12 to be a basic element of culture that is the broadest and most general characteristic of the consumer.

If importance ratings have to do with motivation, it follows that there should be a relation between customer values and these ratings since values are long-term motives. Research devoted to testing this relationship has found it to be true, but the research has largely been limited to the Rokeach system of values. In that system, it is sometimes difficult to see why some of the consumer values should be relevant. Also, the scales specified by Rokeach are intended to be ranked instead of rated. Yet, for a customer to rank two sets—instrumental and terminal—of 18 scales each is too demanding of the respondent under field conditions such as over the telephone. Rating them as equal-interval scales is a solution, however, as Michael Munson has shown.[18] But here, the variance may to be too small unless special attention is given to encouraging the respondents to spread their ratings over the scales.

It is particularly important to know whether the relationship between importance ratings and values actually holds. There is a growing use of values

---

[15] R. J. Calantone and A. G. Sawyer, "The Stability of Benefit Segments," *Journal of Marketing Research*, XV (August 1978), 402–3.

[16] J. U. Farley and others, "Parameter Stability and 'Carry-Over Effects' in a Consumer Decision Process Model," *Journal of Consumer Research*, 8, no. 4 (March 1982), 468 and 70.

[17] T. S. Robertson and Y. Wind, "Organizational Psychographics and Innovativeness," *Journal of Consumer Research*, 7, no. 1 (June 1980), 24–31.

[18] J. M. Munson, "Personal Values: Considerations on Their Measurement and Application to Five Areas of Research Inquiry," in R. E. Pitts and A. G. Woodside, eds., *Personal Values and Consumer Psychology* (Lexington, Mass.: Lexington Books, 1984), pp. 19–22.

by practicing marketers, and no other simple test can logically determine the validity of the values the way importance ratings do. However, there is a missing link between values and importance ratings. This linkage is the social *norms* discussed in Chapter 13. Values will be discussed and then norms. We are not suggesting that values are the only source of consumer differences, but we are saying they are the major source and are being well studied. Consequently, they are something upon which to build, a fundamental understanding of segmentation.

3.3.3 Summary of Theoretical Foundations of Segmentation Bases.

The focus of this section is upon those consumer differences that have to do with buying. It is essential to separate these clearly from differences that can serve as descriptors.

Typically, the consumer's attitude is closely associated with her buying. But both her buying and her attitude can change and, therefore, in a sense are unreliable. Further, her buying is often influenced by factors beyond attitude, such as price and product availability, which weakens buying as a basis for segmenting.

The basis should be as stable as possible. This characteristic of stability is exhibited by her "benefit importance weightings." These weightings are connected to her personal values by her behavioral norms.

3.4   Use of Values in Practice

3.4.1 Introduction.

Values have been referred to repeatedly in previous chapters, and their application was discussed somewhat in Chapter 9. Here we want to review how they are used and the functions they serve since they would likely be a vital part of any serious effort to segment by importance weightings. Lynn Kahle has described the effects of values for consumer behavior very well:

> The very meaning of a product can differ as a function of the values of a consumer. For example, a personal computer may be a necessity for a person who values a sense of accomplishment, a challenge (like a musical instrument) for a person who values self-fulfillment, a frivolous luxury for a person who values self-respect, a status symbol for a person who values being well-respected, a toy for video games to a person who values fun and enjoyment in life, a "toy for the kids" to a person who values sense of belonging, a topic of conversation for a person who values warm relationships with others, and an unattainably expensive item for poor people who value security. Thus, the nature of the product attributes, the personal sales appeals, and the marketing communications will all vary as a function of the value group of primary importance in a certain context. The values linked to a product or service often provide the potential consumer with a basis for comparison shopping.[19]

[19] L. R. Kahle, "The Nine Nations of North America and the Value Basis of Geographic Segmentation," *Journal of Marketing*, 50, no. 2 (April 1986), 44.

Values are postulated here to be the major source of importance weightings. First, we will briefly review the discussion of values as a segmentating tool initiated in Chapters 7 and 8.

3.4.2 Segmentation.
Understanding how values tend to be used in the current practice of segmenting helps one to appreciate the need for them—and also to appreciate the difficulty of validating their use in advertising.

First, for values to be useful in practice, customers must be grouped according to categories of these values. Just to know the value ratings is not enough; the groupings are essential. Ad agency Young & Rubicam uses seven of the nine SRI VALS groups, each with its respective descriptor: need-driven, belongers, emulators, achievers, I—Am—Me, experientials, and societally conscious. Thinking back to the Southwest Airlines example, we might illustrate and view businessmen as "achievers" and local vacationers as "belongers."

Second, the primary need of segmentation is to use consumers' values as guides in all manner of marketing decisions. To facilitate this role, the director of the SRI Value Program not only groups customers by their values but has also developed a thumbnail sketch of a representative person in each of the nine groups.[20] The thumbnail sketches provide both concreteness and vocabulary to the copywriter that is thought to stimulate his creative juices. This role of providing vocabulary to stimulate creative ideas is striking and points to how badly the understanding of language needs to be integrated into marketing analysis, as we have attempted to do especially in Chapters 4 and 12.

There are definite language problems associated with segmentation. Obviously, different words (adjectives) are required to label the benefits for different products. For a car, consumers refer to comfort, cost, and gas consumption. Words describing foods include nutritious, tasty, and inexpensive. Complicating matters for the copywriter, different people may use different words for the same product. In a major study highlighting this point, three groups of people were asked to paraphrase compound names.[21] Taking compound names like "blackbird house," they had to provide a phrase that meant about the same thing. Interestingly, the three groups—secretaries, undergraduate students, and graduate students—had wide diversity in their responses. As the researchers reported, there were large population differences in the capacity to deal with paraphrasistic relations. This provides clear evidence on individual differences in the use of language.

For people making up their own value system to conform to the product they are introducing, a wide array of statistical techniques can be applied, including factor analysis and other clustering techniques.[22] To select meaningful descriptors for these segment categories, the marketer must be aware of demo-

---

[20] A. Mitchell, *The Nine American Life Styles* (New York: MacMillan, 1983).

[21] L. R. Gleitman and H. Gleitman, *Phrase and Paraphrase: Some Innovative Uses of Language* (New York: W. W. Norton, 1970).

[22] A review of segmentation edited by Jerry Wind refers to a number of them, see Wind, "Issues and Advances"; also see B. Tverski and K. Hemenway, "Categories of Environmental Scenes," *Cognitive Psychology*, 15, no. 1 (January 1983), 143.

graphic characteristics. Otherwise, his value system will be useless, since he won't know in media-relevant terms specifically at whom to direct his marketing.

3.4.3 Existing Value Systems.   A number of value systems have been developed and are available to be applied in marketing practice. The SRI VALS system has received by far the greatest attention by practioners.[23] As mentioned earlier in this chapter, the developers of that system very wisely combined it with the annual *Simmons* magazine readership study. In this way the *Simmons'* survey provides the segment descriptors for the VALS measures that make the VALS measures immensely more useful to the practitioner. Another survey covering demographics has been taken for VALS by Arnold Mitchell in 1980.

Rokeach's value system has been the most widely used in academic research.[24] Alfred Boote has developed a number of systems too, some for particular product classes, such as sewing machines.[25] Drawing upon the Rokeach system Lynn Kahle has constructed a set of values from a survey of 2,264 Americans and has used it extensively.[26] As you see in the left stub of Table 15-3, Kahle formulated eight values from Rokeach. Then, from the survey of 2,264 people across the United States, Table 15-3 was derived using the nine Bureau of Census regions. There you see some surprisingly large variations in values across the regions. On self-respect, as first or second in importance, for example, the Mountain region is 29.2% while the West North Central is 16.7%. On every value, there is some variation. For example, he used it to determine if the system of nine areas into which the Bureau of Census divides the United States is more valid. He found that the values did vary across these areas, suggesting that marketing to each of them should be different in many cases as seen in Table 15-3.

3.5   Norms

In Chapter 12 it was said that norms are the action implications of values. A consumer's behavioral norms specify his values toward a specific form of buying behavior such as a particular product or service category. In Chapter 13 it was said that the influence of small groups occurs through the development and enforcement of social norms. Zaltman and Wallendorf point out that small groups influence the following:

1. Whether or not a consumer ever becomes aware of a product.
2. What a consumer learns and believes about a product.

[23] Mitchell, *Nine American Life Styles.*

[24] M. Rokeach, *The Nature of Human Values* (New York: The Free Press, 1973).

[25] A. S. Boote, "Psychographic Segmentation in Europe," *Journal of Advertising Research,* 22, no. 6 (December 1982/January 1983), 19–25; A. S. Boote, "A Close Look at Women Who Intend to Purchase a Sewing Machine," unpublished Report (Singer Co., Stamford, Ct. January 1981).

[26] L. R. Kahle, "The Values of Americans: Implications for Consumer Adaptation," in R. E. Pitts and A. G. Woodside, eds., *Personal Values and Consumer Psychology* (Lexington, Mass.: Lexington Books, 1984) pp. 77–86; and Kahle, "The Nine Nations," p. 43.

Table 15-3 Distribution of Values across Census Regions of the United States*

Values	New England	Middle Atlantic	South Atlantic	East South Central	East North Central	West North Central	West South Central	Moun-tain	Pacific	N
Self-respect	22.6%	18.6%	23.1%	23.4%	20.2%	16.7%	23.8%	29.2%	19.8%	471
Security	21.2	18.0	18.3	26.9	22.1	20.6	23.8	18.1	18.5	461
Warm relationships with others	13.9	16.8	15.7	11.4	16.0	21.6	14.9	15.3	17.6	362
Sense of accomplishment	13.9	13.0	10.7	9.6	11.4	14.7	6.8	8.3	12.1	254
Self-fulfillment	8.0	10.0	10.1	7.8	9.3	8.3	5.5	6.9	15.0	214
Being well-respected	8.8	7.7	9.8	12.0	10.0	7.4	14.0	4.2	3.5	196
Sense of belonging	7.3	8.8	9.2	7.8	7.4	6.9	6.4	13.9	7.0	177
Fun-enjoyment-excitement	4.4	7.1	3.3	1.2	3.5	3.9	4.7	4.2	6.4	100
Total	100.0	100.0	100.0	100.0	100.0	100.0	100.0	100.0	100.0	2235
N	137	339	338	167	430	204	235	72	313	

*$\chi^2(56) = 90.22$, $p = .0025$.

Source: L. R. Kahle, "The Nine Nations of North America and the Value Basis of Geographic Segmentation," *Journal of Marketing*, 50, no. 2 (April 1986), 43. Published by the American Marketing Association.

3. Whether a consumer ever tries a product (independently of what the consumer knows and feels about a product).

4. How a product is used.

5. How satisfied a consumer is with the product's performance.[27]

They also say that a marketing research executive at Joseph Schlitz Brewing emphasizes group influence upon consumer choice because beer tends to be drunk in small groups.

Not a lot of research has been done on small group influence on buying, as you will recall from Chapter 13. The evidence to date is that its effect varies much among products and that it probably does not apply to products low in visibility, complexity, and perceived risk and high in testability.[28] That this exception should occur is not surprising. Little if any attention has been paid to measuring norms directly. The usual practice is to infer them from the consumer's buying behavior.

3.6 Conclusions on Segmentation Systems

The basic idea is that customer values lead to norms of behavior and norms lead to importance weights. It is crucial to recognize that once differences in customer weightings of benefits differ among potential customers for a product are identified, then only half of the problem has been solved: the basis of segmentation. The other half of the problem is typically how to identify the relevant segment descriptors so that marketing effort can be correctly directed.

The benefit weightings are essentially the motivational element of customer buying. Another way to conceptualize these is as making up the customers' goal hierarchy as described in Chapter 5 where it was said to be another way of conceptualizing values, norms, and benefit weightings. The goal hierarchy formulation may appear more meaningful than does the benefit weightings, but it does not focus as sharply upon motivation per se.

Since segmentation is one of the three central features of core strategy we will now apply the basic ideas of segmentation from Chapter 15 to routine problem solving (RPS). Most of the discussion in this chapter has been in terms of EPS and LPS because they are usually the most important decisions for the company. But RPS decisions are by far the most frequent. Also, by using RPS, it is possible to bring together the Chapter 15 point of view and a way of dealing with RPS called "consumer brand categorization," which involves the familiar evoked set and relates it to segmentation.[29]

---

[27] G. Zaltman and M. Wallendorf, *Consumer Behavior: Basic Findings and Management Implications*, rev. ed. (New York: John Wiley & Sons, 1983), pp. 135–36.

[28] J. D. Ford and E. A. Ellis, "A Reexamination of Group Influence on Member Brand Preference," *Journal of Marketing Research*, XVII (February 1980), 125–32.

[29] M. Laroche, J. A. Rosenblatt, and J. E. Brisoux, "Consumer Brand Categorization: Basic Framework and Managerial Applications," *Marketing Intelligence and Planning*, 4, no. 4 (Bradford, England, 1986), 60–74.

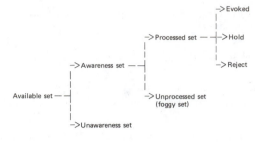

Figure 15-2
Consumer Brand Categorization

SOURCE: M. Laroche, J. A. Rosenblatt, and J. E. Brisoux, "Consumer Brand Categorizations: Basic Framework and Managerial Implications," *Marketing Intelligence and Planning*, 4, no. 4 (Bradford, England, 1986), 60–74. © 1986 by MCB University Press Limited: all rights reserved.

The concept of evoked set—those brands a consumer will consider buying—is one of long standing in marketing.[30] Only recently, however, has it been developed into a systematic way of portraying market segments within RPS. Figure 15-2 presents the several ways that a consumer in RPS categorizes a brand. As you notice in the upper right corner is the familiar "Evoked Set." It is one way, but only one way the consumer categorizes brands. Let us review the additional ways that extensive research have shown are used. With this introduction to categorizing brands let us go back and start at the beginning.

In Figure 15-2 beginning at the left is the "Available set," which is all brands in the category. In the next column, this total set is divided into those the consumer is aware of ("Awareness set") and those she is not aware of ("Unawareness set"). The third column are those the consumer is aware of and has thought about ("Processed set") and those she has not thought about ["Unprocessed set (foggy set)"]. Finally, the "Processed set" is divided three ways: (1) this is the familiar "Evoked set," which are those she would clearly consider buying. (2) This is the "Hold set," which have been evaluated to some extent but not fully. (3) This is the "Reject set," which are those she has fully evaluated and rejected. Hence, she does not consider them at all.

Substantial evidence on the nature of these categories is contained in Table 15-4. At the top and left is the average (mean) "Evoked size" for six widely different categories of products and services. These average from 2½ to almost 6. Also, you see the mean for each of the other three types of awareness sets: "Hold," "Foggy," and "Reject." They vary even more.

In the lower part of Table 15-4 you see confirmation of these buying statuses represented in the four sets by the level of attitude held. As you can see the attitude is substantially higher for brands in the evoked set. Those in the reject set are substantially the lowest, as you would expect. The hold and foggy sets are in between, with hold tending to indicate somewhat higher attitudes than the foggy set.

As you can imagine, where your brand is located—in which set—should make substantial difference in the nature of your market strategy. Let us briefly

---

[30] J. A. Howard, *Marketing Management: Analysis and Planning* (Homewood, Ill.: Richard D. Irwin, 1963), p. 84.

Table 15-4 Mean Set Size and Attitude Across Six Product Categories

PRODUCT CATEGORY	Evoked	Hold	Foggy	Reject
		Set Size		
Toothpaste	2.98	2.86	.95	1.43
Beer	2.52	1.32	1.41	1.33
Universities	3.98	4.83	5.60	5.40
Television	5.16	2.23	3.54	3.02
Fast food	5.74	2.50	2.36	2.25
Microcomputer	2.92	5.92	5.17	3.29
PRODUCT CATEGORY				
		Attitude[*]		
Toothpaste	7.65	4.92	2.38	2.46
Beer	6.75	5.47	5.51	2.50
Universities	7.29	6.63	4.95	4.25
Television	8.02	6.42	5.55	3.94
Fast food	5.74	2.50	2.36	2.25
Microcomputer	7.02	5.48	4.71	3.95

[*] Attitude was measured using a 9-point scale, where "1" represents "very low" and "9" represents "very high."

SOURCE: M. Laroche, J. A. Rosenblat, and J. E. Brisoux, "Consumer Brand Categorization: Basic Framework and Managerial Implications," *Marketing Intelligence and Planning*, 4, no. 4 (Bradford, England, 1986), 60–74.

discuss their strategy implications so that the relevance of the principles will be more obvious.

If your brand is in the "evoked set" of a large number of consumers, you are among the market leaders where the competition is the strongest. If it is an involving product, you would probably advertise the unique benefits of your product. If your brand is in the "hold set" of a number of customers, it suggests that you probably need to improve the quality of your product and advertise this improvement. If it is in the "reject set," you will need a total brand-image change or will have to withdraw it from the market.

If it is in the "foggy set," it is barely at the awareness stage in ordinary marketing parlance. If it has hidden attributes, these can be publicized. If not there is not much to be done about it, but withdraw it from the market. With this brief discussion of relevance of brand categories or strategy to give the categories more meaning, let us apply the principles in detail.

These four sets represent different segments, however, within each of these there may well be segmentation, for example, not all of those consumers who have it in their evoked set will have the same benefit weightings. Consequently, if both levels are exploited, we have represented here a case of *two-level segmentation*. To apply it in practice, the marketer would collect three types of specific data in the survey. First, he would want from each consumer the data indicating what set each brand is in. Second, data or importance weights of benefits would be needed as the *basis* for segmenting. Third, *description* data, typically, demographics, are necessary to identify each segment member in the market.

The data must then be analyzed to reveal the complex segments that may exist. Some kind of clustering techniques such as that contained in "Quick 'n Easy II," a computer guide that accompanies this text, will be useful in accomplishing this. The process of clustering importance weights is more complicated than using intention as the segmenting basis, for example. If the consumers tend to use these benefits in evaluating brands in the product category, each consumer will typically have a set of perhaps three importance weights. Assuming that the importance ratings are on a 1-to-5 scale and that all ratings were 3, 4, or 5, the following sets of scales are possible:

345	334
354	335
435	443
453	553
543	553
534	554

All 11 should be tested for their contribution to explaining differences in consumer product choices. But currently intention is much easier to use.

Once the segments are identified, they can then be fed into the intention (I) variable of the CDM, assuming that data on the other variables of the CDM had also been collected. When placed in the CDM framework, simulations can be derived from all these data. From the simulations, conclusions can be obtained about the optimum elements of the marketing strategy.

4.   INVOLVEMENT

Up to now in this discussion of segmenting the use of the term "involvement" has been downplayed. However, "high involvement" and "low involvement" have become widely used in textbooks; Bloch and Richins present a more formal statement of the concept.[31] There is no question that involvement is relevant. The issue however is whether it is better to apply the concept of involvement to differences among *products* or to differences among *customers*. We believe it is more fruitful for management purposes to treat them as customer differences as we have done in this chapter and as Houston and Rothschild as well as Tybejee suggest.[32]

---

[31] P. H. Bloch and M. L. Richins, "A Theoretical Model for the Study of Product Importance Perceptions," *Journal of Marketing*, 47, no. 3 (Summer 1983), 69–81.

[32] M. J. Houston and M. L. Rothschild, "Conceptual and Methodological Perspectives in Involvement," in S. C. Jain, ed., *Research Frontiers in Marketing: Dialogues and Directions* (Chicago: American Marketing Association, 1978), pp. 184–87; T. T. Tybejee "Refinement of the Involvement Concept: An Advertising Planning Point of View," in J. C. Maloney and B. Silverman, eds., *Attitude Plays for High Stakes* (Chicago: American Marketing Association, 1979), pp. 94–111.

There are a number of reasons for taking this position. First, it is surprising how much buying behavior is explained by the amount of information customers receive even among such low-priced, frequently purchased products as instant breakfast, vegetable bacon, toilet soap, and so on. These are usually thought of as "low-involvement" products, and, relative to cars and houses, they are. In Chapter 2, even with ordinary bread, however, we saw the important role of information. Second, information is a key policy variable for companies, and for public policy as well, as you will see in Chapter 18, and both are concerned with differences across people. Third, we are surprised to see the large magnitude of individual differences in buying behavior, for example, as noted early in this chapter in Table 15-1. We conclude that differences among people are probably greater than are differences across products. Finally, it is possible to determine statistically the magnitude of individual differences in a sample as discussed earlier in the chapter without having to know just what those differences are.[33] If the differences turn out to be important in a particular case, then one is justified in searching for the specific difference variables.

5. VALUES AND STRATEGIC PLANNING

In all the discussion of values up to this point, we have taken a static, unchanging view of them. This is not surprising, because most of marketing takes a short-term view of things. Our attention is devoted to matching products to customer needs (benefits) *now*.

There is an analogous but long-term view, however, that we could take, and the need for it exists in strategic planning. It can be phrased as the problem of matching customer values (which determine benefit importances) with product technology (from which products are derived as discussed in Chapter 8). This requires forecasting values and technology and hence deals with the dynamics of values instead of their static character as required in segmentation for regular short-term planning.

Not much systematic research has yet been devoted to this new and dynamic role of values. Mitchell refers to this dynamic aspect when he observes that people seem to move among the different VALS categories. He goes on to say, "these flow patterns are strongly suggested by available data but, it should be emphasized, are not yet incontrovertibly established."[34] However, Daniel Yankelovich has, for sometime, been interested in this problem of predicting changing values. Yankelovich, Skelly and White, Inc., regularly publishes data on the topic for clients, but values and norms are not clearly distinguished.

The classic Haire and Webster-von Pechman studies illustrate a general approach that might be taken. The two studies are compared in Table 15-5.

---

[33] Carpenter, Farley, and Sugito, "Detecting and Estimating Structural Parameter Differences."

[34] Mitchell, *The Nine American Life Styles,* p. 46.

Table 15-5   Percentage of Respondents Ascribing Characteristics to Shoppers

Ascribed Characteristics	Haire Study			1968 Study		
	Nescafé Shopper (n = 50)	Maxwell House Shopper (n = 50)	chi Square	Nescafé Shopper (n = 22)	Maxwell House Shopper (n = 20)	chi Square
Lazy	48%	4%	22.921*	18%	10%	.010
Poor planner	48	12	13.762*	27	25	.034
Thrifty	4	16	2.778†	36	55	.813
Spendthrift	12	0	4.433‡	23	5	1.436
Bad wife	16	0	6.658§	18	5	.706
Good wife	4	16	2.778*	18	25	.026
Overweight				18	10	.010
Time-saver				32	10	1.808
Does not enjoy homemaking				18	10	.010
Enjoys homemaking				27	40	.298
No imagination				41	30	.172
Single girl, busy				18	10	.010
Brand of coffee mentioned				50	35	.447

* Significant at .10 level.

† Significant at .05 level.

‡ Significant at .01 level.

§ Significant at .001 level.

SOURCE: F. E. Webster, Jr., and F. von Pechman, "A Replication of the 'Shopping List' Study," *Journal of Marketing,* 34, no. 2 (April 1970), 62.

Mason Haire found in the late 1940s that housewives considered users of Nescafe, the first of the instant coffees, as somewhat undesirable women.[35] As contrasted with Maxwell House users, almost 50% of the housewives interviewed considered the Nescafe user to be "lazy" and a "poor planner" while 16% considered her a "bad wife" and only 4% a "good wife." Fred Webster and Fred von Pechman followed up 20 years later with a replication of the Haire study.[36] They found the Nescafe user as seen in Table 15-5 to be much less "lazy" (18% versus 48% in the earlier study) and less a "poor planner" (27% versus 48% earlier). Also, there were just as many who considered her a "good wife" as a "bad wife." Although values were not directly measured by either of the two studies, most of us are willing to infer that the changes in attitudes are a reflection of changes in the respondents' underlying values.

Strategic planning in companies has been severely limited by the inability to make long-term forecasts of demand for products. The fact that marketing

[35] M. Haire, "Projective Techniques in Marketing Research," *Journal of Marketing,* XIV (April 1950), 649–56.

[36] F. E. Webster and F. von Pechman, "A Replication of the 'Shopping List' Study," *Journal of Marketing,* 34, no. 2 (April 1970), 61–63.

has been unable to contribute to this forecasting problem is probably one reason why marketers have in many companies lost out at the corporate level.[37] If we could develop the value-technology relationship to understand the long-term demand problem, we could be of immense help to the finance people who have tended to do most of the strategic planning.

6. OTHER USES OF INDIVIDUAL DIFFERENCES

6.1 Introduction

Our emphasis so far in discussing individual differences among consumers was upon their role in market segmentation. However, those differences play two other important roles as we see next.

6.2 Noise Reduction

Marketers wish to separate customers by their buying-related characteristics to reduce the "noise" in the CDM when describing customer behavior—and for a very practical purpose. To the extent that the model can more fully explain the customer's behavior, the marketer can validate the system as he applies it. To the extent that his model explains everything that happens to buying behavior, it reduces the "noise."

Specifically, by including *individual differences* among customers, the marketer can make the R^2 larger and closer to 1. To the extent that the R^2 in the equations making up the model is less than 1, something else is happening to the customer that is not—but might be—included in the model. Consequently, a prediction from such a simulation can be correct on average but off in a particular instance. This is what we meant when we said earlier that under some circumstances, segmentation is not necessarily the most important reason for identifying individual differences among customers, much less the only one.

6.3 Feedback Analysis

Another reason for wanting to know about individual differences among customers is that this knowledge is needed to *identify* properly the CDM or any other model when extending it to include feedbacks, such as from satisfaction (S) in using the brand to attitude (A) and confidence (C), as discussed in the next chapter.

"To identify" is used here in its mathematical sense where it is related to the principle learned in high school algebra that to solve a set of equations simultaneously there must be as many equations as unknowns. This is a requirement for feedback analysis in Chapter 16. In brief, there must be an individual difference variable in each of your feedback equations. This analysis allows the

---

[37] D. S. Hopkins and E. L. Bailey, "Organizing Corporate Marketing," Report No. 845, (Conference Board, New York, 1984).

marketer to capture accurately, for example, the simultaneous relationships that occur in consumer behavior, (1) among attitude (A), purchase (P), and satisfaction (S), and (2) the reverse direction of satisfaction (S) to attitude (A). Specifically, advertising affects attitude (A), which affects intention (I), which affects purchase (P), which affects satisfaction (S). But at the same time, having bought it and liked it, his attitude (A) will be higher. It also has the immediate practical advantage of enabling you to separate the effect of your advertising from the effect of the quality of the product as you will see in Chapter 16.

7. CONCLUSIONS

Five concepts have been brought together in this chapter to present a more systematic understanding of segmentation in consumer behavior: segmentation bases, segment descriptors, values, norms, and core strategy. The first two are essential for dealing with the practical problem of selecting and utilizing segments. Their use can avoid a lot of misunderstanding with managers.

The second two concepts—values and norms—make up the consumer theory side. Values are the basic source of most segmentation and norms specify those values to specific purchasing behavior, via the benefit importance weights. Values, norms, and benefit importances are summarized in the concept of goal hierarchy.

The fifth—core strategy—connects all four concepts to building marketing strategy. The CDM can be used to bring all five concepts together quantitatively to focus upon the segmentation problem in a practical situation, if the CDM is applied simultaneously to key competitors. Also, with the five concepts as a language aided by the CDM, it is possible to communicate effectively with others in the company about the relevance of this subtle notion of segmentation, so that they will understand it and cooperate in implementing it.

Finally, there are two other uses in addition to segmentation for exploring individual differences among consumers: noise reduction in the study of consumer behavior and doing feedback analysis in consumer behavior such as from satisfaction (S) with the brand to attitude (A) and confidence (C).

Questions

1. Why is market segmentation such a subtle process?
2. Explain the "basis of segmentation" and "descriptors of segments."
3. From the standpoint of the psychological characteristics of the customer, what are the foundations of market segments?
4. How can the CDM be used by management to evaluate which segments are most profitable?
5. The chapter has emphasized segmentation as a reason for understanding differences among customers. What other reasons are there for knowing how customers differ?

CHAPTER 16

Brand Satisfaction
and Other Feedbacks

1. INTRODUCTION

Up to now we have assumed that the effects of information (F) in the Consumer Decision Model (CDM) upon attitude (A), intention (I), and purchase (P) are roughly in that order. This implies that causation is unidirectional, always forward from left to right in the CDM diagram. This assumption immensely simplified our discussion of a complex problem, and only in some relations and under some conditions did we lose much by making that simplification.

In some parts of the system and under some conditions, however, the system does "feed back" upon itself, in fact, as indicated in Chapter 3. This means that causation is occurring both ways, both forward and backward. These are situations where by incorporating these feedbacks into the analysis, a fuller picture of how the customer buys is obtained and the results can be more useful for both qualitative and quantitative analysis. Feedbacks are relevant in a number of ways but particularly so in dealing with both the thinking and the emotional features of consumer behavior. Consequently, the CDM is extended here to include these feedbacks.

The feedbacks occur in at least two major ways. First, there can be a feedback from the satisfaction of *consuming* the product to both confidence and attitude. With a moment's thought, you will recall a commonsense observation. If people buy a brand today, and they are satisfied with it, they are more likely to buy it next time. To understand this tendency as shown in Figure 16-1, a satisfaction variable (S) from purchase (P) and its feedback effect upon attitude

293

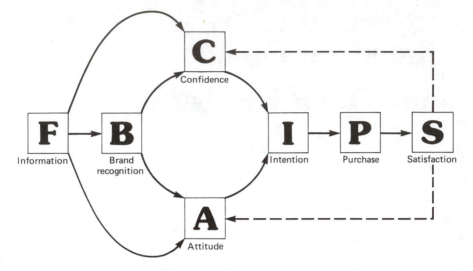

Figure 16-1   Feedback from Satisfaction

(A) and confidence (C) are included. A second feedback is from the elements of the *brand image* (A and C) to information (F). The more commonsense and obvious feedback, from satisfaction (S) with the product to attitude (A) and confidence (C), will be examined first and then the feedbacks to information (F).

2.   FEEDBACK FROM USE OF PRODUCT

The basic notion of the feedback from satisfaction is seen in Figure 16-1. Notice that purchase (P) causes satisfaction (S), and then satisfaction (S) causes attitude (A) and confidence (C). Thus, if the consumer's satisfaction is favorable, he is more likely to buy the brand the next time he buys because his confidence and attitude were increased as a result of this purchase, and these led to increased intention and so increased purchase the next time. The evidence, not surprisingly, is very good on this point. This sensible behavior gives us greater faith in the good judgment of the buyer.

In prior chapters, attention has been focused on the buyers' *anticipation* of purchase (intention) instead of also dealing with his actual consumption and therefore his actual satisfaction. Satisfaction thus extends the CDM to incorporate consumption or use of the brand as well. Technically, the only additional complication required in modeling the satisfaction feedback, or any other feedback for that matter, is that an individual difference variable must be added to each of the equations relating satisfaction to confidence and to attitude as described in Chapter 15.

Consumption can be studied in a much more detailed way than just by incorporating a satisfaction variable alone, but incorporating S is an easy and powerful first step toward learning about the consequences of actual consumption. The inclusion of consumption in the analysis introduces a whole new range of human experience, including the emotions. This was implied in the discussion of motivation in Chapter 4 but was not made explicit. As it has been stated about consumers, "Consumption has begun to be seen as involving a steady flow of fantasies, feelings and fun."[1] Others, too, have argued this more emotional view.[2] This is in contrast to the cognitive or more rational, utilitarian thinking that we have used up to now, except in Chapter 10. For some products such as entertainment and the arts, this emotional level of response may even be a stronger motivation than the more utilitarian. Also, it may be more common under certain conditions than we have thought; for example, it is probably stronger in routine problem-solving (RPS) situations. To deal with this broader range of human feelings requires some additional techniques that have been described by Holbrook and Hirschman.[3]

However, there is also another subtle feature of this feedback. If the buyer's satisfaction from consuming the product is *less* than what he *expected* it to be, does it make a difference in his behavior? This is practically significant, as suggested by the admonition often made by some managers, "Don't overpromise in your advertising!" As John Sculley, the former Pepsico executive who probably saved Apple Computer from bankruptcy observed in 1984, "There was an incredible amount of overpromise in computer advertising, ... People (computer sellers) were promising that the computer was going to save the world."[4]

A simple way of picturing this possibility of disappointed expectation is as in the following equation:[5]

$$A_{t+2} = f(S_{t+1} - A_t) + A_t$$

where

A_t = prepurchase attitude
S_{t+1} = immediate postpurchase satisfaction
A_{t+2} = revised postpurchase attitude

---

[1] M. B. Holbrook and E. Hirschman, "The Experiential Aspects of Consumption: Consumer Fantasies, Feelings, and Fun," *Journal of Consumer Research*, 9, no. 2 (September 1982), 132; see also L. M. Ward and J. A. Russell, "The Psychological Representation of Molar Physical Environments," *Journal of Experimental Psychology*, 110, no. 2 (June 1981), 121–52.

[2] R. B. Zajonc and H. Markus, "Affective and Cognitive Factors in Preferences," *Journal of Consumer Research*, 9, no. 2 (September 1982), 123–31.

[3] Holbrook and Hirschman, "Experiential Aspects."

[4] B. Morgan and C. Horton, "John Sculley: Marketing Methods Bring Apple Back," *Advertising Age*, December 31, 1984, p. 22.

[5] J. A. Howard and J. N. Sheth, *The Theory of Buyer Behavior* (New York: John Wiley & Sons, 1969), p. 147.

The equation was developed after the general idea was discussed at length with some experienced Procter & Gamble executives who from their experience agreed with the principle.

The equation tells us that the buyer has at the moment a favorable expectation (A_t) of how good the brand is. This judgment causes him to buy it. He finds, however, that it is not as good when he tries it as he had expected. Consequently, his satisfaction (S_{t+1}) is low. To the extent that satisfaction (S_{t+1}) is lower than the original attitude, it causes his attitude toward the brand to decline (A_{t+2}). The equation applies just as well when $S_{t+1} > A_t$, as implied earlier, but the negative side—the disappointment—will be emphasized here.

This "disappointment of expectations" has been confirmed and has come to be called the "disconfirmation effect." The buyer has from his experience disconfirmed the quality of the product, and it causes his ensuing attitude to be less as described in the equation. It is well supported by several studies, as summarized by Richard Oliver.[6]

Further, recent evidence suggests that two different levels of thinking operate in the buyer's mind toward satisfaction.[7] One is the usual, rational, calculating type of thinking, and the other is the emotional, feeling, or affective response described earlier in this chapter and also shown in liking the ad as discussed later. Moreover, there may be substantial difference among products in terms of these two levels of thinking about satisfaction. With footwear, for example, only the purchase-specific, rational factors were operative: the extent to which the product's performance met or exceeded expectations. With automobiles both factors operated.[8] The emotional or feeling influence was not large but was clearly significant. Also, a difference in the role of disconfirmation was found between a nondurable and a durable product, specifically between a plant (a chrysanthemum) and a videodisk player.[9] Disconfirmation operated with the plant but not with the videodisk player.

Not only does knowing this feedback tell you the very important fact of how well a product is doing, as judged by the customers who are buying the product, but it also provides some other most essential marketing information. It permits separating the effect of product quality from the effect of your information input. Without knowing the feedback you will assume that information (F) is causing the entire purchase response. When satisfaction (S) is incorporated, the path in Figure 16-1 of $S \rightarrow A \rightarrow I$ and $S \rightarrow C \rightarrow I$ can be compared with the path of $F \rightarrow A$, $F \rightarrow C$, $F \rightarrow B$, $B \rightarrow A$, $B \rightarrow C$, $A \rightarrow I$, and $C \rightarrow I$ to determine

[6] R. L. Oliver, "A Cognitive Model of the Antecedents and Consequences of Satisfaction Decisions," *Journal of Marketing Research*, XVII (November 1980), 460–69.

[7] D. J. Reibstein, C. H. Lovelock, and R. Dobson, "The Direction of Causality Between Perceptions, Affect and Behavior: An Application to Travel Behavior," *Journal of Consumer Research*, 6, no. 4 (March 1980), 370–76.

[8] R. A. Westbrook, "Intrapersonal Affective Influences on Consumer Satisfaction with Products," *Journal of Consumer Research*, 7, no. 1 (June 1980), 49–54.

[9] G. A. Churchill and C. Surprenant, "An Investigation into the Determinants of Customer Satisfaction," *Journal of Marketing Research*, XIX, no. 4 (November 1982), 491–504.

which is larger and by how much. The former measures the effect of the quality of the product, and the latter measures the effect of the advertising.

The thinking process involved in consuming the product may be more complex than the discussion of satisfaction indicates. It has been proposed that, when a customer is unsure she has made the best buy, she is in a state of dissonance, which she attempts to relieve by modifying her judgment of the quality of the product, for example. Robertson et al. conclude that dissonance is more likely to occur in highly involving situations.[10] It remains to be seen, however, whether this self-delusion actually exists.

Another aspect of postpurchase behavior is its power in analyzing the consequences of the extent to which consumers complain about the purchase of a product. There has been substantial discussion on this issue, and some research.[11] For example, Gilly and Gelb find that, if the complaint involves a monetary loss (percentage of price repaid by the company), satisfaction will be more affected when the complaint is settled than if it does not involve monetary issues.[12] Also the more quickly a complaint is resolved the greater the satisfaction. Further, the higher the degree of satisfaction with the complaint response, the greater the increase in level of brand purchase. From this evidence, it is clear that a marketer is well advised to have in his organization a service for receiving complaints, to encourage complainants to notify him, such as by an 800 telephone number, so that he can deal quickly and effectively with them.

In summary, this discussion of feedbacks from using the product has pointed out four contributions of doing feedback analysis in the CDM. First, it may reveal that the motivation for buying is more complex and emotional than the thoughtful, rational motivations assumed in information processing. Second, it permits separating the effects of your advertising from the product quality as an influence upon the consumer. Third, it shows the risks in overpromising the benefits of a product in advertising and other means of communicating with the customer. Finally, it shows how important it is to deal effectively and quickly with customer complaints.

3. FEEDBACK TO INFORMATION

3.1 Introduction

A more complex process is involved in the feedback to information acquisition by the customer. This feedback has been implied whenever we discussed the customer *searching* for information and the role of his *attention* in this process of acquiring information, as we did particularly in Chapter 5. The practical

---

[10] T. S. Robertson, J. Zielinski, and S. Ward, *Consumer Behavior* (Glenview, Ill.: Scott, Foresman, 1984), p. 259.

[11] Ibid, pp. 603–4.

[12] M. C. Gilly and B. D. Gelb, "Post-Purchase Consumer Processes and the Complaining Consumer," *Journal of Consumer Research*, 9, no. 3 (December 1982), 323–28.

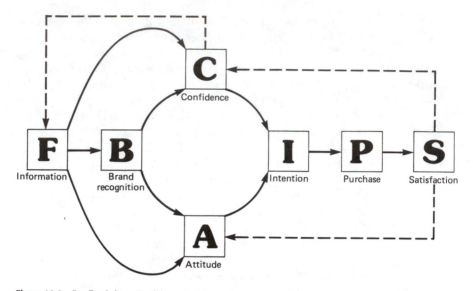

Figure 16-2 Feedback from Confidence to Information

importance of the feedback is that it indicates whether the customer is sensitive to information and to which copy and media a customer is paying attention. In earlier chapters it was said that attention exerts a strong positive influence on whether the exposure to a source of information is effective.

There are two major feedbacks to the customer's information input that influence the amount and kind of that input to his thinking processes, and thus shape his buying behavior. The first of these is from his confidence to his search effort. The second is from his attitude to his search.

3.2 Feedback from Confidence to Search

A key feedback relation is from the buyer's *confidence* to the amount of searching she does. Figure 16-2 shows the relation. As might be expected, it is negative, and so the more confident she is, the less searching she will do. This is interpreted as indicating she searches less *because* she already has information and therefore doesn't need the additional information. A recent study of 1,561 people who bought cars for their own use in the period September–November 1978 supported this negative relationship.[13] So does a study of car purchasing in Australia.[14] Further Reilly and Conover, in a meta-analysis of seven previous studies, "show a high degree of support for a negative relationship with familiarity with a product category and the amount of external search."[15]

[13] G. N. Punj and R. Staelin, "A Model of Consumer Information Search Behavior for New Automobiles," *Journal of Consumer Research*, 9, no. 4 (March 1983), 366–80.

[14] G. C. Kiel and R. A. Layton, "Dimensions of Consumer Information Seeking Behavior," *Journal of Marketing Research*, XVIII (May 1981), 233–39.

[15] J. R. Bettman, "Consumer Psychology," *Annual Review of Psychology*, 37 (1986), 261.

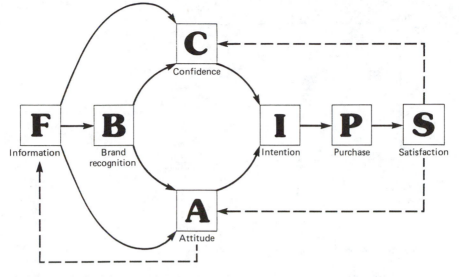

Figure 16-3 Feedback from Attitude to Search

Knowing this negative relationship permits a fuller interpretation of the nature of the buyer's thinking process. For example, if her confidence is low, the buyer will be paying more attention to relevant information, and this can explain why readership scores for advertising are so high.

3.3 Feedback from Attitude to Search

Also, there is a feedback from attitude to search. This relationship is diagrammed in Figure 16-3. It has long been observed in advertising studies: a buyer is more likely to recall having seen an ad about her preferred brand than having seen ads about other brands. Thus, attitude controls information input. The research supporting this issue has been nicely summarized and the feedback further supported.[16] Let us examine the evidence.

Figure 16-4 describes part of the feedback process that we believe is operating in Figure 16-3 because it was carefully tested in the study. The emphasis is upon the role of "attribute importances" for which you could substitute our term "benefit importances." These play a dual role in Figure 16-4. First, they determine what information the buyer searches for and pays attention to, as shown by the upper horizontal arrow (1): that information relating to the most important benefits. As the buyer is confronted with information (cues), she selects out that portion (acquires those cues) that gives her information about the most important benefits. Second, as shown by the lower horizontal arrow

---

[16] M. B. Holbrook, A. A. Velez, and G. J. Tabouret, "Attitude Structure and Search: An Integrative Model of Importance-Directed Information Processing," in K. B. Moore, ed., *Advances in Consumer Research* (Arlington, Va.: Association for Consumer Research, October 1980), Vol. VIII, pp. 35–41.

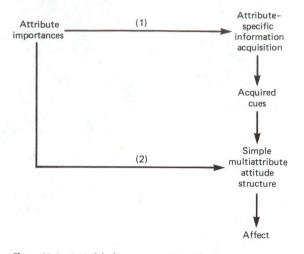

Figure 16-4 A Model of Importance-Directed Information Processing

SOURCE: M. G. Holbrook, A. A. Velez, and G. J. Tabouret, "Attitude Structure and Search:
An Integrative Model of Importance-Directed Information Processing," in K. B. Monroe,
ed., *Advances in Consumer Research* (Provo, Utah: Association for Consumer
Research), Vol. VIII, p. 36.

(2), these same benefit importances determine which benefits will be used by
the customer to form a simple attitude that predicted better than a weighted
attitude (2). This and some earlier studies thus support this notion of the feedback
from attitude (A) to information (F) in the CDM model.

The conclusion of Figure 16-4 that attribute importance directs both
information acquisition and attitude formation was arrived at by an experiment
among students who had bought at least two pop or jazz recordings within the
last six months. They were confronted with information about a number of
attributes of hypothetical recordings and therefore recordings about which they
could not yet have formed a brand concept. With their recent buying experience,
however, the students probably had developed in their mind at least some benefits
of the product category. Hence, these criteria guided their selection of information, which in turn gave them the specific performance information on each
hypothetical product. This chosen information caused them to form their judgments on those attributes toward each product and so form their preference
for the hypothetical recordings in line with the process described in Figure 16-
4. These two conclusions will be used extensively in Sections 4 and 5 to extend
the integration of the attitude and information-processing concepts.

This idea of information selection guided by benefit importances, however, can now can be taken one very important *practical* step farther in terms
of the CDM model in Figure 16-3, where the feedback from attitude (A) to
information (F) is shown by a dashed line. By inserting individual differences
as described in Chapter 15 into this feedback relation, we may be able to identify
market segments of customers that are more attentive to the information. When

these customers are identified in terms of the particular media they use, the advertiser will then know how to concentrate her advertising on these information-receptive customers and also how to modify the nature of the copy content to be included.

Finally, another practical use of feedback analysis, from attitude to information, is to test for the so-called "halo" effect. The "halo" effect is indicated when a customer's strong overall preference for a brand distorts her perception of the information she is receiving about how good the brand is. Specifically, if she strongly likes a brand, this may cause her to rate the performance of the brand on some benefits higher than she actually believes is so. These halo-stimulated evaluations, if not recognized, can obviously be misleading. Halo research has received considerable attention but has been found to vary from situation to situation and sometimes thought to be spurious. Whether it really exists in a specific situation can obviously be important in deciding what action to take based upon the CDM results. By using feedback analysis with the CDM it is possible to measure the extent of the halo effects with substantial ease and accuracy by comparing the customer's stated weights with the weights she actually used as shown by which weights were related to benefit effects on intention (I).[17]

4. IMPLICATIONS OF FEEDBACK

Knowing that the feedbacks exist permits integrating most of Chapters 3, 4, 5, and 6 and spelling out relations that up to now may not have been at all obvious. The two types of feedbacks discussed earlier in the chapter—satisfaction and search—are but pieces of the much bigger picture seen in Figure 16-5, initially shown as Figure 5-2 and Figure 9-2, for setting strategy. Figure 16-5 is an emerging general theory of consumer behavior that builds upon the three foundation concepts of Chapter 2: *product category* as the underlying concept of product hierarchy, *stages of the* product life *cycle* with characteristic types of consumer behavior for each stage, and the *market* where suppliers compete in serving consumers. The theory also incorporates the CDM as the central component and captures most of the contents of previous chapters. It also specifically includes the nature and potential of individual differences among consumers as developed in Chapter 15 such as by modeling each segment separately.

These modifications reflect some further development. First, "choice" has been dropped from Figure 16-5 because its content is captured in intention (I) and purchase (P) of the CDM. Second, the product hierarchy diagram is discarded because it is actually contained in memory as shown in memory (M). Specifically, the process by which the hierarchy develops and is modified is

---

[17] M. B. Holbrook, "Using a Structural Model of Halo Effect to Assess Perceptual Distortion due to Affective Overtones," *Journal of Consumer Research*, 10, no. 2 (September 1983), 247–52.

Information Processing

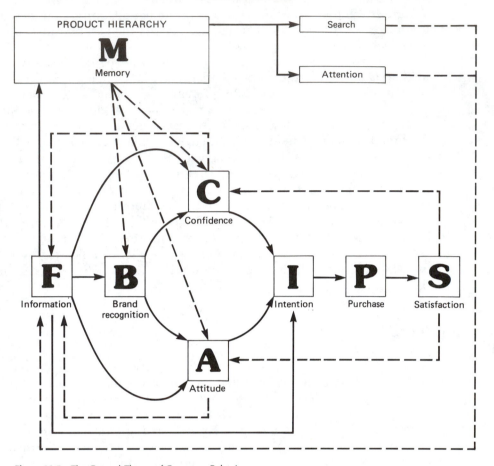

Figure 16-5   The General Theory of Consumer Behavior

contained in the relations of information (F) to memory (M), and memory (M) to brand recognition (B), and attitude (A). If it is well formed, the consumer eminently better understands the brand and will make his purchase decisions accordingly. Further, the hierarchy describes the nature of the competition in the market. Both of these, the consumer and competitor, are essential to building strategy and marketing plans. The hierarchy is also the means by which the consumer orders and makes sense of a complex buying and consuming situation. Thus, the product hierarchy serves a triple role in understanding the consumer.

Third, as you see in Figure 16-5, information feeds back from search and attention to information (F). From F, that information can take either of two routes. It can take the familiar direct bypass route, such as from emotion, to form and activate the ABCs. It can also, however, go to memory (M) and then feed back to form the ABCs.

Finally, when price changes for an RPS consumer, intention (I) is affected without changing attitude (A) first. However, the causal path would be from price to memory (M) and then to intention (I) which to simplify is not shown in Figure 16-5.

5. MEMORY

5.1 Review of Memory

In Sec. 3.3, the strong impact of benefit importances on the way the consumer processes information and forms her attitude toward a brand was described. These attitude components as they develop are stored in her memory so as to be easily accessed when she needs information to consider buying that category of product.

Let us briefly reexamine the concept of memory. There are various views of what memory is but they tend to be consistent with the notion of *limited* processing capacity (short-term memory, STM) and a *single store* (long-term memory, LTM) with an activation power in which *allocations* of that processing capacity are made to the processing of incoming information.[18] LTM is made up of meaningful concepts such as brands and associations or linkages among those brands as in the product hierarchy. It also includes visual imagery such as brand recognition (B) and auditory events.

Short-term memory is where pieces of information are put together to form a new idea. These pieces can be retrieved from LTM or come from the environment via information (F). STM holds this information for only a few seconds, however, when it is either transferred to LTM or lost.

To simplify here we will use the term "memory" (M) and not distinguish between LTM and STM, except when necessary. A major feature of Figure 16-5 to consider is the relation between memory (M) and attitude (A). This relation best represents the needed merger of the information-processing research and concept formation research where "concept" is made up of attitude, brand recognition, and confidence as reflected in Figure 16-5. In the past information-processing scientists did not see attitude as dependable[19] while concept formation scientists did not find the memory variable essential.

In thinking about how to map the memory-attitude relation so that we can better understand the buying process, let us begin with the flow of information into memory (M) from information (F). The consumer has a number of memory strategies that regulate this flow in and out of memory. As marketers, we are concerned with these strategies. The *transfer strategy* is *what* the consumer decides to encode or store in LTM and *how* in the sense of what form, for example, words or pictures. We want to provide the information content and form that will be consistent with that strategy and so enable the consumer to decide to buy. For example, in Sec. 3.3 it was shown how the importance of the benefits

---

[18] J. R. Bettman, *An Information Processing Theory of Consumer Behavior* (Reading, Mass.: Addison-Wesley, 1979), pp. 142–43.
[19] Ibid, p. 209.

shaped the consumer's processing in forming an attitude. The transfer strategy of the consumer's memory would cause the consumer to store in words the more important benefits of a product category to form attitude (A) and to store in picture form the elements by which the consumer recognizes the brand (B).

We are also concerned with the consumer's *placement strategy* of where it will be stored in her memory. She will store the more important benefits so as to be more readily accessible when she considers buying this category and also the particular brand. Less important information would be stored so as to be less accessible. The locations required to support easy access will be in terms of the existing memory structure and the particular associations the consumer makes to relate the new information to that which she already has. In summary, both transfer and placement strategies affect her *retrieval strategy*, the ease and speed with which she can call up this new information when she later thinks about buying our product.

We have been recognizing all along the need to know her *response generation strategy*, which means recognizing that LTM is largely made up of stored fragments of information. By becoming associated with each other, these stored fragments can form a new mental construction such as a new category concept or a new brand concept. Similarly, existing concepts can be modified.

We are also concerned with the consumer's *rehearsal strategy* of holding incoming information in STM while she pulls up information from LTM to combine with the information already in STM and so enables her to understand better the incoming information.

This rehearsal strategy is intimately related to the consumer's *coding strategy* of how she structures information in LTM for rehearsal in STM, that is, what kind of associations does she use to bring different pieces together to make sense of the whole, which is especially essential when she is in extensive problem solving (EPS). As marketers, we want to know the copy, media advertising budget, and sales presentations that will best serve these six strategies.

Having discussed the nature of the information (F) to memory (M) relation, the next order of business is the relations between memory (M) and the ABCs. How do the ABCs form in her memory so that we can capture in our consumer surveys the central part of the consumer's CDM? The specifics of the foregoing discussion of memory have dealt with the As (attitude). We lack for the Bs (brand recognition) and Cs (confidence) the understanding that the study of attitude in the earlier section gave us for the As. Presumably, the same strategies hold for brand recognition (B) and confidence (C). Rehearsal and coding strategies are the core of these two ABCs as well.

Attitude is such an important concept in marketing practice because much of marketing deals with "natural objects" (physical brands) where attitude is effective in understanding and predicting purchase behavior.[20] Services are,

---

[20] W. J. McGuire, "Attitudes and Attitude Change," in G. Lindzey and E. Aronson, eds., *The Handbook of Social Psychology*, 3rd ed. (New York: Random House, 1985), pp. 2, 239.

of course, more ambiguous, but even these—for example, the complex managed cash accounts as you have seen in earlier chapters—tend to become well defined by the marketing process. Also, the timing of buying services tends to be more fixed and so more predictable than is much of human behavior generally.

Easily finding these relationships between memory (M) and attitude (A) for designing marketing strategy will require much more development in how to measure memory.[21] Three areas of memory will now be presented to indicate the current state of memory research. These areas are the familiar recognition and recall, prior knowledge, and structure of memory.

5.2 Recognition and Recall

The first has to do with why consumers sometimes use recognition and at other times use recall in accessing their memory to form a brand image. You will remember that this issue was introduced early in Chapter 3 and has come up in many, many ways in later chapters. Recognition is much easier and serves a purpose different from recall. Recognition underlies brand recognition (B), which enables the consumer to recognize the brand but also serves as a mental "chunk" for building attitude (A) toward the brand and confidence (C) in judging the brand.

This distinction of recognition versus recall can also be used more broadly on the issue of whether ads should be made up of visual stimuli (pictures) and/or verbal stimuli. Bettman reviews the Edell and Staelin research on this issue. You will recall from Chapter 5 that they tested the notion of whether the viewer seeing the verbal portion of an ad as "framing" the picture, that is, viewing the picture as an illustration of the ad, caused the viewer to process the ad differently. When the picture was "framed," the viewer retrieved information from memory and proceeded to evaluate the brand. When the picture was not framed, he did not retrieve information from memory or evaluate the brand. He did store the ad trace but *not* with the product class information. Bettman reports that the "results are an important demonstration that the degree of congruence between the visual and verbal components of a message has a major impact in the processing of the message."[22]

5.3 Prior Knowledge

The second area of memory's role in consumer behavior is illustrated by the familiar product hierarchy concept. Recalling the automobile example with its Ford Escort used in introducing the hierarchy concept, for some people such as "car buffs," this hierarchy can represent a mass of information and therefore a major contribution of memory. But some car drivers, such as those who buy

[21] J. R. Bettman, "Consumer Psychology," p. 265.
[22] Ibid, p. 276.

the same brand purchase after purchase, probably have a very poorly developed product hierarchy of cars.

Another way to look at the product hierarchy is as a special case of the consumer's "prior knowledge." It is *knowledge* that *she has in her memory at any particular moment* as she goes through the buying process. We are thinking here of a time sequence where new information changes memory and the revised memory then changes the nature of the buying process. The key question is in what way and by how much does prior knowledge affect the consumer's current purchasing? Some answers were given to this question in Chapter 2 in discussing evidence supporting the three types of buying over the product life cycle for some products. Consumers with prior knowledge tend to develop three skills. First, they have superior knowledge of existing products, which they can call upon in making purchase decisions. Second, they have a greater ability to encode new information, which increases memory. Third, they have a greater ability to select new information. The consumer with more prior knowledge tends to cluster information by brands in his memory and, further, to cluster brands that are more similar in the benefits they provide.

Further, it has been found that when the information a customer receives about a category is what he expected, he will tend to use "category-based process-ing" of the information. His impressions are made faster, he verbalizes more information about the category but with fewer verbalizations about the benefits. On the other hand, if the original information does not match his expectations about the category, he will use a "piecemeal approach" to processing the informa-tion where he focuses more upon the individual benefits rather than upon the category as a whole.

In the last few years, substantial research on prior knowledge has been done. From it we infer that prior knowledge in many cases probably affects the development of all three variables in the CDM making up brand image: brand recognition (B), attitude toward the brand (A), and confidence in judging the quality of the brand (C), not just attitude.

5.4   Structure and Content

The third area of long-term memory that is beginning to get attention is the most basic—the structure and content of memory. How is it organized?

You will recall that in Chapter 5, Figure 5-4 offered a description of LTM, and it is repeated here as Figure 16-6. We will review it with some care because it is one of the most fundamental ideas of memory as we have already seen. Structure is made up of *nodes* (concepts) and *links* (relations among the concepts). Four kinds of relationships are represented in the diagram: subsets, supersets, overlays, and disjoints. These relations are here also represented in terms of the car product hierarchy to illustrate.

The subjects in the study were asked to answer whether a statement was true or false—for example, "Some birds are animals"—and the issue is how long it took them to answer the question. The answer was true because as

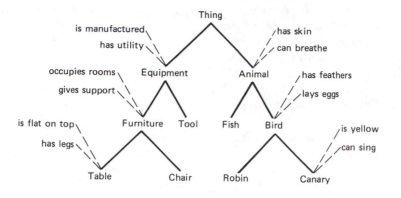

Figure 16-6   A Picture of Long-Term Memory

SOURCE: D. E. Meyer and R. S. Schvaneveldt, "Meaning, Memory Structure and Mental Processes," *Science*, 192 (April 2, 1976), 28. Copyright 1976 by the AAAS.

the diagram shows, birds are a *subset* of animals just as Escorts are a subset of subcompacts. The second was "Some animals are birds," just as some subcompacts are Escorts, which is a *superset* relation. Third, "Some birds are female" is an *overlap* because both animals and birds are female just as Escorts consume little gasoline just as subcompacts do. Finally, "Some birds are tools" is analogous to "Some Ford Escorts are trains," a *disjoint* relation, one bearing no relation to the other. As predicted, the findings were very consistent: the more similar the "things" being compared, the faster the subject could answer, that is, subsets were the fastest for example. The speed in thinking is much greater for similar objects just as repeat purchase (RPS) is faster than LPS.

Memory structure is a difficult area to research. Bettman states that for dealing with content and structure, "there has yet been no convincing empirical demonstration of a measurement scheme that can provide the necessary framework."[23] Rosch and her colleagues, however, have made substantial progress with their categorization research on "natural objects."[24] Leading psychologists are now recognizing the need to model quantitatively memory circuits and networks.[25] In reviewing two recent books on memory development, a leading psychologist states, "One of the many important messages of these volumes is that the exclusive reliance upon laboratory context is likely to result in misleading models of memory development."[26] Perhaps this will prove to be an area where consumer behavior researchers who work in naturalistic settings, namely, the market, will have an advantage. The Committee on Basic Research

[23] Ibid, p. 265.

[24] C. B. Mervis and E. Rosch, "Categorization of Natural Objects," *Annual Review of Psychology*, 32 (1981), 89–115.

[25] R. F. Thompson, "The Neurobiology of Learning and Memory," *Science*, 233 (August 29, 1986), 946.

[26] S. J. Ceci, "Memory Development," *Science*, 231 (March 1986), 1452.

in the Behavioral and Social Sciences of the National Research Council reported in 1982 that the concept of information processing has provided "a framework that shows promise of guiding explorations in the neural substrate, the functioning of the brain as an information processing system, which has to date proved nearly intractable."[27]

This discussion of memory concepts as a background should permit us to articulate our inevitable theories about memory's role in consumer behavior such as in the CDM more sharply and enable us to test them more effectively. Also, the need for real-world instead of laboratory research already mentioned is especially relevant. Direct marketing with its data bases where experimentation can be carried out provides an especially good opportunity for doing this real-world research in a way that has not previously been available.

6.   THREE NEW AREAS OF DEVELOPMENT

6.1   Introduction

With this general description of Figure 16-5 as a review, let us now apply the general theory to three particular issues. The purpose is twofold. The first purpose is to test the theory in terms of whether it can accommodate each of the three new emerging areas.[28] The areas are "liking the ad," "emotional processes," and the "pioneer brand." The second purpose is to develop the theory further.

6.2   Liking the Ad

The first issue is the extent to which the consumer's liking the ad motivates him to buy as contrasted with an ad that tells him favorable information about the important benefits he uses in evaluating the brand as explained in Chapter 3. Such advertising copy was discussed briefly in Chapter 10, and the growing number of entertaining ads seen in practice was referred to there. The Japanese are particularly inclined to emotional appeals. Bernard Barber, executive vice president of McAnn-Erickson in Japan, states that

> Unlike most U.S. advertisers who generally try to explain product form, functions, features and superiority, Japanese advertisers believe communicating information is inherently less persuasive than involving consumers in the emotional aspects of the product and communication . . .[29]

Also, he sees the emotional type of advertising as a global trend.

[27] R. McC. Adams, N. J. Smelser, and D. J. Theiman, eds., *Behavioral and Social Science Research*, Part I, (Washington, D.C.: National Academy Press, 1982), p. 50.

[28] The author is deeply indebted to Professor Donald R. Lehmann for suggesting these three pieces of research as challenges to the theory.

[29] D. Kilburn, "Japan's Sun Rises," *Advertising Age*, August 3, 1987, p. 42.

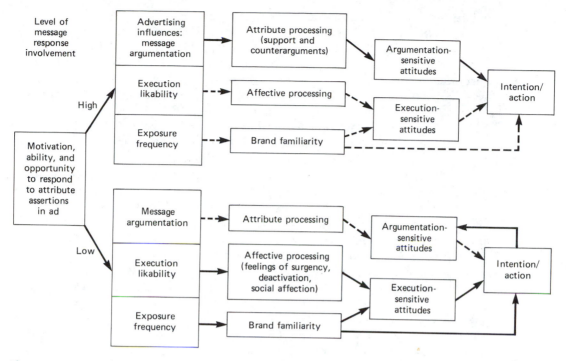

Figure 16-7   Role of "Liking the Ad"

SOURCE: R. Batra and M. L. Ray, "How Advertising Works at Contact," in L. F. Alwitt and A. A. Mitchell,
eds., *Psychological Processes and Advertising Effects* (Hillsdale, N.J.: Lawrence Erlbaum Associates,
1985), p. 39.

Recent evidence indicates that when engaged in a low-involvement buy-ing situation typical of routine buying (RPS) with its three characteristics of little product change, bypassing, and a cyclic pattern of behavior as discussed in Chapter 6, consumers are influenced by no more than their mere *liking* the *ad* even though it tells them nothing about the important benefits of the brand. However, this involves quite a different choice process from the usual high-involvement situation, as Batra and Ray have shown.[30] It is pictured in Figure 16-7 and is related to the "bypass" version of the CDM as discussed in Chapters 6 and 10.

On the left side of Figure 16-7 is a single box, which represents the level of the consumer's message response involvement and to the right are four successive columns. Forty TV commercials were selected from 60 commer-cials, most of which were chosen to represent one of the two extremes of involve-

---

[30] R. Batra and M. L. Ray, "How Advertising Works at Contact," in L. F. Alwitt and A. A. Mitchell, eds., *Psychological Processes and Advertising Effects*, (Hillsdale, N.J.: Lawrence Erlbaum Associates, 1985), pp. 13–43; see also R. J. Lutz, "Affective and Cognitive Antece-dents of Attitude Toward the Ad: A Conceptual Framework," in the same source, pp. 45–63.

ment, high or low; the brand was a market leader or follower so that it would be well known and the commercial stressed either brand attribute superiority ("rational") or likability of the ad ("affective"). One hundred twenty women, more educated and affluent than average, volunteered to participate for a small incentive. After undergoing some preparation procedures, each of these women was shown 4 of the 40 ads and then asked questions that revealed where each ad was located in each of four columns in Figure 16-7.

The results with some exceptions are as indicated in Figure 16-7, where the solid line shows a major influence and a dashed line minor influence. The highly involving ads, in the extreme upper left box, led to "message argumentation." These then led to "Attribute processing" (as shown by the solid arrow to the next box), where the person agreed ("support") or disagreed ("counterarguments") with the ad. These in turn affected those benefits ("Argumentation-sensitive attitudes") of a utilitarian nature, which in turn affected intention to buy ("Intention/action"). This, of course, is nothing more than carefully spelling out a description of our usual LPS utilitarian information processing.

When we turn to the low-involving route in the lower half of Figure 16-7, however, we find a highly useful extension and elaboration of RPS. In the first column and fifth row "Execution likability"—whether they like the ad—comes through with a solid arrow to "Affective processing" and associated feelings or emotions triggered by the liking of the ad. Such emotional responses or feelings are "upbeat surgency, pleasantness, or heartwarming tenderness," for example, one of Procter & Gamble's famous "slice-of-life" ads of a family happily gathered around a family dinner table. These emotions, in turn, affect "Execution-sensitive attitudes," which are hedonic attitudes and related to the ad, instead of the utilitarian attitudes found in the more involving ads. The former refer to an immediate pleasure-displeasure objective, while the latter refer to a longer-term objective requiring more thought to achieve. These hedonic attitudes in turn trigger intention to buy. Finally, "Brand familiarity" on the sixth row affects intention to buy via "Execution-sensitive attitudes," the more hedonic advertising-related attitudes.

This low-motivational-level activity is quite different from that at the high level. As we saw in the RPS level theory of Chapter 6, the consumer does not need the information as badly. Only occasionally does she bother to look around for information, and about a fourth of the consumers never bother to look around at all, buying the same brand month after month. Consequently, liking of the ad can play a role in getting the consumer's attention. Further, the attitudes involved tend to be "execution sensitive" because more emotional benefits are used. In RPS, which is the stable or declining portion of the product life cycle, competing brands are usually very much alike. The emotional differences may be the only differences available for the consumer to use in making her purchase. Figure 16-7 clearly implies that two different types of brand benefits are appropriate: in the high-involvement case they are utilitarian and in the low-involvement case, hedonic.

The notion of "liking the ad" contributes substantially to our understanding of the consumer's response to advertising. This can obviously be helpful to

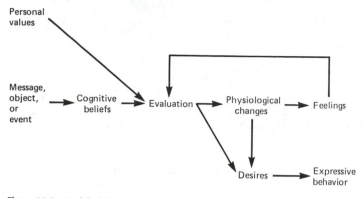

Figure 16-8 Model of the Emotional Process

SOURCE: M. B. Holbrook and J. O'Shaughnessy, "The Role of Emotion in Advertising," *Psychology and Marketing*, 1, no. 2 (Summer 1984), 50.

the manager faced with designing ads in a mature market. Further, it introduces the affective component of attitude toward the brand. It also has relevance for public policy. Does it contribute to the ad's power to take advantage of the consumer so that he needs some protection from it? This is one of the issues we will deal with in Chapter 18, Consumerism.

Here we find consistency with a "bypass" type of behavior discussed in Chapter 6. But we also find an extension in terms of how this low involvement affects response to advertising, namely, the liking of the ad.

6.3 Emotional Processes

Up to now we have emphasized the cognitive aspects of consumer behavior characterized by long-term motivation, which is represented by personal values, social norms measured by benefit importances, and the goal hierarchy. Here we will begin to focus systematically upon the affective, shorter-term, more physiological drives represented by arousal and the emotions generally.

Earlier in the chapter, the feedback from satisfaction was shown to be important in guiding behavior. Further, the satisfaction variable introduced the consumer's consumption experience into the CDM and enables the CDM to go much beyond mere buying behavior to include the consequences of consumption. It is largely in the consumption experience where the consumer's emotions play a significant role and especially in the low-involvement situation of RPS.

In Chapter 10 we learned from Holbrook and O'Shaughnessy that the additional element needed for the consumer to experience emotion are some physiological changes to occur in his process of evaluating (evaluation) the brand and as seen in Figure 16-8.[31] These are such things as changes in the consumer's

---

[31] M. B. Holbrook and J. O'Shaughnessy, "The Role of Emotion in Advertising," *Psychology and Marketing*, 1, no. 2 (Summer 1984), 45–64.

Table 16-1 The PAD Typology of Emotional Content

	Positive	Negative
Pleasure	Joy, friendliness	Sadness, loneliness
Arousal	Vitality, liveliness	Sluggishness, overstimulation
Dominance	Competence, self-fulfillment	Futility, ennui

SOURCE: M. B. Holbrook and J. O'Shaughnessy, "The Role in Emotion in Advertising," *Psychology in Marketing*, 1, no. 2 (Summer 1984), 54.

pulse rate, sweat glands, muscles, hormones, or brain waves. These result in the "Feelings," referred to in Figure 16-8. These "Feelings," in turn, feed back to the brand evaluation process as shown in Figure 16-8 and thus emotional elements enter into the brand evaluation process. We can be more specific in describing these emotions by using the PAD typology (Pleasure, Arousal, Dominance) discussed in Chapter 10 and shown in Table 16-1. There you can see both the positive and negative emotions related to the general category of each one, for example, joy, liveliness, and self-fulfillment, which give PAD a lot more meaning. These are important because most discussions tend to emphasize the negative types of emotions and so miss the positive and appealing emotions that consuming brands can engender.

These two diagrams of Figure 16-8 and Table 16-1 present the basics of the complex but important emotional processes that are especially associated with the consumer's consumption experience. It is not a well-developed area but is now receiving much research attention.[32] For instance, lists of emotional dimensions are emerging that might be used in the CDM, where emotions are the basic reasons for buying. An example will be discussed shortly.

The analysis of emotional data appears at this point to be a little more complicated than for the usual utilitarian benefits. Also, the causal process in the CDM may need to be a little different to accommodate the emotional dimensions. This possibility is implied by Figure 16-8, which contains the feedback from "Feelings" to "Evaluation." This may not prove to be difficult, especially since we are already familiar with having to modify the CDM processes for different stages of the product life cycle. However, the need to include that feedback can be great for products the purchase of which is dominated by emotions (e.g., musical concerts). Further, in many products, if not most, we may find that incorporating the emotional substantially impairs our capacity to explain why our customers buy because emotions may influence purchase even though they do not directly enter into the evaluation of the product, for example, emotions that are encountered in the consumption process but not in the buying process.

[32] For a review of research on emotion, see M. B. Holbrook, "Emotion in the Consumption Experience: Toward a New Model of the Human Consumer," in R. A. Peterson, W. D. Hoyer, and W. R. Wilson, eds., *The Role of Affect in Consumer Behavior: Emerging Theories and Applications* (Lexington, Mass.: D. C. Heath, 1985).

Table 16-2   Proposed SEP Instrument

Dimension	Indices	Items
Pleasure	Faith	Reverent Worshipful Spiritual
	Affection	Loving Affectionate Friendly
	Gratitude	Grateful Thankful Appreciative
Arousal	Interest	Attentive Curious Interested*
	Activation	Aroused Active Excited
	Surgency	Playful Entertained Lighthearted
Domination	Sadness	Sad Distressed Sorrowful
	Fear	Fearful Afraid Anxious
	Skepticism	Skeptical Suspicious Distrustful

* This item was added to complete the Interest index.

Further, to illustrate progress, Holbrook and Batra using 12 women as judges to rate their emotional responses to a series of ads have carefully developed a "standardized emotional profile" (SEP).[33] The SEP is to be used in measuring responses to the nonverbal components of advertising. The elements of it are shown in Table 16-2, with the PAD dimensions down the left column.

There has been growing interest in the emotional dimensions of ads. But a comprehensive view for constructing a battery of emotions suitable to advertising has been absent. The SEP provides this battery. Also, just to have the items as a vocabulary to think and talk with in planning ads can be terribly helpful, especially for the creative people. More concretely, these are potential benefit dimensions of attitude in applying the CDM to products where emotions are the major reasons for buying.

[33] M. B. Holbrook and R. Batra, "Toward a Standardized Emotional Profile (SEP) Useful in Measuring Responses to the Nonverbal Components of Advertising," unpublished paper (Columbia University, Graduate School of Business, New York, Spring 1987).

The authors do not maintain that the SEP will be adequate for all ads; for example, pride and anger are omitted and might have to be included for some ads. But for most ads, the list should be adequate.

This discussion of the emotional clearly extends the theory of consumer behavior by the addition of the "standardized emotional profile." But it is consistent with the theory in that by adding a feedback new behavior results. Further, it has relevance for the public policy of protecting the consumer as you will see in Chapter 18. For example, thinking that some of these emotions in buying may cause some people to take an, "I told you so!" view of them. Marketing, especially advertising, is seriously criticized for causing consumers to buy things they allegedly don't need. For example, the use of emotional ads might cause the Federal Trade Commission, in performing its role of protecting the consumer as discussed in Chapter 18, to rule that such ads are misleading and untruthful and should be prohibited. Alternatively, a better understanding of emotional ads will probably show that FTC regulation is not necessary.

6.4 Pioneer Brand

To be very useful for marketing practice, any theory of consumer behavior must incorporate the concept of competition. It is obviously necessary for management purposes. This need to integrate conceptually the buyer and competition has become sharper, with many companies facing world competition for the first time, and will become still sharper with the integration of company functions required by complete company automation that integrates product design and the production system in manufacturing.

One reason the product hierarchy concept has been developed is to incorporate competition into the theory. There is no question but that the consumer does largely determine the structure (nature) of competition by the way in which she groups or categorizes brands. She forms brand concepts as shown in Figure 16-5 for the Escort and puts similar brands together to form a product category in her mind, and, consequently, the brands within that category compete directly with each other and indirectly with brands in other categories.

But we must be careful and not conclude that she does this categorizing of brands in a very systematic and complete sense. How does she do it? Research has shown that on the continuum made up of the relevant dimensions of the recognition and evaluative characteristics of a product category, there is a typical or middle position called the *prototype*.[34] This notion of the prototype you will recall was introduced in Chapter 4 in describing the horizontal aspects of the product hierarchy.

The prototypical brand is the brand that the consumer uses to refer to in thinking about all other brands in this category. The more prototypical a brand is, the easier the consumer can process information about where the

---

[34] E. Rosch, "Principles of Categorization," in E. Rosch and B. B. Lloyd, eds., *Cognition and Categorization* (Hillsdale, N.J.: Lawrence Erlbaum Associates, 1978), pp. 36–41.

brand is located on the continuum as we saw in discussing the memory structure diagram.[35] Also, there is overwhelming agreement among consumers on how good an example of the category a brand is even when they *dis*agree about where the boundaries are.[36] However, psychological research has also shown that the boundaries of a category are not well defined in peoples' minds.[37]

With this background we can now better understand the nature and relevance of Carpenter and Nakamoto's contention that how consumers form product categories leads to an important marketing phenomenon that we all have observed.[38] They contend that because of the nature of the consumer choice process, the pioneer brand in a category has a great advantage. They point out, for example, that Coca Cola has dominated the soft drink market for more than a century; also, Budweiser in the case of beer and Gerber for baby food for more than 50 years.

Carpenter and Nakamoto's thesis is that this continuing market advantage occurs because the brand that is the innovator becomes the prototypical brand in the category. Later-entering brands are located by the consumer in relation to that prototype. Carpenter and Nakamoto's analysis assumes for their case first that quality is dependent on personal taste or that the relationship between product attributes and performance are not readily observable by the consumer.[39] The difficulty consumers in EPS have in making decisions, described in Chapter 4, and how they form prototypes as discussed earlier, both support this possibility. Second, it assumes that significant market penetration is achieved by the pioneer, before other brands in this category enter the market.

To verify the validity of their contention, Carpenter and Nakamoto designed an experiment with consumers. They found that when quality was subjective, the pioneering brand had a significantly greater advantage. Carpenter and Nakamoto also suggest, however, that a later entrant to the market can also develop an advantage by creating a *sub-category*. The process would occur in the same way but the attributes of the brands would be somewhat different. This possibility has not been tested but follows logically from their research. It is well to bear in mind, however, the necessary two characteristics required: consumer benefits must not be well defined, and one brand must have been in the market far enough ahead that it has the opportunity to establish a strong following before competitors enter.

In summary, knowing how consumers form their prototypes and how these prototypes operate extends the theory by giving us a foundation for understanding the principle of the pioneer brand for purposes of both management and public policy needs. Also, the principle is consistent with the theory of prototypicality.

[35] Ibid, p. 39.

[36] Ibid, p. 36.

[37] Mervis and Rosch, "Categorization of Natural Objects."

[38] G. S. Carpenter and K. Nakamoto, "Market Pioneers, Consumer Learning and Product Perceptions: A Theory of Persistent Competitive Advantage," unpublished working paper (Columbia University, New York, November 1986).

[39] Ibid., p. 5.

7. SUMMARY

The main purpose in this chapter was to show how the basic assumption of the CDM that all causation goes one way could be dropped and the CDM made more widely applicable as a consequence. Two types of feedback were shown: from satisfaction (S) and to information (F).

This feedback concept was then extended to complete the integration of the two streams of consumer behavior knowledge: the concept formation approach and the information-processing approach. The results were shown in Figure 16-5, which indicated considerable extension of the theory to provide a fuller understanding of consumer behavior.

Finally, three new areas of research—liking the ad, emotional dimensions of buying, and the pioneer brand—were used both as a test of the theory and to extend it.

A great amount of research remains to be done in mapping out the nature of the relations in the theory of Figure 16-5. Are they strong or weak and under what conditions: EPS, LPS, and RPS? These are needed to tell us the greatest payoff on the relations that require us to know whether they are linear and/or interactive, as will be described in Chapter 17. More accurate market simulations will be the result.

An enormous amount of very basic research will be required, for example, how to measure memory. We know very little about the role of emotions in the purchasing-consuming process. Nor are the role of signs in communicating understood. These are some of the very basic problems to be solved by future basic research.

Questions

1. What is the practical relevance of the four advantages of doing an analysis of feedback from the customer's usage of the product?
2. What is the advantage for the marketing manager to have the much more complex theory of Figure 16-5 compared with the simple CDM of Chapter 3?
3. When is liking the ad likely to be a significant determinant of buying behavior?
4. How might you use the standardized emotional profile (SEP)?
5. What is the relevance of the prototype concept to the Carpenter and Nakamoto notion of a "pioneer brand"?

CHAPTER 17

Nonlinear Relations and Interactions Add Insight

1. INTRODUCTION

In Chapter 16 there was considerable evidence of increasingly complex relations. In this chapter the tools for dealing with most of these complex relations will be presented.

Dr. Herbert Krugman, manager of public opinion research at the General Electric Company for several years, asserted more than a decade ago that, for a consumer, two to three exposures to an ad is optimal.[1] He said that the first exposure had much effect; the second, less effect; the third, still less; and the fourth, no effect. When this is shown graphically, Figure 17-1 is derived.

Figure 17-1 describes what Krugman was saying. It is a nonlinear relation as contrasted with the linear relations used in describing the Consumer Decision Model (CDM) in Chapter 3. The purpose of this chapter is to explain what nonlinear relations are, how they operate, and how they can be used in setting marketing strategy and plans. If the line in Figure 17-1 were straight, each exposure would be having an equal effect. Most relations of the CDM are usually like that. However, some may not. If they are not linear, you can be making a serious mistake by assuming that they are linear.

You can see the consequences of this mistake in Figure 17-2. The importance of nonlinear relations is not at first obvious. In Portland, Oregon, General

---

[1] H. E. Krugman, "Why Three Exposures May Be Enough," *Journal of Advertising Research*, 12, no. 6 (December 1972), 11–14.

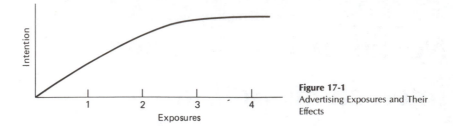

Figure 17-1
Advertising Exposures and Their Effects

Foods had an instant breakfast drink in test market against Carnation, which had been in the market there for about two years. The actual I → P relation as shown by the solid curve looked like that in Figure 17-2.

Let us draw in the dashed line to represent what it would have looked like had a linear (straight-line) relation been used. If intention is low (less than "2" on a 1-to-5 scale), as one would expect in extensive problem solving (EPS) and perhaps even in limited problem solving (LPS), and using the actual relation, a major increase in intention will have little effect upon purchase as you can see. If you were being simplistic and using the straight line, you would greatly *overstate* the benefit of spending money in advertising to increase intention (I). On the other hand, if the mean intention (I) was "3," and you used the straight line, you would *greatly understate* the true benefit of increasing advertising. Here the true curve—the solid curve—shows that increasing intention one point would have a major increasing effect on purchase.

So, if you're wondering whether an increase in advertising will be profitable, the answer when the line is nonlinear will all depend on the current average level of consumers' intention to buy the brand, a crucial fact that would be completely hidden if you had used a straight line. For consumer durables, however, instead of packaged goods like instant breakfast, Manu Kalwani and Al Silk have shown that the relationship between intention (I) and purchase (P) does tend to be linear.[2]

Nonlinear relations are often encountered. In earlier chapters, especially 5 and 6, you have seen a number of examples from instant breakfast. Rajeev Batra and Mike Ray found them repeatedly in their study of how advertising works.[3] Earlier we discussed how Morris Holbrook had designed a way to combine both compositional (conjoint analysis) and decompositional (linear compensatory like the CDM) approaches. In applying this creative idea to emotional product benefits he found substantial nonlinearities.[4] Gary Lillien and Phil Kotler con-

[2] M. U. Kalwani and A. J. Silk, "On the Reliability and Predictive Validity of Purchase Intention Measures," *Marketing Science*, 1, no. 3 (Summer 1982), 243–86.

[3] R. Batra and M. L. Ray, "How Advertising Works at Contact," in L. F. Alwitt and A. A. Mitchell, eds., *Psychological Processes and Advertising Effects* (Hillsdale, N.J.: Lawrence Erlbaum Associates, 1985), pp. 13–43.

[4] M. B. Holbrook, "Integrating Compositional and Decompositional Analyses to Represent the Intervening Role of Perceptions in Evolving Judgments," *Journal of Marketing Research*, XVIII (February 1981), 16.

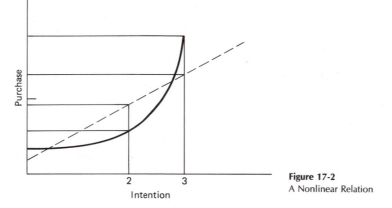

Figure 17-2
A Nonlinear Relation

clude that causal models like the CDM can be more easily developed with nonlinear relations than if the effort is confined to linear relations.[5]

You have seen the usefulness of nonlinear analysis in previous chapters, especially Chapters 5 and 6. It becomes particularly useful in interpreting the more complex models that were just discussed in Chapter 16 involving feedbacks. Further, it is interesting from the author's experience how quickly practicing managers come to understand them and make use of nonlinear relations when they are shown graphically, not in mathematical form. How easily they used them came as a pleasant surprise.

It's generally believed that the wide use of LISREL, a statistical method, in model building has discouraged taking advantage of the contributions of nonlinear analysis.[6] The lack of research interest in it requires us to rely here mainly on one study for evidence. However, Michel Laroche, who has probably done the leading nonlinear research, has recently prepared a computer program to do nonlinear analysis that renders the task much easier.[7]

2. INSTANT BREAKFAST STUDY AS ILLUSTRATIVE EXAMPLE

To see which relationships are nonlinear—and how they work in a consumer's response to a food item—let us review the evidence from General Foods' introduction of Post Instant Breakfast, a part of which we have just discussed.[8] By working through this evidence step by step, you will have a better understanding of how nonlinear relations can make the CDM more useful to you in designing marketing strategy and plans. The purpose here is not to show you how to

---

[5] G. L. Lillien and P. Kotler, *Marketing Decision Making: A Model-Building Approach* (Cambridge, Mass.: Harper & Row, 1983), p. 128.

[6] Rajeev Batra has stated this view in conversation; see ibid., pp. 127–28.

[7] M. Laroche, "A Method for Detecting Non-Linear Effects in Cross-Sectional Survey Data," *The International Journal of Research in Marketing*, 2 (1985), 61–72.

[8] M. Laroche and J. A. Howard, "Non-Linear Relations in Complex Model of Buyer Behavior," *Journal of Consumer Research*, 6, no. 4 (March 1980), 377–88.

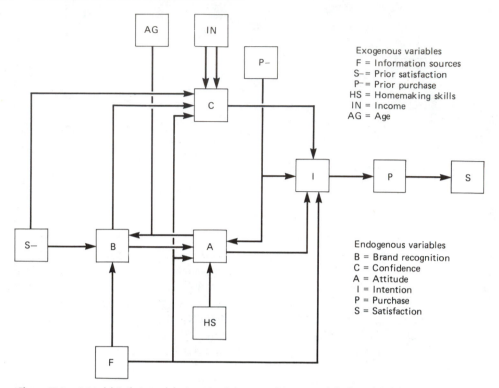

Figure 17-3 A Model Built Around the Learning Subsystem of the Howard-Sheth Model of Buyer Behavior

Source: M. Laroche and J. A. Howard, "Nonlinear Relations in a Complex Model of Buyer Behavior," *Journal of Consumer Research*, 6, no. 4 (March 1980), 378.

carry out a nonlinear analysis with the CDM but to show you its meaning and implications.

The General Foods data are from two different brands of a sample of about 800 families in a test market in Portland, Oregon. Post (PIB) was a new brand, whereas Carnation (CIB) had been in the market for more than two years. Both the linear and nonlinear relations for the data for both brands are given for the same multiple-equation model shown in Figure 17-2. It is a modified version of the CDM as you will see if you examine Figure 17-2 carefully. Both the exogenous, or external, and endogenous variables are shown.

The CDM may not look familiar in this form because at the time of the study the CDM was not as well developed. As you will note, for example, the crucial role of satisfaction (S) in affecting attitude (A) is missing. However, the influence of satisfaction (S) upon attitude (A) is indirectly reflected in prior purchase (P-). But except for this omission, the usual CDM relations are shown. The inclusion of the individual difference or segmenting variables is revealing. Age plays a very small role whereas income is stronger and homemaking skills are substantially stronger and positive. A description of the question by which each variable was elicited in a telephone interview is contained in Appendix 17-1, which can make the variables more meaningful to you.

All the specific equations of the analysis are available from the original source, but the significance of the relationships is much more easily seen and understood in the graphic form of Figure 17-3, and the discussion will be in terms of this graphic form.

3. OVERVIEW OF RESULTS OF NONLINEAR ANALYSIS

From Table 17-1 you can obtain a judgment as to which equations are truly nonlinear because the R^2s for the two relations, linear and nonlinear, are put into ratio form to facilitate comparison. CIB is Carnation Instant Breakfast and PIB is General Foods' Post Instant Breakfast. To ensure that the results were not accidental, two subgroups of 266 people each were selected randomly from the total sample, and these are called group 1 and group 2. Ratios of approximately 1.00 indicate linear relations, while those ratios substantially greater than 1.00 indicate nonlinear relations. We conclude from Table 17-1 that intention (I) to purchase (P), equation (5), as shown in Figure 17-2, is clearly nonlinear. Purchase (P) to satisfaction (S), equation (6), probably is, but not so strongly. The other four equations, however, are linear. But even this conclusion holds true only for all respondents together. Shortly, we will often find that in each case for a part of the respondents, however, the relation is nonlinear.

Table 17-1   Ratios of Nonlinear to Linear R^2s

Equation Number	Group Number	CIB			PIB		
		Wave 1	Wave 2	Wave 3	Wave 1	Wave 2	Wave 3
(1) (F → B)	1	N/A*	1.43	1.21	N/A	1.33	1.26
	2	N/A	1.35	1.26	N/A	1.26	1.12
(2) (B → A)	1	1.01	1.12	1.13	1.15	.996[†]	.971[†]
	2	1.01	1.03	1.01	.915[†]	1.14	1.09
(3) (F → C)	1	N/A	1.02	.995[†]	N/A	1.01	.985[†]
	2	N/A	.999[†]	1.02	N/A	1.02	1.09
(4) (A → I)	1	.995[†]	1.02	1.05	1.09	1.10	1.04
	2	1.02	.990[†]	1.01	1.03	1.17	1.12
(5) (I → P)	1	N/A	1.57	1.18	N/A	1.70	2.89
	2	N/A	1.57	2.21	N/A	1.50	2.98
(6) (P → S)	1	1.65	1.07	N/A	1.54	1.01	N/A
	2	1.62	2.73	N/A	1.29	1.47	N/A

* Not available.

[†] Showed a decrease in R^2.

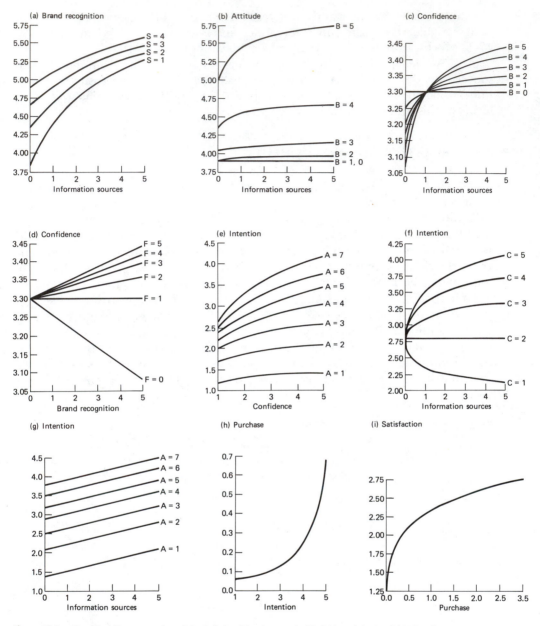

Figure 17-4   Graphical Representation of the Relationships Among the Variables of the Model Using the Results for CIB

SOURCE: M. Laroche and J. A. Howard, "Nonlinear Relations in a Complex Model of Buyer Behavior," *Journal of Consumer Research*, 6, no. 4 (March 1980), 384.

4. INTERACTIVE RELATIONS

The consequences for marketing strategy, as you will see, can be just as profound when two variables interact as were the simple nonlinear relations that we have already discussed. The heart of interactivity is the extent to which the independent variables in each equation such as confidence and attitude both affecting intention are independent of each other or whether they *interact* with each other to have a joint effect on the dependent variable of intention. Some evidence indicates that this interaction is found in the two important variables of price and advertising. If price is high, increasing advertising will have a different effect than when price is low.

The simple CDM as presented in Chapter 3 assumes, of course, that confidence and attitude are independent of each other. What the truth was for buyers of CIB in Portland, Oregon, can be seen in Figure 17-4. In all but two diagrams—(i) and (h)—in Figure 17-4, there are two independent variables and one dependent variable. These diagrams with two independent variables reveal the extent of interaction if any. These diagrams will be presented individually and in enlarged form in the following pages to make it easier for you to analyze them. Carnation is used in Figure 17-4 instead of Post because, being longer in the market, CIB relations are stronger.

As you may recall from Chapter 6, for each relationship the sample was broken into groups. For example, the upper left-hand corner of Figure 17-4, pictured separately in Figure 17-5, shows the effect of information sources (F) upon brand recognition (B). Here, the sample is broken into four levels (groups) of satisfaction (S). There we see that the four levels of satisfaction (S) are not parallel: S = 1 is much steeper than is S = 4. This *lack of parallelism* means that information sources (F) and satisfaction (S) are interacting together jointly to cause brand recognition (B). What may be happening is that people with higher satisfaction (S) are more likely to have been using the brand and already have formed their brand recognition (B), so that information sources (F) are less likely to have an effect upon B.

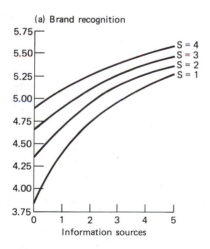

Figure 17-5
Information and Satisfaction Cause
Brand Recognition

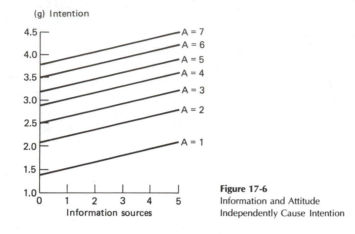

Figure 17-6
Information and Attitude
Independently Cause Intention

Contrast Figure 17-5, however, with Figure 17-6. In Figure 17-6 both information (F) and attitude (A) are affecting intention (I), but their effects are completely independent of each other as shown by the parallel lines, which indicates that there is no interaction.

5. USE OF NONLINEAR RELATIONS

The relevance of nonlinear relationships was shown earlier in this chapter, as well as in Chapter 6. Let's now use the instant breakfast data to show their application in five ways in order to make clear their relevance.

First, we discussed the intention (I) to purchase (P) relation at the beginning of this chapter. In Figure 17-7, you see that it is actually nonlinear. Also, that it is strongly nonlinear is clearly seen in Table 17-1, where the R^2s for the linear and nonlinear equations are put into ratio form. R^2, you will recall, is a measure of how much of the variance in the dependent variable is explained by the independent variable. The R^2 of equation (5), I → P, for PIB in wave 3

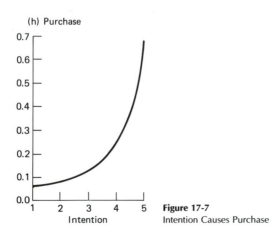

Figure 17-7
Intention Causes Purchase

is almost three times as large as the R^2s for the linear equation (2.89 for group 1 consumers and 2.98 for group 2 consumers). Knowing that this nonlinearity exists is obviously important. Imagine that you are consulting with General Foods on this new product. In your analysis you do a CDM simulation on the assumption that the intention (I) to purchase (P) relation is linear when, in fact, it is as shown in Figure 17-7. For the low values of I as mentioned earlier, your estimate of the increased profit contribution that could result from increasing advertising would be greatly *overstated* as emphasized earlier. On the other hand, for the *high values* of I, your simulation would *greatly understate* the actual gain in profit contribution from increasing advertising.

Second, by using nonlinear analysis we can show that, though some relations are linear for the sample as a whole, in contrast to intention (I) to purchase (P), they do exhibit some specific interdependent relations that are nonlinear. These can be very useful by providing a deeper understanding of the buying process. Let us examine a relation of this type involving brand recognition.

If you look at Figure 17-8, you will see that when brand recognition (B) has a low value, 0 or 1, an increase in information will have little or no effect upon attitude. Once brand recognition (B) has become large (B = 5), however, indicating the buyer is fully informed about the visual characteristics of CIB, then increases in information (F), particularly in the early stages of the formation of the brand image, will cause a large increase in attitude. This conclusion is particularly striking here, because you will note in Table 17-1, that the information (F) to attitude (A) relation, which is a critical relation in the CDM, was so weak that it was omitted. However, for customers with high brand recognition (B) values, the relation for low values of information (F) is strong and only weakens at high values of information (F). Here it can readily be seen how much more understanding that combining nonlinear and interactive analysis together can give you. Further, you see in Figure 17-9 that the information (F) and brand recognition (B) also interact in affecting confidence (C) just

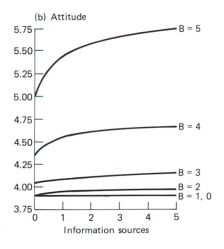

Figure 17-8
Information Sources and Brand
Recognition Cause Attitude

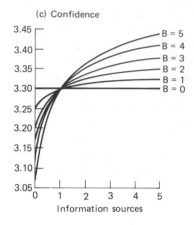

Figure 17-9
Information and Brand Recognition
Cause Confidence

as we said in Chapter 3. The interactive relations, however, are not as strong as those in Figure 17-8.

In earlier chapters we have repeatedly emphasized the significance of brand recognition and made it a part of the CDM. This topic has been stressed because marketing practice and marketing researchers have ignored it as an essential element in a buyer's choice of brands. Even psychologists interested in the attitude concept have paid but scant attention to it. We see here that this neglect has been serious.

Third, the nonlinear analysis in Figures 17-8 and 17-9 together show the *order* in which the marketer should emphasize brand recognition (B), attitude (A), and confidence (C) in applying advertising and other promotion. Specifically, this finding of increasing effect of information (F) on attitude (A) with increasing B in Figure 17-8 suggests that early in the introduction of a brand, the marketing effort should be devoted to creating a physical image of the brand in the buyer's mind. Don Armstrong, vice president of J. Walter Thompson, believed this and as a consequence tried for a number of years to get Ford Motor merely to advertise pictures of the new model cars for the first three months of introduction and then later advertise its good qualities. In Chapter 3, it was stated that buyers form an attitude more easily when they have a physical image of the brand. Later, once brand recognition (B) has been developed, effort should go toward increasing attitude (A), the buyer's evaluation of the benefits of the brand.

That the foregoing argument is valid can be seen in Figure 17-5, where information has a large effect on brand recognition when satisfaction is low, but a small effect when satisfaction is high. Thus, consistent with the first argument, emphasizing brand recognition (B) is justified only when the consumer is first introduced to a brand, before he has had the opportunity to use it and find himself satisfied.

Turning back to Figure 17-9, you see that marketing attempts to boost confidence are probably not justified until brand recognition has increased. However, the differences are not as great as with attitude. Figure 17-10 shows that when attitude (A) is large, confidence (C) has a powerful and consistent large effect on intention (I). Consequently, we can conclude from the evidence

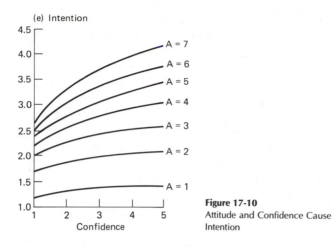

(e) Intention

Figure 17-10
Attitude and Confidence Cause
Intention

here that in introducing a new brand, promotion should go first to increasing brand recognition, then attitude, and finally confidence. Thus, you see three pieces of information supporting the idea that brand recognition builds first, then attitude, and finally, confidence.

Fourth, in Figure 17-11 as we saw in Chapter 6, information (F) has a much greater effect on intention (I) as confidence (C) increases. However, increasing attitude (A) has no effect on information's (F) influence on intention (I) as seen in Figure 17-6. This you will recall is where the thinking process is bypassed by consumers in routine problem solving (RPS) as developed at length in section 4 of Chapter 6. Further, a fairly large number of buyers in this market are probably in RPS because Carnation had entered the market more than two years before Post was introduced and instant breakfast was a relatively unimportant, simple, inexpensive product class that customers would quickly learn how to buy. This suggests that promotion (F) to increase intention (I) should be used in RPS.

Unfortunately, we don't know from this analysis exactly what kind of

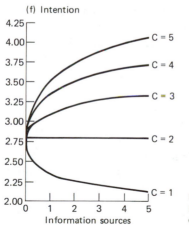

(f) Intention

Information sources

Figure 17-11
Information Sources and Confidence
Cause Intention

information will serve this function because, as you see in Appendix 17-1, information (F) as determined here is a combination of several sources of information, not just advertising. Increasing attitude (A) will not likely have much effect because attitude is already strong. However, as we learned in the theory of routine problem solving (Chapter 6), about three-fourths of the customers tend to shop around periodically, and these could be affected by atttitude information. Also, increasing attitude (A) will, as we see in Figure 17-10, cause confidence (C) to have a still greater effect upon intention (I).

Finally, information (F) is such a key variable since it is a major source of our marketing impact that, one should ask how nonlinear its effects are. Table 17-1 suggests that information (F) to brand recognition (B) is somewhat nonlinear although nothing like intention (I) to purchase (P). Information (F) to attitude (A) is not shown in Table 17-1, because for all respondents together, F has little effect upon A. However, this is very important and is seen only when the interactive relations of information (F) and attitude (A) of Figure 17-8 are examined. When the consumer is high on another independent variable, namely, brand recognition (B) as in Figure 17-8, information (F) has a strong nonlinear effect on attitude (A). In this situation, our linear estimates of sales and advertising effects could be quite wrong. For those consumers with high brand recognition (B), and when information (F) is on the low side, the effects of information (F) will be greatly understated if a linear relation is assumed. When information (F) is on the high side and brand recognition (B) is high, the effects of increasing information (F) will be overstated. Thus, for certain consumers, those with high brand recognition (B), information (F) can be having a strong effect but only if information (F) is low.

In summary, it is clear that knowledge of nonlinear relations can be useful in at least five different ways, and probably others. These are predicting sales (purchases) from intention (I), showing how some consumers respond much differently from others, explaining the order in which each element of the ABCs of marketing should be applied, supporting the point that bypassing can be occurring in an RPS market, and further developing the role of the vital information (F) variable. Our scope of evidence has been narrow being confined to a single product category, but the conclusions applied to two different brands at different stages of development in the same category. However, you would want to check these out on your own product class before applying them with great confidence. Nevertheless, these results are suggestive of the nature of the importance of nonlinear and interactive analysis.

6. VEGETABLE BACON

With another product, a vegetable bacon innovation that General Foods later introduced into test market, these same nonlinear relationships were confirmed except that information (F) to confidence (C) was not significant and information (F) to brand recognition (B) was linear.[9] The latter is not surprising, since with

[9] Francine Mandel, "Final Project," unpublished paper (Columbia University, New York, Spring 1980).

instant breakfast data, the relationship was the least nonlinear, as seen in Table 17-1.

7. LINEARITY OF BENEFITS

One of the important questions is whether any of the *individual* benefits making up attitude (A) are nonlinearly related to intention (I). If one is, then incurring the cost of increasing that benefit beyond a certain point would be unwise if, for example, the relationship is upwardly convex. Both sets of data that have been examined here—instant breakfast and vegetable bacon—indicate a linear relation between the total attitude and intention. But if some of the specific benefits making up attitude were nonlinear, they could be canceling out and so yielding a total linear relationship. For example, in an examination of a modified version of the vegetable bacon product, researchers found evidence of nonlinearity in individual benefits.[10] Specifically, in one benefit of the product—palatability—there was a strongly positive relationship between it and intention (I) up to a point, and beyond that, the effect surprisingly became negative. The relationship between another benefit—convenience—and intention (I) was linear throughout. A third benefit—no fat—was nonlinear, but in a peculiar form: it was positive, then leveled off, then again became positive.

More evidence is needed to permit greater generalization of nonlinear results. All that is needed is a great number of nonlinear analyses to be applied so that generalizations about when nonlinearities and interactions are likely to exist can be developed. Now that ordinary least squares regression is more accepted relative to LISREL, these nonlinear analyses should be forthcoming.

8. CONCLUSIONS

Nonlinear models are very powerful, both in their own right and also for their subsidiary capacity to reveal interactions—indirect effects—among variables. They can contribute to the precision of estimates made using the CDM to predict marketing effects. But they should be applied only after you have acquired a working familiarity with the simpler linear system of the CDM.

Except for important decisions, the linear CDM should be used because it is simpler to work with. However, as mentioned earlier, the significance of nonlinear relations seems to be readily understood by practicing managers when shown diagrammatically as in Figure 17-2, which encourages their use. Further, if the results are to be used in a major strategy issue and you have had no previous experience with the product category, the relations should be tested for both nonlinearities and interactions. If they exist, they can have a major impact on choosing a strategy, as seen repeatedly in this chapter.

---

[10] Rene E. Mora, "Estimation of a Nonlinear Multi-Attribute Attitude Model," unpublished paper (Columbia University, New York, Spring 1977), Table I, p. 10.

Questions

1. How would you describe the differences between a linear and a nonlinear relation?
2. Illustrate the consequences of assuming when applying the CDM that the I → P relation is linear when, in fact, it is quite nonlinear.
3. How is the interactive analysis useful in formulating marketing strategy and plans?
4. What does nonlinear analysis suggest about the order in which the "ABCs of marketing" (attitude, brand recognition, and confidence) should be developed?
5. In what way is nonlinear analysis particularly useful in understanding the effects of information (F)?

Appendix 17-1

Symbol	Variable Name	Operational Definitions
F	Information sources	Have you talked with anyone about the products? Have you received a sample? On how many media have you seen the product advertised?
B	Brand recognition	Do you think Instant Breakfast comes in powder, in a box, in many flavors, a drink, packaged in individual portions? (This is approximated by product class recognition.)
C	Confidence	How confident are you in your ability to judge the product? (5) Extremely confident (4) Very confident (3) Somewhat confident (2) Only slightly confident (1) Not confident at all
A	Attitude	How do you like this product? I like it / I do not like / 7 6 5 4 3 2 1 / very much / it at all
I	Intention	How likely are you to buy the product in the next month? (5) Definitely will (4) Probably will (3) Not sure one way or the other (2) Probably will not (1) Definitely will not
P	Purchase	Number of units purchased at each period and for each product
S	Satisfaction	Satisfied when used: (1) Not satisfied (2) Slightly satisfied (3) Quite satisfied (4) Extremely satisfied
AG	Age	Age of housewife in years.
IN	Income	Total income of household. (1) Under $2,500 (2) $2,500–3,999 (3) $4,000–5,999, (4) $6,000–7,999 (5) $8,000–9,999 (6) $10,000 and over
HS	Homemaking skills	How good would you say you are at other tasks of home making? (1) Poor (2) Fair (3) Good (4) Very good (5) Extremely good (6) Excellent

SOURCE: M. Laroche and J. A. Howard, "Nonlinear Relations in a Complex Model of Buyer Behavior," *Journal of Consumer Research*, 6, no. 4 (March 1980), 386–87

CHAPTER 18

Public Policy and the Consumer

1. INTRODUCTION

The Consumer Decision Model (CDM) and its supporting theory enables you to take a broader and deeper look at marketing. The broader look is the public policy view of protecting the consumer that all marketers need to know. The deeper look is the social acceptability of marketing.

In a sense these two extensions of the CDM go beyond what we ordinarily think of as a course in consumer behavior. However, the theory summarized in the CDM is badly needed to aid in understanding these two important issues. Since the CDM can throw new light on both issues, we would be remiss if we ignored these two contributions of our tools.

The role of the CDM in the public policy of consumer protection will be examined first, because it lays a foundation for the second issue, the social acceptability of marketing.

2. PUBLIC POLICY FOR THE CONSUMER

2.1 Introduction

Substantial background on consumer policy is essential to appreciating fully the role of the CDM in public policy. Three general areas are involved: why consumer policy is important to marketers, what the institutions are that our society has provided to protect the consumer, and how consumer policy has developed and is continuing to evolve.

2.2   Consumer's Interest Essential to Management

Understanding the consumer's point of view aids marketing managers in several respects. First, a marketing manager armed with theoretical concepts that make up the CDM and its supporting theory can be immensely valuable to his company if it faces an antitrust or consumer protection charge from some source. Traditionally, marketing personnel have played a limited role in these cases. The author observing this once asked an attorney for the case he was involved in why this was so. The attorney quickly replied, "They are of little help to us." This attorney meant that the traditional intuitive and qualitative approach that companies have taken toward marketing has not taught the ability to articulate the understanding needed to deal with regulatory issues, an understanding that the CDM and related concepts and techniques can provide.

Second, the marketing manager concerned with an understanding of the consumer's interest can sometimes persuade the more senior executives in his company that by providing consumers with products they need, the company's own interest can be better served.

Third, the marketing manager is more likely to be aware of his company's needs and be asked to be involved in public policy issues if he participates in trade association activities. In the late 1960s, for instance, when the consumerism movement was at its zenith and the House Commerce Committee was holding public hearings on how Congress should protect consumers, George Koch, president of the Grocery Manufacturers of America, played the leading role by working with Congress and urging his members to change their practices. Any marketing manager who could articulate the true nature of the consumer market had a golden opportunity to serve his company, his industry, and himself, simply by making an effective presentation before the House Commerce Committee. Of course, to be effective, he had to have a logical argument well worked out.

2.3   Institutions for Consumer Protection

A number of institutions in our society are designed to protect the consumers' interests. The traditional one is, of course, the market as discussed in Chapter 2. "It is the function of a market to bring together buyers and sellers who wish to exchange goods and money."[1] In most markets, consumers, because they are so numerous, often lack access to information and, not being organized, are in a sense the weaker party. Thus, there is concern for "protecting the consumer from the seller" in the market and the Federal Trade Commission is an outgrowth of this concern. Also, other institutions—particularly those that regulate markets—have evolved. Among them are nutritional labeling, unit pric-

---

[1] G. J. Stigler, *The Theory of Price* (New York: Macmillan, 1952), p. 56.

ing, substantiation of advertising, corrective advertising, and comparative advertising.

The first of these, nutritional labeling, is a federal mandate that the seller tell the consumer the nutritional qualities of a product, in a certain standard format on the package, with which you are already familiar, as seen on food items.

Unit pricing, required in some states, makes the seller specify the price of a brand *per unit* of weight or volume; this is intended to help the consumer make meaningful price comparisons among brands.

Substantiation of advertising, mandated by the Federal Trade Commission, says the seller must be able to support his advertising claims by providing objective evaluations. Recently the FTC "ordered Bristol-Myers Co. and Sterling Drug, Inc., to drop ads saying tests show their Excedrin, Bufferin, and Bayer aspirin brands are more effective than others unless they have two clinical studies to back up the claims."[2]

Corrective advertising, another device for encouraging truthful advertising, requires the seller to admit in future advertising that his past advertising was untrue. (Firestone Tire and Rubber Company, for example, was charged with failing to tell consumers that its tires are not safe under all conditions. As a consequence, it agreed to spend $750,000 to inform consumers that "no tires are safe under all conditions of use" and "proper tire safety depends upon the consumer taking specific steps.")[3]

Finally, there is comparative advertising. A seller, in his advertising, compares his product explicitly with a competitor's product by name. Quite common today is to see an ad that says, "Our brand X is better than our competitor's brand Y." Bob Pitofsky, as director of the Bureau of Consumer Protection, a unit of the Federal Trade Commission, in 1972 declared that comparative advertising, if it is truthful, is not only legal but also in the consumer's interest. Prior to this statement by Pitofsky it was generally held that comparative advertising was unfair competition and therefore illegal. Since then comparative advertising has burgeoned as you will see if you watch national advertising. Later, more will be said about comparative advertising.

In addition to these specific areas of protection there is a substantial body of consumer policy. The FTC is the chief source of the federal consumer policy, and we will confine our discussion largely to that agency. (Of course, the FTC is not the sole source of federal consumer policy: the Attorney General's Office also oversees antitrust, and the Food and Drug Administration (FDA) deals with many issues of consumer protection.) Let us review that policy in some detail.

FTC policy is a mixture of more traditional antitrust doctrine and more recent doctrines about consumer protection. The FTC has a division responsible for each, Antitrust and Consumer Protection. Antitrust approaches consumer

---

[2] *The Wall Street Journal* (New York edition), July 21, 1983, p. 29.

[3] Editorial, "Ad Boycott Is Bad Medicine," *Advertising Age*, February 23, 1976, p. 16.

protection by ensuring that markets are competitive and so deals with the adequacy of consumers' *options* in the market; Consumer Protection, however, by and large has to do with the adequacy of *information* available to the consumer for choosing among those options in the market. These two aspects are brought together by the three different views of the consumers' decision—marketing, economics, and psychology (Chapter 2)—and these can be especially useful in explaining consumer policy. For example, knowing the economists' viewpoint is essential. It provides a highly useful philosophic framework and economists' thought processes are similar to those of the lawyers who carry out the regulations. This is no accident. Economic theory has provided the guiding rationale at FTC and Justice since the 1950s; unfortunately it contributes little to understanding the consumers' information requirements. This latter is the role of marketing and psychology.

2.4 Stages of Consumer Policy

2.4.1 Introduction. Total consumer policy—this blend of antitrust measures and consumer protection—has gone through two stages—pure competition versus monopoly and market structure—and it is now into the third. The public policy of consumer protection is also now undergoing major change. If marketers are to play a responsible role in shaping that policy, they should be familiar with these three stages.

2.4.2 Pure Competition versus Monopoly. Before 1930, companies were evaluated by the FTC in terms of their effect on the consumer by two broad concepts: pure competition and monopoly, which can be described in terms of Figure 18-1, where in FTC cases the buying "industry" is consumers and the selling "industry" is usually manufacturers. In "pure competition," industry rivals in the market are sufficiently numerous, and brands sufficiently alike so that no one firm has significant control over the price of his product in that market. This condition is described in Figure 18-1 by two dimensions, "Fewness of competitors" (many) and "Degree of product differentiation" (not at all differentiated). Consequently, every company has to meet the market price. In a "monopoly," the exact opposite of pure competition, one company sells an entire product category in the market, and, of course, there is no product differentiation. Hence, the company is able to exert control over the price. In both cases before 1930, the structure of the market was defined simplistically, as the number of sellers. So, although three dimensions of interindustry competition are shown in Figure 18-1, only one of these three dimensions—number of competitors—was really taken seriously in consumer policy before 1930.

Let us now deal with intraindustry competition and assume that you are one of the sellers in Figure 18-1. Within your sellers' industry on the right, you face a competitive situation made up of a value on each of the three dimensions: fewness of companies, degree of domination as indicated by share distribution, and degree of product differentiation. However, public policy's role in

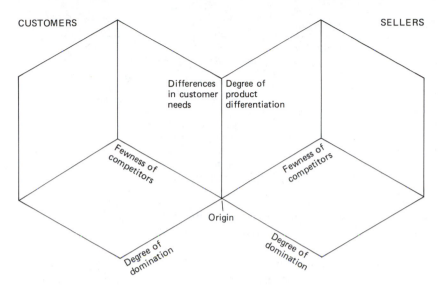

Figure 18-1   Interindustry Competition

serving the consumer before 1930, thus, was simply to maintain competition in an industry and do this in terms of a market structure with only one dimension: number of competitors. If there were many competitors, that was good. However, if there were only a few, as *usually* happens in a mature industry, that was bad.

The idea was that if an industry departed from the model of pure competition and moved toward the model of monopoly by acquiring a large share of the market, it should be forced back into line by the government. This could be done by breaking up the individual companies each into two or more independent companies. This became the accepted way for the government to achieve consumer protection.

There were two flaws in this early approach to protecting consumers by using "adequate options in the market" as the device. Lewis Engman, a former FTC chairman, stated, "Because economic theory binds the means (structure of the market) and end (industrial performance) so tightly together into a causal relationship, we tend to measure only the causal factors, to focus on the means (market structure) rather than the desired ends (industrial performance)."[4] They focused upon modifying the market structure and largely ignored whether the good results that were supposed to occur from that change in market structure actually did occur. The significance of this flaw, which will become clearer shortly, was that the public policy goal became one of maintaining competition per se *instead* of protecting the consumer as originally intended. The second flaw was that "number of sellers" alone as a measure of competition was too one dimensional; additional dimensions of the market such as shown in Figure 18-1 were

[4] Lewis Engman, before the Antitrust Section of the American Bar Association, Honolulu, August 14, 1974.

Table 18-1 Market Structures

Degree of Differentiation \ Number of Sellers		Many Sellers	Few Sellers	One Seller
Undifferentiated product		Pure competition	Pure oligopoly	Monopoly
Differentiated product		Monopolistic competition	Differentiated oligopoly	

needed to make market competition more realistic. These two flaws led the FTC to turn to the "market-structure approach."

2.4.3 Market-Structure Approach. In 1950, impelled by the need to correct these flaws, the market-structure approach, which had been earlier developed by economists, especially Edward S. Mason and his students at Harvard, became government policy. The FTC as well as the Attorney General's Office accepted it as the guiding doctrine.

A number of market structure concepts made up the new approach. A new market dimension was introduced: product differentiation as shown in Figure 18-1. One seller could differentiate his product from another firm's product in the eyes of the consumer. On the basis of the two dimensions—degree of product differentiation and number of competitors—five theoretical market structures resulted as you see in Table 18-1. These five structures encompassed all possible competitive situations—if one assumed competition on the buying side of the market. This, of course, is true of the consumer market if there are no large intermediaries such as retailing or wholesaling chains.

Also, the market-structure concept included the notion of "workable competition," an idea articulated by J. M. Clark, a leading economist in the 1940s:

> The main implication of a program of workable competition is to decide, on the basis of the specific information available for individual industries, what degree of competition is obtainable by methods of practical policy without substantial loss of *technological efficiency* at the time when the policy is adopted and does not presumably create a degree of *uncertainty* such as would offset the advantages.[5]

"Workable competition" proposed that the economic performance of the companies making up each industry subject to question be *investigated* to determine the quality of their performance in the market. This concept caused regulators' attention to be focused upon whether better performance would actually result

[5] W. Fellner, *Competition Among the Few* (New York: Alfred A. Knopf, 1949), pp. 289–90.

Table 18-2   Analytic Framework of Market-Structure Approach

Industry Structure	→	Competitive Behavior	→	Industry Performance
Number of companies		Dimensions of rivalry		Profit levels
Degree of domination		(e.g., price, advertising)		
Degrees of				Progressiveness in
differentiation				cost reduction
Barriers to entry				
Stage of PLC				

from a change in structure that the government enforced. This contrasted sharply with the older doctrine that pure competition is good and monopoly is necessarily bad and that, therefore, the large companies in the industry should be forced into the mold of pure competition without bothering to investigate whether their performance was, in fact, bad.

The "market-structure economists"—or "industrial-organization economists," as they were often called—explicitly distinguished between three related elements of the market—the *structure* of the market (Figure 18-1), competitive *behavior*, and market *performance*, as indicated in the top row of Table 18-2. Their basic assumption was that a given industry structure led to certain competitive behavior, which in turn yielded a particular level of economic performance by the companies making up that industry. Each element had a number of dimensions as shown in the columns of Table 18-2.

The definition of industry structure was soon made more elaborate when other dimensions such as "degree of domination" and "barriers to entry" were included as in Figure 18-2. Another new dimension had to do with the nature of industry demand—whether it was expanding, stable, or contracting; this was a precursor of our concept of a product life cycle on which Arthur Burns, another well-known economist, had written his dissertation in the 1930s. For example, in a declining industry, monopoly may be much more socially desirable than competition because a company by becoming larger can reduce its costs.

Expanding the dimensions of competition stimulated research projects, which investigated a number of industries to test the validity of the market-structure concept. Clearly, the broader market idea had substantial appeal to policymakers, such as the FTC commissioners, for it gave them a systematic rationale that was extremely useful in the political arena. Specifically, they could use it to answer legislators' complaints from their constituents. As implied in Table 18-2, it was now possible for the government to use either or both of two approaches. It could change the *structure* of the industry and so change marketing competitive behavior and thereby improve performance of the companies. Alternatively, it could act directly upon a company's competitive behavior by *prohibiting* it from that undesirable competitive behavior so as to improve its performance.

Now let us see the relevance of the market structure approach when applied in a landmark case. By 1970, the availability of product information to

Table 18-3 Cited Companies and Their Share of the Cereal Market

Company	Share as of 1970 (%)
Kellogg	45
General Mills	21
General Foods	16
Quaker Oats	9
	91

the consumer had become accepted by the Congress as the most important element of consumer protection. However, there was nothing in the market structure theory of Table 18-2, column 3, like "adequacy of consumer information" to accommodate this dimension. The cereal case described in Table 18-3 was the first attempt to integrate the consumer's need for product information as a performance dimension into the modern market-structure view. As the case evolved in the courts over a 10-year period, the original purpose for bringing the case, which was to incorporate consumer information as an element of industry structure unfortunately was lost in the legal proceedings. Yet, it was still implicit in the charge that advertising was a barrier to entry as discussed next.

The FTC, under Chairman Miles Kirkpatrick, first proposed that all four of the cereal companies (see Table 18-3) be "broken up" (dissolved). One of the charges leveled in support of dissolution was that their advertising was *excessive* and *untruthful*. In the past, dissolution was proposed only by the Antitrust Division, and charges of untruthfulness were handled by Consumer Protection. But the FTC held in this case that excessive advertising was a barrier to entry, keeping out other competitors.

As for the development of policy in the case, the FTC charged that *advertising* converts true product competition into *trivial product competition*, and by implication, therefore, this advertising is not only a waste of society's resources but also damaging in other ways. Evidence used to support this charge was that 120 "trivial" new products had been introduced between 1950 and 1970. It was not explained just why they were "trivial." The commission also questioned how retail shelf space was allocated to the industry, but the nature of the shelf-space arrangement, because it was not well specified in the FTC complaint, is omitted from the exposition here.

Finally, the FTC complained that competitors had been bought up by these companies over the 30-year period (1940 to 1970), during which the industry's behavior was being examined as the basis for the complaint. The FTC felt that this contributed to monopoly.

The FTC staff finally proposed, specifically, that three new companies be made from Kellogg, that General Mills and General Foods each spin off one new company, and that Quaker Oats be left as is. The FTC's logic was as follows: the structure of the industry is clearly concentrated, in that the four companies, especially Kellogg, controlled the market as indicated by the market shares in Table 18-3. This concentration was allegedly a result of advertising, which acts as a barrier preventing other companies from entering the market. The FTC thus alleged that the existing companies competed on dimensions other than price—specifically, advertising and dubious product improvement, for example. "Good" rivalry on price was replaced by "less desirable" rivalry on the less competitively risky elements of the marketing mix, advertising, and product improvement. The FTC presumed that the companies had colluded, at least tacitly (discussed shortly), to avoid price competition.

Curiously, the FTC didn't explicitly analyze why, in the presence of a furious pace of product innovation, no new firms and no private brands had penetrated the industry to any extent. Instead, it simply concluded that advertising had been the barrier to entry—advertising that it claimed was untruthful, directed at children (who were said to be less discriminating in evaluating brands than adults), and aimed at supporting trivial instead of desirable changes in the product. So the FTC concluded that the protection from competition afforded by this concentrated structure and by advertising as a barrier to entry led to excessive profits: a 10-year average of more than 20% return on equity. The FTC's proposed answer to this "bad" performance was, as indicated, to dissolve three of the four companies into smaller companies.

As the cereal case evolved, it came to be called the "shared monopoly" case. This sprang from the usual assumption that, whenever a few companies exist in a market, they tacitly coordinate their behavior—through price leadership, for instance—and act as a single monopolist, thus "sharing the monopoly power." The FTC was careful not to insist that heavy brand advertising was unlawful, but it did say that, as a group, the companies were exploiting every possible market segment. The commission even claimed that this last contention was supported by testimony from the Leo Burnett Company, Kellogg's advertising agency. According to the commissioners,

> Using consumer statements of brand similarities and competitive relationships, Burnett created a multidimensional map on which various brands were represented by flags arrayed in a relationship to one another in a manner described by consumers.

From this common marketing research practice and other evidence already discussed, the FTC concluded that the cereal companies were able to keep out competitors and still charge excessive prices, hence achieve excessive profits.

By implication, the FTC claimed that the consumer was prevented by advertising pressures, from adequately discriminating among brands, and so from taking advantage of a lower-priced or better quality brand that a potential competitor might provide. Thus, although the FTC presented no evidence that the customer was not able to acquire the information he wanted from the advertis-

Table 18-4   Market-Structure Analysis Applied to Cereals

Industry Structure		Competitive Behavior		Industry Performance
Distribution of firm by number and size				Excessive profits
Kellogg	45%	Heavy	Trivial product	Undesirable pro-
General Mills	21%	advertising →	development	gressiveness in
General Foods	16%			product (trivial im-
Quaker Oats	9%			provement)
				Untruthful advertising directed to chil- dren
Barrier to entry: advertising				

ing, it concluded that because of the advertising, entry from outside the industry was impossible.

Let us summarize the market structure approach with the cereal case as background. Historically, there have been two disparate elements in our national consumer policy: the first element, antitrust activity, is intended to provide the consumers with adequate options (products and services) in terms of price, quality, and number of products. The second element, consumer protection, is designed to provide the consumer with adequate information for evaluating these options. The enormous need for an adequate theory of consumer behavior is obvious here. One of the FTC commissioners, Mary Gardiner Jones, sensed this need when she told a consultant, "We here at the Commission need for regulating consumer protection what we already have for antitrust, the market structure rationale."[6] This need is very great because the FTC like all administrative agencies must be able to defend its actions to the public and especially to members of Congress. Constituents inquire of their congressional representative why the consumer policy is what it is, and the representative calls the FTC for an answer.

The FTC intended to merge the two elements of antitrust and consumer protection in the cereal companies case as shown in Table 18-4. In so doing, it treated advertising as a structural characteristic of the market, since it was purportedly a barrier to entry. For the first time, the FTC included product information—its truthfulness and the nature of its recipients (children)—as performance criteria in an antitrust case. But actually, as the case proceeded, this explicit role of consumer information as a performance dimension was lost. Indeed, it became clear that there were two flaws in the FTC's logic. First, it was falsely presumed that companies compete through advertising only on trivial dimensions of a

---

[6] J. A. Howard was the consultant. For a full report see J. A. Howard and J. Hulbert, *Advertising and the Public Interest: A Staff Report to the Federal Trade Commission* (Chicago: Crain Communications, 1973).

product, and, second, it wrongly judged that consumers were so affected by advertising that the advertising had the potential to become such a barrier to entry. That charge by the FTC was made at the time only because an adequate theory of consumer information processing—such as that found in Chapters 4, 5, and 6 and that support the CDM—was not then available. As stated earlier, at least one of the commissioners, and probably all of them, recognized this need.

2.4.4 New Directions of Consumer Policy.   Fortunately, as of the last two or three years, a modified version of the conventional market structure policy is emerging. The basic idea of market structure as being made up of three elements is still firmly held. What is changed are the commissioner's beliefs as to what kind of competitive structures and competitive behaviors will lead to what kind of industry performances.

The FTC dropping the cereal case is one example of the change. The Justice Department dropping the suit against IBM is another. Even more important was the FTC's response to the DuPont case. In it, the Commission asserted that

> The essence of the competitive process is to induce firms to become more efficient and to pass the benefits of the efficiency along to consumers. The process would be ill-served by using antitrust to block hard, aggressive competition that is solidly based on efficiencies and growth opportunities even if monopoly is a possible result.[7]

This statement is, as you can see, a far cry from the 1948 Supreme Court decision, which said that

> Monopoly power, whether lawfully or unlawfully acquired, may itself constitute an evil and stand condemned.[8]

The most important of the new directions, however, for our purposes, is the new position being taken by the FTC that will be discussed later in connection with the consumer. It is hoped that it will ultimately lead to an effective integration of antitrust and consumer policies. However, there are two other aspects of the problem, technology and the supply side generally, that needed elaboration.

Technology was an important factor. A major factor in bringing about the new direction in public policy has been the recognized impact of foreign competition in stimulating the country's growing awareness of the increasing role of technology in industrial competition. There have been some dramatic instances of high technology enabling American industry to compete more effectively abroad, such as in computers. The emergence of high technology contrasts

---

[7] "The New Case for Monopolists," *Business Week*, December 15, 1980, p. 58.
[8] Ibid.

with some other industries, especially autos, that have sustained significant losses to foreign competitors, with consequent mass unemployment. The role of technology as the basis for market development was discussed at length in Chapter 8.

Let us now examine the impact of these developments, technological and otherwise, on thinking about both the supply and demand sides of a company that have brought about this changing public policy.

There was a very interesting supply-side development. Joseph A. Schumpeter, as long ago as 1913, saw the subtle role that technology plays in competition. He made a sharp distinction between the inventor, who creates the new idea, and the innovator, who promotes the new idea and its consequent product in the marketplace. He then proceeded to show the neglected, but crucial, role of the innovator.[9] Basically, he believed that innovation—especially product innovation—is a driving force in desirable competition and also serves to generate economic development.

According to Schumpeter, when a company creates a "new commodity"—in our terms, a new product category—it must promote heavily to get its radically new product accepted. As Schumpeter put it, "The great majority of changes in commodities consumed have been forced by producers on consumers, who, more often than not, have resisted the change and have had to be educated up by elaborate psychotechnics of advertising."[10]

To compete effectively with the innovator, other companies must each provide an improved offering. As a result, innovations cluster in an industry, and consumers respond by changing their buying habits to accept these new products and services. Thus, innovation and imitation of the innovator both impart a healthy dynamism to market behavior. The conventional market-structure view neglects or at least downplays this dynamism. However, once in a while, "progressiveness" is included in the performance column as shown in Table 18-2 to incorporate this dynamic element.

Most of us accept the notion that innovation is beneficial to society. But it is possible to be much more specific about those benefits, as Table 18-5 makes clear. Here, you see the results of 20 different innovations: 12 industrial products, 4 consumer products, and 4 industrial processes. In the right-hand column is the rate of return to the innovator. In the middle column is the rate of return to society. Only two respondents listed a negative return to society—this was because of an adverse effect on the environment. But even one of these products led to a later innovation, which had a positive return for both the innovator and society.

As you notice, the median social return (99%) is very high, a point that has been confirmed by other studies. Another key finding, according to the study, was this:

[9] J. A. Schumpeter, *Business Cycles*, Vol. 1 (New York: McGraw-Hill, 1939). Schumpeter's work is now receiving greater attention. David Dickson, "Technology and Cycles of Boom and Bust," *Science*, 219, no. 4587 (February 1983), 933–36.

[10] Schumpeter, *Business Cycles*, p. 87.

Table 18-5 Discounted Cash Flow of Return on Innovations (Rate of Return, %)

Innovation	Social	Private
Industrial products		
A	62	31
B	Negative	Negative
C	116	55
D	23	0
E	37	9
F	161	40
G	123	24
H	104	Negative
I	113	12
J	95	40
K	472	127
L	Negative	13
Consumer products		
M	28	23
N	62	41
O	178	148
P	144	29
Industrial products		
R	103	55
S	29	25
T	198	69
U	20	20
Median	99	27

SOURCE: J. G. Tewksbury, M. S. Crandall, and W. E. Crance, "Measuring the Societal Benefits of Innovation," *Science*, 209, no. 4457 (August 1980), 659. Copyright 1980 by the AAAS.

Marketing strategy often had an important effect on private rate of return, which in turn strongly affected social benefit. Passing on substantial savings to the customer, determined in part by pricing policy, often substantially increased private return by increasing rate or depth of penetration of the market. Also, marketing strategies that result in lower capital investment for the purchaser of the new product or lower prices also often increased private return.[11]

As the quotation implies, a marketing manager who has the capacity to innovate is playing an important social role. His marketing strategy can clearly contribute to innovation.

A caveat to the discussion of technological change, however, is that the American public is less enthusiastic about its benefits today than it was in earlier decades. In comparing public attitudes of 1957 versus 1979, we see a

[11] J. G. Tewksbury, M. S. Crandall, and W. E. Crane, "Measuring the Societal Benefits of Innovation," *Science*, 209, no. 4457 (August 1980), 659.

major decline in the proportion who thought that "the benefits of scientific research have outweighed the harmful results."[12] However, among the better informed, the drop was considerably smaller—from 96% to only 90%; among the less well informed, the decline was from 87% to 66%. More recently, opinion has shifted back more favorably toward innovation.[13]

Now that we have justified from the supply point of view the need for a change in public policy, let's turn to the demand side. The customer is in a stronger position vis-à-vis the seller than has been usually thought. In fact it is useful to think of the customer or demand side as actually driving the supply side. This is especially meaningful when we think of the role of the customer's product hierarchy in determining who the competitors are in a market. In fact, it has been found that customers have a greater effect on company profits than do competitors.[14] Here is a potential role for consumer theory even in understanding the supply side of the market. For example, one of the long-standing antitrust questions has been how to measure competition in a market. This is one aspect of what the customer's product hierarchy is all about as we saw in Chapter 4. Also, in Chapter 10 the model of competitive vulnerability was shown to provide a direct measure of competitive impact upon another company.

The demand issues were critically important, and these make up the second major flaw of the conventional market-structure approach to competition: the lack of a theory of consumer behavior, specifically, a theory of how customers process information they receive from advertising and other marketing sources. Such a theory is necessary, since there is clearly inadequate understanding of the role of information in protecting the consumer. As a guide to the development of public policy, we must have a rationale to explain how a consumer uses information. Put another way, antitrust and consumer protection should be integrated, and the theory of consumer behavior presented in Chapter 16 and shown as Figure 18-3 here can facilitate this integration as discussed in the paragraphs that follow.

The lack of a consumer behavior theory should not be surprising, because the conventional market-structure approach evolved out of economics, where buyer preferences were perceived as a given instead of being explained as discussed in Chapter 2. Here we see why as asserted earlier that economics is inadequate in forming public policy. Kelvin Lancaster, a Columbia University economist and a pioneer in understanding consumer demand, summarized the situation as follows:

> The economist's theory of consumer choice is built on the concept of the preferences of the individual and devotes great attention to the study of the presumed

---

[12] John Walsh, "Public Attitude Toward Science Is Yes, But . . .," *Science*, 215 (January 13, 1982), 270.

[13] C. Norman, "Broad Public Support Found for R & D," *Science*, 222, no. 4630 (December 23, 1983), 1311.

[14] G. Carpenter, "Product Quality, General Promotion and Profitability," Unpublished working paper (Center for Marketing Studies, U.C.L.A., Los Angeles, 1983).

structure of these preferences. Are preferences innate? Are they entirely due to social conditioning? Can they be influenced by advertising or propaganda? Do individuals know their "real" preferences, or do they have to learn what they are from experience? How stable are these preferences? Do behavioral changes due to major environmental changes represent a shift in preferences or an adjustment within a grand pattern of preference? In spite of the crucial role of preference in economic theory, economists have no real answers to questions such as these, and generally speaking do not even ask them within the ordinary context of economic theory.[15]

Lancaster emphasized that economists must understand how these preferences are formed to deal with many important problems, but he left it up to the consumer behavior researchers to really do the explaining as Figure 18-2 does in using attitude (A) as the basis of preferences. He did the pioneering work in consumer behavior in economics when he developed the notion of consumer technology, which as described in Chapter 2 corresponds in a way to the limited problem-solving theory dealt with in Chapter 5. His other contribution was to ensure that the assumption of "separability"—the assumption that consumers have the capacity to form a product category concept—got more attention than it had previously received in economics. You will recall that Chapters 4 and 5 implicitly stress separability in discussing how the customer's product hierarchy evolves as described in Figure 18-2. For a more prescriptive view of how consumers ought to behave as viewed by an economist, see Ratchford.[16]

There are broadly two kinds of consumer protection issues: adequacy of information and truthfulness of information. The first has received relatively little attention, the second, a lot of attention. To clarify the difference between the two, adequacy can be termed "processability," the ability of the consumer to process it and learn from it. Let us deal with this first.

Consumer theory provides useful guidelines in public policy dealing with processability as Bettman nicely points out.[17] As discussed in Chapters 4 through 6, a basic question is whether in a particular situation, consumers use attribute processing or brand processing. Second, given their decision which to use, the question is how they carry it out. Three types of methods are available: (1) use of stored rules versus constructive processes, (2) where the processing occurs (in-store or before shopping), and (3) whether they use recognition or recall.

Which of these patterns they actually use in a concrete situation depends upon the stage of decision: routine (RPS), limited (LPS), or extensive problem

---

[15] K. Lancaster, "Theories of Consumer Choice from Economics: A Critical Survey," project on Synthesis of Knowledge of Consumer Behavior, RANN Program (Washington, D.C.: National Science Foundation, April 1975), p. 50.

[16] B. T. Ratchford, "The Value of Information for Selected Appliances," *Journal of Marketing Research*, XVII (February 1980), 14–25; B. T. Ratchford, "The New Economic Theory of Consumer Behavior: An Interpretive Essay," *Journal of Consumer Research*, 2, no. 2 (September 1975), 65–75.

[17] J. R. Bettman, *An Information Processing Theory of Consumer Choice* (Reading, Mass.: Addison-Wesley, 1979), pp. 306–16.

Information Processing

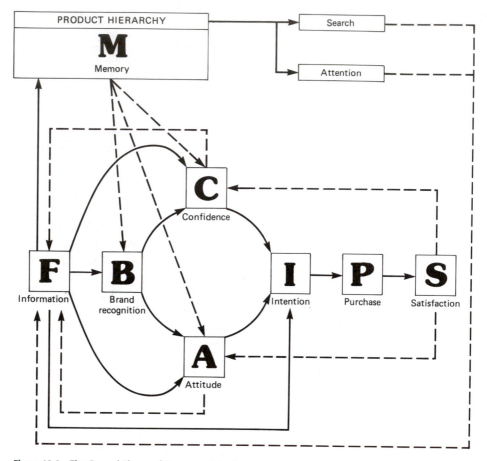

Figure 18-2   The General Theory of Consumer Behavior

solving (EPS). Let us take RPS first, which Bettman calls "brand choice with much prior experience," where the consumer tends to use brand processing and use stored rule, recall, and prior methods. This is an easy choice situation; he can use recall from his memory, and he can pick up information outside the store and handle it easily, unless of course, there has been a major product change. He can process even the brief TV message because he already has chunks in his memory about the brands in his evoked set. He tends to use stored rules instead of constructing them for the occasion.

RPS is the one major area of buying where many observers have expressed concern for consumer protection. This is in stable, mature industries, where buying is largely repeat purchase within the customer's evoked set, and where the supplier makes relatively few changes in product. It is probably here that most of the economists' serious criticism has been focused. In such a situation, why should there be advertising? Let us use aluminum foil to illustrate the critics' view. In a study of the aluminum industry by John Stuckey at Harvard,[18] he applied Michael Porter's definition of "convenience goods" in analyzing the consumer foil section of the aluminum industry. These are "Goods with relatively low unit price, purchased repeatedly, for which the consumer desires an easily accessible outlet."[19]

In the case of what Porter calls "convenience goods," the trade-off, as he sees it, typically amounts to consumers relying heavily upon manufacturer's advertising messages for information. The consumer's choice in convenience goods is relatively unobjective, he concludes, and this gives the manufacturer the opportunity to supply subjective information to convey the brand's "image" via the mass media at low message per dollar cost. This, of course, amounts to alleging that brand differentiation *without substance* occurs via advertising. Furthermore, Porter alleges a manufacturer can via his marketing successfully lower the cross-price elasticity of demand for his brand and hence can price it above cost and earn "differentiation rents." These rents allegedly are not eroded by the retailer, because, given the manufacturer's advertising, the retailer has minimal impact upon the consumer's interbrand choice.

If consumers' aluminum foil is a "convenience good," then its manufacturers have the opportunity to earn differentiation rents. However, we saw in Chapter 6 that of a sample of 21 consumer products, consumers were least brand loyal to aluminum foil. Stuckey concludes: "The product differentiation of Reynolds Wrap is probably not in society's interest, because it commands a price premium but is not a superior product in a functional sense."[20] In a class where this case was being discussed, one of the students pointed out that Reynolds has a more convenient package.

In terms of the Dutch study discussed in Chapter 6, Stuckey's conclusion might be valid for the roughly 20% who did not shift. As we saw in the Dutch study, however, about 80% of the consumers surveyed are periodically in and out of the market for a particular brand. Advertising is meeting a consumer information need.

Having examined the RPS buying situation, let us turn to LPS, "brand choice with little prior experience or other processing difficulties." Here, a consumer would be expected to use attribute processing instead of brand processing, to use constructive decision rules, to do his information processing in the store, and to use recognition methods instead of recall. Out-of-store advertising alone would be less than adequate. If it were combined with an in-store display organized by attribute it would help substantially. Perhaps better would be to put in the ad the benefits of processing the information and then direct consumers to the special in-store display where the information can be found. Further, the information should be organized to facilitate processing by attribute and

[18] J. A. Stuckey, *Vertical Integration and Joint Ventures in the Aluminum Industry* (Cambridge, Mass.: Harvard University Press, 1983).

[19] M. Porter, *Interbrand Choice, Strategy and Bilateral Market Power* (Cambridge, Mass.: Harvard University Press, 1976), p. 24.

[20] Stuckey, *Vertical Integration*, p. 287.

checked or preprocessed information; for example, the consumer could be provided with summary brand ratings.

Finally, for the case of EPS, "product category choice," consumer education efforts that encourage the consumer to use standards across categories will help. Booklets available from the store manager that compare categories on relevant attributes are desirable. Advertising suggesting that these can be obtained from the store manager can contribute still further. However it is done, EPS presents a difficult choice situation for the consumer. Also, where the benefits are not well defined and one brand is well ahead of succeeding brands in entering the market, the first brand may become the prototypical brand and so have an advantage, as shown in Chapter 16.

Product labeling presents an information problem that may fit either of the three stages. Also, it is a problem that has become increasingly important with the growth of technology, as has been recognized by the American Association for the Advancement of Science as affecting the health and safety of the consumer. Calling heavily upon consumer behavior research, Susan G. Hadden has done a careful extensive report on the public policy implications of product labeling.[21]

Interestingly, public policy and self-regulation aren't the only ways of avoiding monopoly. A built-in barrier to monopolies may be the boundary around product classes that customers create in their own minds. As we saw in Chapter 6, to simplify their choice, customers may exaggerate the product that is really "out there" in the market; that is, they imagine dimensions that may not apply to all brands. In such a case, customers may shift their product class boundaries as their values change, and thus create a much more dynamic competitive situation than is apparent.

Having dealt with adequacy of information, let us turn to the issue of truthfulness. In earlier chapters we have assumed information to be truthful. Yet information is not necessarily truthful, and whether it is can make a difference in the operation of a market. Most important, it misleads and cheats the customer. Also, the results of untruthful information are probably a less responsive, more slowly adapting, less effective market. In addition, false information can mean less reward for the seller of the superior product. Furthermore, truthfulness is essential to responsive markets that support technological change. Finally, the FTC has used advertising substantiation and corrective advertising both of which were discussed at the outset of the chapter to ensure truthfulness in advertising.

In recent years, there has been criticism of the FTC's policy of advertising substantiation, namely, that advertisers must have evidence to support product claims made in their ads. Many believe the policy has become weaker in protecting the consumer. In response, General Foods has taken industry leadership and issued a warning to the FTC. Kent Mitchell, vice president at General Foods, wrote that to weaken this requirement "would remove the guarantee of advertis-

---

[21] S. G. Hadden, *Read the Label: Reducing Risk by Providing Information* (Boulder, Colo.: American Association for the Advancement of Science and Westview Press, 1986).

ing legitimacy on which consumers and advertisers depend."[22] Also, he "made detailed suggestions for 'clarifying and simplifying' substantiation requirements to reduce costs of complying."[23] He also asserted, "Among competing producers, claim substantiation acts as a hedge against the unjustified claim of a competitor."[24] Or, as put more acerbically by Stanley Cohen, an editor of *Ad Age*, "An industry which pioneered in supporting 'truth in advertising' since the turn of the century is not going to be easily sold on new statutory language that makes cheating less risky."[25]

Former Chairman Miller's view of the FTC's current position is "We haven't made changes in the overall standard. We're just applying it more intelligently. The demagogues are saying that because the Commission is not going out and flogging people with a bullwhip that it's backing away."[26] One of the cases cited to support the argument that the FTC is "backing away" from stiff enforcement is

> In 1974, the FTC prohibited Sterling Drug from claiming that its Lysol spray disinfectant could prevent the spread of colds. The agency said there was little scientific certainty about the claim.
>
> A new agreement reached with Sterling Drug in March, 1983 would permit a limited version of the claim if the company eventually has enough evidence to support it. Sterling won the FTC concession by citing a single new experiment that some of the commissioners criticized as inconclusive.[27]

Advertising substantiation can be expensive and bothersome for a company charged with lack of it, but corrective advertising can be damaging. In the case of Sun Oil, for example, in 1972, the company would have been directed to devote 25% of its advertising budget to the correction and face the public embarrassment of running the corrective ads. However, it is a way of penalizing a company and undoing the damage of an untruthful ad.

Opponents of corrective advertising argued that corrective advertising will not achieve its objective. A recent careful study, however, indicates that it can achieve the desired objective. Mizerski, Allison, and Calvert using a CDM multidimensional type of measure of attitude shown in Table 18-6 illustrates their findings.[28] As you see there, Listerine was used in the carefully arranged naturalistic experiment to measure the effects of corrective advertising on all the dormitory residents of a large state university.

---

[22] "GF Goes to Bat for Ad Substantiation Rule," *Advertising Age*, January 11, 1982, p. 6.

[23] Ibid.

[24] Ibid.

[25] Editorial, "Why Industry Wants Miller to Slow Down," *Advertising Age*, March 29, 1982, p. 16.

[26] *The Wall Street Journal* (New York edition), July 21, 1983, p. 29.

[27] Ibid.

[28] R. W. Mizerski, N. K. Allison, and S. Calvert, "A Controlled Field Study of Corrective Advertising Using Multiple Exposures and a Commercial Message," *Journal of Marketing Research*, XVII (August 1980), 341–48.

Table 18-6 Test of Corrective Advertising

Dependent Variables	EXPERIMENTAL GROUP ($n = 48$) Mean	CONTROL GROUP ($n = 49$) Mean	F	P≤
Beliefs about Listerine				
Kills germs (b_1)	4.67	5.10	1.58	.212
Leaves mouth refreshed (b_2)	5.12	4.65	2.00	.160
Fights colds and sore throats (b_3)	3.58	4.61	6.64	.012
Long-lasting effects (b_4)	4.39	4.45	.03	.868
Belief salience				
Kills germs (a_1)	4.98	4.77	.29	.593
Leaves mouth refreshed (a_2)	5.42	4.84	2.45	.121
Fights colds and sore throats (a_3)	4.48	4.57	.05	.823
Long-lasting effects (a_4)	5.46	4.77	3.62	.060
Perceived honesty of Listerine	4.76	4.50	.79	.374
Overall affect/attitude	4.27	4.00	.53	.460
Intention to purchase Listerine	39.80	33.98	.74	.390

SOURCE: R. W. Mizerski, N. K. Allison, and S. Calvert, "A Controlled Field Study of Corrective Advertising Using Multiple Exposures and a Commercial Medium," *Journal of Marketing Research*, XVII (August 1980), 346. Published by the American Marketing Association.

Table 18-6 lists both the Listerine product benefits and benefit importances. "Fights colds and sore throats" was the benefit used in the corrective advertising. In the experimental group, the target benefit rating is significantly lower than is the control group benefit (3.58 versus 4.61). Thus, the corrective effect was achieved. But the importance weighting of that benefit was unaffected. Equally important, none of the other three benefits was affected either on the performance rating or on the importance rating. Also, there has been concern that a corrective ad damages the consumer's view of the company's integrity, a conclusion found in a previous study. As you can see, there is no effect seen in "Perceived honesty of Listerine." The final two items, total attitude and intention, show no effects either. The conclusion from this study is that corrective advertising does achieve its desired effects but does not have the undesirable effect that others thought it might. Thus, corrective advertising is a desirable feature of consumer policy.

Many people now believe that self-regulation of advertisers has been more effective than generally recognized in the past. The national advertising division of the Council of Better Business Bureaus, which is responsible for handling complaints, says that, out of almost 2,000 investigations over the past 10 years, only 2% of advertisers appealed to the advertising review board rather than change or discontinue the ads. Out of that 2%, no advertiser has refused to follow the recommendations of the board.[29] Most people also believe, however,

[29] S. Thurm, "Comment," *Association of National Advertisers, Washington Edition*, December 1981, p. 2.

that self-regulation would have been less effective if the FTC had not had the power to proceed against untruthfulness. Knowing that the FTC has this power, companies have probably been more inclined to follow self-regulation.

The enforcement of untruthful charges, however, is technically not easy, as you might expect. This is seen in a recent federal court decision involving Procter & Gamble's private suit against Chesebrough-Ponds for claiming benefits in its advertising for skin lotion products:

> Although the tasks of evaluating scientific product tests may be challenging and distrustful because of the technical and theoretical nature of the procedures involved and the intricate statistical analysis needed to derive qualitative inferences and conclusions from the data, the court is under just as much of a duty to consider and weigh such evidence as it is to analyze economic or scientific evidence in a complicated patent or antitrust case.[30]

This was the higher court's answer and reprimand to a lower court judge who had complained that federal courts are not the place for settling advertising disputes, which by their nature supposedly are not of serious import. Companies involved in comparative advertising cases are increasingly turning to private suits via the Lanham Act, which permits a company to go directly to court to stop competitive ads it considers deceptive. Going to the FTC is said to be time consuming and uncertain.

Proving whether an ad is intrinsically untruthful or deceptive in its benefit claims can be difficult because of our lack of objective criteria. To deal with this issue, the FTC following the 1938 legislation operationalized "untruthful" as "deceptive." David Gardner has developed a logic for using the multiattribute measure of attitude, the centerpiece of the CDM, as a measure of deception.[31] Russo, Metcalf, and Stephens have developed the procedures for applying a related version and applied it.[32] Further research is needed for someone with a strong interest in the deception problem. Horton nicely reviews the research on deception.[33]

In Chapter 16 the question was raised whether emotional advertising takes unfair advantage of the consumer. Little is known, and it, too, will need to be researched.

Probably once companies learn more about customers' needs for information through research and how to satisfy those needs based on consumer behavior theory, they will decide to become more competitive by providing even better information. General Electric has made such a move, which *Advertising Age* has

---

[30] N. Giges, "Judge Reprimanded for Jibe at Ad Case," *Advertising Age*, November 19, 1984, p. 57.

[31] D. M. Gardner, "Deception in Advertising: A Conceptual Approach," *Journal of Marketing*, 39, no. 1 (January 1975), 40–46.

[32] J. E. Russo, B. L. Metcalf, and D. Stephens, "Identifying Misleading Advertising," *Journal of Consumer Research*, 8, no. 2 (September 1981), 119–31.

[33] R. L. Horton, *Buyer Behavior: A Decision Murking Approach* (Columbus, Ohio: Charles E. Merrill, 1984), pp. 424–28.

referred to as "Gutsy and smart. . . . It takes a degree of boldness for hard goods manufacturers to move into the marketing of repairs programs."[34] To cite another example, General Electric Co. announced in September 1982 a major "customer information" program.[35] Six two-page magazine ads will describe a number of GE information programs, including an 800 phone number, which allows consumers to call computer-assisted "experts" in the "G.E. Answer Center" any time of day. Also, the ads inform consumers about the "G.E. Home Library," which contains booklets on redecorating, redesigning, and installing kitchens; lighting; and home video equipment. The company planned special ads to support those individual programs. Procter & Gamble has used the 800 phone number effectively.

Finally, there is the issue of new communications technology. Another influence increasingly brought to bear upon the concept of competition and consumer protection is the advance in this technology. Cable and satellite systems have generally improved market communication, thus creating a more sensitive marketplace. At the same time, however, the efficiency of communications networks is raising greater questions about the need to protect children from advertising.

The Surgeon General's Office issued a report on the effect of TV on children a decade ago, and a recent report by the same source confirms that "television violence very likely causes some children to become more aggressive, at least in the short run."[36] We believe, however, that this problem highlights the more general issue of the role of parental responsibility in our society. With modern TV, the child is subjected to a wide variety of influences, some of which may need regulating. The problem is still serious, but it should not be viewed as uniquely a marketing burden that advertisers should bear.

The FTC has been trying to deal with the issue of children's commercials since the late 1970s. You will recall that it was an issue in the cereal case. The FTC attracted its share of critics, who ridiculed the Commission with being a "national nanny" for children. Finally, in early October 1981, the FTC dropped the effort, saying it wasn't sure it could resolve the factional disputes or devise an enforceable remedy even if it decided something was needed.[37]

2.5   Conclusions on Public Policy

At the outset of this chapter, many reasons were given why a marketing manager is well advised to know the nature of consumer protection policy. A resurgence of interest in consumer protection can be expected.

[34] Editorial viewpoint, "GE: Gutsy Endeavor," *Advertising Age*, September 28, 1981, p. 16.

[35] *The New York Times*, June 29, 1982, Business Section.

[36] "TV Report Affirms Violence Aggression Link," *Science*, 216, no. 4552 (June 18, 1982), 1299.

[37] "Kiddie TV Rule Dies," *Advertising Age*, October 5, 1981, p. 117.

Table 18-7   Merging Antitrust and Consumer Information Approaches

Structure	Behavior	Performance
Number of firms	Advertising	Adequacy of information
Firms' domination	Promotion	
Product life cycle	Pricing differentiation	Truthfulness
Ease of entry	Research and development	Progressiveness in product
Ease of exit		

There is a great need for additional research on the nature of the consumer protection problems. There has been substantial research of this complex area that Robertson et al. thoughtfully and systematically review,[38] but not a lot of progress. However, a new journal, *Journal of Public Policy and Marketing*, has been initiated by the University of Michigan to stimulate research in this area.

One of the more prominent areas has been the satisfaction research. You will recall from Chapter 16 how the analysis of feedback from satisfaction (S) with brand in use to attitude (A) and confidence (C) enabled us to separate the effect of advertising from the effect of the quality of the product in shaping consumer evaluations of brands. Also, in Chapter 16 we discussed how to model advertising effect when it exaggerates the quality of the product. This more precise measurement illustrates the potential for future research.

Finally, now that antitrust effort has become more focused upon the role of protecting the consumer it would seem appropriate to merge the traditional market structure approach and the general theory of consumer behavior as shown in Figure 18-2. Table 18-7 illustrates how this might be done by making truthfulness and adequacy of information major performance criteria. The theory of consumer behavior shown in Figure 18-2 would be a framework for such research. Effort will have to be devoted to the dimensions of each element: structure, behavior, and performance. For example, six possible dimensions for advertising were proposed to the FTC: timelessness, intelligibility, relevancy, completeness, truthfulness, and accuracy of target audiences.[39] Four of these—relevancy, completeness, truthfulness, and accuracy of target audiences—were actually recommended. Also, the market-structure concept if combined with product hierarchy and competitive vulnerability can be highly useful for designing strategy as well.

[38] T. S. Robertson, J. Zielinski, and S. Ward, *Consumer Behavior* (Glenview, Ill.: Scott, Foresman, 1984), Chapter 23.

[39] Howard and Hulbert, *Advertising and the Public Interest*, pp. 86–87 and 96.

A splendidly creative example is provided by Fornell and Robinson.[40] They did an extensive study of 23 industries in which they compared the degree of concentration in an industry and the level of consumer satisfaction/dissatisfaction in terms of price and quality. Using consumer satisfaction as a measure of the industry's performance is new. They found no relation between the two influences upon the consumer, unfortunately, but their work is very suggestive of what might be done.

3. SOCIAL STATUS OF MARKETING

3.1   Introduction

You saw implied in the cereal case discussed earlier great concern about the helplessness of the consumer against the onslaught of the marketer's advertising. The concern was phrased in terms of a barrier to entry. Entry was blocked supposedly because the consumer was misled by the advertising. This concern may sound strange to you because in previous chapters, you have seen evidence that the consumer has remarkable information-processing capacity. He has a set of cognitive mechanisms and patterns of behavior that enable him to select the relevant from the irrelevant. But only recently have we come to know this, and even now it is little understood in society generally.

How much of this knowledge is being used in practice even now? Very little! Further, marketers haven't had the concepts to explain marketing even to others in the company much less to the public generally. It is not surprising then that they have been criticized as engaging in socially questionable activity, with advertising and selling representing dubious ethical behavior on their part. Consequently, it is also not surprising that in some circles, marketing is of doubtful social acceptability.

To raise a general question about the social acceptability of this profession is not new. As Steiner put it almost a decade ago, "Society honors those who build better mousetraps but suspects those who market mousetraps better."[41] An effort has recently been made to develop and produce annually an "Index of Consumer Sentiment Toward Marketing."[42] This will provide a generally available measure of consumers' feelings toward marketing.

We will first discuss some of the sources of this view and then examine the relevance of the CDM and associated theory of Table 18-7 and techniques for the view.

[40] C. Fornell and W. T. Robinson, "Industrial Organization and Consumer Satisfaction/Dissatisfaction," *Journal of Consumer Research*, 9, no. 4 (March 1983), 403–12.

[41] R. L. Steiner, "The Prejudice Against Marketing," *Journal of Marketing*, 40, no. 3 (July 1976), 2.

[42] J. F. Gaski and M. J. Etzel, "The Index of Consumer Sentiment Toward Marketing," *Journal of Marketing*, 50, no. 3 (July 1986), 71–81.

3.2 Sources of the View

There are two general sources of the social unacceptability of marketing. First, as previous pages in this chapter have indicated, we have a substantial history of concern about protecting the consumer. It would not be surprising that practitioners of this questionable activity of marketing, which the consumer needs protection from, would feel some social sting as a consequence. Advertising has probably felt it the most. As the dean of one of our well-known business schools a number of years ago said to the chairman of his marketing department, "Teaching advertising in a business school is like teaching prostitution in a sociology department." Quite recently, a federal judge complained that truthfulness in advertising cases were too trivial for the federal courts to deal with as we saw earlier. In a review of views toward advertising held by humanists and social scientists, Richard Pollay quotes Robert Heilbroner as follows:

> If I were asked to name the deadliest subversive force within capitalism, the greatest single source of its waning morality, I would without hesitation name advertising. How else should one identify a force that debases language, drains thought and undoes dignity.[43]

Second, and, in a sense, the opposite of the first, marketers are sometimes viewed as less effective members of the management team in a company. As Robert K. Mueller, chairman of Arthur D. Little, recently asserted, many CEOs today put their marketers "into a narrow role of creative, right-brain, non-analytical, advertising-oriented, over-promisers of sales and profits."[44]

Both these sources give a basis for raising doubts about the social acceptance of marketing.

3.3 Relevance of CDM

That marketing can be damaging to the consumer has become a more focused and well-informed concern. It now focuses heavily upon truthfulness and should also focus upon adequacy of information. The CDM brings to bear a wealth of associated theory and techniques that can help in answering these questions of public policy for consumer protection. The theory suggests that consumers are remarkably able with their information-processing capacities to make sense of information from advertising or any other source. However, more research is needed to give us a clearer picture of the problem of deceptive advertising, now that we are better able to define it and measure it.

---

[43] R. W. Pollay, "The Distorted Mirror: Reflections on the Unintended Consequences of Advertising," *Journal of Marketing*, 50, no. 2 (April 1986), 30.

[44] R. K. Mueller, "Profitability: A Result Not a Target," *The Conference Board*, Marketing Conference (New York, October 20–21, 1982), p. 13.

The *need* to strengthen marketing's role in the management team is clear. As we saw in the study of 20 innovations, marketing strategy often had an important positive effect on the private rate of return, which in turn strongly affected the benefit that society derived from those innovations. The possibility of strengthening marketers as members of the management team clearly exists. As middle management learns these concepts and techniques and the computer skills to apply them in designing marketing strategy, this potential will be exploited and their role rewarded accordingly. The middle managers will find from that experience that their intuition and splendid insights can be more systematically and fruitfully combined—the artistic and the systematic—to better serve their organization, either profit or nonprofit. Further, these ideas have been extended to apply to the higher levels of management as well.[45]

Finally, these two consequences interact. To the extent that it becomes clear to the public that marketing practices are actually modified, where necessary to better serve the consumer, the general social status of the marketer will improve. To the extent that the marketer becomes more effective as a member of the management team, he can with greater ease, bring about those modifications in company practice that are needed to bring it in line with the consumers' needs. Also, to the extent that the marketer is more highly valued socially, he will be more respected within the organization.

4. CONCLUSIONS

Parts I and II set a logical framework for dealing with consumer behavior issues. The heart of this framework was the simple Customer Decision Model, which ties the pieces together.

In Part III the CDM was combined with the concept of core strategy and applied to designing marketing strategy to four different market conditions: extensive problem solving, limited problem solving, routine problem solving, and buying by the formal organization. A conclusion is that to the extent that managers can use these principles, they can more effectively persuade others in the organization to accept them.

Part IV was devoted to developing an additional framework for extending the CDM to incorporate the important possibility that consumers in a particular market will be different from each other in their buying habits. If so, they offer a segmentation possibility.

Part V extended the CDM in five additional directions. First, individual consumer differences and segmentation were added. Second, feedbacks were incorporated, and in the process a much fuller systematic description of consumer behavior was developed.

[45] F. D. Honn and J. A. Howard, "Marketing Theory in the Modern Corporation," in G. Frazier and J. N. Sheth, eds., *Contemporary Views in Marketing Practice* (Lexington, Mass.: D. C. Heath, 1987).

Third, nonlinearities and interactions that had been introduced piece-meal in earlier chapters were developed further. A general conclusion was that, especially if the marketing problems are important and the product category unfamiliar, the relations should be tested for nonlinear possibilities. Their conse-quences can be too misleading to ignore.

Fourth, the issue of consumer protection was introduced. Its history was developed at length because public policy is changing and the contributions of well-informed marketing people are seriously needed to guide that develop-ment.

Finally, there was some discussion of the social acceptability of marketing as a field of endeavor and the contribution that theory could make to the accept-ability of that field.

Questions

1. It is said that there are six institutions designed to protect the consumer. Would you explain how each one operates to achieve this?
2. How would you describe the current policy of protecting the consumer?
3. Compare and contrast the "convenience good" concept of economists with the "pioneer brand" concept discussed in Chapter 16.
4. Has the government policy of protecting the consumer from untruthful ads been adequate in your judgment? Please explain.
5. Marketing, especially advertising, is sometimes said to be less socially useful than the other functions of business. What is your judgment on this issue and why?

Glossary

Active synthesis   When the consumer combines the key physical characteristics (recognition) and evaluative characteristics (attitude) of the brand.

Advertising self-regulation   Handled through the National Advertising Council of Better Business Bureaus, a private agency, which receives advertising complaints and decides whether the ad is untruthful. If it decides the ad is untruthful, the advertiser is asked to change or discontinue the ad. The advertiser has the choice of complying or appealing to the review board of the Bureau.

Advertising substantiation   The Federal Trade Commission requires that a seller must be able to support the claims that are made in the seller's advertising about the benefits of the product and service.

Affect   Usually defined as feeling, emotion, mood, and temperment. "Drive" is also used. It is useful to think of it as short-term motivation in contrast to values that constitute long-term motivation.

Attacker's advantage   The notion advanced by Richard Foster that the firm with the innovation always has an advantage because the firms producing the existing product are lulled by past satisfactory performance.

Attention   The allocation by a consumer of his/her information processing capacity to a particular stimulus.

Attitude   A consumer's enduring and learned predisposition to behave in a consistent way toward an object, based on his liking for that object.

Boredom problem solving   The belief that consumers shift among brands when in RPS because they are bored. It is contrasted with an instinctive way of getting information to adjust to changes in the market.

Brand image   The consumer's total understanding of a brand in terms of how it is recognized and valued, and with what assurance.

Brand loyalty   The extent to which consumers shift among brands; specifically, it is the inverse of the amount of shifting.

Brand recognition   The mental picture a consumer forms, by which she recognizes a brand when she comes into contact with it and with which the consumer's liking and confidence become associated.

Buying center The group of people in a formal organization, such as a company, whose function is to buy for that organization.

Bypass behavior Consumers "bypass" the thinking process of using brand recognition (B), attitude (A), and confidence (C) in their buying behavior and instead go directly from information (F) to intention (I).

Categorize To classify a brand in the mind so that the consumer can more easily recognize and evaluate the brand.

Central vs. peripheral routes Advertising can have either of two causal effects. When the buying decision is involving, it can have a central effect where the buyer thinks about the alternatives and judges them in utilitarian terms. When the decision is not involving, the buyer's attitude changes because of emotion or simple decision rules requiring little if any thinking.

Choice by processing attributes (CPA) The buyer considers the individual benefits in making a choice instead of merely considering the brand as a whole.

Choice by processing brands (CPB) In choosing among brands the individual does not consider the individual benefits of a brand but makes an overall choice.

"Chunk" A particular amount of information that has psychological significance to the consumer in that the consumer will then build upon that "chunk" as she learns more about the product.

Cognition Any process whereby a consumer becomes aware or obtains knowledge of a brand or category.

Cognitive response The consumer's response to an ad in terms of the thoughts that came to mind when he saw the ad as contrasted with what he recalled from the ad.

Comparative advertising Under Federal Trade Commission rules, in an ad a seller is free to compare his product with that of a competitor by *name* as long as the statements are truthful.

Competition, direct and indirect Direct competition exists in the choice of brands when consumers have a product category concept in their thinking. Choice among categories represents indirect competition and the higher the category in the product hierarchy, the more indirect the competition.

Competitive vulnerability The sensitivity of one competitor to any of the other competitors in the market.

Concept attainment The mental process that occurs when a consumer develops a concept of brand. It is exemplified by limited problem solving.

Concept formation The mental process that occurs when the consumer develops a concept of a product category. It is exemplified by extensive problem solving.

Concept utilization The mental process that a consumer uses to think about a concept that he/she had previously attained. It is exemplified by routine problem solving.

Confidence The consumer's degree of certainty that his evaluative judgment of a brand or category is correct.

Conjoint measurement A technique for identifying relevant attributes of a product that might be converted into benefits for consumers. It is called a decompositional approach to identifying the attitude elements in the CDM.

Consumer behavior How consumers think and act in buying and consuming products and services from both profit and nonprofit organizations.

Consumer behavior theory A simplified abstract representation of consumers' actual buying that can guide a researcher in deciding what data to collect, how to analyze that data, and how to interpret the results of the analysis in designing marketing strategy.

Consumer decision model (CDM) A simple six-variable representation of consumer behavior. It merges the streams of psychological research, concept formation, and information processing, and can readily be expanded to capture more complex features of the market.

Core strategy   The benefits that consumers want in a product, a description of the consumers who want those product benefits, a description of each of the competitors who can supply the product so that the manager can put these together in such a way that the result will give a competitive advantage.

Corrective advertising   If a company runs untruthful advertising, it can later be required to run ads saying that what was said in the original ad was not true.

Cultural norms   The action implications of a person's values that, in consumers, lead to weighted benefits.

Culture   The material and behavioral arrangements, such as values, language, and beliefs, whereby a society achieves greater satisfaction for its members.

Cyclic behavior   The tendency of consumers to buy one brand for a period and then cycle back into the market to consider, and often buy, another brand.

Decision rule   A guiding rule of thumb that consumers use in processing information when choosing a category or brand.

Diffusion process   The process by which innovations spread to members of the social system.

Direct marketing   When a product is sold by the producer directly to the consumer without passing through an intermediary such as the retailer.

Evaluation   The process by which the consumer judges the quality of a brand.

Evoked set   Those brands the consumer has in his memory, that he considers acceptable and that he will consider when contemplating a purchase of the category.

Expectations   The consumer's beliefs about what certain information will tell her based on her experience. These are contained in her product category image. If the information agrees, she needs only limited processing, but if it disagrees, she must process the information in more depth, thus her attention and search processes tend to be much more efficient.

Extensive problem solving   Buying behavior exhibited by consumers who are buying an unfamiliar category of brand. It is characterized typically by the need for substantial information and time to choose because the consumer must form a concept of a new category.

Feedback   Most consumer behavior models are recursive, meaning that the causation flows one way. The CDM in its simple form is such a model. However, actual behavior is often nonrecursive, which means it "feeds back" upon itself. This "feedback" refers to when a consumer buys a brand and in the consuming process learns to like it even better. This feedback has the further implication that it introduces the emotional, feeling, affective response in contrast to the usual cognitive, rational, thinking type of response.

Formal organization   A type of social group like the family and other informal groups but the within-group relations are much more fixed and influential in shaping its buying behavior.

"Framed" picture   When the visual stimulus is clearly related to the purpose of the ad, thereby helping to convey the intended message of the ad.

Framing   The practice of using a visual stimulus in an ad where the picture is related to the purpose of the ad.

Goal hierarchy   The overall structure that gives the LPS and RPS consumers direction and is made up of values, norms, and benefit importances.

High-benefit users   Current users of a product who have a stronger unmet need for a product attribute or product concept than does the average user and so can be an important future user.

Husband-wife buying unit   Many buying decisions are made jointly by husband and wife. These have been studied to determine the relative influence of husband and wife during the stages of decision—"problem recognition," "search for information," and "final decision"—for a great variety of products.

Industrial conversion framework   A framework for describing a formal organization by a representation of the purchase, resource conversion, and marketing processes of a firm. It exists in either unitary (single firm) or dyadic form (two interacting firms). It can serve as a framework for applying the CDM.

Information   Here defined as used in the CDM, which emphasizes the percept that is caused by a stimulus rather than the stimulus itself.

Information adequacy   Has to do with whether it is enough information and whether it is in a form that the consumer can process to understand its meaning.

Information truthfulness   A quality essential to avoid misleading and cheating the consumer, to obtain a responsive market to improvements such as new technology, and to reward the seller of the superior product to encourage improvement.

Innovation   A new brand in a new category of brands requiring extensive problem-solving behavior on the part of the consumer.

Innovation, diffusion of   The process by which a new category is disseminated through a society. This process conforms to a logistic curve. A key question is the speed of the diffusion and this has been increasing.

Intention to buy   The mental state that reflects the consumer's plan to buy some specified number of a particular brand in some specified time period.

Interaction process   The social interaction that occurs in face-to-face contact between a salesperson and a client.

Internal search   Retrieving information from memory as contrasted with searching the environment for information.

Kernel sentence   A simple, declarative, active, and affirmative sentence. It is the form in which information is stored in the consumer's memory.

Lead users   A type of buyer with needs that are not now prevalent but can be predicted to become general and so are a key source of future consumers of a new category.

Lexical or word knowledge   A group of adjectives for recognizing and evaluating brands within a category.

Limited problem solving   Buying behavior exhibited by consumers buying a new brand in a familiar category. It is typically characterized by considerable information seeking and time to choose.

Marginal satisfaction   The principle that consumers will buy additional units if the price is lowered, and that operates only when a brand has some market protection.

Market   A place where buyers and sellers interact in the process of exchanging goods. Practically, it is a relationship because most buying and selling is carried on at a distance, not in one place.

Market structure and consumer protection   The basic idea that if an industry has a favorable structure—several sellers, without one dominating, and no barriers to entry or collusion—the sellers will behave in a competitive way and so protect the consumer from monopoly.

Marketing's social acceptance   Marketing in the past, especially advertising, has sometimes been seriously criticized as contrary to the public interest, e.g., causing the consumer to buy something he or she should not buy. As marketing has become better understood (more acceptable) with the expanding role of technology and the consumer's capacity to handle information, this criticism has lessened.

Marketing strategy   A timeless thinking and organizing framework that guides the development of marketing plans for some definite time period, such as quarterly or annually, and that links the company's objectives to the performance achieved by the execution of those plans.

Market structure approach   A way of regulating industry in the interests of the consumer by using the structure of the industry as a causal entity affecting its behavior and, in turn, its performance in terms of the consumer's interest. Consumer behavior theory is needed to specify the kind of performance that is desirable and the kind of company behavior that will yield that desirable performance.

Media   The means by which information (F) is transmitted to the consumer. It can be words, pictures, or music.

Memory   Memory is a multiple storage place for information, including sensory memory, short-term memory, and long-term memory. Sensory memory is momentary only. Short-term memory is where the consumer's externally obtained information combines with information retrieved from his long-term memory, which represents "thinking." Memory plays a dominant role in brand concept formation (recognition, attitude, and confidence).

Memory strategies   A number of processes that the consumer uses to regulate the flow of information in and out of his memory. These are very useful in thinking about the function of memory in buying.

Model   A simple representation of a complex set of activities.

Motivation   The process by which motives cause behavior. It is convenient to distinguish between long-term motives growing out of values and short-term motives derived from physiological processes such as hunger and sex, often referred to as affect and arousal.

Nonlinear relations   The relations among the variables in the simple CDM are assumed to be linear. However, some of them are found under some conditions to be nonlinear. Also, nonlinearity introduces the possibility that some relations are interactive where two or more variables interact in influencing a third variable.

Norms, behavioral   The normative dimensions of a society's culture. These are the culturally approved attitudes and behaviors, the weighted benefits of the CDM, and the action implications of a consumer's values.

Nutritional labeling   The federal law states that in some items, especially foods, the seller must disclose the nutritional qualities of a product in a standard format on the package.

Operational definition   A description of the operations and procedures to be used in obtaining the measurement of a variable in a model.

Personal reinforcement   A principle from the theory of attribution in psychology that when a person is labeled as, e.g., "a charitable person," he sees himself as being more charitable as a consequence.

Phased strategy   When the consumer first uses choice by processing the brand to form an evoked set and then uses choice by processing attributes to choose from within that evoked set.

Polar adjective   An adjective that has a polar opposite, e.g., alone–together, active–passive, etc.

Practical knowledge   Information that sets the framework, typically the product category concept, within which the lexical knowledge operates for the consumer to recognize and evaluate a particular brand in that category.

Prior knowledge   The knowledge that a consumer has in her memory at any particular moment as she goes through the buying process.

Product benefits   Those characteristics of a category and/or brand that consumers value and so use in deciding whether to buy.

Product category   A group of brands that consumers view as close substitutes for each other.

Product diffusion   The study of the process of how a new category is accepted throughout society. Research indicates that it can be described as a logistic curve.

Product life cycle   The stages that a product category passes through, including introduction, growth, and maturity.

Product hierarchy   A structure in the buyer's mind made up of related brands and categories. It has vertical and horizontal dimensions. The vertical is made up of levels in the hierarchy: basic, superordinate, and subordinate. The horizontal is across a given level.

Prototypical product   The brand that is located as the middlemost brand on the continuum in the consumer's mind, made up of recognition and evaluative characteristics.

Purchase   The consumer's actual purchase or financial commitment to purchase a certain number of units of a brand or category during some specified time period.

Recognition   The process of imagery by which the consumer recognizes a brand as contrasted to the way in which she evaluates a brand. Evaluation requires recall, which is much slower than recognition.

Recursive model   A model that explains only one direction of events as contrasted with a model that explains events in both forward and backward directions.

Reference group   A number of consumers who have common goals and who interact with each other over a period of time. They constitute an informal group that influences consumer choice.

Routine problem solving   Buying behavior characterized by consumers buying a brand they have bought before. It is typically characterized by little or no information seeking and is performed quickly.

Satisfaction feedback   Satisfaction is the response of the consumer after consuming the brand. It is often an emotional response and so may have different effects on overt behavior than a more rational response.

Search   When the consumer is motivated to expose one or more of her sense organs to information about the category or brand.

Segmentation bases   The consumer's characteristics that cause her to prefer one brand over another. These are contrasted with segmentation descriptors.

Segments, descriptors of   Characteristics that can be used for identifying market segments and focusing marketing effort on particular segments as required in designing marketing strategy. These are contrasted with bases of segmentation.

Separability   The economist's assumption that consumers can group brands into product categories so as to simplify their buying. It is the basis of the economist's concept of an industry.

Shared monopoly   In an oligopoly market, the competitors can coordinate their behavior by such means as price leadership. One company, usually the largest, sets the price and others follow by setting the same price. This is essentially sharing the fruits of a monopoly.

Social class   People interacting in the social system of a community evaluate the participation of those around them on a scale of prestige. The members of the community are explicitly or implicitly aware of the ranking and can translate their evaluations of such social participation into social-class ratings.

Standardized emotional profile   A set of emotional indices for measuring consumer responses to the nonverbal components of advertising; a comprehensive list of potential benefit dimensions of attitude for applying the CDM to products where emotions are the major reasons for buying.

Standardized language   The technical language often used by members of the buying center in a company.

Structural model   A model that is based on a theory.

Subculture   A category of people who share a sense of identification distinguishable from that of the total culture. In the U.S., these tend to be blacks, Hispanics, and whites.

Substantiation of advertising   The Federal Trade Commission can direct companies to substantiate the claims they make in their advertising.

Two-level choice   The consumer must, at least implicitly, first choose at the product category level and then at the brand level.

Type of information   There are two types of knowledge: practical vs. lexical.

Unit pricing   In some states, to protect the consumer sellers are required to specify the price of a brand per unit of weight or volume. This facilitates making price comparisons.

Values   A type of belief, centrally located within a consumer's total belief system, about how he or she ought and ought not to behave. It is more than an attitude, often underlying it.

Vulnerability model   A representation of the competitive process that provides measures of the intensity of the vulnerability of one competitor to another.

Author Index

Subject Index